Es agradable saber que hay personas especiales como tú, que quieran conocer mi país, Espero algún día lo podamos compartir.

Con Cariño

María Carolina Q.

I-/98

Fotografías
Archivo Editorial Colina

Textos
Gloria Lucía Fernández G.
Editorial Colina

Diseño y Diagramación
Alex Amelines
SHS Comunicación Visual S.A.

Preprensa Digital - Zetta Colina
Impreso en Colombia por Editorial Colina
Comercialización Hola Colina

Medellín
✆ 266 32 11 ▪ Fax 266 03 97 ▪ Apartado ✉ 3674
Santafé de Bogotá
✆ 217 04 55 ▪ Fax 235 68 19 ▪ Apartado ✉ 52171 Zona 2
ISBN 958-638-205-2

¡Colombia!

Índice

Paisajes de todos los Climas 8
Azul de mar, costas e islas 12
Agua viva de ríos y lagunas 15
El país de las flores y las aves 18
Campo y ciudad, dos caras de la misma Colombia 21
De los caminos de herradura a los aeropuertos internacionales 24
Algo de Historia 27
Riquezas de las entrañas de la tierra 32
Aromas y colores de sus campos 36
Industria a toda Marcha 40
El país de todas las Sonrisas 44
La expresión de su gente 47
¡Aquí hay fiesta! 50
Colombia para recorrer 52
Parques arqueológicos y naturales, una opción turística diferente 55
¡Venga! 58

Este es un viaje por un hermoso país que en 1'138.914 de kilómetros cuadrados de superficie, disfruta de todos los climas posibles: desde los más ardientes de los valles y desiertos, hasta los de las silenciosas nieves perpetuas.

Un país donde viven aproximadamente 37 millones de personas de los más variados tipos humanos, con sueños de paz y trabajo para todos. Gente que habita ruidosas y progresistas ciudades, o pueblos que parecen dormir al arrullo de los años.

Recostada en el extremo noroeste de América del Sur, Colombia recibe al norte la caricia del Mar Caribe, alegre y soleado, y al occidente las olas majestuosas del Pacífico llegan a playas inmensas, tras las cuales se extiende una selva imponente y húmeda. Países hermanos son Panamá, Venezuela, Brasil, Perú y Ecuador, con los que limita al noroccidente, oriente, suroriente, y sur, respectivamente.

Por su extensión, Colombia ocupa el cuarto lugar entre los países suramericanos, y el vigésimotercero en todo el mundo. Ninguna nación europea, excepto Rusia, la excede en tamaño. Sus puntos extremos son Punta Gallinas en el norte, Boca de San Antonio al sur, la Piedra del Cocuy en el este, y Cabo Manglares al oeste.

En este marco la población colombiana, una de las más numerosas de América del Sur, habla el idioma español y realiza sus transacciones con el peso, la moneda nacional. El sistema de gobierno es la democracia participativa, y la vocación republicana de Colombia es una de las más antiguas y sólidas del continente americano.

Administrativamente el país está dividido en 32 departamentos. Santafé de Bogotá es la capital del país, y del departamento de Cundinamarca.

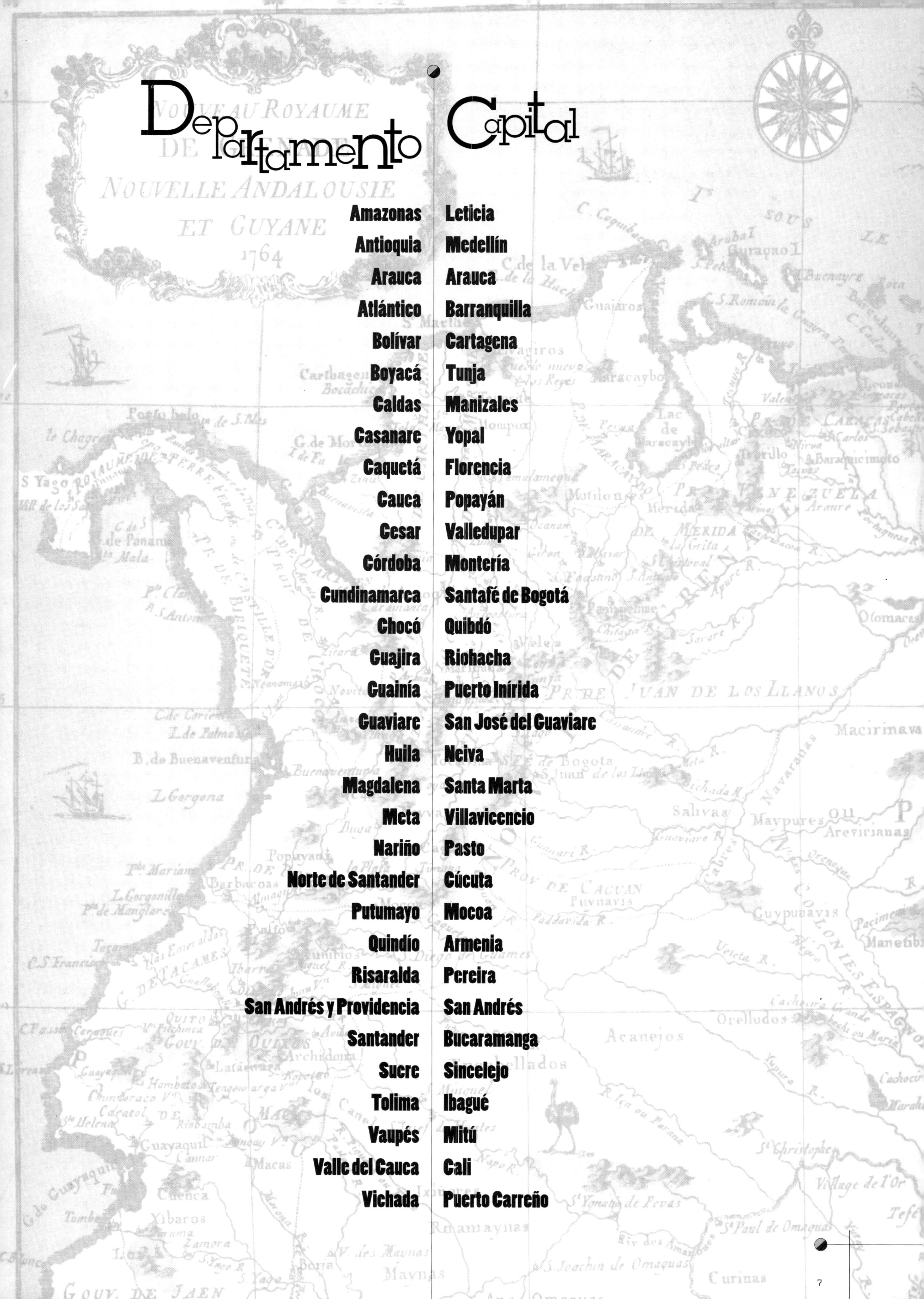

Departamento	Capital
Amazonas	Leticia
Antioquia	Medellín
Arauca	Arauca
Atlántico	Barranquilla
Bolívar	Cartagena
Boyacá	Tunja
Caldas	Manizales
Casanare	Yopal
Caquetá	Florencia
Cauca	Popayán
Cesar	Valledupar
Córdoba	Montería
Cundinamarca	Santafé de Bogotá
Chocó	Quibdó
Guajira	Riohacha
Guainía	Puerto Inírida
Guaviare	San José del Guaviare
Huila	Neiva
Magdalena	Santa Marta
Meta	Villavicencio
Nariño	Pasto
Norte de Santander	Cúcuta
Putumayo	Mocoa
Quindío	Armenia
Risaralda	Pereira
San Andrés y Providencia	San Andrés
Santander	Bucaramanga
Sucre	Sincelejo
Tolima	Ibagué
Vaupés	Mitú
Valle del Cauca	Cali
Vichada	Puerto Carreño

todos los Paisajes todos los Climas

Sierra Nevada del Cocuy, Henry Mariño

Desafiantes montañas, donde la niebla de los páramos cubre con su silencio el frailejón y la nieve. Llanuras verdes y libres, que se extienden más allá de lo que la vista pudiera contemplar. Cálidas playas de arena blanca, donde desembocan ríos que corren por valles ardientes. Todos los paisajes posibles existen en un solo país, Colombia, que por su posición geográfica en el trópico, y por las cordilleras que la cruzan, tiene el privilegio de ser múltiple y variada en sus bellezas naturales.

Por el Nudo de los Pastos, en el departamento de Nariño, penetran los Andes a Colombia, y forman dos cordilleras: la Occidental y la Central. Más al norte, en el Nudo de Almaguer, nace la cordillera Oriental. Colombia es el país americano con el mayor número de sistemas orográficos, y gran parte de la actividad nacional se desarrolla en sus cordilleras y en los valles que las separan.

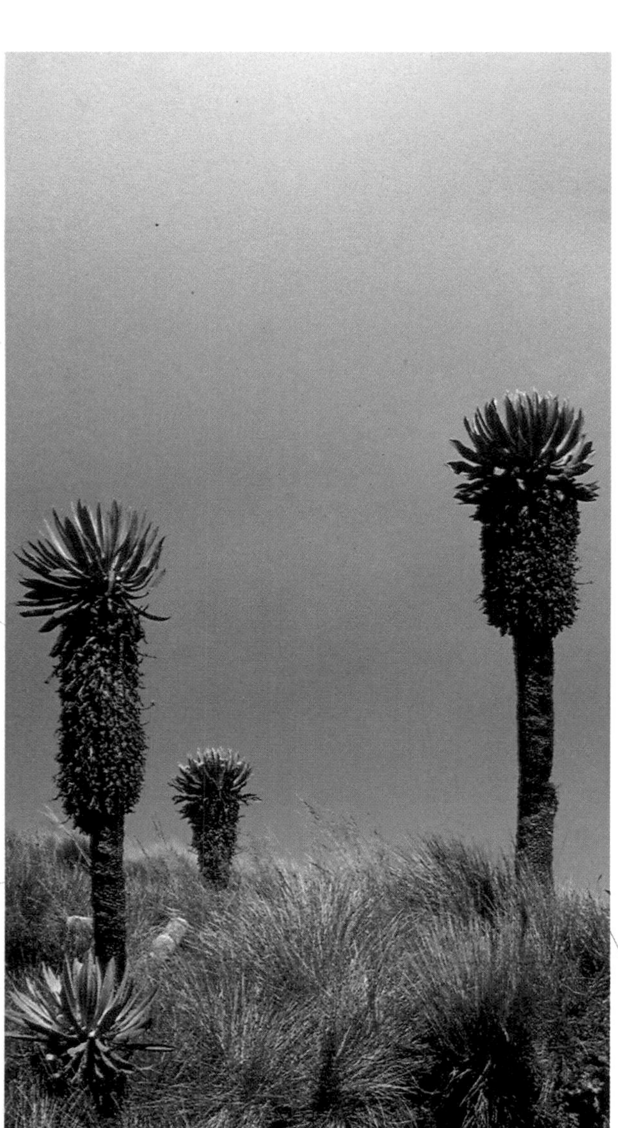

Paisaje de páramo, *Jorge Hurtado*

La cordillera Occidental respalda las húmedas selvas del Chocó. En la Central, el Parque Nacional de los Nevados eleva al cielo sus picos eternamente cubiertos de nieve. Los nevados del Tolima, Quindío, Santa Isabel y el Ruiz, son hermanos de no menos de 30 volcanes activos e inactivos que se enfilan en esta cordillera, la más antigua de las tres. El páramo más extenso del mundo, el de Sumapaz, está en la cordillera Oriental, con su mayor elevación, la Sierra Nevada del Cocuy.

La Sierra Nevada de Santa Marta, al norte, es uno de los tres sistemas montañosos autónomos de Colombia, y es el conjunto orográfico litoral más alto del mundo. En ella se eleva como un reto el pico Cristóbal Colón, la mayor cima del país, con 5.775 metros. Pero si la Sierra Nevada es hermosa en su imponencia, la Serranía de la Macarena, al suroriente, es uno de los más importantes recursos naturales de Colombia. Declarada Reserva y Parque Nacional, la Serranía de La Macarena guarda elementos de fauna y flora únicos, por su situación de puente ecológico entre las zonas andinas y las llanuras selváticas del Orinoco y el Amazonas. Igualmente importante es la Serranía del Baudó, situada al occidente del departamento del Chocó, en una de las zonas con mayor precipitación pluvial del planeta.

Al oriente del país, abarcando el 60% de su territorio se extienden los llanos, un mar verde de 400.000 Kms cuadrados. La calidez de su clima parece justificar el espíritu independiente y cordial del llanero. La mitad sur de los llanos la constituye la cuenca amazónica, una hermosa región de bosques vírgenes, caudalosos ríos, extraños animales y mucho misterio.

Taganga, *Ramiro Posada*

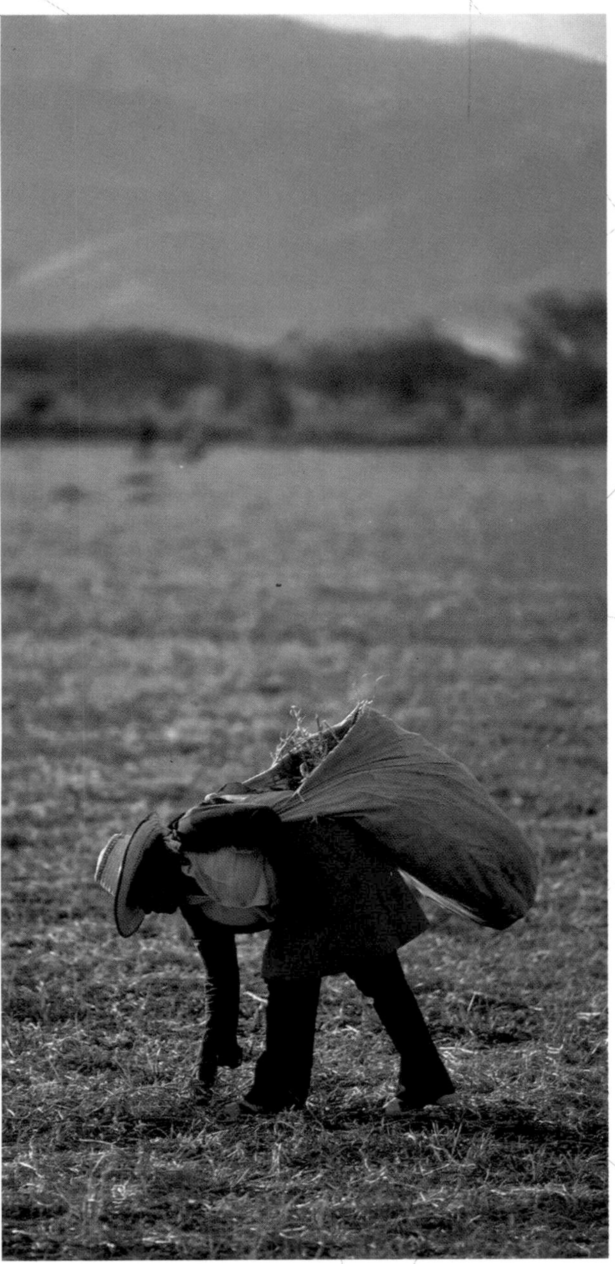

Valle del Cauca,
Patrick Rouillard

Complementando este mosaico de paisajes y climas, las dos zonas costeras constituyen cada una un mundo aparte. Al norte, la región caribe es la bullanguera, la visitada por cientos de turistas año tras año. Cálida y húmeda en el sur con sus vastas plantaciones de banano, se torna seca y árida hasta llegar al ardiente desierto de La Guajira. Pese a que la economía de la región se basa principalmente en la ganadería, la llanura Caribe es también sitio para grandes ciudades como Barranquilla, Cartagena y Santa Marta, que han permitido el desarrollo de la industria y la agricultura intensiva.

En contraste, la zona del pacífico parece ser un paraíso de silencios. Su clima cálido y húmedo se debe a su baja altura sobre el nivel del mar y a las casi constantes lluvias que la bañan: aproximadamente doce mil milímetros anuales, uno de los niveles más altos del mundo. La pesca y los recursos madereros son las principales fuentes de ingreso de una región que aún tiene mucho por ofrecer en crecimiento y desarrollo.

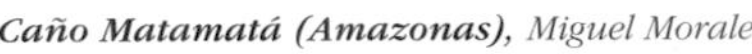

Caño Matamatá (Amazonas), *Miguel Morales*

Selva chocoana, *Camillo Volpe*

Desierto de La Tatacoa (Huila),
Jorge Hurtado

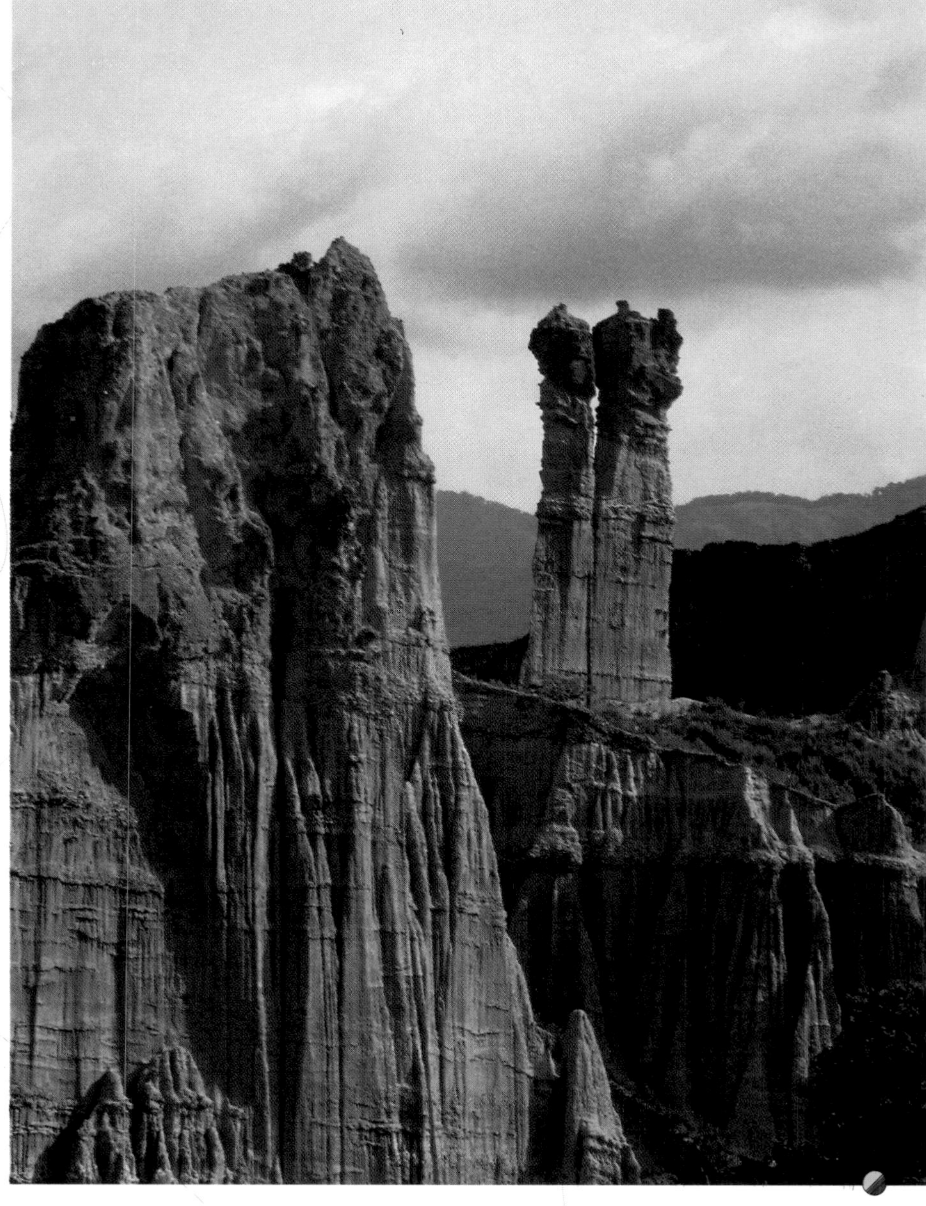

Esta variedad en el relieve geográfico determina que Colombia goce prácticamente de todas las temperaturas. Según la altura sobre el nivel del mar, cinco climas marcan en el país las costumbres y hasta tipos humanos de su gente. Hasta los 1.000 metros, la temperatura es cálida (más de 24 °C) como en las zonas costeras, los llanos orientales, selvas húmedas, y los valles interandinos. Entre los 1.000 y 2.000 metros, el clima templado, de 24 °C a 17 °C, hizo que la mayoría de las ciudades colombianas nacieran en los lugares donde es posible disfrutarlo. De 2.000 a 3.000 metros se vive un clima frío, entre 17 °C y 12 °C en los altiplanos, vertientes y cumbres menores del país. Por encima de los 3.000 metros están los páramos, escasamente habitados, con temperaturas menores de 12 °C. Más arriba, sobre los 3.500 metros, los nevados y sus bajísimas temperaturas imposibilitan cualquier asentamiento permanente.

Salvo las modificaciones debidas a la altura, la posición tropical de Colombia le permite disfrutar un clima más o menos constante.

Azul de mar, Costas e islas

Scooner Bay (San Andrés),
Jorge Navas

Cormoranes y flamingos (Guajira),
Miguel Morales

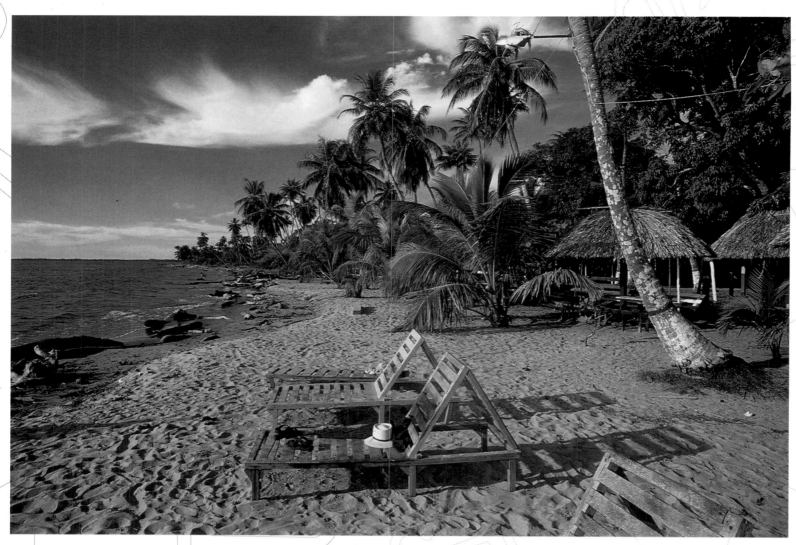

Necoclí (Antioquia),
Juan Carlos Balcázar

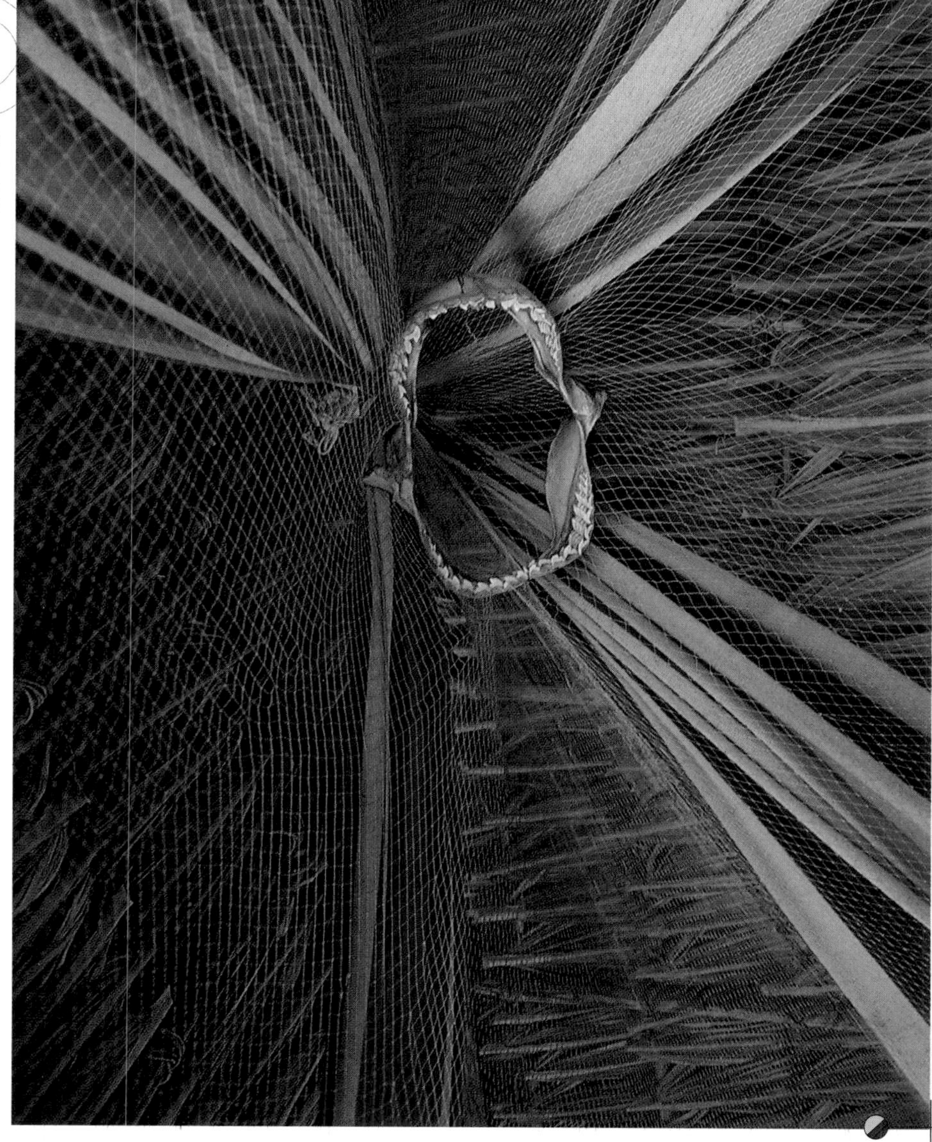

Fauces de tiburón con hamacas. Cartagena (Bolívar),
Edgar Garcés

Como si fuera un caballito de mar, Colombia cabalga sobre las aguas de dos océanos. Riqueza pesquera, facilidades para el comercio exterior, sol, playas y alegría, son algunos de los regalos que las olas del Atlántico y el Pacífico le traen cada vez que llegan a sus costas.

Más de 140 playas de muy diversos tipos se reparten en las dos zonas costeras, haciendo de Colombia un país especialmente atractivo para el turismo. La caribe, de 1.600 kilómetros, se extiende desde la orilla occidental del Golfo de Urabá hasta Castilletes, en La Guajira. Toda la alegría de Cartagena o Santa Marta, las arenas blancas de Coveñas o Moñitos, la soledad salvaje del Cabo de la Vela, atraen temporada tras temporada a turistas de todo el mundo. La costa pacífica, menos activa turísticamente, pero con playas de indescriptible belleza, extiende sus 1.300 kilómetros entre la frontera con Panamá al norte, y la desembocadura del río Mataje en límites con Ecuador, al sur.

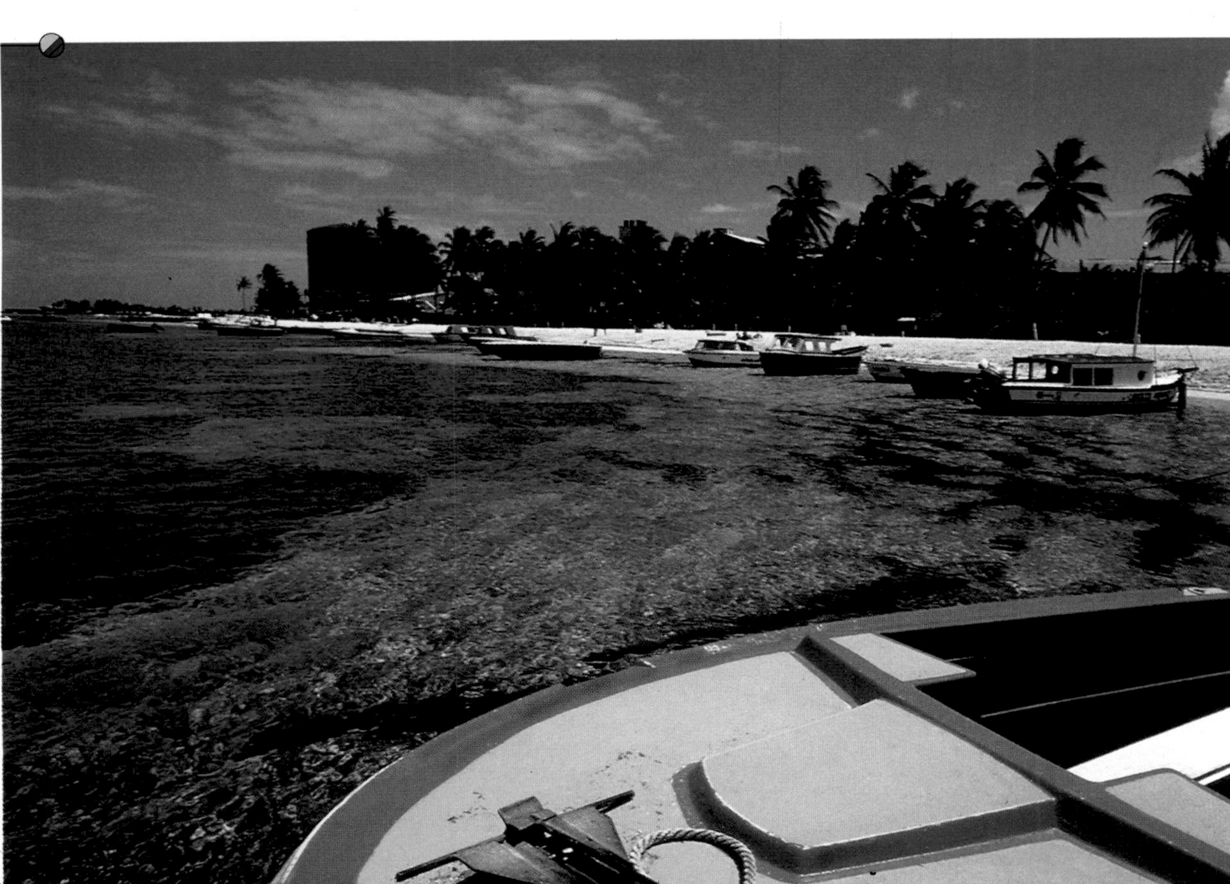

Bahía de las Sardinas (San Andrés), *Patrick Ruillard*

A 480 kilómetros de las costas colombianas, y en medio del Mar de las Antillas está el archipiélago de San Andrés y Providencia, explosión de azules que integra uno de los más importantes centros turísticos en el Caribe. Otras islas colombianas en el Atlántico son Santa Catalina, Tierra Bomba, Barú, Isla Fuerte, Salamanca, Islas del Rosario, San Bernardo y los bancos de Serrana, Serranilla, Quitasueño y Rosalinda.

En el océano Pacífico, la Isla de Gorgona es un centro de investigación bioecológica, luego de ser una prisión de máxima seguridad. Hoy la vegetación cubre los muros y las rejas y la isla es un paraíso para los delfines, las ballenas, y todo el que quiera hacer un turismo tranquilo y diferente. Otras islas en el Pacífico, tan hermosas como Gorgona, son Malpelo y Gorgonilla.

Nuquí (Chocó), *Camillo Volpe*

Agua Viva de ríos y lagunas

Coconuco, Camillo Volpe

En América sólo el Brasil y Canadá aventajan a Colombia en la cantidad de ríos que recorren su territorio. Unos torrentosos y cortos, otros extensos y mansos, la mayoría de los ríos colombianos nacen en las frías cumbres de los páramos andinos, y forman cuatro vertientes principales: la Atlántica, la Pacífica, la del Orinoco y la del Amazonas.

El Río Grande de la Magdalena, o río Magdalena, es el principal del país, y el río interandino de mayor longitud en América del Sur. Ha sido desde siempre el eje de la nación y antes de las carreteras o el transporte aéreo, fue la principal vía colombiana, la que facilitó la comunicación con el exterior y dio salida a productos tan importantes como el café en el siglo XIX. A lo largo de sus riveras surgieron pueblos y ciudades, y puede decirse que buena parte del desarrollo colombiano navegó por sus aguas.

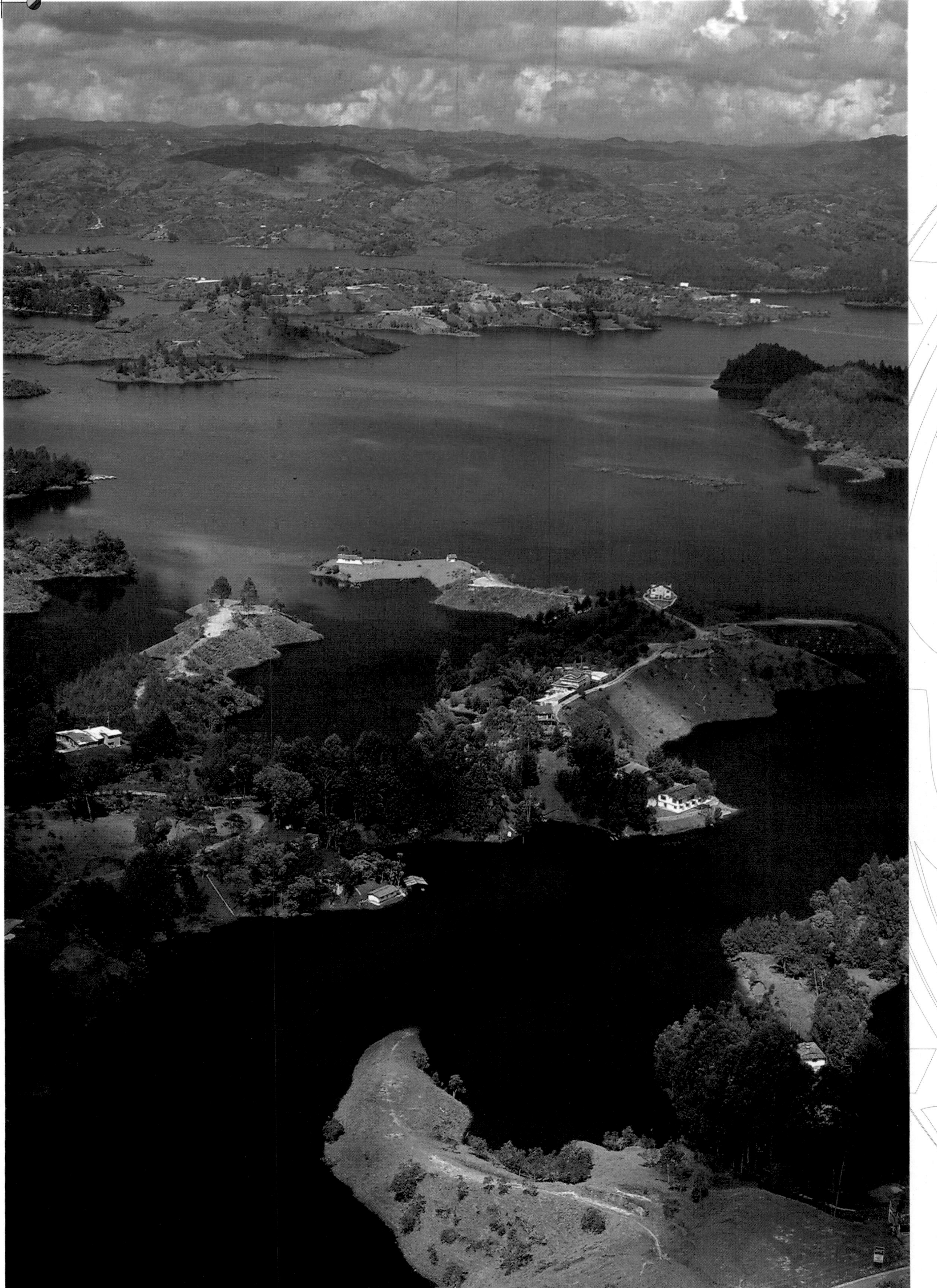

Embalse del Peñol (Antioquia), *Juan Carlos Balcázar*

Junto con el Magdalena, muchos otros ríos colombianos fertilizan sus orillas, y forman hermosos valles. 8.180 kilómetros de ellos son navegables y permiten la comunicación con extensas zonas del país. Algunos como en Antioquia, el Chocó y la Orinoquía, arrastran en sus aguas oro y platino. Otros rompen montañas como el Patía, o llevan la vida y el progreso a zonas selváticas, como el río Caquetá. Con el Magdalena, el Cauca forma la depresión de Mompós, una región de ciénagas riquísimas en recursos pesqueros. Por el contrario, el río Vinagre, que nace cerca del volcán Puracé, no crea vida a su paso: sus aguas, ricas en ácidos y azufre, forman en su desembocadura con el Cauca una barrera química que niega cualquier posibilidad a los peces o las plantas. El San Juan y el Patía son el río más largo y el más caudaloso, respectivamente, de todos los que en América del Sur desembocan en el Pacífico. Y el río Atrato, con relación al tamaño de su cuenca, es uno de los más caudalosos del mundo.

Pero no sólo los ríos conforman la inmensa riqueza hidrográfica de Colombia. Cientos de lagunas y ciénagas salpican su territorio. La Ciénaga Grande de Santa Marta y la de Betancí en la llanura caribe, junto con las lagunas de Suesca, Tota, Guatavita, la Cocha, Zapatoca y Fúquene en la región andina, son algunas de las muchas que se reparten en todo el país y constituyen el medio de subsistencia de gran cantidad de colombianos.

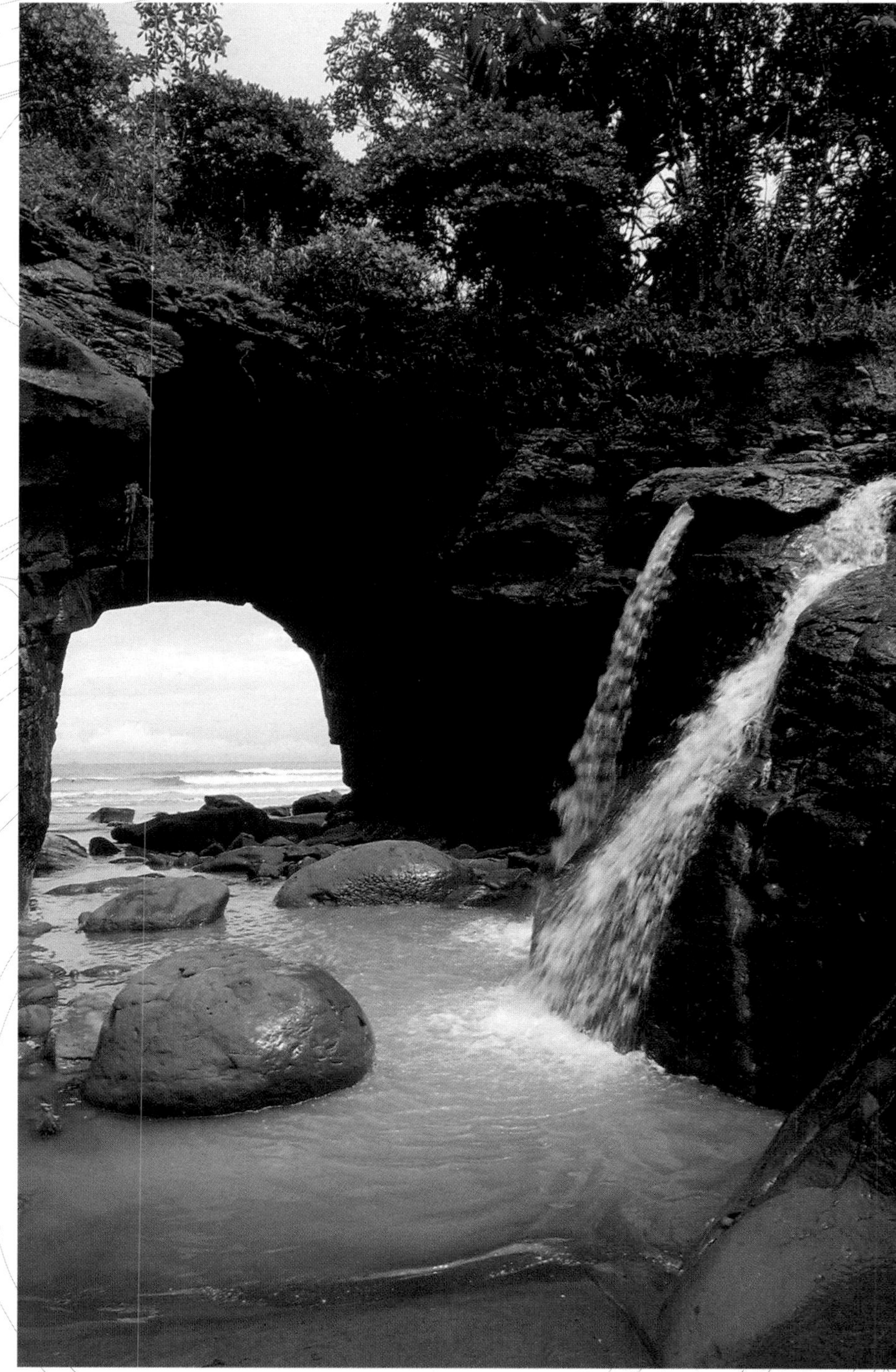

Paisaje chocoano, *Jorge Hurtado*

Túquerres (Nariño), *Camillo Volpe*

El país de las flores y las aves

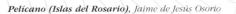

Pelícano (Islas del Rosario), Jaime de Jesús Osorio

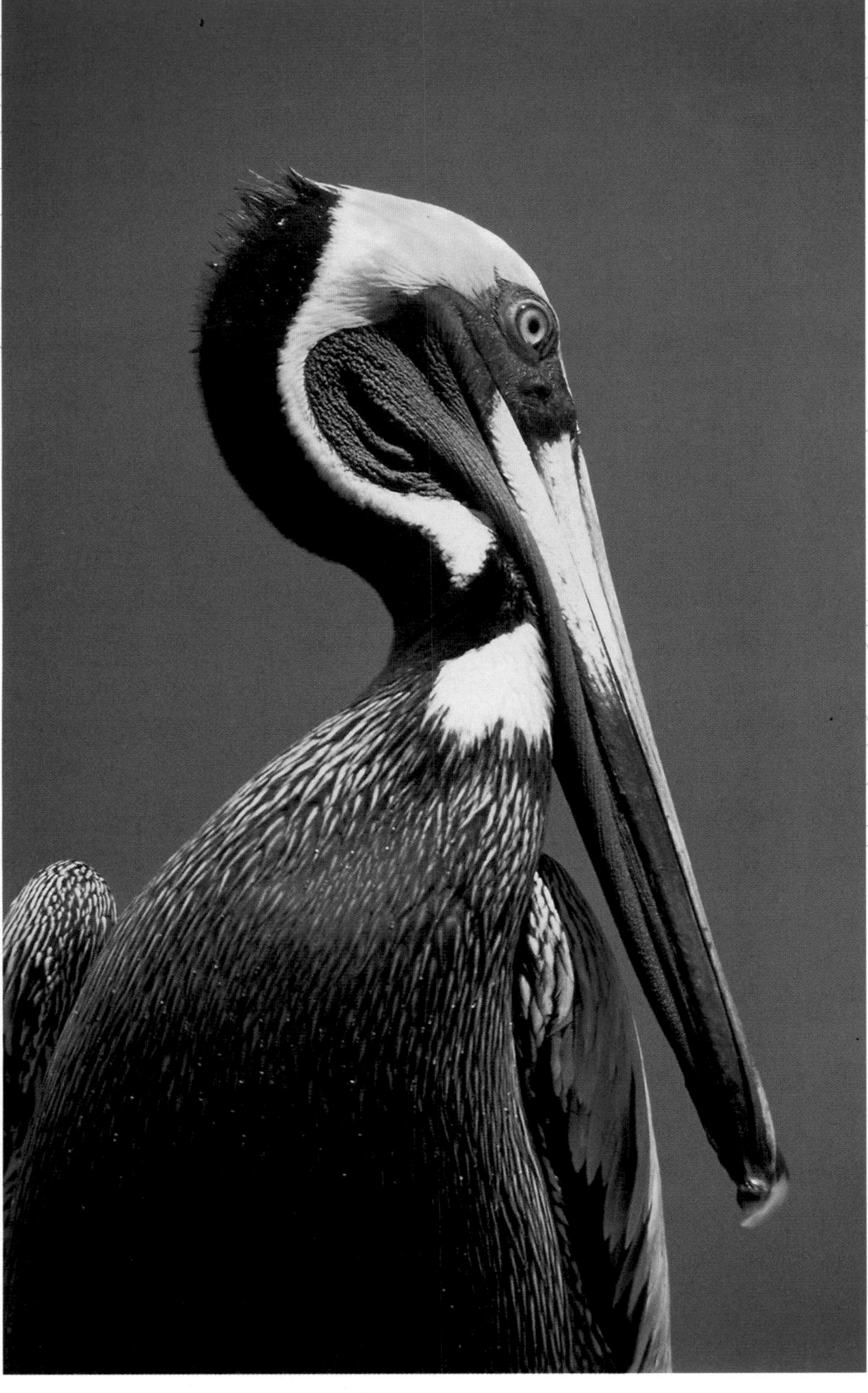

El 72% de la superficie colombiana, equivalente a 46 millones de hectáreas, representa la superficie forestal del país. De esta cantidad, doce millones son aprovechadas de manera permanente, pero la tala de árboles, unida a las quemas, hacen que anualmente un millón de ellas se pierdan.

Selvas tropicales cubren gran parte del país con una vegetación aparentemente inagotable. Bajo este manto está la zona del mundo más rica en especies vegetales, insectos y aves: Colombia es el territorio de más variada vegetación en América, el que alberga la mayor cantidad de especies de aves en el mundo entero (2.700), y el tercero en variedades de loros y guacamayas.

La corocora. Caño Limón (Arauca), *Thomas McNish*

En Antioquia, el Parque Nacional de las Orquídeas encierra no menos de 200 especies distintas, que son apenas una muestra de la inmensa variedad de especies vegetales que crecen a lo largo y ancho del país. La mayor extensión de páramos del mundo está en Colombia, y en ellos el frailejón es un ejemplo de adaptación al medio ambiente, al igual que la victoria regia, el loto gigante que crece en las aguas de la zona amazónica.

Pero si estos recursos vegetales son frágiles y requieren un cuidado ecológico adecuado, la variedad de especies animales que pueblan el país no lo son menos. Colombia posee tres de las cuatro especies de danta que existen, hoy en claro peligro de extinción. Más de 200 especies de lagartos conviven con tortugas, babillas, iguanas y caimanes. En el Amazonas vive uno de los peces más pequeños del mundo, el carnero, de sólo 1.5 cms, y en el Chocó, la rana Cocoi es considerada la más venenosa del planeta. Junto con la rana Arlequín, que vive en los páramos colombianos y es el batracio que en todo el mundo reside a mayor altura, constituyen casos únicos de la fauna universal.

Narciso de agua (Amazonas), *Miguel Morales*

Cóndor de los Andes, Miguel Morales

145 especies y subespecies de colibríes comparten el cielo con 76 especies de aves rapaces, de las que el cóndor de los Andes fue alguna vez el rey. Hoy quedan algunos ejemplares en la Sierra Nevada de Santa Marta y en inmediaciones del volcán de Sotará. Como el cóndor, en Colombia quedan algunos ejemplares de un animal muy especial: el oso de anteojos, el único del hemisferio sur.

En el Amazonas habitan dos clases de primates poco comunes: el mono tití enano, el más pequeño del mundo, y el mono de noche, el único entre los simios con hábitos nocturnos. Chigüiros, jaguares, dantas: especies animales que constituyen riqueza tanto o más que cualquier recurso económico, y que hacen del colombiano, un territorio especialmente mimado por la naturaleza.

Cayeno (Amazonas), Miguel Morales

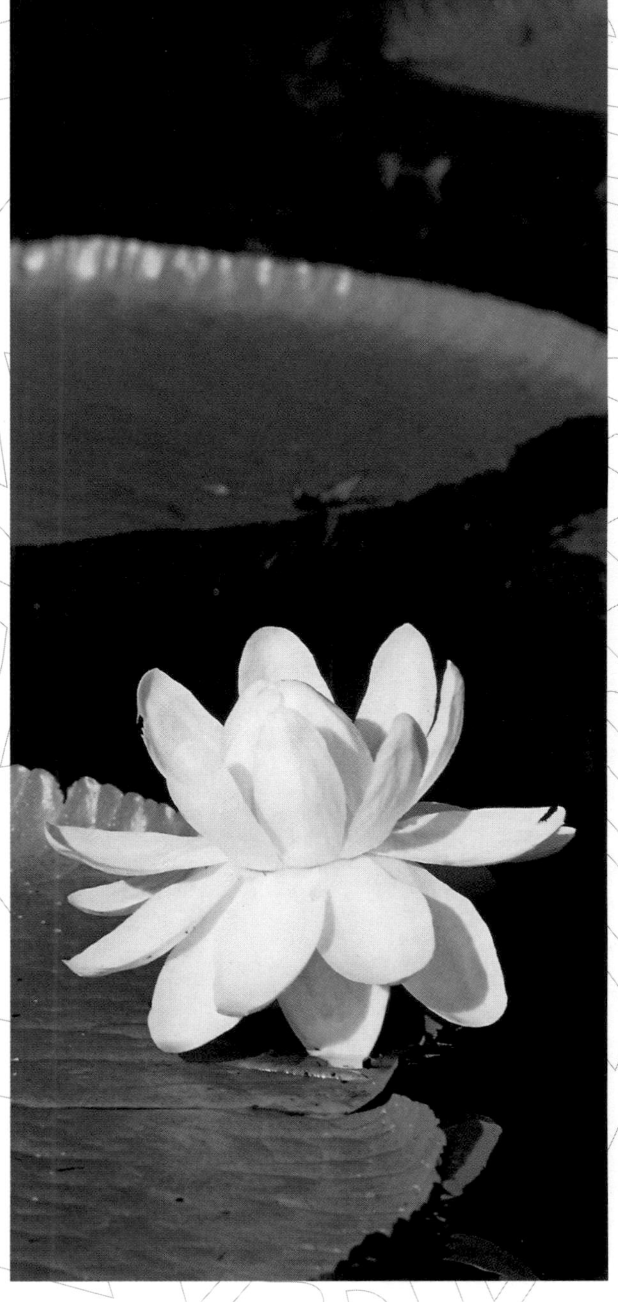

Victoria Regia (Amazonas), Miguel Morales

Campo y ciudad, dos caras de la misma Colombia

Medellín (Antioquia),
Juan Carlos Balcázar

Hasta hace pocas décadas la mayoría de los colombianos vivía en las zonas rurales. Hoy, casi el 67% de la población habita en los centros urbanos. Y sin embargo Colombia es un país de vocación agraria, con más de veinte millones de hectáreas cultivables atendidas por la tercera parte de su población total.

Las ciudades colombianas han experimentado un crecimiento continuo desde el siglo pasado. Muchas de ellas nacieron a la vera de los caminos, o fueron fundadas por colonos emprendedores que abrieron las selvas a golpe de hacha. Casi todas copiaron el esquema español de la plaza central y la distribución por manzanas. En Colombia, las iglesias forman a su alrededor espacios nuevos, y cada población del país tiene su plaza o parque principal, además de uno o dos barrios tradicionales que crecieron alrededor de la parroquia: La Candelaria en Bogotá, San Antonio en Cali, Prado en Medellín, o Manga en Cartagena.

Finca cafetera.
Chinchiná (Caldas),
Miguel Morales

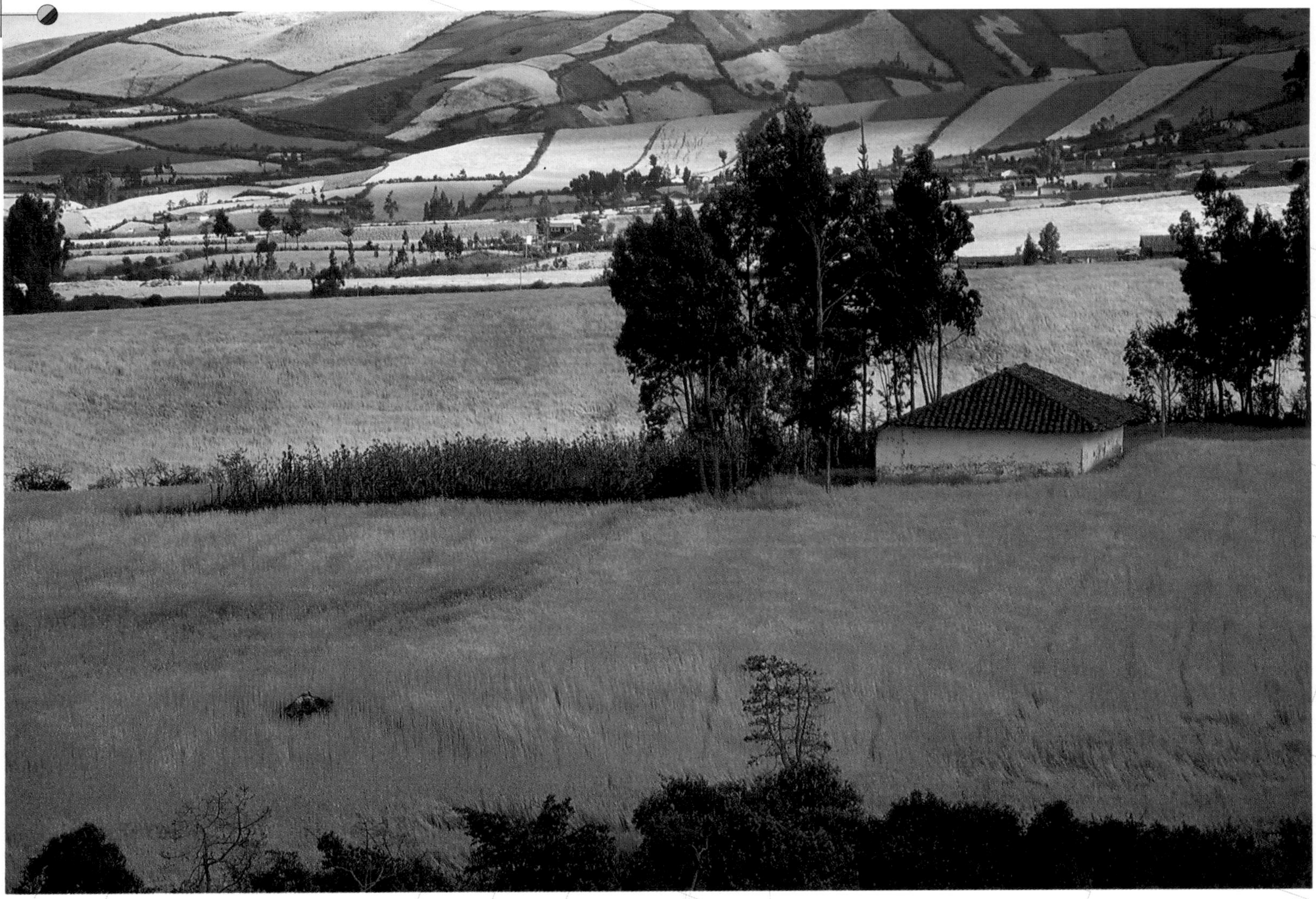

Cultivo de trigo (Nariño), Miguel Morales

Centro Internacional (Santafé de Bogotá), Miguel Morales

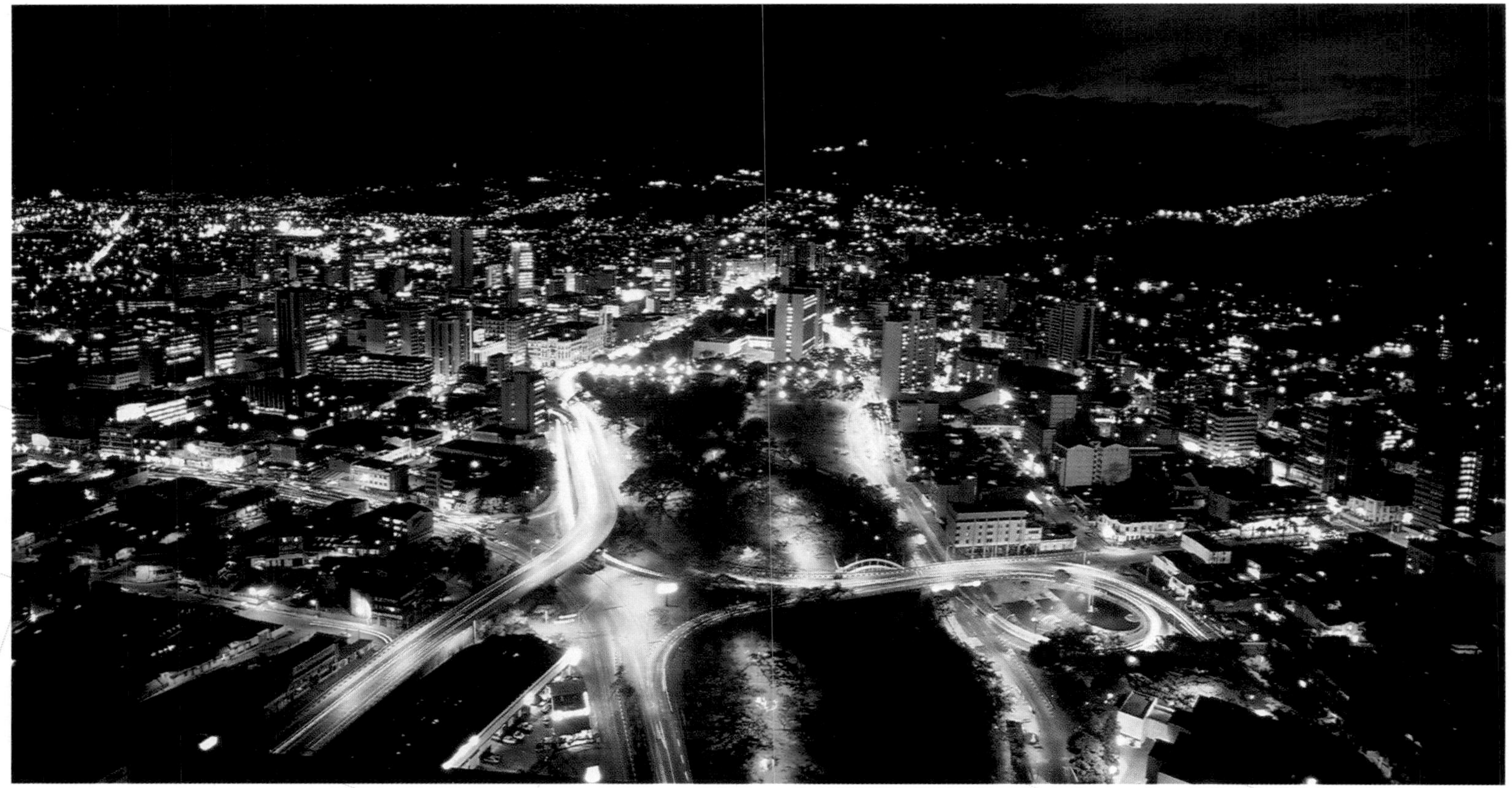

Cali (Valle), *Juan Carlos Balcázar*

De arquitectura heterogénea, como sucede en un país joven y abierto a toda clase de influencias, las ciudades colombianas, a pesar de su progreso, guardan rincones amables donde todavía es posible sentirse individuo. Siete de ellas sobrepasan ampliamente el medio millón de habitantes: Bogotá, Medellín, Cali, Barranquilla, Cartagena, Bucaramanga y Cúcuta. En las tres primeras el fenómeno de la conurbación es consecuencia de su acelerado crecimiento.

Grandes o pequeñas, cada una de las ciudades del país tiene su importancia y su personalidad propia, que se traduce no sólo en aspectos externos como la arquitectura o los servicios públicos, sino también en las costumbres y en el temperamento de sus habitantes. A pesar de que los centros urbanos concentran gran parte de su actividad comercial, industrial y financiera, Colombia obtiene de las zonas rurales gran parte de sus recursos, y no hay prácticamente ningún colombiano que no tenga sus inmediatas raíces en algún pequeño pueblo perdido en la inmensidad de la geografía nacional.

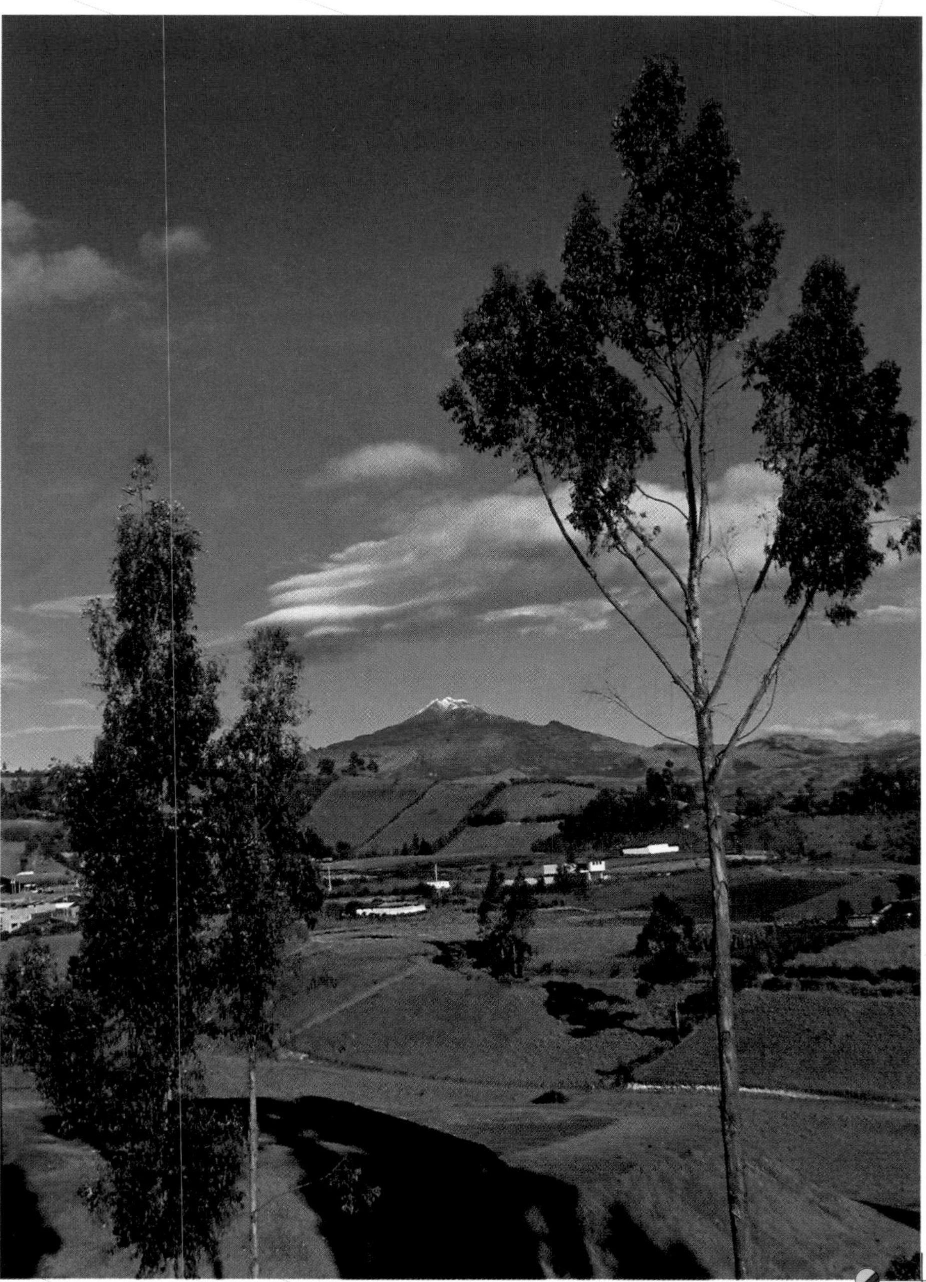

Nariño, *Craig Duncan*

De los Caminos de herradura a los aeropuertos internacionales

Uno de los índices de progreso de un país es la cantidad y operatividad de sus medios de comunicación. Esto es particularmente cierto para una nación como Colombia, cuya difícil geografía obstaculizó por mucho tiempo su desarrollo y mantuvo aisladas extensas zonas de su territorio.

Durante la colonia, viajar de Cartagena a Santafé de Bogotá era una auténtica odisea. Los caminos reales, que se empezaron a construir sólo a partir de 1825, atravesaban selvas, profundos abismos y torrentosos ríos, en un viaje que duraba semanas enteras. Sólo a finales del siglo XIX el ferrocarril vino a hacer un poco más rápidas estas comunicaciones, desarrollando vastas zonas y facilitando la exportación de productos agrícolas. Su actividad se vio desplazada por la actual red de carreteras y por la aviación nacional, que nacieron casi a la vez en la década del 20.

Barichara (Santander), *Camillo Volpe*

Bolombolo (Antioquia),
Juan Carlos Balcázar

Actualmente buena parte de la carga y los pasajeros se movilizan por carretera, en un sistema formado por troncales: la occidental, la central, la costera, la pacífica, y las carreteras bolivariana y panamericana. Esta red vial mantiene vivo el pulso económico del país, y conecta sus centros con zonas que de otra manera permanecerían aisladas.

Los puertos más importantes del país son Buenaventura y Tumaco en el Pacífico, y Cartagena, Barranquilla y Santa Marta en el Atlántico. Los principales aeropuertos, y los que registran mayor movimiento, son El Dorado en Bogotá, Ernesto Cortisoz en Barranquilla, José María Córdoba en Medellín, Alfonso Bonilla Aragón en Cali, y Rafael Núñez en Cartagena.

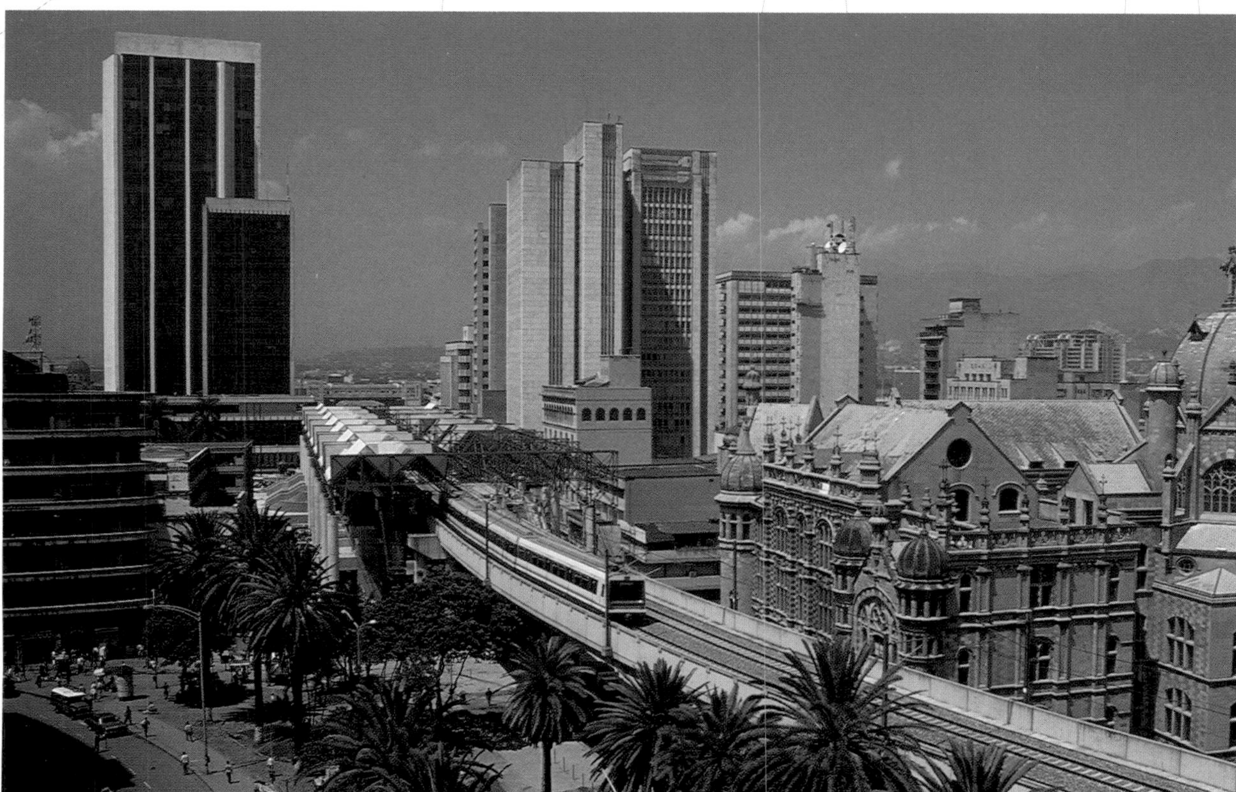

Medellín (Antioquia),
Manuel Hormaza

Aeropuerto Ernesto Cortizos.
Barranquilla (Atlántico),
Henry Mariño

Además de estos hay gran número de aeródromos locales en ciudades intermedias y otras poblaciones, que hacen del transporte aéreo el segundo en importancia después del terrestre.

Aeropuerto José María Córdoba.
Rionegro (Antioquia),
Patrick Rouillard

Algo de Historia

Muchos siglos antes de que llegaran los españoles a América, ya en Colombia habitaban diversas culturas indígenas. Su posición geográfica la hizo territorio de tránsito para los diversos pueblos que ocuparon Suramérica. Estos primeros rastros de ocupación humana se remontan a 10.000 años antes de nuestra era. Las comunidades que alcanzaron mayor desarrollo vivían en los llanos y laderas de la región andina, e intercambiaban sus productos con los pobladores de las costas.

Para 1492, se calcula la población precolombina en 850.000 personas, distribuidas en los diversos grupos.

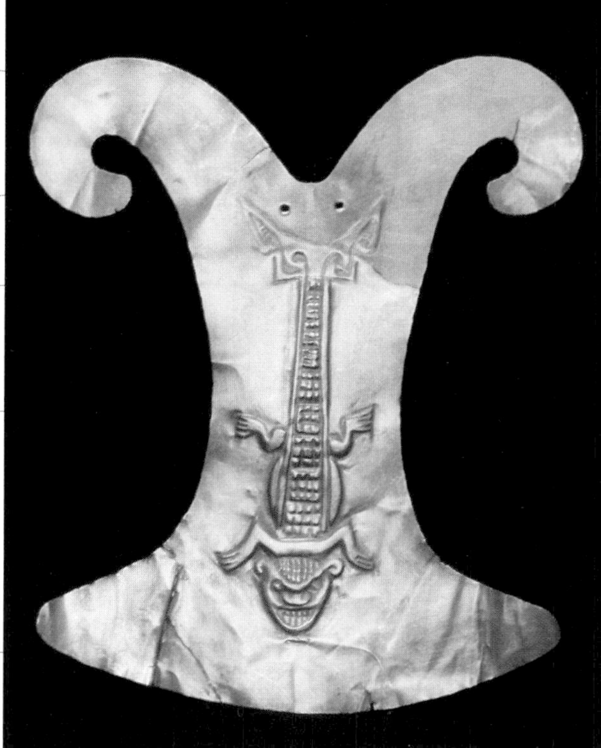

Pieza de Tierradentro. Santafé de Bogotá (Cundinamarca), *Archivo Museo del oro*

Los chibchas fueron posteriores a la cultura agustiniana que floreció entre los siglos II y III d.c. y que desapareció dejando como un mudo mensaje la estatuaria que puebla el Parque Arqueológico de San Agustín. Los taironas ocuparon la Sierra Nevada de Santa Marta, y desarrollaron avanzadas tecnologías en agricultura. Los quimbayas y calimas, y en general todos los pueblos precolombinos, dominaron las artes de la cerámica y la orfebrería. Un pequeño rastro de su trabajo se conserva en el Museo del Oro en Bogotá. Todos estos grupos poseían formas organizadas de gobierno, y establecían alianzas y pactos políticos entre sí. A partir de la conquista su actividad fue poco a poco reducida, sus tesoros saqueados, su territorio ocupado, y en general su identidad perdida en un proceso de aculturación. Este período de conquista va de 1509 a 1550, y es en estos años cuando se fundan la mayoría de las ciudades colombianas.

Durante la colonia, las audiencias, presidentes y virreyes representaron el poder real. La agricultura y la explotación del oro sustentaron la economía del país. Santafé de Bogotá era la capital del virreinato de la Nueva Granada, y el 20 de julio de 1810, fecha del grito de independencia, contaba con menos de 50.000 habitantes.

Fuente de Lavapatas. San Agustín (Huila), *Miguel Morales*

Entretejido casa indígena Kogui.
Sierra Nevada de Santa Marta,
Manuel Hormaza

La Campaña Libertadora al mando del General Simón Bolívar culminó el 7 de agosto de 1819 con la batalla del Puente de Boyacá. Todo el siglo XIX sería una época de ajustes políticos y económicos, caracterizados por sucesivas guerras civiles que alcanzaron su clímax con la Guerra de los Mil Días, entre 1899 y 1903, año en que Panamá se independizó de Colombia.

Los primeros años del siglo XX estuvieron determinados por largos periodos en el poder de los dos partidos políticos tradicionales, el liberal y el conservador. Esta lucha creó un clima de violencia política que se recrudeció especialmente entre 1948 y 1953, a raíz del asesinato del líder liberal Jorge Eliécer Gaitán. A estos duros años puso fin una dictadura militar entre 1953 y 1957, tras la cual liberales y conservadores acordaron el establecimiento de un Frente Nacional, en el que se alternarían sucesivamente en el gobierno, por un período de 16 años: 1958 a 1974.

Indígena Guambiano. Silvia (Cauca), *Camillo Volpe*

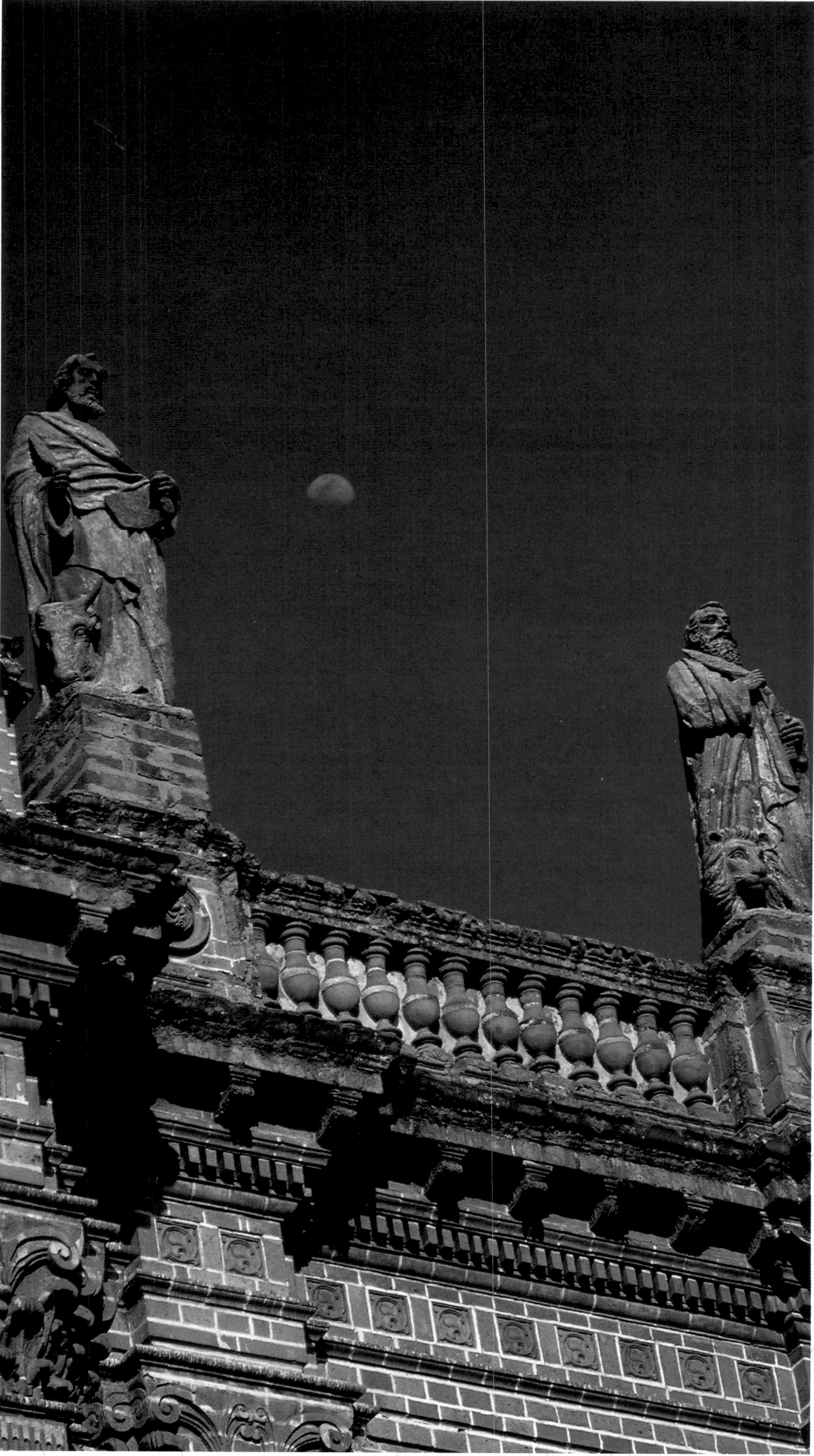

Iglesia de San José. Medellín (Antioquia),
Juan Carlos Balcázar

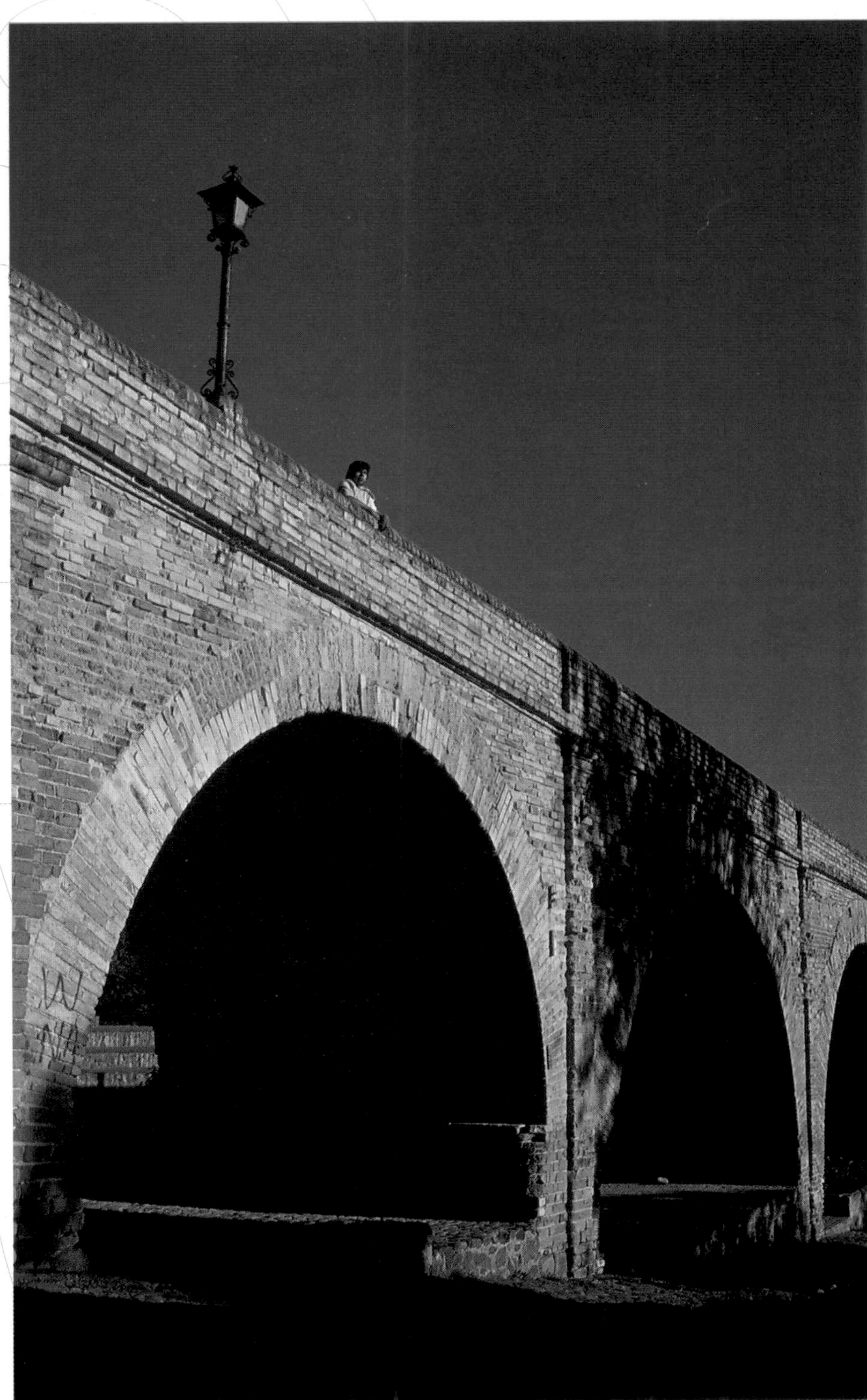

Puente del humilladero.
Popayán (Cauca),
Markus Oertly

Barco de los espíritus. Cultura Emberá.
Museo Etnográfico Madre Laura.
Medellín (Antioquia),
Juan Carlos Balcázar

Túquerres (Nariño), *Camillo Volpe*

Terminado el Frente Nacional los dos partidos tradicionales, junto con nuevas fuerzas políticas que han surgido, luchan por gobernar el país dentro del más recto marco democrático.

La constitución vigente en Colombia fue redactada en 1991 por una Asamblea Nacional Constituyente. Por medio de ella se establece que la nación es una república unitaria, cuyo gobierno se compone de tres poderes independientes entre sí: Ejecutivo, Legislativo, y Judicial.

La constitución consagra la libertad de cultos. La flor nacional es la orquídea, y la palma de cera del Quindío es el árbol que representa al país.

El Himno Nacional fue escrito por el presidente Rafael Núñez, y su música compuesta por Orestes Sindici. La bandera está formada por tres franjas; amarilla, azul y roja, y el escudo representa las riquezas naturales, la libertad y la importancia marítima del país.

La fiesta nacional, que conmemora el Grito de Independencia, se celebra cada 20 de julio.

Salto del Tequendama (Cundinamarca), *Henry Mariño*

Riquezas de las entrañas de la Tierra

Oro, plata, platino, esmeraldas, plomo, cobre, asbesto, carbón, calizas, azufre, fosfatos, todos duermen muy adentro, bajo el suelo colombiano, esperando regalar sus maravillas. Muchos de estos yacimientos han sido explotados desde tiempo inmemorial. El oro, por ejemplo, enriqueció gran parte del país gracias a las cuadrillas que, en su búsqueda, fundaron pueblos y abrieron caminos. Mucho antes, los habitantes precolombinos lo elevaron a la categoría de objeto artístico. La calidad y cantidad de vetas y de oro de aluvión que posee el país, lo lleva a ocupar el noveno lugar en el mundo y el tercero en Iberoamérica por la magnitud de su producción.

Compitiendo en belleza, las esmeraldas colombianas son las más apreciadas en el mercado internacional.

Colombia produce el 95% de las esmeraldas que se comercializan en el mundo. Las minas de Muzo, Coscuez, Peñas Blancas, Chivor o Gachalá en Boyacá, son famosas por producir las más hermosas esmeraldas que se puedan conseguir.

Ecopetrol (Barrancabermeja), *Henry Barbosa*

Manaure (Guajira),
Patrick Rouillard

Más al norte, en la costa atlántica, la naturaleza vuelve a mostrar su generosidad en las salinas de Manaure, Galerazamba y Pozos Colorados, algunos de los pocos sitios de la geografía mundial que son salinas naturales de carácter permanente.

Colombia es dueña de 15 mil millones de toneladas de carbón, la mayor reserva de Iberoamérica. Gran parte está localizada en El Cerrejón (departamento de La Guajira), la mayor explotación a cielo abierto del mundo, con una extensión de 76.000 hectáreas divididas en tres zonas.

Máscara Precolombina, colección I.C.A.N. (Santafé de Bogotá),
Juan Carlos Balcázar

Manaure (Guajira),
Patrick Rouillard

En 1951 nace la Empresa Colombiana de Petróleo, ECOPETROL, encargada del manejo del recurso petrolero del país. Desde 1969 la empresa estableció los contratos de asociación, que han permitido la localización de importantes yacimientos. Los principales pozos se encuentran en el Catatumbo y Zulia cerca de Venezuela; en el Putumayo, y en Arauca. En esta región se localizó en 1983 el campo Caño Limón y posteriormente el de Cusiana, los mayores hallazgos petroleros en los últimos quince años.

La producción de estos campos ha permitido a Colombia convertirse en exportador de petróleo, y hoy el sector de los hidrocarburos es uno de los principales generadores de divisas para el país.

Pozo petrolero. Llanos orientales, *Patrick Rouillard*

El Cerrejón (Guajira), *Patrick Rouillard*

Aromas y Colores de sus Campos

País de campos y cultivos, de campesinos, pequeñas parcelas e importantes agroindustrias. País de la tierra, Colombia obtiene grandes recursos del sector agrario, y buena parte de sus niveles de exportación los alcanza con sus productos: café, banano, flores y caña de azúcar.

Hace más de 200 años llegó a las montañas colombianas el café. Con excepción de la costa atlántica, se cultiva en todo el país, especialmente en los departamentos de Antioquia, Caldas, Quindío y Risaralda. El colombiano, es el mejor café suave del mundo, y su volumen de producción lo coloca en un ventajoso segundo lugar, después del Brasil.

Túquerres (Nariño), *Camillo Volpe*

Ipiales (Nariño), *Camillo Volpe*

Después del café, la mayor extensión de área cultivada se dedica a la caña de azúcar para la producción de panela, sin embargo desde principios del siglo los ingenios azucareros compiten con la panela en importancia. El Valle del Cauca es una de las pocas zonas en el mundo que permite el cultivo de caña todo el año.

En volúmenes de exportación el banano ha escalado posiciones, hasta ocupar el segundo lugar dentro de las no tradicionales. Las comercializadoras colombianas han ampliado los mercados que abarcan hoy los EE.UU., Europa, y el Medio y Lejano Oriente. Las zonas bananeras de Urabá y el Magdalena producen fruta de primera calidad, que representa significativos ingresos anuales.

Tunja (Boyacá), *Camillo Volpe*

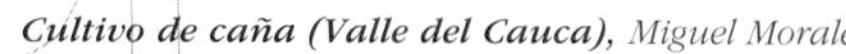

Cultivo de caña (Valle del Cauca), *Miguel Morales*

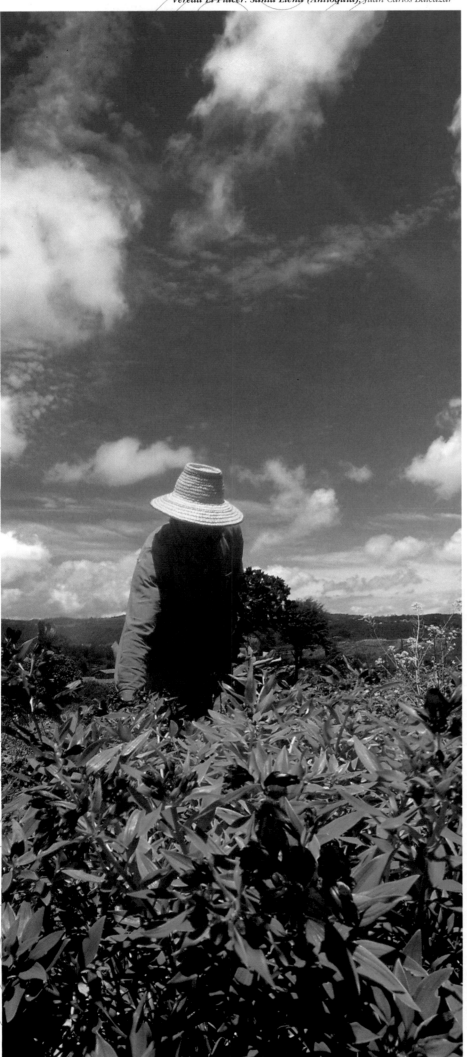

Vereda El Placer. Santa Elena (Antioquia), *Juan Carlos Balcázar*

Hermosas flores colombianas llevan mensajes de amor a personas de lejanos países. La explotación de flores ha irrumpido con fuerza, hasta el punto que hoy, Colombia es el segundo productor de flores en el mundo.

70 variedades de claveles, 70 de rosas y 150 de pompones, son cultivadas en sus invernaderos. Medalla de Oro en el Chelsea Flower Show de Londres en 1989, las flores colombianas llegan a los mercados de EE.UU., Europa, Canadá, Arabia Saudita, Kuwait, Australia, Trinidad y Tobago, Guadalupe, Surinam y Panamá, entre otros.

Café. Génova (Quindío), *Miguel Morales*

Iza (Boyacá),
Manuel Hormaza

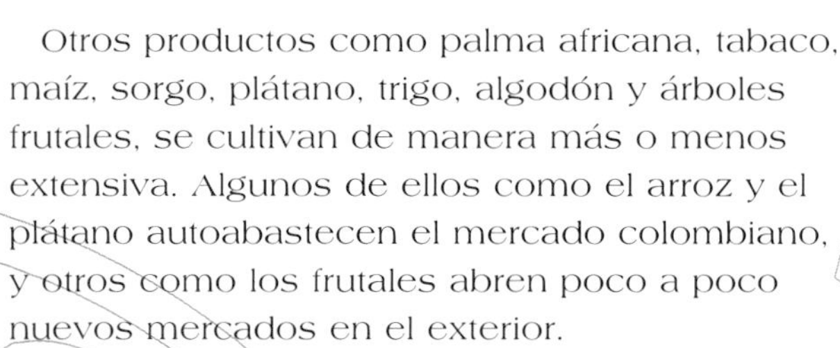

Otros productos como palma africana, tabaco, maíz, sorgo, plátano, trigo, algodón y árboles frutales, se cultivan de manera más o menos extensiva. Algunos de ellos como el arroz y el plátano autoabastecen el mercado colombiano, y otros como los frutales abren poco a poco nuevos mercados en el exterior.

En las cálidas llanuras del norte del país, en los valles interandinos, en los vastos llanos orientales y en las mesetas montañosas, aproximadamente 30 millones de cabezas de ganado ocupan más de veinte millones de hectáreas y son fuente de ingresos para el país.

Ipiales (Nariño), *Camillo Volpe*

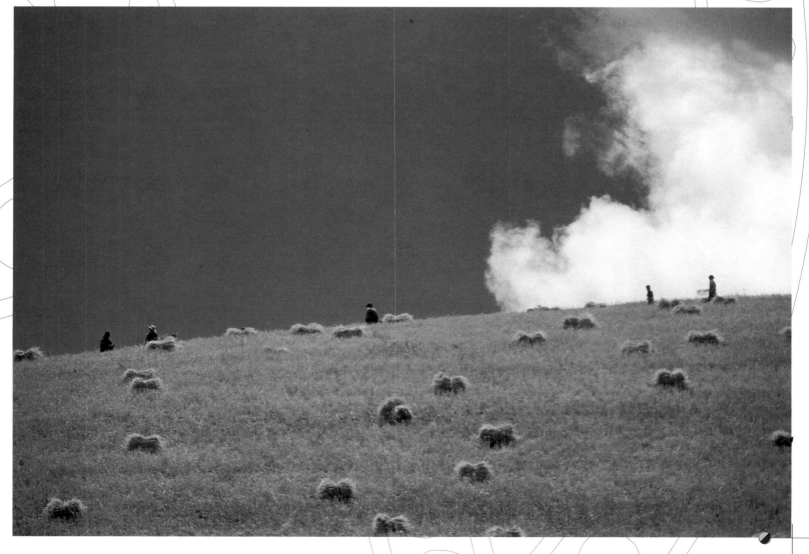

Industria a toda Marcha

Un colombiano de hace cincuenta años no reconocería hoy el paisaje de las ciudades donde vivió. Antes tranquilas, más parecidas a pequeños pueblos que a urbes, las ciudades colombianas de hoy han concentrado en las últimas cinco décadas la inmensa mayoría de los establecimientos fabriles del país. Bogotá, Medellín, Cali y Barranquilla son los principales centros industriales, pero más y más ciudades intermedias se suman al crecimiento del sector manufacturero.

Zona industrial de Barranquilla (Atlántico), *Jaime Borda*

Planta Coltejer. Rionegro (Antioquia), *Gabriel Carvajal*

Planta Industrial (Valle del Cauca), *Patrick Rouillard*

La diversificación ha sido una nota importante en los últimos cincuenta años. Empresas tradicionales como la textil y la cervecera, han visto desarrollarse nuevas industrias.

Es el caso de las productoras de alimentos y bebidas, las siderúrgicas, la automotriz, la del petróleo y sus derivados, la industria del cuero, la química y muchas más, que han registrado un crecimiento significativo no sólo en volumen de producción, sino en la calidad de los artículos que ofrecen, y que les permite competir en buenas condiciones en el comercio mundial.

Cementos Diamante (Tolima),
Juan Carlos Balcázar

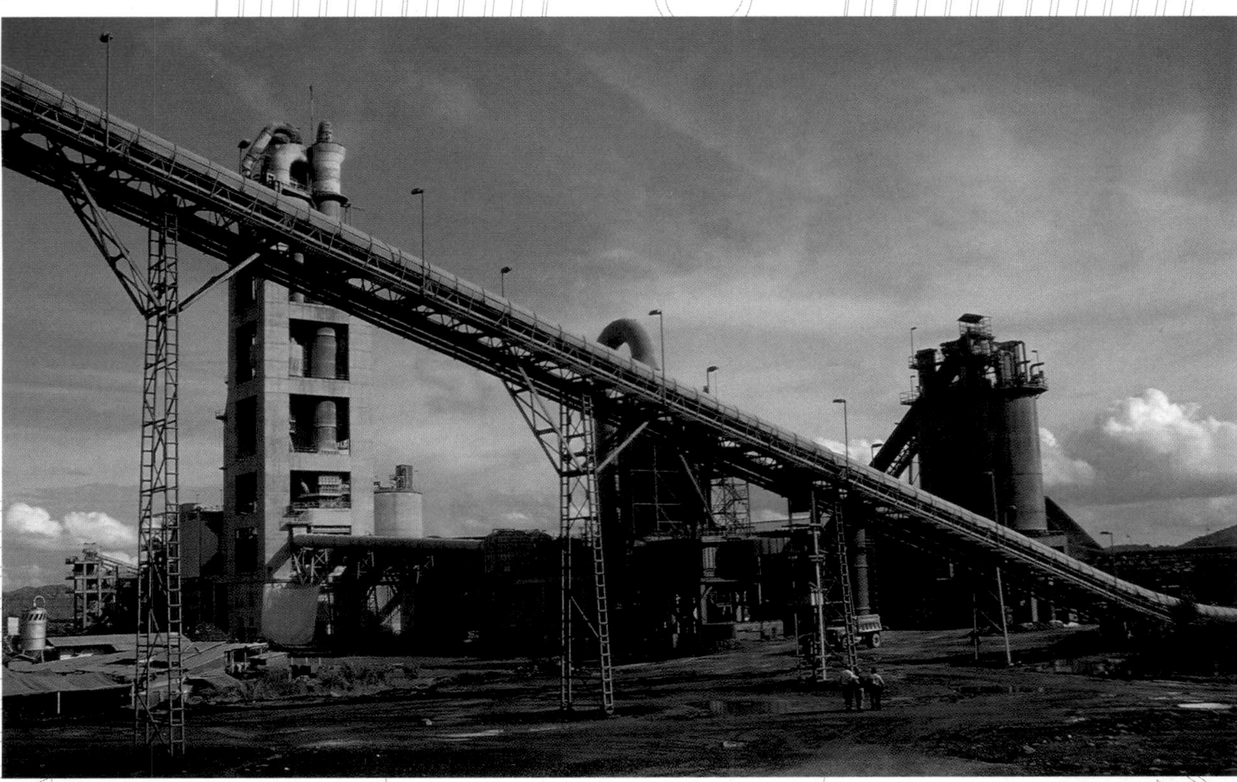

Hidroeléctrica del Guavio (Boyacá)
Juan Carlos Balcázar

Hidroeléctrica La Tasajera. Girardota (Antioquia), *Juan Carlos Balcázar*

Zona industrial de Mamonal. Cartagena (Bolívar), *Jaime Borda*

A pesar de que sus exportaciones tradicionales están constituidas por el café y el petróleo, Colombia ha realizado un esfuerzo por diversificar sus líneas de venta al exterior, y por insertar de manera efectiva su economía en la fuerte competencia de los mercados internacionales.

El país de todas las sonrisas

Bolívar (Antioquia), Camillo Volpe

¿Qué se puede decir de los colombianos?

Tejedora de Canastas. Guacamayas (Boyacá),
Manuel Hormaza

Jardín (Antioquia),
Camillo Volpe

Que son hospitalarios, recios y trabajadores. Que la gran variedad de tipos humanos que llenan de color la geografía nacional, la llenan también de sueños, risas y costumbres diferentes.

Mestizos, zambos, mulatos, negros, indios y blancos se mezclan y conviven, y le dan a Colombia ese toque de variedad en todas sus manifestaciones. Haciendo a un lado estereotipos, en cada zona se baila, come, lucha, trabaja, ríe y espera de manera diferente. El frío, la calma y los silencios de los altiplanos parecen pertenecer a un mundo aparte del bullicio, el calor y la alegría desbordante del Caribe.

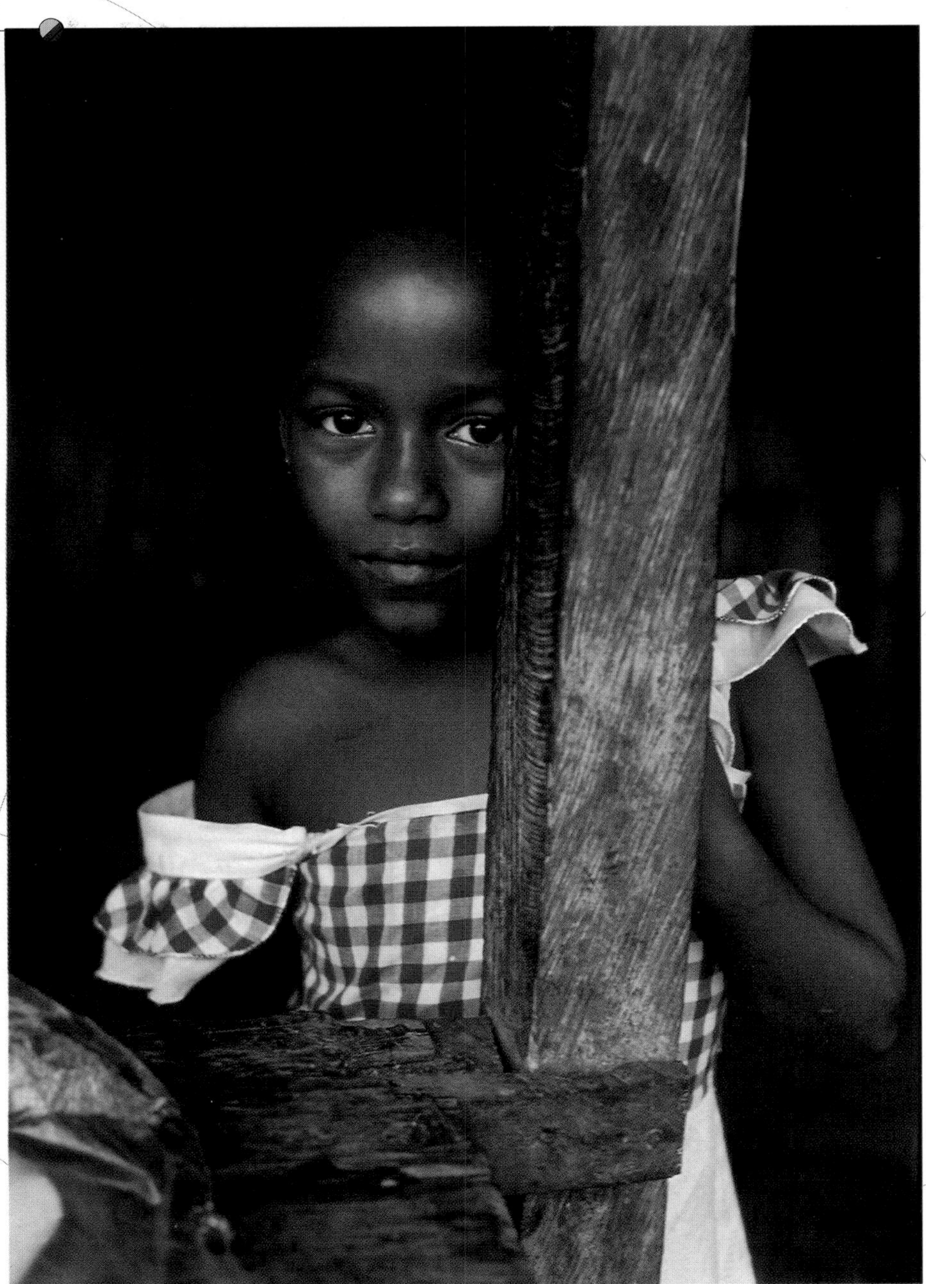

En 1825, año en que se hizo el primer censo, sólo había 1'223.598 colombianos. En el primer tercio del siglo XX esta cifra se dobló, y en el censo de 1985, casi 30 millones de personas poblaban el país.

A finales del siglo pasado, y en un proceso que aún continúa, el país abrió sus puertas a inmigrantes de todo el mundo: ingleses, alemanes, españoles, turcos, palestinos, todos encontraron en ésta una nación amable que los acogió como a hijos propios.

Tal vez por eso no sea importante saber que Colombia es el segundo país en población de América del Sur. Probablemente sea más significativo conocer que este territorio, abierto a dos océanos, formado por montañas y llanuras, está poblado por gente que tiene sus raíces dispersas en mil culturas, que se funden y expresan de diversas maneras en la vida diaria y las esperanzas de todos los colombianos.

Bahía Solano (Chocó),
Jorge Hurtado

Jardín (Antioquia), *Camillo Volpe*

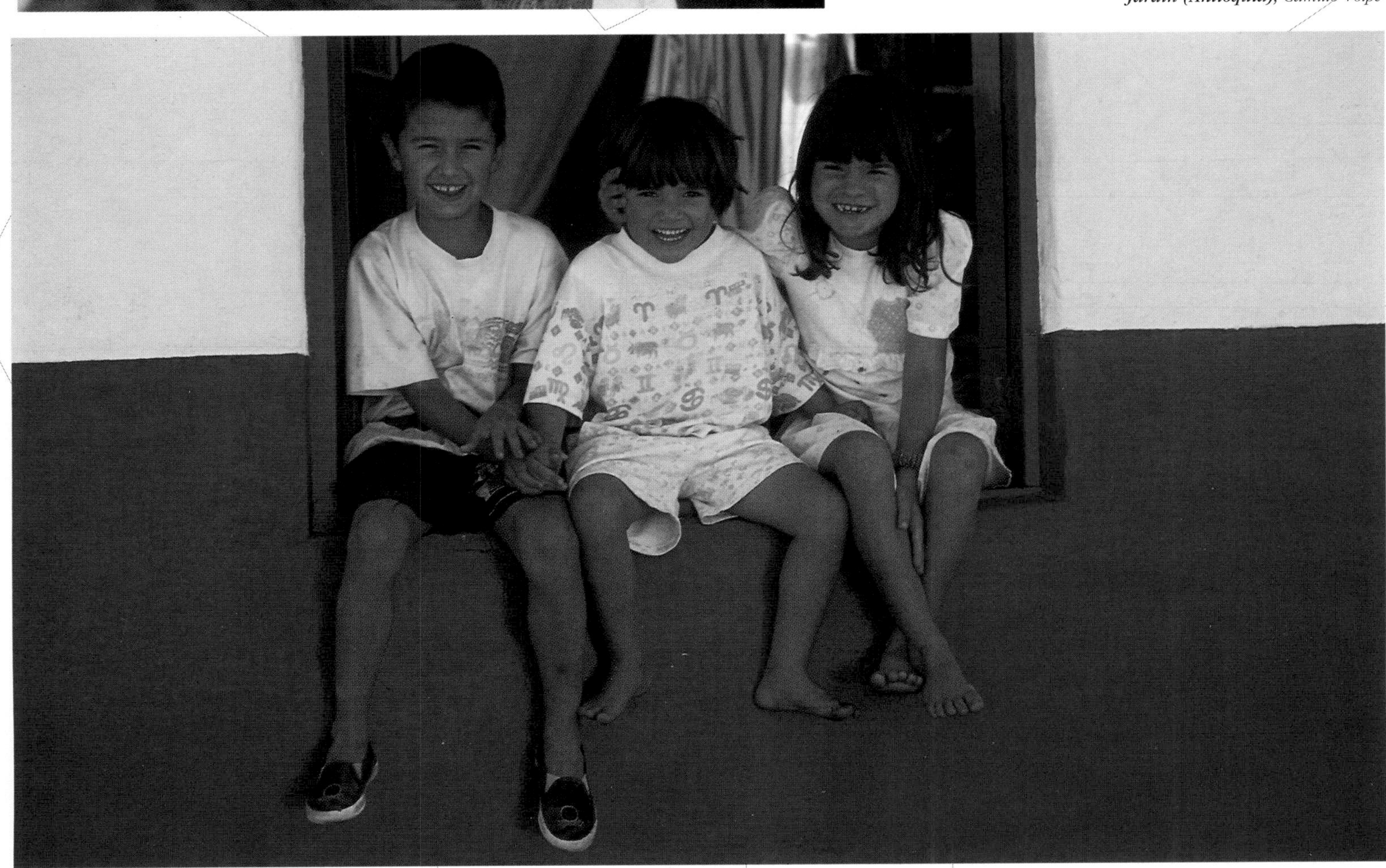

La expresión de su gente

Ipiales (Nariño), Camillo Volpe

La gran variedad de tipos humanos, unida a la diversidad de climas y regiones, hacen del folclor colombiano uno de los más ricos del continente. Esta riqueza se manifiesta en sus artesanías, su música y bailes, en la variedad de su gastronomía, o en las fiestas que con mil motivos diferentes congregan a los colombianos.

Objetos tan autóctonos como el sombrero "vueltiao" de Sampuez o las hamacas de San Jacinto, comparten honores con muchos otros artículos en el reconocimiento internacional. Pañolones y tejidos de Cundinamarca son enlazados con la misma delicadeza de los muebles y objetos de mimbre del Tolima. El carriel antioqueño es toda una tradición, y procede de la misma gente que en Santa Fe de Antioquia elabora joyas en oro de la más pura filigrana. En Pasto, la artesanía de madera, tratada con el famoso barniz de Pasto, presenta un original acabado. No menos valiosas son las artesanías en cerámica que se realizan en Boyacá, las mochilas Arhuacas con sus diseños y técnicas precolombinas, las molas cunas o las mecedoras de Mompós.

Tejido de hamacas. Morroa (Sucre), Juan Carlos Balcázar

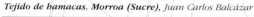

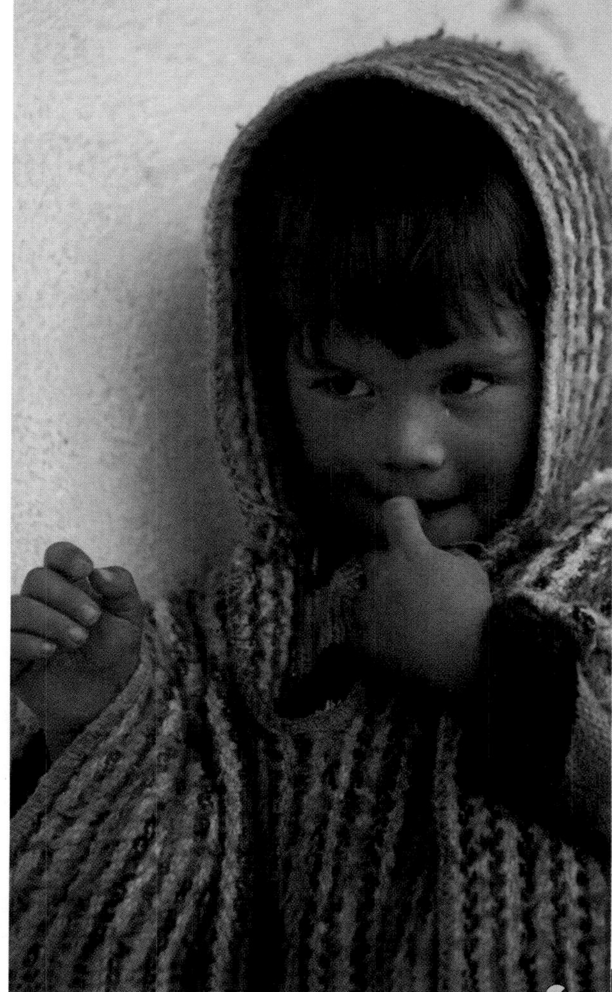

Pamplona (Norte de Santander), Camillo Volpe

Boyacá, Camillo Volpe

Pero si la artesanía colombiana es rica en su variedad, miles de melodías expresan los sentimientos propios de cada región. El baile nacional y originario del país es la cumbia. También de la costa atlántica son conocidos el mapalé, el merengue, el porro y el bullerengue. El bambuco es el baile típico de la zona andina junto con el sanjuanero, la guabina, la danza, la contradanza, todos con marcada influencia española. El vallenato es una expresión folclórica que poco a poco ha conquistado espacio, y hoy tiene vigencia y reconocimiento internacional. Crónica cantada del diario acontecer de la gente, su instrumento inseparable es el acordeón.

***Dosquebradas (Risaralda),** Camillo Volpe*

Tenza (Boyacá), Manuel Hormaza

Cestería en fique. Guacamayas (Boyacá), Manuel Hormaza

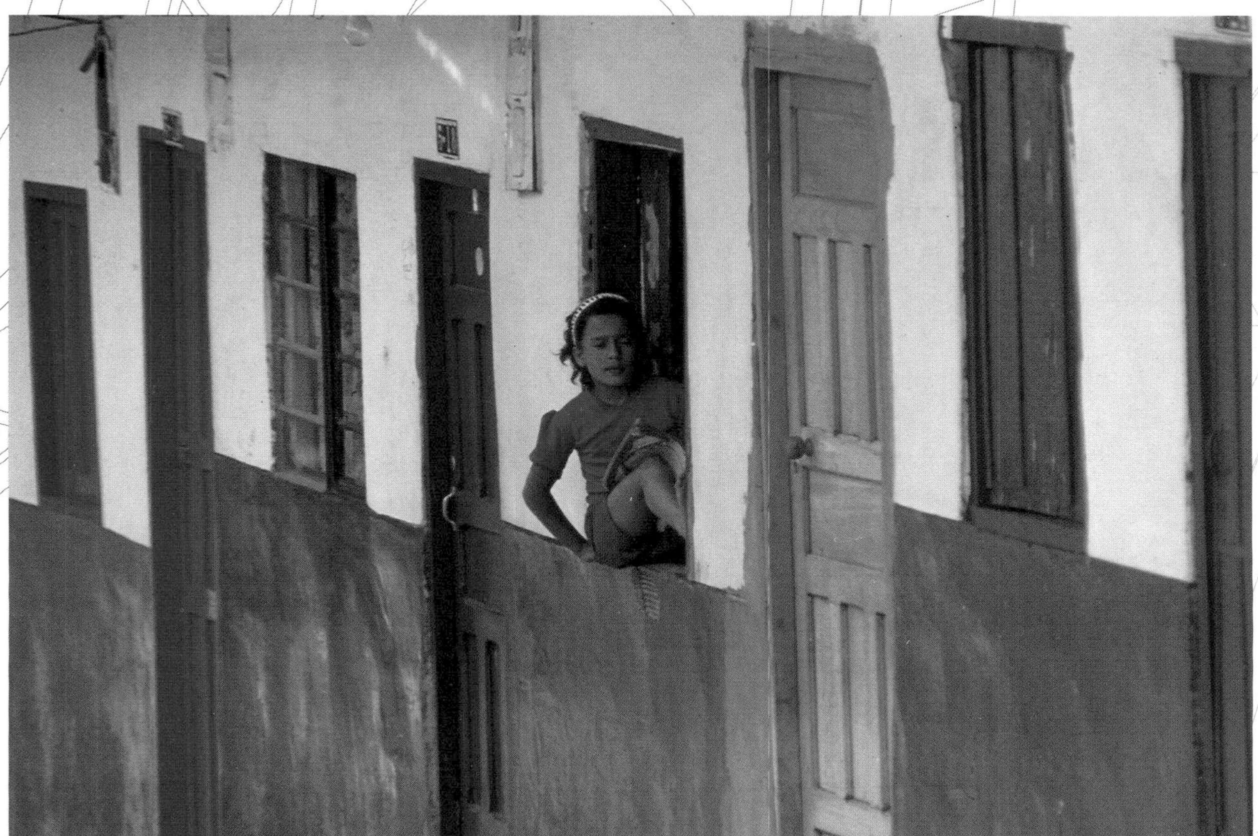
Jardín (Antioquia), Camillo Volpe

Pitalito (Huila),
Camillo Volpe

Silvia (Cauca), Camillo Volpe

La cocina colombiana es toda una amalgama de elementos negros, españoles e indios, y sus ingredientes se basan principalmente en productos como el maíz, el fríjol, el plátano o la papa. La bandeja paisa, el sancocho, los tamales, la lechona tolimense, el ajiaco, el mote, las carimañolas o la arepa de huevo son manifestaciones de una nación que tiene su esencia justamente en su multiplicidad.

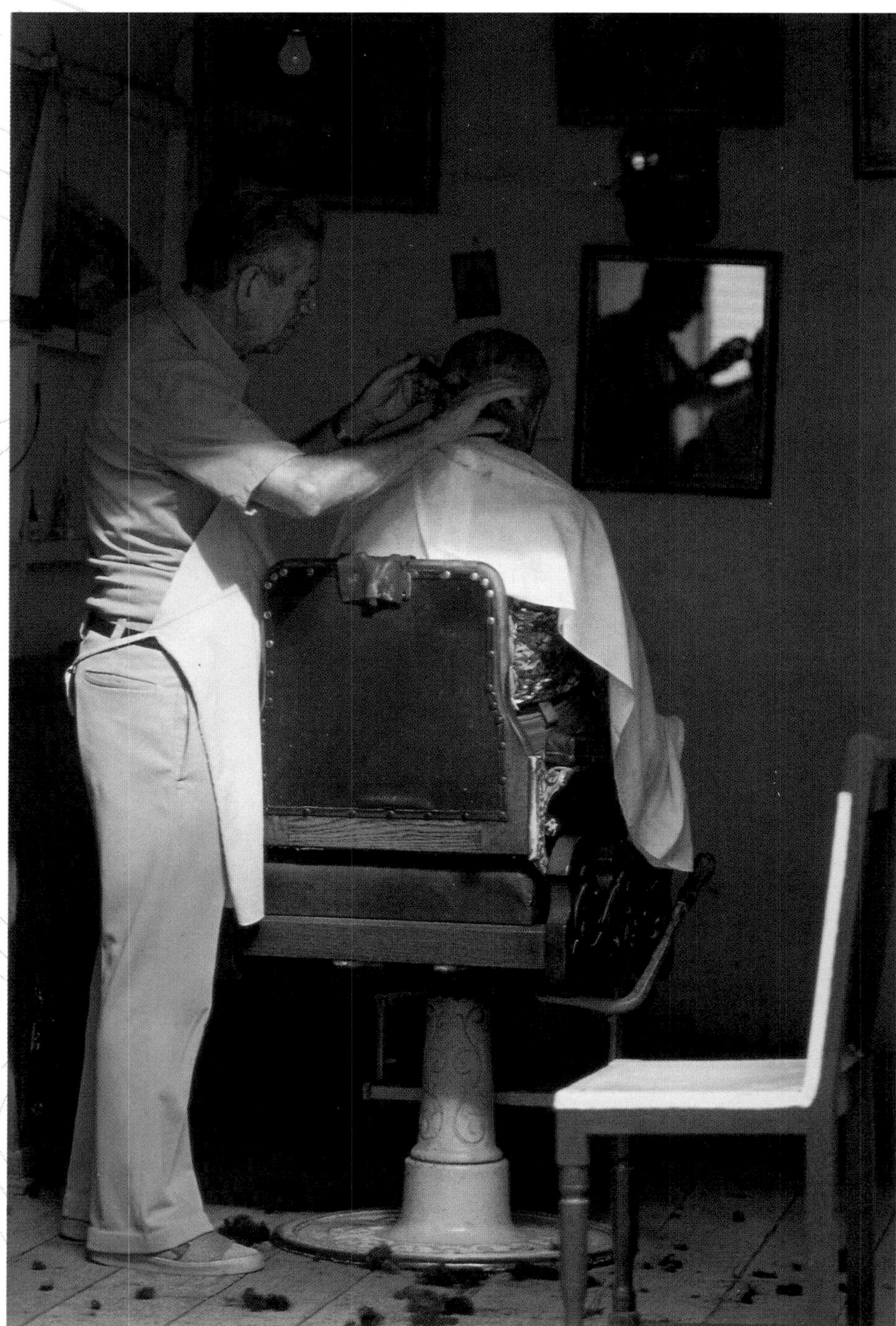

Jericó (Antioquia), Camillo Volpe

Tunja (Boyacá), Camillo Volpe

Plato típico,
Ana Lucía Pérez

¡Aquí hay fiesta!

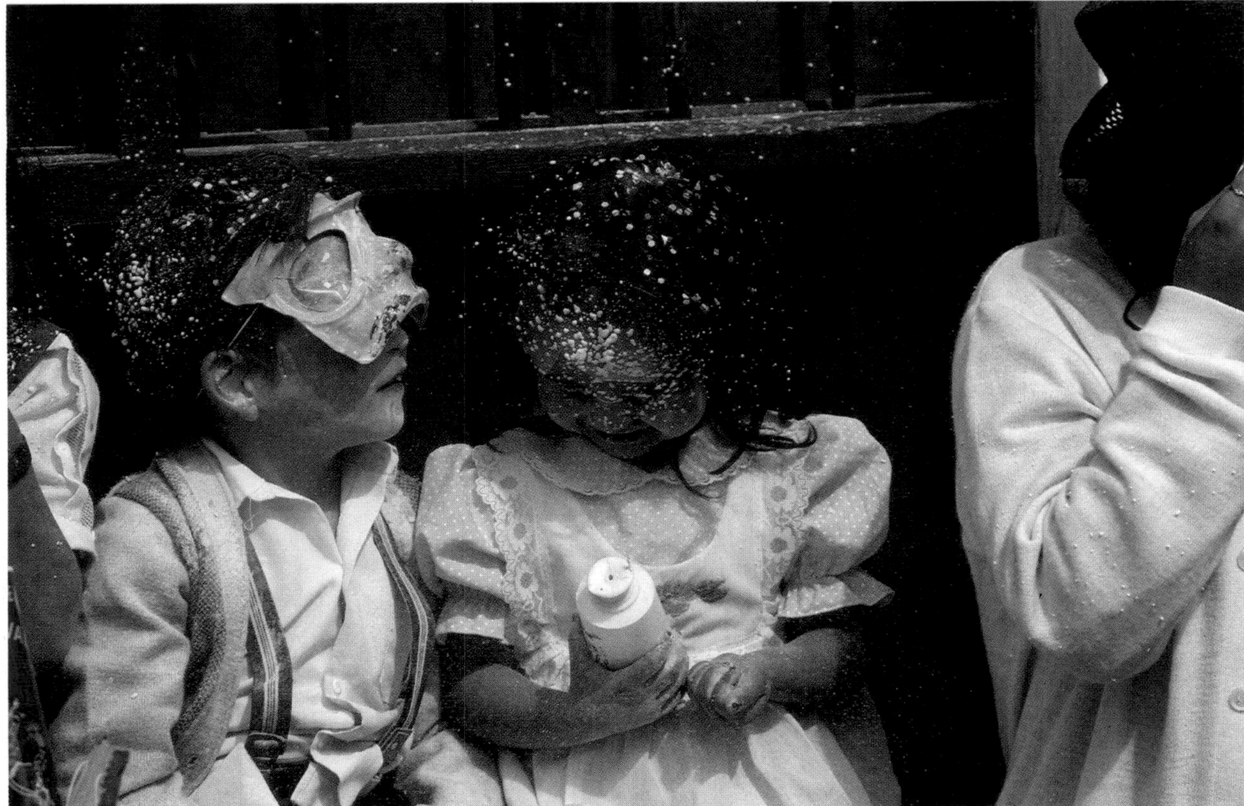

Carnaval de blancos y negros. Pasto (Nariño), Patrick Rouillard

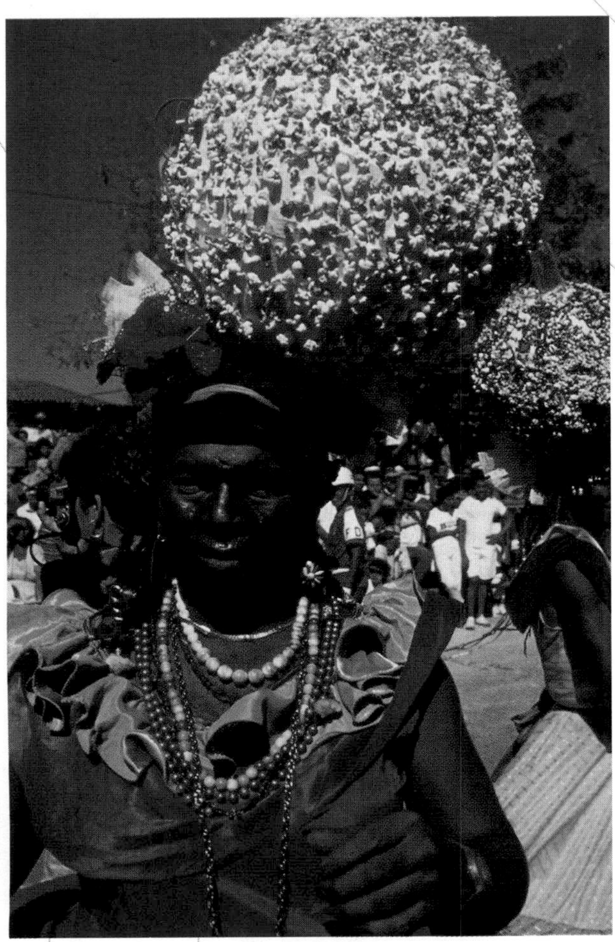

Carnaval de Barranquilla (Atlántico), José Miguel Gómez

Cada año, entre febrero y marzo, una ciudad completa se paraliza. Barranquilla se torna aún más bullanguera, y la gente llena las calles en una explosión incontenible de alegría: aquí la orden es divertirse. El Carnaval de Barranquilla es tal vez la fiesta más popular de Colombia. La guacherna, la gran parada, los congos, los disfraces y máscaras o el hombre caimán, llevan a todo el mundo la imagen de este pueblo alegre, hospitalario y descomplicado como ninguno. Con una alegría diferente, cada agosto Medellín se llena de flores traídas por los silleteros que bajan de sus montañas, en un desfile tradicional y auténtico. En enero, las calles de Pasto son tomadas por el Carnaval de blancos y negros, y así cada mes del año, sin parar...

Colombia es un país de carnavales, de gente que celebra, y siempre hay un espacio y un tiempo para salir de fiesta a las calles.

ENERO
Sirenato del Mar, Tolú
Reinado Internacional del Café, Manizales
Festival Nacional de la Trova, Manizales
Carnaval de Blancos y Negros , Pasto

FEBRERO
Carnaval de Barranquilla

MARZO
Semana Santa, Popayán
Festival Internacional de
Música Religiosa, Popayán
Festival Internacional de Música
del Caribe, Cartagena

ABRIL
Festival Vallenato, Valledupar

MAYO
Festival Nacional de Intérpretes
de la Canción, Ginebra (Valle)

JUNIO
Reinado de la Ganadería, Montería
San Juan y San Pedro, Neiva

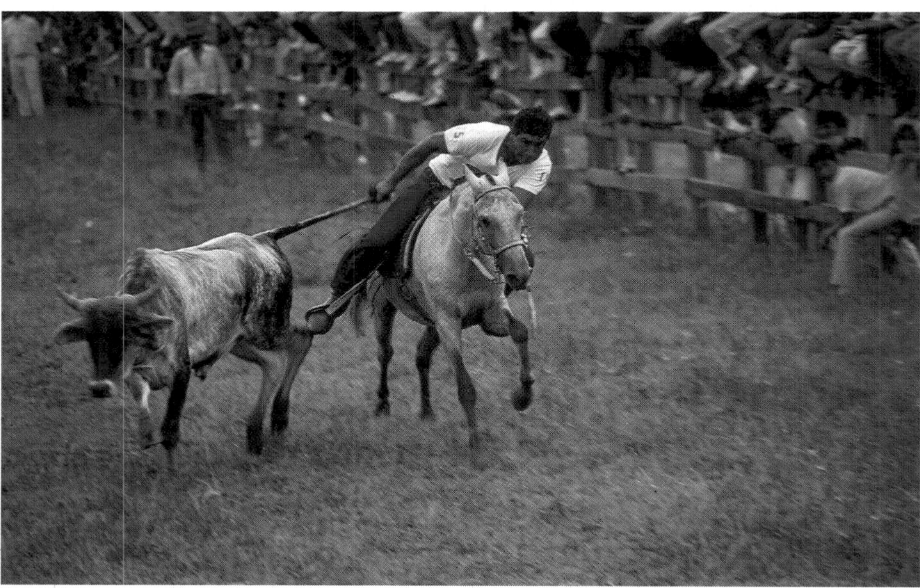

Coleo llanero. Acacias (Meta), *Miguel Morales*

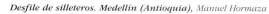

Desfile de silleteros. Medellín (Antioquia), *Manuel Hormaza*

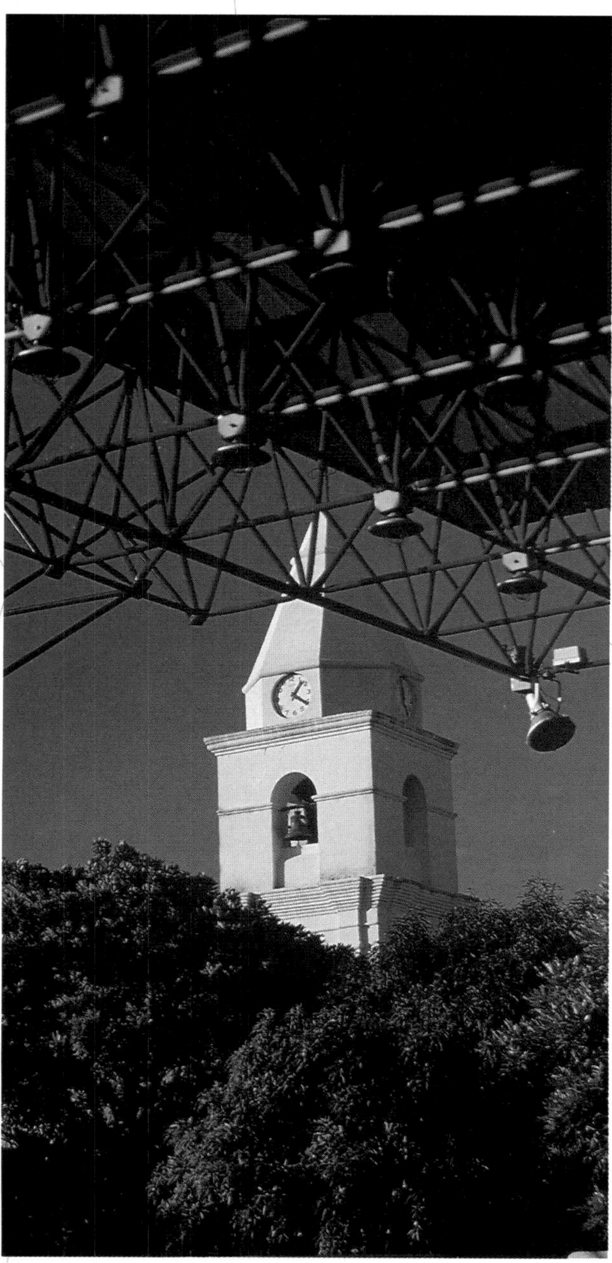

Plaza principal de Valledupar (Cesar), *Juan Carlos Balcázar*

JULIO
Festival Folklórico del Pacífico, Buenaventura
Concurso Internacional de Pesca, Leticia

AGOSTO
Feria de las Flores, Desfile
de Silleteros, Medellín
Fiesta del Mar, Santa Marta
Concurso Nacional de Cometas,
Villa de Leyva

SEPTIEMBRE
Concurso Nacional de Bandas, Paipa

OCTUBRE
Reinado Nacional del Turismo, Girardot

NOVIEMBRE
Reinado Nacional de la Belleza, Cartagena
Fiesta del Coco, San Andrés
Festival del Acordeón, Sincelejo

DICIEMBRE
Feria de la Caña de Azúcar, Cali

Colombia para recorrer

Chocó, Camillo Volpe

No importa el estilo de turismo que se quiera realizar, Colombia ofrece todo un abanico de atractivos. En el caribe, Barranquilla, Cartagena y Santa Marta son enclaves turísticos por excelencia. Barranquilla, "La puerta de oro de Colombia", es una ciudad joven e irreverente, en la que se mezclan etnias y estilos arquitectónicos. De acelerado desarrollo y crecimiento económico, Barranquilla recibe con amabilidad y sin protocolos a aquellos que la visitan. Con más hondas raíces en el pasado, Cartagena nació como fuerte militar en el Caribe, condición que aún testimonian sus murallas. La ciudad es el principal centro turístico colombiano, y su hermosa arquitectura colonial le valió ser declarada Patrimonio Histórico de la Humanidad por la UNESCO. Sus playas de El Laguito o Bocagrande atraen turistas del mundo entero. Santa Marta combina las comodidades de una gran ciudad con el encanto de la naturaleza. Sitios históricos como la Quinta de San Pedro Alejandrino, donde murió el Libertador Simón Bolívar, realzan el atractivo de las playas de El Rodadero o las del Parque Tairona. San Andrés es un paraíso en el Caribe: sus habitantes, amables y hospitalarios, están siempre dispuestos a compartir las riquezas naturales de las islas que tienen la suerte de habitar.

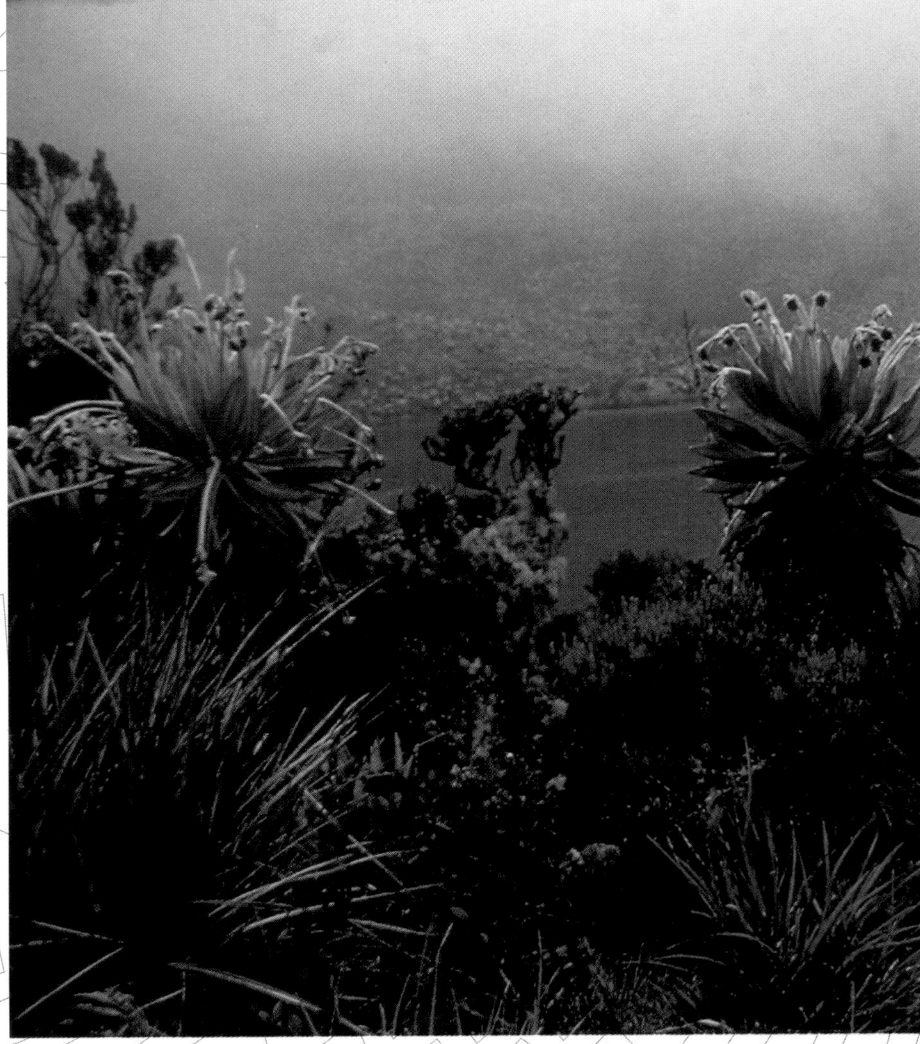

Laguna sagrada de San Pedro de Iguaque (Boyacá), *Henry Mariño*

Con un toque diferente, las ciudades del interior tienen también un encanto propio. Santafé de Bogotá conserva todo el sabor de su pasado colonial en muchas de sus casas y calles, al lado de avenidas y edificaciones que delatan su acelerado desarrollo. Entre sus museos, el Museo del Oro merece especial atención. Este centro guarda una de las más completas colecciones de orfebrería precolombina. Cientos de figurillas, narigueras y pectorales testimonian la sabiduría de unas culturas que tuvieron su auge hace ya muchos siglos. Importante en todo el mundo, la muestra del Museo del Oro es la colección más grande elaborada en este material.

Medellín es la segunda ciudad del país, y parece resumir en ella toda la heterogeneidad de Colombia. Ciudad de grandes e importantes industrias, maneja también un comercio de magnitud significativa, y un movimiento cultural con proyecciones nacionales. Es una de las urbes colombianas con mayores índices de crecimiento económico. Compitiendo en importancia, Cali ofrece múltiples atractivos turísticos. Situada en un valle de incomparable belleza, y gozando de un clima ideal, se perfila como uno de los centros urbanos más importantes del país. La belleza de sus mujeres es proverbial, y la alegría de la salsa es telón de fondo para las actividades que desarrolla: industria, cultura, música y alegría, todo se vive en Cali al mismo ritmo febril.

Cerro de Monserrate.
Santafé de Bogotá (Cundinamarca), *Ana Lucía Pérez*

Iglesia La Candelaria y edificio Coltejer. Medellín (Antioquia), *Manuel Hormaza*

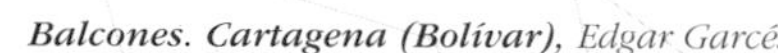

Balcones. Cartagena (Bolívar), *Edgar Garcés*

Paisaje caribe, *Craig Duncan*

Si se quiere, más allá de sus grandes centros urbanos, Colombia ofrece una infinita gama de posibilidades. El verde de Boyacá parece extenderse como una manta sobre la cual, aquí y allá, poblaciones como Villa de Leyva, Monguí o Paipa conservan todo el encanto de su pasado histórico.

Al sur, la región amazónica es un mundo aparte, abierto a aquellos que estén dispuestos a conocer algo diferente. Leticia, la ciudad más austral del país, ofrece toda la infraestructura adecuada para el inicio de esta aventura.

Villa de Leyva (Boyacá), *Camillo Volpe*

Parques arqueológicos y naturales, una opción turística diferente

San Agustín (Huila), *Craig Duncan*

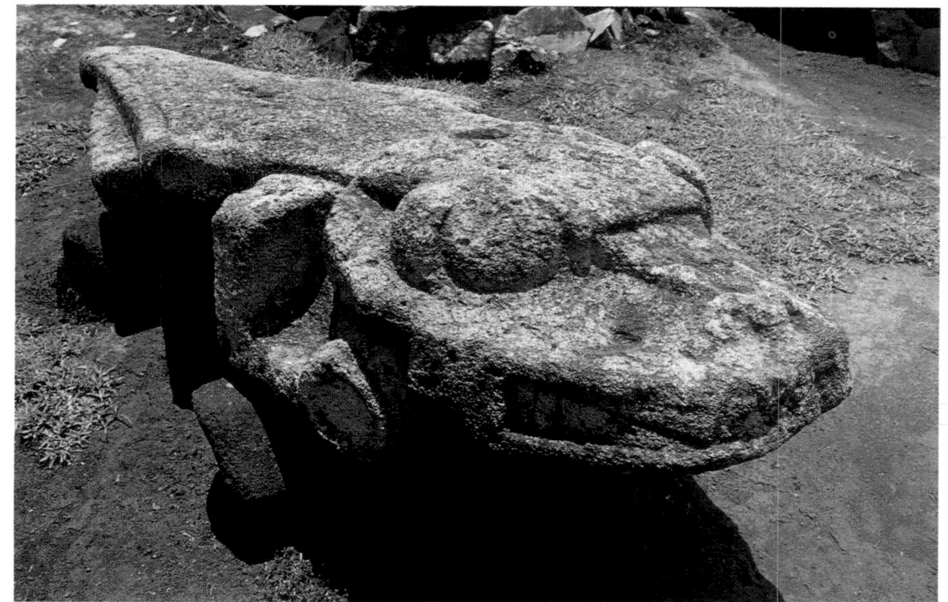

3'950.000 hectáreas del territorio colombiano están consagradas al cuidado y preservación de la naturaleza o de tesoros arqueológicas de incalculable valor. El parque Arqueológico de San Agustín, en el Huila, guarda un testimonio histórico de importancia continental. En 2.000 kilómetros cuadrados reúne estatuas de piedra, tumbas y fuentes ceremoniales elaboradas por una cultura, la agustiniana, que se borró en la historia sin dejar el menor rastro.

En Tierradentro, en el departamento del Cauca, es posible visitar alrededor de 200 hipogeos, últimos vestigios de la cultura precolombina que habitó la región.

Sierra Nevada del Cocuy (Boyacá), *Alvaro Pescador*

Parque Natural de los Nevados, Ramiro Posada

El Parque Natural Tairona, el más visitado del país, esconde en un rincón de sus 383.000 hectáreas a Buritaca o Ciudad Perdida, el más importante hallazgo arqueológico que se ha hecho en América Latina en los últimos tiempos. Situada a más de cinco mil metros sobre el nivel del mar, está conformada por grandes mesetas o terrazas comunicadas entre sí por caminos de piedra. Igualmente existen rastros de un sistema de irrigación altamente tecnificado.

Nibiyaka. Sierra Nevada de Santa Marta, Manuel Hormaza

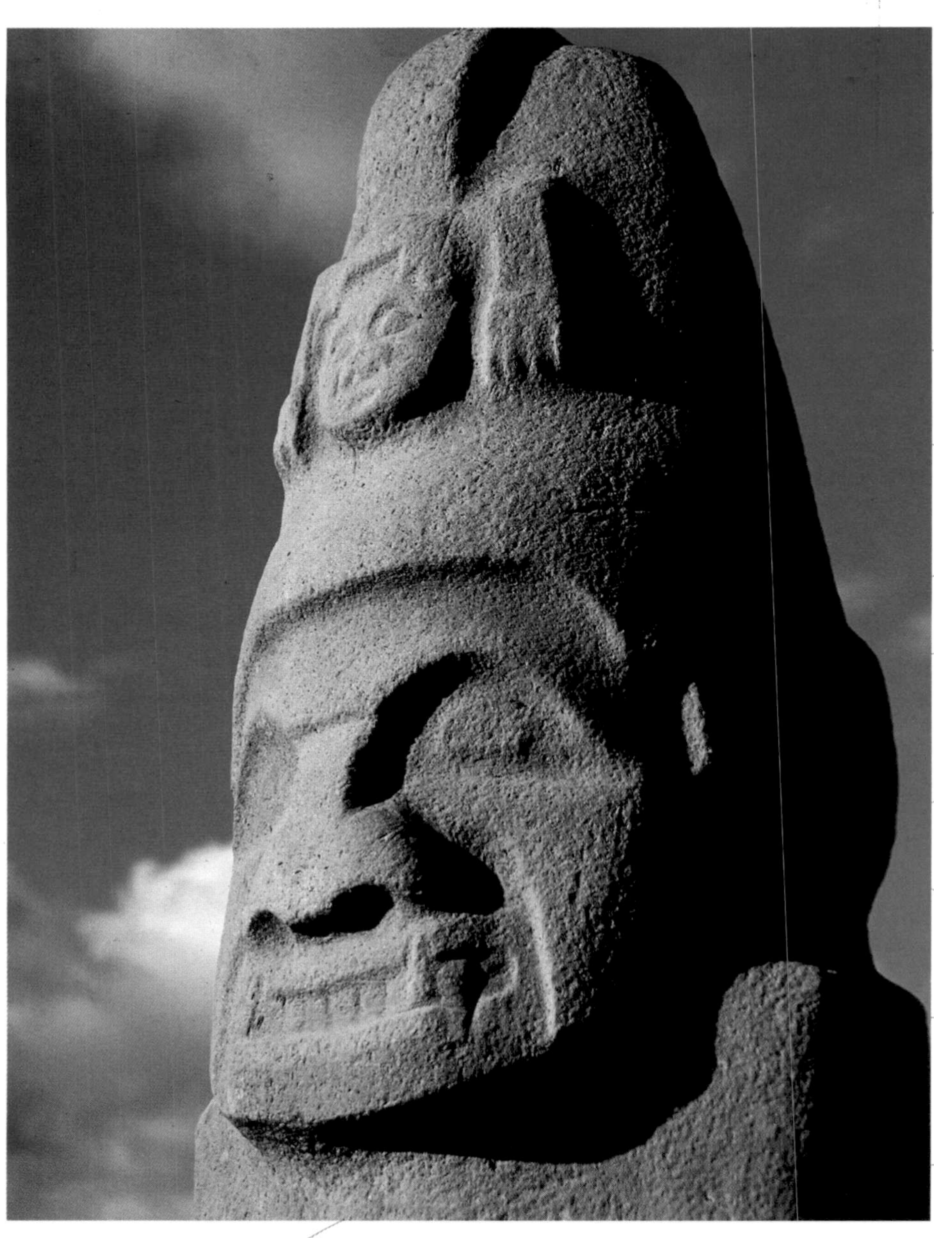

Tan valiosos como los arqueológicos, los parques naturales ocupan gran parte de la geografía nacional. El Parque Nacional Islas del Rosario es uno de los más visitados por sus arrecifes de coral y la posibilidad de practicar pesca submarina. En el Parque del Puracé nacen cuatro importantes ríos colombianos: Cauca, Magdalena, Patía y Caquetá, y en el Parque de los Nevados es posible la práctica del montañismo en cualquiera de sus picos: Tolima, Quindío, Santa Rosa, Santa Isabel y el Ruiz.

Este sistema de parques y reservas naturales, conformado por casi un centenar de ellos, agrega un atractivo adicional a Colombia al permitir y promocionar un turismo no contaminante y respetuoso de la naturaleza. A través del Inderena, entidad encargada de su cuidado, es posible el trámite de permisos especiales para visitar cualquiera de estas zonas de reserva ecológica.

San Agustín (Huila),
Markus Oertly

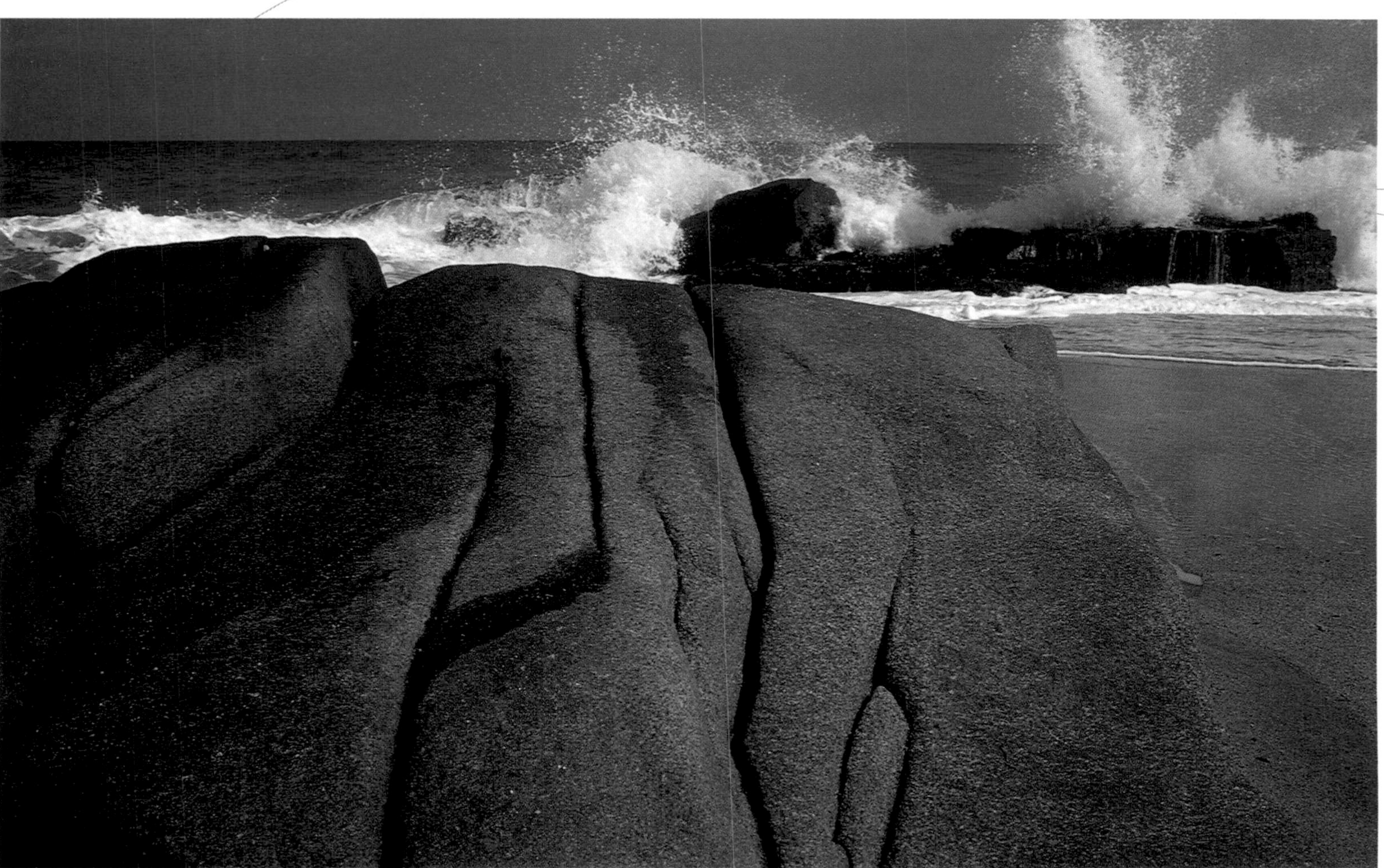

Parque Tairona (Magdalena), *Nicolas Bright*

¡Venga!

Manglares, Craig Duncan

Esta es la culminación de este viaje imaginario. ¿Por qué no iniciar el real? Colombia está allí, amable y lista para recibir a sus amigos.

Aeropuertos internacionales en las principales ciudades son la puerta de entrada. Desde allí, basta decidir qué camino tomar para que se inicie la aventura. Cualquiera que sea el plan, Colombia tiene la posibilidad de satisfacerlo.

¿Hoteles de cinco estrellas, con todo el brillo y la actividad de ciudades cosmopolitas? Allí están: basta elegir uno.

San Pedro de los Milagros (Antioquia), *Juan Carlos Balcázar*

¿Pequeñas y tranquilas hosterías en alguna población alejada del ruido y de la prisa? Decídase: a la orilla del mar, o en las cumbres andinas, las hay con todas las características y atractivos.

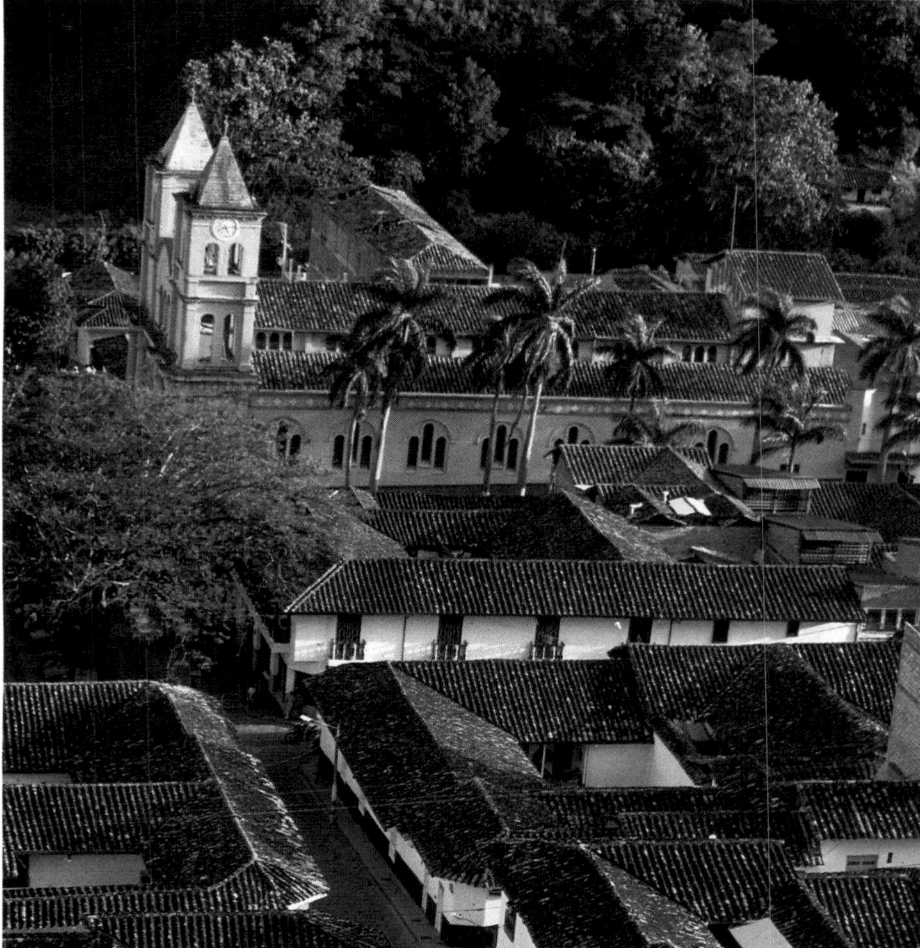

Bolívar (Antioquia), *Camillo Volpe*

¿Una carpa, aire libre e independencia? Kilómetros y kilómetros de naturaleza esperan para contar sus secretos.

¿Bullicio, fiestas, carnaval? Difícilmente existe una gama más amplia de opciones para elegir.

Venga. Este es un país rico. Rico en climas y paisajes. En flores, olores, sabores y frutas. En historia y arte. En recursos naturales, y sobre todo, rico en gente. Ellos están esperándolo a usted, para compartir ese territorio de sueños y maravillas que es Colombia.

Chocó, *Craig Duncan*

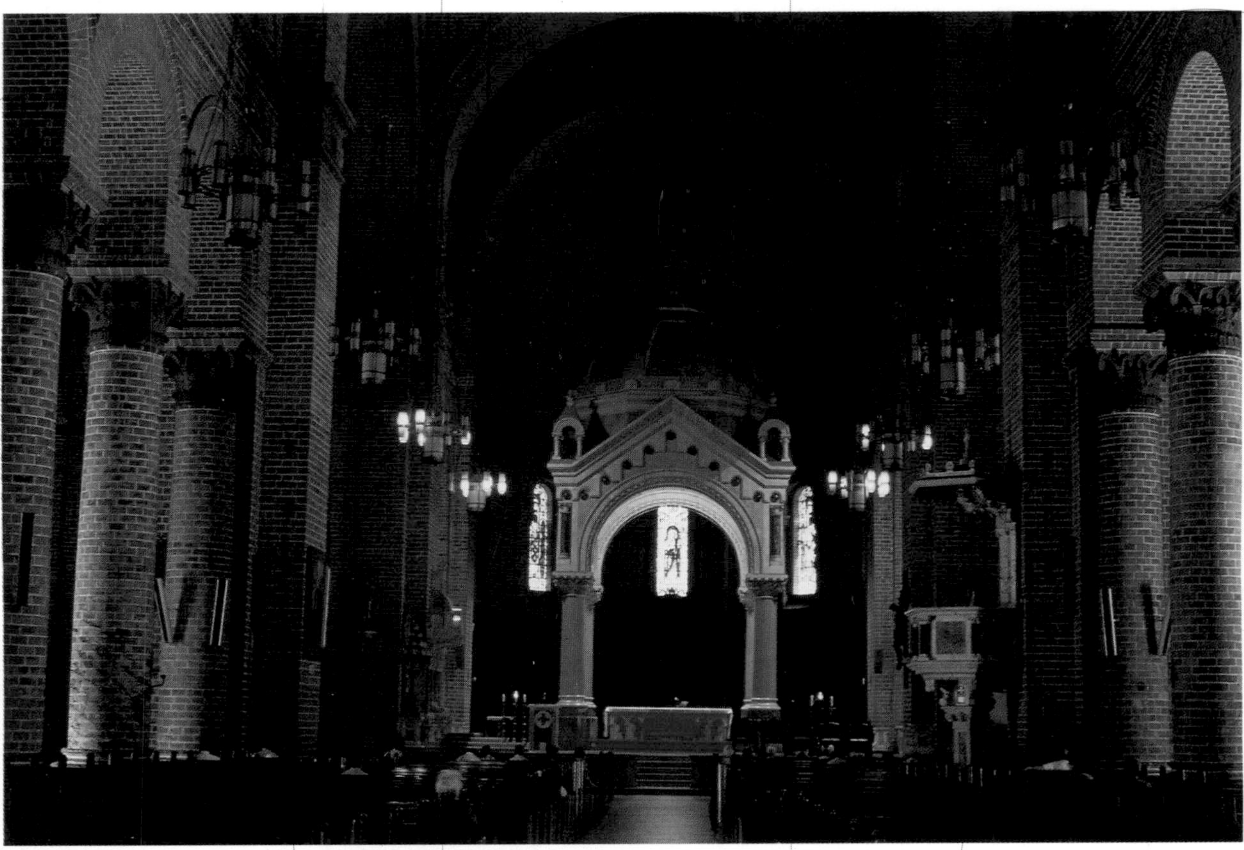

Santuario de Monserrate.
Santafé de Bogotá (Cundinamarca),
Miguel Morales

Espinal (Tolima), *Camillo Volpe*

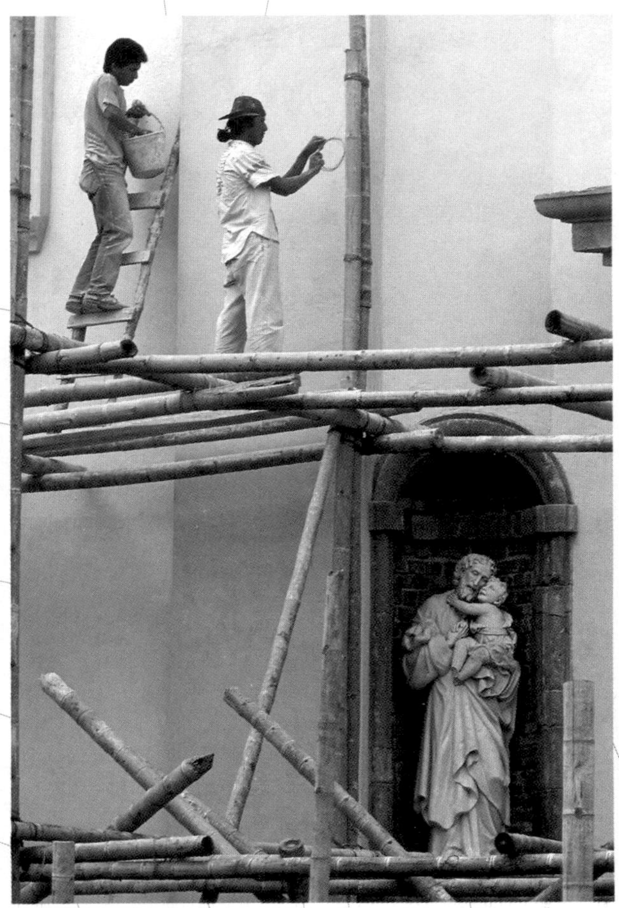

Popayán (Cauca), *Camillo Volpe*

THE COLLECTOR'S DICTIONARY OF GLASS

BY THE SAME AUTHOR

English Tableglass
English and Irish Cut Glass
Paperweights and other Glass Curiosities

A Beilby Goblet, formerly in the collection of Frances L. Dickson and purchased in 1961 at Sotheby's by Messrs. Delomosne and Son Ltd. for the record sum of £1,820. (Reproduced by kind permission of the owner, Mr. J. F. Wells)

THE COLLECTOR'S DICTIONARY OF

GLASS

BY

E. M. ELVILLE

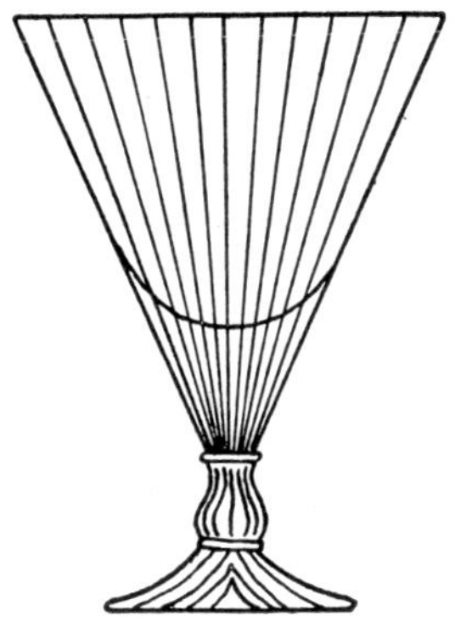

COUNTRY LIFE

LONDON · NEW YORK · SYDNEY · TORONTO

Published for Country Life Books by
THE HAMLYN PUBLISHING GROUP LIMITED
LONDON · NEW YORK · SYDNEY · TORONTO
Hamlyn House, Feltham, Middlesex, England

Second edition 1967
Second impression 1969

Printed in Great Britain by
Billing & Sons Limited
Guildford and London

PREFACE

COLLECTING antique glass has become an increasingly popular pursuit during the present century, not only in this country, but in many countries abroad. As in the case of other branches of collecting, a great deal of literature has been published on the subject, but most of the books and articles which have appeared have in general been of a specialised kind, each dealing with one or at most a few of the many branches of glass art.

It has long been apparent, therefore, that there is need for a comprehensive treatise of the subject, giving at the same time some indication to the collector of the prices at which specimens change hands in the sale rooms. This has now taken shape in the present volume, presented in the form of a dictionary for quick and easy reference.

The dictionary was at first intended to embrace the forms of glass art that could be found in antique shops throughout Britain, and should therefore basically refer to glass of the British Isles. While this idea has not been fundamentally changed, however, it became obvious as the work developed that the keen collector would tend to seek specimens of foreign glass that may have influenced the development of native styles. This would apply not only to collectors in this country, but also to those from abroad.

The dictionary has therefore been extended to include introductions to the antique glass of America, France, Germany (including Bohemia), Holland, Sweden and Venice.

It will be readily appreciated, however, that in a subject with such a vast background as glass, it is impossible to include in a single volume all its many forms and styles in detail. Indeed, with such a wealth of information at the disposal of the writer, the great difficulty has been not what to include but what to leave out.

If, however, the details on any subject given in the dictionary are considered by the reader to be insufficient for his requirements, then he can if necessary consult the books which have specialised on particular subjects.

For example, *Rare English Glasses of the 17th and 18th Centuries*, by J. Bles; *Irish Glass*, by M. S. D. Westropp; *A History of English and Irish Glass* (two volumes), by W. A. Thorpe; *Glass Through the Ages*, by E. B. Haynes, which contains a detailed classification of English drinking glasses; *English and Irish Cut Glass, 1750-1950*, by the present writer, a monograph dealing with English and Irish cut-glass in particular, etc. Such books are included in the Selected Bibliography at the end of the dictionary.

There is an Introduction to the dictionary which gives an outline of the early history of glass and which covers its development up to the Venetian period. It is from this period that the dictionary proper begins, and subjects are thereafter treated in alphabetical order.

My grateful thanks are due to the following collectors and owners who have kindly allowed me to illustrate specimens or who have supplied me with information for this dictionary: Her Majesty the Queen, Sir Hugh Chance, Mr Derek Davis, Mr J. W. Edwards, Mr A. Amory Houghton, jnr., Mr Paul Jokelson, the late Mr John Northwood, jnr., Mr J. Perret, the late Mr C. E. Ramsden and Mr Laurence Whistler.

My thanks are also due to the authorities of Museo Vetrario, Murano, The British Museum, London, The Royal Albert Museum, Exeter, The National Museum, Dublin, The Science Museum, London, The Victoria and Albert Museum, London, The Corning Museum of Glass, New York, The Central Museum, Northampton, The City Art Gallery, Bristol, The Rijks Museum, Amsterdam, The Tolson Memorial Museum, Huddersfield, The Laing Art Gallery, Newcastle-on-Tyne, who have granted me permission to reproduce photographs from their collections.

My thanks are also due to the following Companies and Bodies for valuable assistance: Messrs Central Press Photos, Ltd., Messrs Christie, Manson & Woods, Ltd., Messrs Arthur Churchill, Ltd., Messrs Corning Glass Company, New York, Messrs Cristalleries de Baccarat, Paris, Messrs Cecil Davis, Ltd., Messrs Delomosne & Son, Ltd., Messrs Mallet & Son, Ltd., Messrs Orrefors Glass Company, Stockholm, Messrs Parkinson & Spencer, Ltd., Messrs James Powell and Sons (Whitefriars), Ltd., Messrs Sotheby & Co., Ltd., Messrs Stevens and Williams, Ltd., Messrs Stuart and Sons, Ltd. and Messrs Steuben Glass Company, New York. Also to the Editors of *Country Life*, *Country Life Annual*, *Glass*, and the *Bulletin of the Paperweight Collectors' Association*, for kind permission to use material which has been published from time to time in articles from my pen.

In conclusion, I have acknowledgments to make to Mr Victor Leonard Marshall, the young artist who has so kindly provided the line drawings.

SELECTED BIBLIOGRAPHY

BATE, P.
English Tableglass, London, 1905.

BERGSTROM, E. H.
Old Glass Paperweights. London. 1947.

BLES, J.
Rare English Glasses of the 17th and 18th Centuries. London, 1926.

BUCKLEY, F.
History of Old English Glass. London, 1925.
The Glass Trade in England in the Seventeenth Century. London, 1914.

BUCKLEY, W.
Diamond Engraved Glasses of the Sixteenth Century. London, 1929.
European Glass. London, 1926.
The Art of Glass. London, 1939.

CHARLESTON, R. J.
Dutch Decoration of English Glass. *Transactions of the Society of Glass Technology*, Vol. xli, pp. 229-243t (1957).
Michael Edkins and the Problem of English Enamelled Glass. *Transactions of the Society of Glass Technology*, vol. xxxviii, pp. 3-16 (1954).

CHIPMAN, F. W.
The Romance of Old Sandwich Glass. New York, 1932.

CHURCHILL, ARTHUR AND CO.
Glass Notes.
History in Glass. London, 1937.

DILLON, E.
Glass. London, 1907.

ELVILLE, E. M.
English Tableglass. London, 1951.
English and Irish Cut Glass. London, 1953.
Paperweights and other Glass Curiosities. London, 1954.
Opaque-White Glass of the 18th and 19th Centuries. *Country Life*, vol. cvi, pp. 1297-1299 (1949).
The History of the Glass Chandelier. *Country Life Annual*, pp. 200-204 (1949).

FLEMING, A.
Scottish and Jacobite Glass. Glasgow, 1938.

FRANCIS, G. R.
Old English Drinking Glasses. London, 1926.

GRAHAM, F.
Thoughts on Early British Glass. *Apollo Annual*, pp. 79-82 (1948).

GRAY, J. M.
James and William Tassie. Edinburgh, 1894.

GUTTERY, D. R.
Broad-Glass to Cut Crystal. London, 1956.

HARTSHORNE, A.
Old English Glasses. London, 1897.

HAYNES, E. B.
Glass Through the Ages. London, 1948.

HOGAN, J. H.
The Development in the Design of English Glassware during the Last Hundred Years. *Transactions of the Society of Glass Technology*, vol. xx, pp. 735-740 (1936).

HONEY, W. B.
English Glass. London, 1946.
Glass. London, 1946.

HORRIDGE, W.
The Rose and Emblems on Jacobite Drinking Glasses. *Transactions of the Circle of Glass Collectors*, No. 56.

HUGHES, G. B.
English, Scottish and Irish Tableglass. London, 1956.

IMBERT, R. and AMIC, Y.
Les Presse-Papiers Français. France, 1948.

JANNEAU, G.
Modern Glass. London, 1931.

JOKELSON, P.
Antique French Paperweights. New York, 1955.

LEE, MRS RUTH WEBB
Early American Pressed Glass. New York, 1931.

MCGRATH, R. and FROST, A. C.
Glass in Architecture and Decoration. London, 1937.

MCKEARIN, H. and G. S.
American Glass. New York, 1941.
Two Hundred Years of American Blown Glass. New York, 1949.

MARSON, P.
Glass. London, 1918.

MOORE, N. HUDSON
Old Glass, European and American. London, 1926.

NESBITT, A.
Descriptive Catalogue of the Glass Vessels in the South Kensington Museum. London, 1878.

NEUBURG, F.
Glass in Antiquity. London, 1949.

NORTHWOOD, JOHN II
John Northwood. Stourbridge, 1958.

PELLATT, A.
Curiosities of Glass Making. London, 1894.

PERRET, J. B.
The 18th-Century Chandeliers at Bath. *Connoisseur*, vol. cii, p. 187 (1938).

PLAUT, J. S.
Steuben Glass. New York, 1948.

POLAK, A. D.
Gammelt Norsk Glass. Oslo, 1953.

POWELL, J.
Glass-Making in England. Cambridge, 1923.

RACKHAM, B.
A Key to Pottery and Glass. London, 1940.

ROBERTSON, R. A.
Chats on Old Glass. London, 1954.

ROCHE, S.
Mirrors. London, 1957.

SCHMIDT, R.
Das Glas. 2nd Ed., 1922.

SOTHEBY & CO.
Catalogues.

THORPE, W. A.
A History of English and Irish Glass, 2 vols. London, 1929.
English Glass. London, 1935.
English and Irish Glass. London, 1927.

WESTROPP, M. S. D.
Irish Glass. London, 1920.

WHISTLER, L.
The Engraved Glass of Laurence Whistler. London, 1952.

WINBOLT, S. E.
Wealden Glass. Hove, 1933.

ILLUSTRATIONS

1. Drawn stem glass with elongated 'tear' *page* 14
2. Wineglass stem showing early air-twist formation 14
3. Early air-twist of imperfect formation 14
4. Ale glass with perfectly formed air-twist stem 15
5. Two-piece glass with knopped air-twist stem 15
6. Three-piece wineglass with air-twist stem 15
7. Three-piece glass with air-twist stem and white enamelled bowl 15
8. Three-piece glass with unusual air-twist stem 15
9. Three-piece wineglass with knopped air-twist stem 15
10. Ale glass with unusual air-twist stem 16
11. Ale glass with air-twist stem 16
12. Ale glass with white opaque-twist stem 16
13. Ale glass with bowl engraved with hops and barley motif 16
14. American whale oil lamp with cover 17
15. American 'Lacy' pattern pressed dish 17
16. American whale oil lamp with 'Lacy' pattern base 18
17. American pressed bowl on stand 19
18. American vase with 'Favrile' decoration 19
19. American vase in 'Aurene' style 20
20. American vase in 'Aurene' style 20
21. Typical seventeenth-century English baluster-stemmed glass 21
22. Group of baluster-stemmed glasses 22
23. Light Newcastle baluster-stemmed glass 23
24. Balustroid glass with inverted baluster 23
25. Earliest English 'sealed' bottle, dated 1657 25
26. English 'sealed' bottle, dated 1690 25
27. 'Sealed' bottle with 1770 date 26
28. Pair of eighteenth-century bottles 26
29. 'Sealed' bottle with 1785 date 26
30. Bristol white opaque vase and cruet bottles painted in enamel colours 29
31. Bristol tea caddies painted in enamel colours 29
32. Bristol vase painted in enamel colours 29
33. Signature of I. Jacobs, Bristol 30
34. Dark blue Bristol decanter 30
35. Pair of dark blue Bristol toilet bottles 30
36. Dark blue Bristol wineglass cooler 31
37. Dark blue Bristol finger bowl *page* 31
38. The Buggin bowls, *circa* 1676 32
39. Replica by John Northwood, sen., of Portland Vase 33
40. Cameo plaque of Aphrodite by John Northwood, jun. 33
41. Cameo vases by George Woodall and Alphonse Lecheveral 33
42. Group of cameo vases by various artists 34
43. Early glass candelabra 35
44. Pair of candelabra, *circa* 1770 35
45. Candelabra with notched shaft 36
46. Candelabra blending rococo and Adam styles 36
47. Regency style candelabra 36
48. Pair of candelabra, *circa* 1800 36
49. Regency candelabra and ornamental stands *en suite* 37
50. Heavily cut candelabra of the Regency Period 38
51. Candlestick from first quarter of eighteenth century 38
52. Candlestick from the Adam period 38
53. Group of candlesticks showing development from 1780 onwards 39
54. Group of candlesticks from Irish period 39
55. Early eighteenth-century candlesticks 39
56. Glass described as a champagne glass or alternatively as a sweetmeat glass 40
57. Champagne glass, *circa* 1869 41
58. Venetian chandelier of the seventeenth century 42
59. Venetian chandelier with naturalistic motifs 43
60. Thornham Hall chandelier, *circa* 1732 43
61. Six-light chandelier, *circa* 1765 44
62. Four-light chandelier, *circa* 1775 44
63. Six-light chandelier, Adam period 45
64. Six-light chandelier, Regency period 45
65. Eight-light chandelier, *circa* 1820 46
66. Central chandelier from the group in the Throne Room, Buckingham Palace 47
67. Wroxton Abbey chandelier, *circa* 1815 48
68. Chimney glass, eighteenth century 49
69. Chimney glass with painted overmantel 50
70. Chimney glass in scroll giltwood 51
71. Glass oil clock lamp, eighteenth century 52

72. Comfit glass, alternatively described as a small sweetmeat glass *page* 54
73. Comfit glass or small sweetmeat glass 54
74. Cordial glass with drawn stem 56
75. Cordial glass with air-twist stem 56
76. Cordial glass with opaque-twist stem 56
77. Group of cordial glasses 57
78. Queen Anne Coronation glass, 1702 58
79. Newcastle glass celebrating coronation of George II in 1727 58
80. Glass celebrating coronation of George III in 1760 58
81. Smelling bottle by Apsley Pellatt with bust of William IV 59
82. Pressed amber dish celebrating Jubilee of Queen Victoria in 1887 59
83. Sketches of glass designed for Queen Victoria Diamond Jubilee, 1897 60
84. Glass made at the time of Coronation of Edward VII in 1902 60
85. Glass articles made for coronation of Edward VIII which, owing to his Abdication, were not circulated 61
86. Goblet made to celebrate coronation of George VI 61
87. Glasses made in celebration of coronation of George VI 62
88. Goblet made to celebrate coronation of Elizabeth II 63
89. Glasses made to celebrate coronation of Elizabeth II 63
90. Range of glasses designed for coronation of Elizabeth II 63
91. Roman cup found at Barnwell, Cambridge, second century A.D. 65
92. Hedwig glass of eleventh or twelfth century 66
93. Engraved beaker by Gotfried Spiller, *circa* 1700 67
94. Glass-cutter at work on cutting wheel 67
95. Wineglass cut in shallow diamond pattern 68
96. Wineglass with cut stem 68
97. Wineglass with stem fluted and notched 68
98. Perfume bottle with cut 'Brunswick' star motif 69
99. Sugar bowl, probably Waterford, with typical cut motifs 69
100. Perfume bottle cut with alternate panel motif 69
101. Decanter cut in relief diamond pattern 70
102. Enlarged cut motif showing imperfections 71
103. Bottle-green door-stop 73
104. Bottle-green door-stop 73
105. Wineglass with bowl engraved by Frans Greenwood, signed and dated 1720 75
106. Wineglass engraved by David Wolff, *circa* 1780 *page* 77
107. Wineglass engraved by David Wolff, *circa* 1780 77
108. Wineglass engraved by G. H. Hoolaart, *circa* 1780 77
109. Goblet painted in enamel colours by Beilby of Newcastle-on-Tyne 78
110. Reverse of goblet shown in Fig. 109 79
111. Wineglasses painted by the Beilby Family 80
112. Group of wineglasses painted by Beilby Family 81
113. Two views of decanter painted in enamel colours and signed by Beilby 81
114. Glasses probably painted by Beilby Family 82
115. Decanters and wineglass painted by Beilby family in white enamel 82
116. Royal Oak goblet dated 1663 84
117. Exeter Flute, engraved 'God Bless King Charles The Second' 85
118. Sketches of John Greene's glasses, *circa* 1672 86
119. Ravenscroft roemer bearing the seal of the raven's head, *circa* 1677 87
120. Punch bowl and cover with decoration 'nipt diamond waies,' *circa* 1685 87
121. Selection of glassware and picture taken from the Great Exhibition Catalogue of 1851 88
122. Group of vases popular during last quarter of the nineteenth century 89
123. Example of diamond point engraving by Laurence Whistler 90
124. Sketches of nineteenth-century decanters and rummers 91
125. Sketches of nineteenth-century wineglasses and bowls 92
126. Roman bowl of mosaic glass, first century A.D. 94
127. German goblet of latticinio glass 94
128. Venetian ewer, sixteenth century 95
129. Reproduction of Verzelini goblet 97
130. Reproduction of Royal Oak Goblet 97
131. Faked William III glass 98
132. Reproduction of colour-twist stem 98
133. Reproduction of colour-twist stem 98
134. Louis XVIII carafe and drinking glasses 100
135. Charles X carafe 101
136. Candelabra from the Palace of the Czars 101
137. Drinking glass from formal dinner service of the French President 102
138. Vase by René Lalique 102
139. Vase signed by Emile Gallé of Nancy 102
140. Flushed glass by Daum of Nancy 102
141. Bohemian engraved tankard 103
142. German goblet or 'stangenglas' 104
143. Zwischenglaser 104
144. Reichadlerhumpen in enamelled colours 104

145. Cylindrical cup enamel painted by Johann Schaper *page* 105
146. Tankard painted in enamel colours by Johann Schaper 106
147. Beaker enamel painted by Gottlob Samuel Mohn 106
148. Group of Bohemian glass taken from the Great Exhibition Catalogue, 1851 107
149. Glass with incised-twist stem 108
150. Inkwell in millefiori glass, Stourbridge 109
151. Impressed marks on base of Irish decanters 110
152. Waterford decanters 111
153. Cork Glass Co. decanters 111
154. Waterloo Co. Cork decanters 112
155. Belfast decanters 112
156. Irish salad bowl 113
157. Irish salad bowl 113
158. Irish salt-cellars 114
159. Irish jugs 114
160. Irish jugs 115
161. Irish mirror 116
162. Irish mirror 117
163. Jacobite portrait glass 118
164. Jacobite portrait glass 118
165. Jacobite rose glasses 118
166. Jacobite rose glasses 119
167. Jacobite rose glass 120
168. Jacobite glasses with thistle emblem 120
169. Jacobite FIAT glasses 121
170. Jacobite AMEN glass 121
171. Jelly glasses, early eighteenth century 122
172. Jelly glass, middle eighteenth century 122
173. Glass oil lamp, early eighteenth century 123
174. Glass oil lamp with multiple wick holders 124
175. Glass hanging lantern, late eighteenth century 124
176. Lacemaker's lamp 124
177. Lacemaker's condensing globe 124
178. Lynn or Norwich wineglass 126
179. Lynn or Norwich glass 126
180. Glass marbles 127
181. Open-cast working in Yorkshire clay deposit 129
182. Fireclay pots for melting crystal glass 131
183. Pot-maker constructing glasshouse melting pot 131
184. Model of modern glass-melting furnace 132
185. Model of twelfth-century glass melting furnace 132
186. Model of sixteenth-century glass melting furnace 133
187. Mirror signed by John Gumley, dated 1715 134
188. Chippendale mirror 134
189. Chippendale mirror 135
190. Mirror in giltwood frame 135
191. Mirror in Adam style 136
192. Oval mirror in Adam style 136
193. Convex mirror, turn of eighteenth century 137
194. Group of Nailsea articles *page* 139
195. Nailsea jug in flecked style 140
196. Nailsea jugs with encircling white bands 140
197. Gimmel flask and bellows flask in Nailsea style 141
198. Nailsea rolling pin 141
199. Early wineglass of opaque-twist stem style 144
200. Goblet with opaque-twist stem 144
201. Wineglass with corkscrew opaque stem 144
202. Glass with opaque-twist knopped stem 144
203. Five-piece wineglass 144
204. Baccarat millefiori paperweight 145
205. Baccarat dark blue overlay paperweight 145
206. Baccarat millefiori paperweight 145
207. Group of Baccarat paperweights with flower motifs 146
208. Baccarat bouquet paperweight 147
209. Baccarat bouquet paperweight 147
210. Baccarat butterfly paperweight 147
211. Baccarat strawberry paperweight 148
212. St Louis yellow overlay paperweight 148
213. St Louis snake paperweight 148
214. Group of St Louis paperweights featuring different motifs 149
215. Group of Clichy paperweights featuring different motifs 151
216. Modern English paperweight 153
217. Modern Scottish paperweight 153
218. Plain straight-stemmed glass with tear 155
219. Plain straight-stemmed glass of robust make 155
220. Portland or Berberini Vase 156
221. Posset cup and cover 157
222. Ratafia flute glass with opaque-twist stem 158
223. Ratafia flute glass with air-twist stem 158
224. Ratafia flute glass with engraved bowl 158
225. Roemer in soda metal inscribed 1663 159
226. Roemer with the raven's head seal 160
227. Rummer engraved with the bust of Nelson 160
228. Goblet after the roemer style 160
229. Rummer engraved with Sunderland Bridge 160
230. Rummer popular at middle of the nineteenth century 160
231. Rummer popular at time of Great Exhibition in 1851 160
232. Pair of salt-cellars with three supporting feet 161
233. Pair of salt-cellars, *circa* 1740 162
234. Salt-cellar with boat-shaped bowl 162
235. Ship's four-hour sand glass 164
236. Set of four sand glasses in wooden frame 164
237. Silesian-stemmed wineglass with initials GR on shoulder of stem 166
238. Italian wineglass with moulded stem 166

239. Wineglass with eight-sided Silesian stem *page* 166
240. Sweetmeat glass with moulded stem 167
241. Single flint glass, *circa* 1690 168
242. Group of pre-Ravenscroft soda glasses 168
243. Soda glasses popular in John Greene's time 169
244. Tie woven from coloured glass threads 169
245. 'Valor Cup' engraved at Steuben Works, New York 170
246. 'Merry-go-Round' bowl engraved at Steuben Works, New York 171
247. 'Gazelle Bowl' engraved at Steuben Works, New York 172
248. Engraver at work on 'Merry-go-Round' bowl 172
249. Pair of vases engraved at Steuben Works, New York 172
250. Bowl engraved at Orrefors Works, Sweden 173
251. Bowl engraved at Orrefors Works, Sweden 173
252. Bowl engraved at Orrefors Works, Sweden 174
253. Early sweetmeat glass in cut style 175
254. Sweetmeat glass with opaque-twist stem 175
255. Sweetmeat glass with knopped opaque-twist stem 175
256. Glass salver holding tall sweetmeat and eight jelly glasses *page* 176
257. Interior view of sweetmeat glass in Fig. 256 176
258. Epergne with suspended sweetmeat glasses 176
259. Taperstick or tea candlestick in cut style 179
260. Toddy lifter for serving punch 180
261. Victorian coloured vase lustre 181
262. Venetian wineglass with twisted baluster stem 181
263. Venetian tazza 182
264. Venetian sweetmeat glass 182
265. Venetian wineglass in white and blue glass 183
266. Two Venetian wineglasses with scrolled stems 184
267. Verzelini goblet dated 1577 185
268. Verzelini goblet dated 1581 185
269. Verzelini goblet dated 1586 186
270. Verzelini tazza dated 1580 187
271. Sketch showing stages in process of making a wineglass 188
272. Glass-maker at work 189
273. Gaffer at work in his glass-maker's chair 189
274. Bowl forms 190
275. Yard-of-Ale glass 191

INTRODUCTION

GLASS is one of the most remarkable and fascinating substances known to man. It can be produced of the transparency of water, and as devoid of colour; it can be made as opaque as china, colourless or tinted with every known hue. Its peculiar properties of fluidity enable it to be fashioned into any elegant shape while hot either by hand methods or swift moving machines. While plastic, it can be manipulated as easily as the clay of the potter; it can be cut with scissors like cloth or drawn into threads thinner and stronger than the finest silk. It can be rolled into plates or drawn into sheets. But whatever process is used, it still retains the smooth and shining surface acquired on cooling that defies artificial reproduction.

It is generally accepted today that the origin of glass lies far back in the pre-history of the Eastern Mediterranean countries, most probably Egypt. The earliest glass vessels certainly owe their origin to that country, probably in the fifteenth century B.C. Before that period, at least as early as four thousand B.C., beads of stone were glazed by the Egyptians.

The earliest glass vessels that can with some certainty be dated are three vases with the cartouche of King Thotmes III (1501-1449 B.C.). One of these vases is in the British Museum, a second in the Munich Antiquarium, and a third in the Metropolitan Museum of Art in New York. All three are of turquoise blue glass.

Similar specimens from this period indicate that the art of glass-making and of its decorative techniques had reached a high standard of efficiency. Egyptian vessels of coloured glass found a ready market in the Middle East countries. This naturally led to the spread of knowledge, and as a result glass-making began to be practised in other countries bordering the Mediterranean. Rapid development did not occur, however, until the foundation of Alexandria in 331 B.C. by Alexander the Great after his conquest of Asia Minor, Palestine and Egypt.

Alexandria then became the centre of the glass-making industry and she quickly captured the export markets which had been for so long enjoyed by Egypt. Her extensive export trade, indeed, reached as far as England and Scandinavia.

It would appear from specimens extant that in all probability it was Alexandrian glass-makers who, about the beginning of the Christian era, introduced their craft into Rome. From the great mass of records from the pre-Christian era, it is evident that the early Romans were not as interested in glass as were their successors of the first century A.D. onwards. The first mention of glass, indeed, was in a speech by Cicero in 54 B.C., but after the conquest of Egypt by the Romans in 27 B.C., glass began to reach Rome in great quantities.

There are several reasons why Roman interest in glass and glass-making began to extend about this period. Without doubt, the greatest factor was the discovery, just before the Christian era, of the technique of blowing glass. The earlier method of making glass vessels had been to prepare a core of earth or clay on which were wound threads of hot plastic glass. The mass was heated and, while soft, smoothed with a spatula and allowed to cool. The clay core was then withdrawn and any adhering clay removed. An alternative method was to dip a clay core into a crucible of molten glass and to remove the clay after the glass had cooled.

Vessels from this period in bright, multi-coloured patterns can be found in almost any museum today. They fall into three main categories: a cylindrical or cigar-shaped phial, or *alabastron*; a pear-shaped vessel with a pointed base, or *amphora*; and a jug, or *aenochoe*, which had a flat base to make it suitable for standing. These jugs were usually provided with a small handle.

The discovery that a hot mass of glass attached to a hollow metal tube could be blown into a spherical shape revolutionised the art of making glass vessels. Its simpler technique not only cheapened the product, but immensely increased its scope. Moreover, the possibility of variety in shape and decorative treatments were very soon apparent.

The second important factor in the development of glass-making in Rome was the increasing wealth and luxury which accompanied the establishment of the Roman Empire. Samian ware had been the most decorative kind of pottery available, and although full use was made of its limited properties, it had not the same appeal as glass.

The development of glass-making in Rome was rapid and the art eventually reached a stage of artistic attainment which in certain directions has never been excelled. Only perhaps in the present century has glass been used for more purposes and on such a scale as in the early Roman Empire.

Glass vessels of all colours were made both in transparent and the opaque variety, some of pure colours and others of mixtures of one colour with another. The combination of colours was effected by superposition, of which the Portland Vase is the outstanding example (*see* PORTLAND OR BERBERINI VASE) or by combining several colours in such a manner that they traversed the entire thickness of the glass. The latter style includes filigree and millefiori, which are discussed in the dictionary under their respective headings.

Knowledge of glass-making spread very rapidly after the establishment of the Roman Empire, along the valley of the Rhône to Gaul, to the districts bordering the Rhine, and finally to England. Indeed, glass-making was attempted in every province that fell under the Roman yoke.

Roman penetration into the known world was without doubt the main influence in the spread of knowledge of glass-making, and Rome was almost wholly responsible for establishing the European tradition of glass-making which has survived to this day.

Even after the sacking of Rome in A.D. 410, the Roman art in glass was by no means submerged. Constantine's new capital, Byzantium, had been established in A.D. 300, and in spite of the fact that its culture and, indeed, its official language after the middle of the sixth century A.D. was Greek, the glass-making tradition was fundamentally Roman.

Syrian and Alexandrian competition in trade in glassware was met and successfully overcome; Byzantium became the centre of world trade. But its glass changed in name only; what had formerly been known as Roman glass was now called Byzantine.

The rise of Islam threatened for a time the Roman tradition. During the seventh century, Islam had conquered Arabia, Syria, Egypt, Persia and Armenia, and by the end of the century it not only dominated Africa, but had besieged Byzantium and was to do so again early in the eighth century. As a result, it was Syrian glass that was affected; it became less Roman and more Islamic.

It is significant, however, that it was following this period that there was a general decline in the art of glass-making throughout the known world. In Europe it degenerated into a crude peasant art, such as the *Waldglas* (forest glass) of Germany, which persisted in various centres throughout the mediaeval period until the Renaissance.

The capture of Byzantium by the Franks and Venetians in 1204 was not the beginning of Venetian glass. There had already been Venetian glass-makers in the eleventh century, who, records show, had had contact with Alexandria, but by the thirteenth century the Venetian industry was well established.

It is from this period that modern history in glass begins. At the time of the Renaissance, Venetian craftsmen, operating from closely guarded Murano, dominated the world in glass, but by the end of the seventeenth century its secrets had passed over the Alps to the mountain fringe of Bohemia. In a very short space of time knowledge of glass-making had spread all over Europe.

It is from this period also that the dictionary begins, and the history of Venetian glass will be found under its own title.

This introduction to the dictionary, however, cannot be left without further emphasis on the Roman tradition. It is certainly true that the Venetian art of glass-making which formed the springboard of our modern knowledge was an independent development, but it was inspired in form and in many of its treatments by Roman art in glass. In many respects Venetian glass may be regarded as a progressive development of the Roman art. Indeed, in most phases of European glass-making up to the present time, there can be traced the influence of a period in which artistic merit and aesthetic appeal were of the highest order, and one which has successfully withstood the many challenges which have from time to time affected all other branches of art.

THE COLLECTOR'S DICTIONARY OF GLASS

ABSOLON, WILLIAM, OF GREAT YARMOUTH. William Absolon, an independent enameller, appeared to have worked at Great Yarmouth towards the end of the eighteenth century and probably in the beginning of the nineteenth. He painted clear, blue and opaque glass in gilt and enamel colours, a speciality being cream jugs. Some of his work was initialled.

A collection of his work was preserved in the Yarmouth Museum, but unfortunately all specimens were destroyed by enemy action during the second world war. There are some mugs, however, preserved at the Victoria and Albert Museum, which bear the mark of Absolon. They are painted with the inscriptions 'A Trifle from Yarmouth' and 'Success to the Cruizer and Capt Hancock' with initials. A third specimen is a small beaker with slightly outward-sloping sides, decorated in gold, now mostly rubbed off, and inscribed 'A Trifle from Yarmouth For my dear Emily'.

Other glasses by Absolon, such as tumblers and rummers, recently changed hands for sums between £22 and £36.

ACID ENGRAVING.
See ENGRAVING.

ADAM, ROBERT (1728-1792). Robert Adam, architect and designer, was the second son of William Adam, who had a large architectural practice in Scotland.

Robert went to Italy when he was 26 and, after four years' study, returned to England to practise in London. He specialised on decoration and furniture, his theory being that only by including such items within his province could an architect obtain a complete and harmonious result. So great was his influence that he revolutionised the character of applied arts in this country.

Rococo, Chinese and Gothic styles were abandoned by cabinet makers and were superseded by designs which Adam himself had drawn. Indeed, the whole range of household equipment was covered by Adam's designs, including glassware of all descriptions; vases, lamps, epergnes, sconces. candlesticks and lanthorns came within the province of his designs, and all other sorts of glassware showed his influence. (*See* CANDELABRA, CANDLESTICKS, CHANDELIERS, LANTHORNS AND GLASS LAMPS, MIRRORS, PIER GLASSES and TASSIE, JAMES AND WILLIAM.)

AIR-TWIST STEMMED GLASSES. Foreign influences can be detected in most English styles. It is true that they were absorbed almost as soon as they were adopted and reproduced with a strong native flavour, but the idea of the air-twist and its subsequent development was peculiarly English. Indeed, glasses of this group maintain a more exclusively English origin than any others. Air-twist decoration was the most aesthetically effective of all forms of glass adornment; it displayed the beauty of glass as glass without the necessity for any applied work; it was inherent, a creation of the glass-maker himself at the furnace.

The air-twist stem is generally regarded as fortuitous in origin. It developed from the enclosed 'tear' or 'bubble of air', but this was an international decorative feature.

The formation of a tear was a quick and easy operation for the glass-maker. Using a blunt metal tool, he merely dented the surface of the metal he was working and covered the depression with a second layer of glass; the air entrapped in the depression rapidly expanded with the heat and formed a spherical bubble which became elongated into pyriform shape when the stem was being drawn. A specimen is shown in Fig. 1.

The next step obviously was to introduce a multiplicity of these simple tears, and specimens are found where a slight twist has been given to the stem causing the elongated tears to run partly round it. The stem illustrated in Fig. 2 shows how this occurred, although it is not necessarily an early example. The final step to the simple air-twist did not require a great deal of imagination.

The period during which air-twist stems began to make their appearance has been the subject of much discussion, but 1740 is the date usually given by writers as a 'safe' date for air-twists. At this period the air-twists were almost exclusively applied to the drawn two-piece glass mainly with the trumpet type of bowl; first, because it was probably the only current glass which lent itself to air-twist decoration and, secondly, because at that time the glass-maker was not sufficiently experienced to apply it to other styles. The twists were irregularly formed with threads widely spaced. Some specimens are found in which the length of the air-twisted portion of the stem is quite short and others in which an air spiral appears to have run into the surface of the stem causing a groove like an isolated thread of an incised twist stem.

The specimen shown in Fig. 3 is a good example of early imperfections; the spacing and thickness of the threads are faulty and, in addition, the threads themselves terminate a good half inch below the solid base of the bowl. They trail off indecisively at the bottom of the stem.

1. *Drawn stem glass with elongated 'tear'.* 2. *Stem of a wineglass showing elongated 'tears' in slightly twisted formation, the early development of the air-twist stem.* 3. *Air-twist stem glass showing imperfections when the style was first introduced such as variations in spacing and thickness of the air spiral.*

The art of forming the simple air-twist was quickly mastered, however, and an example of the perfectly executed air-twists which appeared later is shown in Fig. 4. Here the spacing and thickness of the threads are uniform, the multiple air spiral is carried well into the solid base of the bowl, and its termination at the base of the stem is definite.

Most two-piece glasses had straight stems, but occasional specimens are found with knops; these were probably experimental glasses. They are marked by a bell bowl, a waisted style introduced after the accession of George I of Hanover in 1714, in combination with a knopped stem. A specimen is illustrated in Fig. 5. The air spiral begins in the base of the bowl, but it is squeezed out in the constriction above the knop. There should be the same number of spirals in the base of the bowl and in the stem if a specimen is a two-piece one.

Glasses of this type were, on the whole, not very successful in the making and, no doubt in order to obtain greater variety and finish, a break was made from the two-piece glass to the lighter three-piece style in which the bowl, stem and foot were separately made. Exactly when this change occurred is debatable. Some writers claim it had nothing to do with the transition in style caused by the glass-makers' efforts to develop the air-twist stem, but was the direct result of the Glass Excise Act of 1745, which resulted in a decrease in the size of all drinking glasses.

Whatever the cause, there is no question that the result was an improved technique. The three-piece glass allowed a much wider range of bowl and stem form, and, as the stem was made separately, it had the additional advantage of simplifying the making of the air spiral itself and of offering a greater variety. Examples of this period are shown in Figs. 6, 7 and 8.

The real beauty of the air-twist stem, however, was not really displayed until the glass-maker developed the technique of making air-twist stems with knops. Such perfection was attained that not only were air-twist stems adorned with a series of several knops, but the knops themselves were formed on the stem in such a way that the continuity of the air-spiral was not broken. A specimen is shown in Fig. 9.

The three-piece glass also allowed the glass-maker a wide choice of bowl form, and every known shape was offered with an air-twist stem. There was very little variation in the feet. The folded foot was commoner in two-piece than in three-piece glasses and the domed foot, occasionally found with the earlier style, is comparatively rare with three-piece glasses.

An unusual glass is that shown in Fig. 10. The bowl and straight part of the stem are drawn as in the two-piece glasses. The knop at the base of the stem contains air beads and the foot is domed, an unusual feature on what is really a three-piece glass.

There is a considerable variation in the type of air-spiral, although the multiple spiral, the first to make its appearance, remained very popular throughout the air-twist period. E. B. Haynes in *Glass Through the Ages* (1948), pp. 202-205, has divided air-twist stems into six sections:

1. Knopped two-piece glasses with single series twist.
2. Unknopped two-piece glasses with single series twist.
3. Unknopped two-piece glasses with double series twist.

Two leaves to each barley stalk.

Four leaves to each barley stalk.

Five leaves to each barley stalk.

Only one barley ear and one hop bloom with a single leaf. This type is very rare.

Only one barley ear and hop bloom with two leaves; engraving oil gilt.

Two barley ears, one leaf only to hop bloom; this type is rare.

Barley ears doubled, four, and a single leaf to each stalk; rare.

Two hop blooms dependent from two barley stalks; very rare.

Two ears of barley only, but sideways and not crossed, no hops; extremely rare.

Four ears of barley only, crossed, no hops; very rare.

The normal type of ale glass was engraved with two single ears of barley 'in saltire'—that is, with the stalks crossed diagonally and with a single leaf on each stalk on one side of the glass, with a single hop bloom with two leaves on the reverse side. Ale glasses also appeared with short stems with an annular knop below the stem, but the bowl shape remained the same and was engraved with the usual hops and barley motif. There were other styles with very short stems or without any stem, the bowl being attached to the foot. Finally, there was a giant ale over a foot in height with the capacity in proportion.

Towards the end of the century, ale glasses appeared with cut stems and with ovoid bowls. The stems of these glasses were usually unknopped and hexagonally faceted, or cut with vertical flutes. The latter was a very popular style.

Ale glasses vary considerably in price. Those with unengraved bowls and plain stems change hands between £2 and £3. Engraving with hops and barley somewhat increases the value. Rare ales, however, have been known to fetch good prices. One with funnel bowl set on a four-sided Silesian stem and folded foot, seven and three-eighth inches high, changed hands for £43. Another with round funnel bowl on a baluster stem with angular knop, bell knop and folded foot, nine inches high, realised £52. An ale glass enamelled by Beilby with hops and barley motif realised £44 a few years ago.

AMERICAN GLASS. As may be expected, glass was slow in developing in the American Colonies and the land which was eventually to become the United States. Glass was a luxury and the products produced were those required for the necessities of life. There was no real attempt to produce colourless glass, at that time the aim of the European glass-makers, and for the seventeenth and eighteenth centuries at least, the American glasses were attractively coloured in greenish or bluish tones rather similar to the German waldglas.

The first record of glass-making appears to be in 1608/9 at Jamestown in Virginia, and for the next one hundred years or so there were five or six attempts to produce glass in different parts of the country.

It was not until the eighteenth century was well advanced, however, that traditional American types became established. The first of these is known today as the 'South Jersey Type', which began at Salem County, New Jersey, where Caspar Wistar set up a glasshouse in 1739. Wistar himself was not a practical glass-maker and as there were no trained men in the country, he had to seek them abroad. The main products of the factory would appear to have been window glass in the commoner sizes, lamp glasses, and most sorts of bottles, snuff and mustard bottles, and various size retorts.

To this factory also are ascribed jugs and other vessels in

14. *American whale oil lamp with cover. Height $4\frac{3}{4}$ inches.* circa *1820.* (*Corning Museum of Glass, New York.*) 15. *American pressed dish in 'Lacy' pattern, a style developed by Deming Jarves in the early nineteenth century at the Boston and Sandwich Glassworks, Massachusetts.* circa *1830.* (*Corning Museum of Glass, New York*)

16. *Whale oil lamp with pressed base in 'Lacy' pattern attributed to Massachusetts area, probably Boston and Sandwich Glassworks.* circa *1830.* (*Corning Museum of Glass, New York*)

clear and coloured glass, ranging from green tints to deep olive green, pale aquamarine blue, amber and opaque white. Ware produced from opaque white glass often had striped patterns similar to the 'Nailsea' style (*see* NAILSEA GLASS). The South Jersey type, however, was shared by other factories such as Millville, in South New Jersey, as well as in New York and elsewhere in New England.

Caspar Wistar was succeeded by his son Richard, who continued to operate the factory until 1780. There was an advertisement in the *Pennsylvanian Journal*, dated 11th October, 1780, which stated that 'the glass manufactury in Salem County, West Jersey, is for sale, with 1500 acres of land adjoining. It contains two furnaces with all the necessary ovens for cooling the glass, drying wood, etc.'

The second important tradition in early American glass is known as the 'Stiegel Type'. Henry William Stiegel, a native of Cologne, settled in America in 1750 and founded his glasshouse in Mannheim, Pennsylvania, in 1765. He chose foreign workmen, mainly from England and Germany, and produced tableware in both lead and soda-lime glass, decorated after the English and Continental fashion, in enamel, by engraving and pattern moulding.

Stiegel had three glasshouses and much of the business he conducted is known from the day books and ledgers which he kept, now in the possession of the Historical Society of Pennsylvania. The glasshouses produced bottles and window glass, but as experience grew, it is clear from Stiegel's account books that every conceivable type of article for the table was produced: decanters, tumblers, salts, beer glasses, sugar boxes, cream jugs, vinegar cruets, smelling bottles, wine glasses, candlesticks, blue flower jars are a few that may be mentioned.

Opaque glass was also produced at the Stiegel factories such as white, yellow, blue, green, brick red and black. These opaque colours were used as enamels for coloured decoration for such designs as birds, conventional floral decoration, animals, ships and various inscriptions. The enamelled pieces were usually of clear glass although some were blue tinted.

Two- and three-piece moulds were employed for producing this type of blown ware, and it soon became the most popular form on the market. Fluting, reeding and diamonding were also alternative patterns. One of the most popular vessels of the Stiegel type was the cylindrical tumbler or flip glass. It was a moulded shape, decorated with vertical flutes, and finished with conventional border patterns in wheel engraving. Decanters very similar to the Bristol type were also in great demand.

Other factories followed the Stiegel fashion, especially in Ohio and Pittsburgh districts, probably the most important being that of the Boston and Sandwich Glass Company, founded in 1825 by Deming Jarves, which flourished until 1887.

To Jarves and an associate Hiram Dillaway, who joined him in 1828, may be credited the perfection of the process of pressing glass, several patents being granted for the process from 1827 onwards. The process of pressing glass has become one of the most important methods of manufacture since that time. Jarves's first patent was granted on 1st December, 1828, and part of it reads as follows: 'To make articles of glass by the method in which they now are, and therefore have been manufactured, a mould, giving the shape and ornamental impression, has been required for each article manufactured.'

Hinged metal moulds as an alternative to free blowing had been used for many years. Glass articles were made in such moulds, blown with fluting and diamond patterns, and although other glass-makers had experimented with the idea of mechanically pressing molten glass into shapes and patterns since 1825, it would appear that Jarves was the first to appreciate the possibilities of the mass production of household glass-ware in the pressed style.

The new process was immediately popular, especially as the early glass was of lead or barium metal of fine quality, and within a few years the technique of pressing was sufficiently improved to imitate English and Irish cut-glass. But the American 'Lacy' patterns—elaborate designs imitating embroidery —were very popular alternatives. An example is shown in Fig. 15.

Most of the early pressed glass falls into the lacy category, and there is no doubt that it was an attempt to establish a technique of glass manufacture in a class of its own. It may have been inspired in the first place by the cut article, but the lacy patterns were by no means reproductions of it. Indeed, the intricate design of many of the lacy patterns was such that they could not have been cut by a cutting wheel.

17. *Pressed bowl on stand. The marks caused by the joints in the mould have been obliterated by fire polishing.* circa *1830.* (*Corning Museum of Glass, New York.*) 18. *Vase in 'Favrile' style evolved by Louis C. Tiffany of New York.* circa *1900.* (*Corning Museum of Glass, New York*)

Another popular fashion which grew from the innovation of pressed glass was door knobs and furniture knobs. Jarves obtained a patent in 1829 for a new style of pressed glass knob, provided with a glass screw instead of a metal one. These door knobs were decorated with heavy vertical ribbing and in fancy designs, and in some cases were in opalescent glass.

For many collectors, the lamps, candlesticks, vases and similar ware which were wholly or partially of pressed glass are now extremely popular. Glass lamps made prior to 1820 were free-blown, for it was not until 1827 that the first patent appeared relating to the pressed process. These free-blown lamps were provided with sturdy stems and feet, the knops being of the annular or ball variety. In most cases there was just a single knop. Later, however, the lamps were provided with pressed bases in lacy and stepped patterns. The step bases were usually hollow and fluted on the inside and had stems of different length. As many as eight steps were provided on the bases of some specimens. An example is shown in Fig. 16.

An alternative variety was the style described as the cup-plate base. They were so named because they were pressed in moulds similar to some of the early ones used for the production of cup-plates. They were inverted during manufacture of lamp bases so that the pattern on the underside of the cup-plate would appear on the top of the base for the lamp.

It was probably not until the middle of the nineteenth century that standard pressed patterns began to appear on the American market. The earliest of the new designs known to collectors of today are Ashburton, Argus, Bigler, Brooklyn, Diamond-Thumb print, Excelsior, and Waffle.

Frank W. Chipman (*The Romance of Old Sandwich Glass*, 1932) refers to an order list dated 1840 for goblets, champagnes and wines in raised diamond and other patterns. These articles were described as fire polished. Fire polishing, indeed, is a process that is necessary even today with some types of pressed glass. It has already been explained that two- or three-part moulds were used in the pressing process. Even when a mould was new and the two halves fitted closely together, a seam would be discernible at the join on the pressed article. In order to eliminate these seam marks and lack of smoothness characteristic of the pressing process, the articles were submitted to the heat of an intense flame for a short period. This superficial melting obliterated the marks of the moulds or any tools used in the pressing process, as shown in Fig. 17.

The raised diamond pattern, which stayed in popularity until well towards the end of the nineteenth century, was obviously an imitation of the strawberry diamond and relief diamond patterns used during the period of Irish Glass, 1785-1850.

Many of the pressed articles produced towards the end of the nineteenth century were in coloured as well as clear glass. Floral designs were very popular. Variegated shades of different colours such as purple, yellow, blue and green were often blended together; this was known as 'marble' glass.

Some three hundred different patterns of pressed tableware have been listed in a book by Mrs Ruth Webb Lee, *Early American Pressed Glass*, 1931. The book included a list of ninety different pressed patterns which were produced at the Boston and Sandwich Glass Company belonging to Deming Jarves.

This period of the development of pressing glass in America is of particular interest to the student of glass and the collector. Methods which from time immemorial have remained unchanged were discarded, and in the time required by the craftsman to produce one article by hand, hundreds were produced by the machine to an exact pattern. American ideas and ingenuity had, in a few decades, mechanised an ancient art into a vast industry.

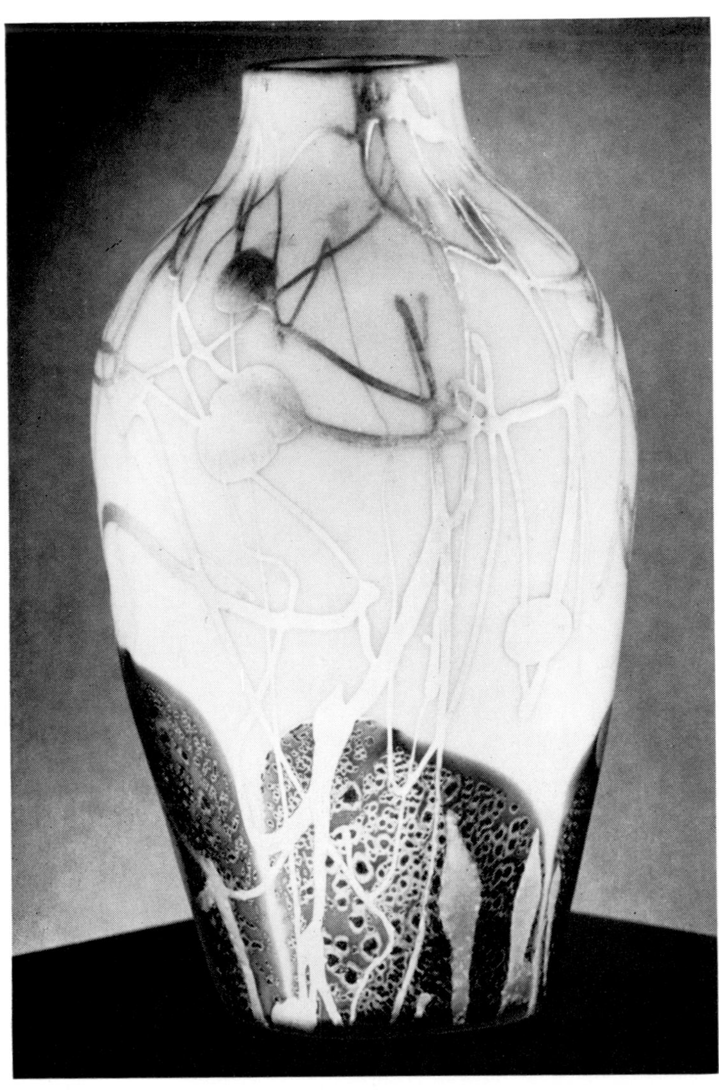

19. *Vase in 'Aurene' style developed by Frederick Carder, who founded the Steuben Glassworks, New York, in 1903.* circa *1920.* (*Corning Museum of Glass, New York.*) 20. *'Aurene' vase by Frederick Carder. Steuben Glassworks, New York.* circa *1920.* (*Corning Museum of Glass, New York*)

That any American glass-maker could pause in the midst of this intensive business of mass production to consider the artistic work of Continental craftsmen seems surprising. Yet such was the case. Louis C. Tiffany of New York, inspired by the artistic achievements of the French worker, Emile Gallé, of Nancy (*see* FRENCH GLASS), set up a factory in 1892 for the production of artistic tableware made in the chair, or 'off hand', in the traditional manner. He employed a large variety of shapes of classical outline, in both plain and coloured cased glass, some of which were fashioned with great ingenuity and charm. The more classical examples of his art featured naturalistic motifs, such as leaves, tinted with the amber glow of the setting sun or slender vines which appeared to be submerged in a shimmering stream.

In addition, Tiffany evolved a method of decoration as original and individualistic as those of Gallé himself. The technique depended on the formation of a metallic lustred or iridescent surface, produced by reheating the glass after manufacture in the chair and spraying it with the atomised solution of the salts of tin or iron. By means of this special treatment, the surface of the glass was split up into infinitesimal metallic patches, each separated by shallow surface cracks. Much of this style of ware appeared under the trade name 'Favrile' and some specimens were signed 'L. C. Tiffany' or were initialled 'L.C.T.' Examples of this work are collectors' pieces. Some specimens are preserved in the Victoria and Albert Museum, London. One from the Corning Museum of Glass is shown in Fig. 18.

In 1903, only a few years after Louis Tiffany set up his glasshouse, Frederick Carder, an English glass-maker from Stourbridge, founded the Steuben Glassworks at Corning, in the south-west corner of the state of New York. The sole object of this glasshouse was the production of art glass in a wide variety of shapes and colours. Iridescent glass, under the trade name 'Aurene', was made at the Steuben factory, and gold ruby and tinted opaque glasses were also popular alternatives. Specimens are shown in Figs. 19 and 20.

In 1918 the Steuben glasshouse merged with the Corning Glass Company, but little progress was made in the development of art glass. No consistent style evolved; glass was blown, cut and engraved into a variety of ponderous and over-complicated forms of indifferent quality in both material and workmanship.

In 1933, however, the company concentrated on flawless

crystal glass as a medium. The services were engaged of Sidney B. Waugh, the sculptor, to exploit the inherent beauty of the glass in imaginative design. The change in policy met with immediate success. The famous art glass of Steuben which emerged from this beginning is discussed under STEUBEN GLASS.

ANNEALING OF GLASS. When a glass article has been fashioned either by hand or by machine, it is in a very unbalanced state of temperature. Some parts of the glass article will be relatively hot, and will still easily become misshapen, while other parts will have become rigid. If the article is allowed to cool from the condition in which this initial inequality of temperature exists, it can only do so by the setting up of a stress between adjacent parts. Glass in such a stressed condition is liable to spontaneous fracture or, when subjected to some sudden change of temperature, such as washing in warm water, may easily crack or break.

The article is therefore annealed in order to avoid the presence of stress. In this process, the glass is first heated to a uniform temperature throughout its mass, when any initial stress present can be eliminated, and when this has been achieved, allowed to cool slowly at a uniform rate so that all parts of the glass vessel follow the same temperature gradient.

The annealing of glass is a delicate and important operation and upon its success depends the behaviour of the article during its useful life. Fortunately, badly annealed articles can be detected by the aid of optical instruments; in modern glassworks, a routine test is carried out to prevent defective articles from being placed on the market.

The annealing process is conducted in most modern establishments in a heated chamber known as a 'lehr', some sixty feet long, through which passes a continuous conveyor belt. The articles to be annealed travel slowly along the conveyor, passing through gradually diminishing temperatures, until they finally emerge from the chamber sufficiently cool to be handled.

ARSENIC.
See MATERIALS USED IN GLASS-MAKING.

AVENTURINE OR SPECKLED GLASS.
See COLOURED GLASS and VENETIAN GLASS.

BAILLIE, LADY GRISELL. Lady Grisell Baillie, a Scottish diarist, kept a careful record of her visits to London and described in considerable detail the arrangement, content and character of the various glasses used at functions she attended. *The Household Books of Lady Grisell Baillie*, 1692-1733, Scottish History Society, Vol. 1, Edinburgh (1911).

For example: 17th December, 1722, Lord Carlile's Dinner party: 'Dessert, Jelly 6 glasses, 3 of biskets hipd as high betwixt each two glasses, a high scaloped glass in the middle.'

Another example: 15th March, 1727, Lord Mountjoy's Dinner party: The centre of the dessert table had 'a scolloped glass cornered brim'; both ends had 'the same cornered brim'd glasses as in the middle'; both sides had 'the same corner'd brim glasses as the rest, also glass broad cream bowls'.

An idea of the cost of glass vessels in the early part of the eighteenth century can be gained from the following entries in Lady Baillie's household books.

Jan, 1715	A dozen wines	6/-
	Two ale glasses	1/-
	Two cruets	1/-
	Two flint-crested flasks	3/-
	Black bottles	2d less
May, 1715	One dozen wines	8/-
	Two glass mugs	2/-

BALUSTER STEMMED GLASSES. Soon after Ravenscroft established his glass-of-lead in 1676, drinking glasses began to appear in great quantity. New glasshouses sprang up all over the country to exploit the new lead metal; existing glasshouses discarded their soda metal and adopted Ravenscroft's medium (*see* ENGLISH GLASS, HISTORY OF).

Among the first to appear were drinking vessels with the baluster style stem. The true baluster formation, of course, was copied from a motif in Renaissance architecture. It had been popular in the time of John Greene, who had imported glasses from Murano between the years 1667 and 1672. For the most part, however, the baluster motif was the inverted form, such as is shown in Fig. 21, and was a purely English version of the Venetian urn-shaped stem. It was from this simple motif that all other stem forms developed.

Drinking vessels and other forms with baluster stems are, for many reasons, of great importance to the student of glass. They mark the beginnings of styles which can claim to be distinctly English; they were among the first vessels to be fashioned from Ravenscroft's newly discovered glass-of-lead; they gave dignity to the short period which has been described by some as the greatest English achievement in the art of glass. There is perhaps one further point of importance to the collector; balusters constitute the earliest type of drinking glass of which he will be fortunate enough to acquire anything like a series.

21. *Typical example of the early baluster style, with inverted baluster stem, tear and base knop. Height 8¼ inches.* circa *1695.*

22. *Group of baluster stemmed glasses showing from left to right: acorn knop, inverted baluster, also inverted baluster, annular knop above a cylinder knop, and cylinder knop. All have a base knop above a folded foot.*

The classification of baluster stems generally accepted today is that given by W. A. Thorpe in his book, *A History of English and Irish Glass*, London, 1929, Vol. 1, pp. 178-180. Some of the more important forms are given below in the order in which they are thought to have appeared, although the dates are not necessarily those given by Thorpe.

Baluster Stems	
Inverted Baluster	1682-1710
Drop Knop	1690-1710
Angular Knop	1695-1715
Ball Knop	1695-1715
Annulated or Triple-ring Knop	1700-1725
Mutiple Knops	1700-1720
True Baluster	1710-1730
Acorn Knop	1710-1715
Mushroom Knop	1710-1715

Typical specimens are shown in Fig. 22.

The above groups may be further sub-divided into sections depending on the formation of the stem, and the classification can be extended still further to include various bowl forms and foot formations.

Although the glass-maker offered a great variety of stem formations, he was less ambitious when it came to the bowls. The general style was a conical-shaped bowl with either straight sides or sides slightly curved at the base. They are known by various writers as (*a*) straight-sided, straight funnel or conical bowls, such as shown in Fig. 21, and (*b*) round funnel bowls. These two styles accounted for the great proportion of the bowls among the early balusters, but when the stems were elaborated about the turn of the seventeenth century, there was a tendency to adopt the German waisted bowl. The tendency increased after the accession of George I in 1714, and in the later baluster styles, such as those with the baluster and acorn knopped stems, the waisted bowl appeared in every other glass.

The feet in all types of baluster glasses were either folded or domed and folded. The fold in the very early types was somewhat thin, following the Venetian practice, but after 1690 it developed into a thick and wide rim in keeping with the generous proportions of the stem and bowl. The plain foot increased in popularity during the baluster period from one in every ten glasses to twice that ratio by 1730.

The domed and terraced foot appeared in the series but, although an artistic attempt of promise, for some reason it did not prosper. Terracing is found only on fairly thick feet and was a feature executed in the chair and not by moulding. As the term suggests, the foot rises from the rim in a series of steps or terraces to a domed centre where it joins the stem.

The glasses which marked the early baluster period were robust, capacious, well-proportioned vessels, but of a plainness and simplicity that enhanced rather than marred their dignity.

The early glasses did not vary much in form, but after the turn of the century the glass-maker was not slow in offering variety, and he learnt to do so without necessarily altering

23. *Typical light Newcastle baluster or balustroid. This glass was engraved by the Dutch artist, Jacob Sang.*

24. (Extreme right) *Balustroid showing elongated form of inverted baluster.*

form. Although the early balusters were quickly elaborated into numerous stem styles which almost defy classification, the logical relationship between bowl, stem and foot necessary to maintain an artistic balance remained fundamentally unchanged for some years, apart from the tendency to lengthen the stem at the expense of the bowl. Indeed, it was this growing tendency to lengthen the stem that eventually brought about the elaboration of the inverted baluster, a characteristically short stem style, into heavy knops of numerous shapes. The glass-maker borrowed from the ornate designs used in architecture, adopted Continental ideas, and was inspired by natural motifs, but he combined them all into so many varieties of stem that attempts to classify them have been the despair of writers for over half a century. Indeed, the classification in the list of the nine varieties already given can be subdivided still further into something like fifty other varieties.

As an example may be quoted glasses with inverted baluster stem. There are at least a dozen known modifications of this simple motif, such as an inverted baluster alone, inverted baluster with a knop at the base, or a knop above the inverted baluster, a knop above and below the inverted baluster, and two knops over an inverted baluster with a knop at the base. The rarest of all the inverted balusters are those with the acorn and mushroom motif.

The baluster glasses developed gradually into the lighter variety classified as balustroids. These glasses are discussed under that heading.

Among the balusters the large goblets realise the highest prices. For example, one with a straight-sided bowl set on an inverted baluster stem, with large air bead and a ball knop at the base, terminating in a domed and folded foot, similar to that shown in Fig. 21, realised £75. This was an exceptionally large glass, over thirteen inches high and weighing nearly four pounds. Smaller examples of the same style fetch correspondingly lower prices. One eight inches high fetched £20.

Wines with baluster stems of similar style to those glasses already described, between six and seven inches in height, have realised between £7 and £9.

BALUSTROIDS. There was a gradual transition early in the eighteenth century from the heavy baluster type of stem to a smaller and lighter style of the same type. These glasses are known today among collectors as balustroids. This transition, and the tendency for the stems themselves to lengthen at the expense of the bowl, had already begun early in the century.

George I had ascended to the throne in 1714 and a style of stem new to English glass was introduced in his honour from the Continent. This was known as the Silesian stem (*see* SILESIAN-STEMMED GLASSES). This factor may also have been partly responsible for the transition to the lighter balustroid form.

It is thought that the lighter balusters were made at Newcastle, whereas the balustroids became more or less a national style portraying the natural evolutionary changes undergone by the baluster form.

Three out of every four glasses of the balustroid type fall into two well-defined groups; they are (*a*) those in which simple knopping occurs as single knops or in multiple form, such as the specimen in Fig. 23, and (*b*) the elongated form of the inverted baluster as the example in Fig. 24. There are others which are much on the lines of the traditional balusters, but of lighter and less emphasised formation.

Glasses with simple knopping constitute at least half the balustroid series. A knop can occur in the form of a single knop, usually in the centre of the stem, where it can be either of the bulbous variety or swelling, but also as a shoulder knop or a base knop. Glasses in this group can have two knops in the stem, one in the centre and the second usually as either a shoulder knop or a base knop. Other varieties with two knops in the stem are rare. Glasses with three knops in the stem, shoulder, centre and base, are fairly common, but those with a greater number are scarce.

The second group which have the elongated form of the inverted baluster have this feature either alone or in combination with other knopping, such as the simple bulbous type, angular and annular knops; but in all cases the knops are very much less emphasised than those appearing in the baluster group.

Glasses in which a true baluster usually appears include the so-called Kit-Kat glasses. They take their name from a picture by Kneller of members of the famous club drinking one of their toasts. The picture shows the balustroid type of glass used at that time and, as was the custom, the glasses were held by the feet and not by the stems.

The balustroid group consist mainly of wines, although gins are well represented, while ales are relatively scarce. The most popular bowl forms are the round funnel and waisted styles. Ogee bowls are fairly common, but other bowl forms are scarce. Folded feet occur on four glasses out of five, but the domed variety is reserved for glasses which, although probably intended for sweetmeats, are often called champagnes.

Balustroids usually change hands between £4 and £6. As an example, one seven inches high with a stem with mushroom knop above an inverted baluster with domed foot, realised £4. Another with cup bowl supported on a collar knop above a teared ball knop on a domed and folded foot, the glass five inches high, fetched £6.

BATCH. Batch is the term applied to the mixture of raw materials which, when melted, produces glass. The batch for a typical lead crystal glass, for example, is as follows:

Sand	1000 parts
Red Lead	660
Potash	330
Saltpetre	40
Borax	30
Arsenic	3
Decolouriser	Very small quantity

The ingredients are accurately weighed and then thoroughly mixed either by hand or by power-driven machines to a condition ready to be charged to the furnace.

It has been found difficult in practice to break up the cords and streaks which tend to develop when the batch is melting, without the addition to it of a proportion of broken glass or 'cullet', as it is termed in the trade. This is a fortunate circumstance for the glass-maker, as a certain amount of glass is always broken during manufacture, accumulated as waste or rejected during final inspection because of some defect. The cullet is collected, cleaned, and a definite weighed quantity added to the batch before it is charged to the melting furnace. Cullet, therefore, must be considered as a definite constituent of the batch itself.

Some of the ingredients of the batch decompose during the melting process to give off gas. For example, in the batch given here, the potash ingredient evolves about one-third of its weight as carbon dioxide, which, forcing its way to the surface of the molten glass, exerts a powerful stirring action on the mass, so improving the homogeneity of the product. Saltpetre and borax also evolve gases during the melting process.

BEADS.

See MARBLES OF GLASS.

BEILBY, WILLIAM (1740-1819) and **MARY** (1749-1797). The Beilby family of Newcastle-on-Tyne were among the most famous of the enamel painters of the eighteenth century. William Beilby, sen. (1706-1765) was born at Scarborough, but later moved to Durham where he established a good business in the city as a jeweller and silversmith. He married in 1733 and brought up a family of seven children, five sons and two daughters, all of whom appeared to have inherited the artistic talent of their father. William Beilby, jun. and Mary were the only members of the family, however, who appear to have practised enamelling on glass.

About 1760 the family removed to Newcastle-on-Tyne where Ralph Beilby (1743-1817), a wood engraver and a younger brother of William, took on an apprentice, one Thomas Berwick, who in 1777 was taken into partnership with Ralph. Berwick later wrote an autobiography, *A Memoir of Thomas Berwick, Written by Himself*, London and Newcastle (1862), in which he recorded details of the Beilby family.

When Berwick joined the Beilby household about 1767, he records that both William and Mary Beilby, who would then have been aged twenty-seven and eighteen respectively, 'had constant employment of enamel-painting of glass'. William had learned the art of enamelling in Birmingham, where he had worked for a time with an enamel box-maker.

During his apprenticeship with the Beilby family, Berwick became attached to Mary, but in her early twenties she unfortunately had a paralytic stroke which appears to have made her an invalid.

The first enamelled work on glasses appeared about 1762, the decoration being of an heraldic nature in coloured and white enamels, and there can be no doubt that such glasses were decorated by William, as Mary at that time would have been only thirteen. It is known that Ralph Beilby was an heraldic engraver and probably influenced his elder brother William in the style of glasses he painted.

About 1774, however, the style changed and the scope was widened to include naturalistic motifs, rustic subjects, landscapes and conventional and fanciful scenes. No doubt Mary Beilby assisted in the enamel painting of these glasses, but it is not possible to distinguish the work of William from that of Mary, as in all cases the signature is merely 'Beilby'.

The brother and sister left Newcastle-on-Tyne after the death of their mother in 1778, when they settled in Fifeshire, and apparently discontinued their work.

The numerous glasses painted by the Beilbys are discussed under ENAMELLED GLASS.

BELLOWS.
See Nailsea Glass.

BELLS.
See Nailsea Glass and Musical Glasses.

BETTS, THOMAS (d. 1767). A glass-cutter and merchant of London who started business as a glass grinder and polisher of mirrors. First mention of him is in 1738 in a shop at Bloomsbury. Shortly after, however, he widened his scope and changed his premises to the King's Arms Glass Shop, Charing Cross, where he employed Andrew Pawl, a Bohemian glass-cutter. Pawl left the Betts establishment in 1744, but not until Betts himself had become initiated into the finer points of using the cutting wheel.

Fortunately, a fairly good idea can be gained of the type of business carried on by Thomas Betts between the years 1747 and 1761 from the series of Bills and Bill-heads collected by the late Sir Ambrose Heal, which contain descriptions and prices of articles supplied by Betts. These include most glass articles used on the table such as cruets, wineglasses, stoppered decanters, beer tumblers, champagne quart decanters, water glasses and carafes.

Some idea of the reputation of Thomas Betts can be gained from an advertisement in a York newspaper in 1773, six years after his death, in which an apprentice of his, John Shoulter of Lincoln, stated that he had been 'apprentice to the late Thomas Betts of London' (Francis Buckley, *Glass*, Vol. V, 1928, p. 299). (*See* Champagne Glasses.)

BISHOPP HAWLEY.
See English Glass, History of and Single Flint Glasses.

BLOW-IRON.
See Wineglass, The Making of.

BLUE GLASS.
See Bristol Glass, Coloured Glass, and Venetian Glass.

BOHEMIAN GLASS.
See German and Bohemian Glass.

BORIC OXIDE.
See Materials Used in Glass-making.

BOTTLE GREEN PAPERWEIGHTS.
See Door Stops or Bottle Green Paperweights.

BOTTLES. Collecting old bottles is a pursuit popular in this country, especially in regard to the 'sealed' variety, but much more so in America, where collectors abound and the variety is boundless.

The glass bottle has a long and honourable history. The discovery in the first century A.D. that a hot mass of glass attached to a hollow metal tube could be blown into spherical shape at once gave rise to the first blown bottle, and the specimens of Roman bottles extant are eloquent testimony today of the vast quantities that must have been produced at the time.

25. *The earliest intact example of a sealed bottle. It is dated 1657. It is preserved in the Central Museum, Northampton.* 26. *Seventeenth century bottle with seal inscribed 'Cha. Turnor 1690'. (Central Museum, Northampton)*

27. *Eighteenth-century sealed bottle, inscribed on the seal 'Jno Andrews 1770'.* 28. *Eighteenth-century bottles, illustrating change in form. That on the left is inscribed on the seal 'I Swift Dean 1727' and that on the right 'Bernard Shaw 1802'.* 29. *Eighteenth-century bottle with the initials and date 'A T 1785' on the seal.*

These Roman bottles and those produced through the Middle Ages were inspired in size and variety of shape by their counterparts in metal and pottery. It was, however, not until Sir Robert Mansell assumed control in this country of glass manufacture in 1623 that a break occurred in the similarity. The long-necked, bulbous bottle was the first of its kind and bore no resemblance to the then popular London delft bottle for 'Whit' (probably white wine) or its stoneware counterpart.

Up to Mansell's time, bottles had been made in thin green glass, and it was not until the manufacture of bottles in dark green glass, which occurred somewhere about 1630, that the glass bottle came into general use. Whether credit can be given to Mansell for making the glass bottle a popular receptacle for wine is a debatable point. Some writers give the credit for adopting what was then a new shape to the London retailers. They already had an understanding with Mansell in 1630 and five years later were incorporated by Charter as the Worshipful Company of Glass Sellers. It has been stated by W. A. Thorpe that their wine bottles did for the bottle industry what Ravenscroft's glass-of-lead did for drinking glasses.

It is from this period that the history of the development of the bottle can very clearly be traced. It was a fortunate custom from the seventeenth century for bottles to be 'sealed'. The seal took the form of an impressed medallion, such as is shown in Figs. 25-29, which was attached to the bottle either at the base of the body or shoulder. The seal may be an owner's mark or that of a merchant, or it may indicate a particular brand. The most sought after seals are those with name, place and date.

The earliest known seal is dated 1652, but it is without its parent body. The earliest intact specimen extant is dated 1657. This is a tall bottle with slightly depressed bulbous body and a long tapering neck. It is preserved in the Central Museum, Northampton, and is shown in Fig. 25.

This style of bottle, often described as the 'shaft and globe', was popular up to nearly the end of the seventeenth century. It is the most elementary of glass forms. Its shape tended to change somewhat towards the end of the century, the body becoming straighter and the shoulder more pronounced. The raised shoulder led to a shortening of the neck, and later this feature became more accentuated and led, just before the end of the seventeenth century, to the 'onion style'. This bottle shape had a low squat body and at first a very short neck. The neck, however, later increased in length and the bulbous body gradually changed to a straighter and much more upright style.

The style had now developed into what is known today as the 'slope and shoulder bottle' and this style was popular from 1715 up to the middle of the eighteenth century. The tendency for the sides to become straighter continued; by the middle of the century the shape had developed into what may be termed the 'cylinder' style.

It was about this time that 'binning' was introduced—that is, the storing of wine bottles on their sides in racks or bins. Obviously the earlier styles did not lend themselves to this practice, but the cylinder style, with its straight sides, could be easily and economically stored in bins. For this reason, the cylinder style is still the popular shape today for bottles for wine and other liquids.

A sealed bottle of the eighteenth century normally changes hands between £1 and £2. (*See* BOTTLES, PERFUME AND SMELLING and SCOTTISH GLASS.)

BOTTLES, PERFUME AND SMELLING. Glass vessels intended to contain perfume have been known from the earliest times, at least the sixth century B.C., when the Egyptian glass-makers, intent on extending their business with Greece, may well have made glass vessels for Lydian perfumes (Honey, *Glass*, 1946, p. 19).

After the technique of blowing glass vessels had been mastered by the Roman craftsmen in the first century B.C., the glass vessel became the article of general utility for storage, carrying and exporting such liquids as wine, oil, medicine and perfumes.

Islamic glass of the ninth and tenth centuries, found some years ago by German archaeologists during excavations at Samarra, included bottles intended for perfume, as well as bowls and other shapes. They were cut in representation of animals and arabesque foliage in a manner which displayed profound knowledge of the art of decorating glass by cutting. Some were pear-shaped in blue and green glass.

The Venetian craftsmen made perfume and sprinkler bottles during the sixteenth and seventeenth centuries.

Glass bottles for perfume were advertised fairly frequently during the eighteenth century in this country under the general term 'smelling bottles'. They included the commercial phials of ordinary glass made for the sale of scent, ladies' toilet bottles for the dressing table, and springel glasses or casting bottles for scattering scent about the room. In addition, fancy glasses were sold at fairs for cottage ornaments and curiosities and as token bottles used as lovers' gifts, usually engraved with initials on each side. Small decorative scent and smelling bottles usually mounted with silver and gold were noted as early as 1716.

In the days when fainting was a fashionable female accomplishment, the business in smelling bottles must have been a successful one. For example, Jackson and Sons of Clerkenwell Green (1768-1800) specialised in cut smelling bottles at their 'Case Wickered and Cut Smelling Bottle Manufactury', and several other cutters, both in London and the Provinces, mentioned them in their lists. 'Cut smelling bottles of all colours' were advertised as early as 1752, and in 1766, Haedy, a London cutter, mentions 'Sweet-water Bottles for the Ladies' Toilets' in his list of cut glass articles. This latter notice refers, no doubt, to the sets of bottles for toilet caskets, a popular form being a rectangular bottle, about five inches in height, cut with a single trellis motif round the middle. 'Lavender Squares' were mentioned in a sale in London in 1771.

Scent bottles were made in great numbers and in a variety of shapes at the Pellatt establishment. One of the standard styles now found is a flat, pear-shaped flask between four and five inches in height with a ground-in mushroom stopper. One side of the flask has an incrustation embedded in the wall and the other is invariably embellished with cut motifs, such as strawberry diamonds or relief diamonds. The sides often show pillar fluting either plain or with diamond cutting. A typical example is shown in Fig. 81. (*See* CORONATION AND OTHER ROYAL COMMEMORATIVE GLASSES.)

Blue toilet bottles can also with some certainty be ascribed to Bristol. The gold-mounted scent bottles shown in Fig. 35 (*see* BRISTOL GLASS) are typical of the Bristol style. They are painted in enamel colours in the fanciful style favoured by Michael Edkins.

Bright green glass scent bottles in similar style and decoration to the blue ones just referred to were also made at Bristol. White glass of a presumed Bristol type was also used for scent bottles and what were then catalogued as 'etwee smelling bottles'. Some are cut in faceted style, others bearing enamelling and gilding of pastoral figures and naturalistic flower motifs. Honey (*Glass*, 1946, p. 114) suggests that this style of scent bottle, which chiefly dates from after 1770, was inspired by Sèvres porcelain; they are particularly well represented in the Schreiber Collection.

The Irish glasshouses also produced perfume and smelling bottles. The Waterford list included 'bottles for smelling salts'. A typical specimen is shown in Fig. 100.

It is impossible to describe the many shapes and sizes of perfume and smelling bottles appearing in the nineteenth century; the smallest noted is a cut bottle one inch in height, including a silver cap, but bottles up to six inches in height, cut with the usual motifs, were quite common. Typical specimens, as in Figs. 98 and 100, show elaborate but nonetheless excellent craftsmanship. It was characteristic of this period that no space on the surface of an article should be unadorned and the more elaborate the cut effects, the more the article was esteemed.

Scent bottles have changed hands up to £10 each. Those by Apsley Pellatt, with bust portraits of Shakespeare, Princess Charlotte, Washington, William IV (*see* Fig. 81) and others, fetch the higher prices.

BOWES, SIR JEROME, d. 1616.
See ENGLISH GLASS, HISTORY OF.

BOWL FORMS. The various bowl formations found on drinking glasses of the eighteenth century are given in WINEGLASS, THE MAKING OF, Fig. 274.

BOWLS AND BASINS. Since ancient times the glass bowl has been called upon to supply nearly all human requirements. The glass 'Bolle' or 'Bason' figured in the household inventories of Henry VIII, John Greene imported glass bowls from Venice, and Ravenscroft made them from his glass-of-lead.

The eighteenth century found an extended use for them, including finger bowls, bowls for sweetmeats, goldfish, punch, fruit, salad, butter, sugar, basins for candles with rings to fix them in; in 1766 Christopher Haedy advertised 'basons of all sorts, the greatest variety ever seen'.

Bowls have fetched anything in price up to £90, depending on their description and rarity. Details are given under their respective headings.

BOWLS, BUGGIN.
See BUGGIN BOWLS.

BOWLS, SALAD.
See IRISH GLASS.

BRANDY TUMBLERS. There is very little written on the subject of glasses used for brandy. The late seventeenth-century style is shown on John Greene's designs for glasses ordered from Morelli of Murano during the period 1667-1672 (Sloane MS. 857. Papers relating to the Glass Sellers). The style of the glass then used, according to Greene's designs, was a cylindrical tumbler about as high as it was wide.

Ravenscroft's Price List (Wholesale, dated 29th May, 1677), which has been preserved among the records of the Glass Sellers' Company, shows an item: Brandy glasses of the same, 2-oz, 6s.

'Of the same' refers to ribbed and plain styles.

It is pointed out by Thorpe (*A History of English and Irish Glass*, 1929, Vol. I, p. 127) that a 'brandy in Mr Mason's Collection (*see* Plate XXV in his book) weighs 2¼-ozs.' It has a gadrooned base and is in soda metal of the period about the second half of the seventeenth century.

There is no mention of brandy tumblers in any of the eighteenth-century notices, although in *Aris's Birmingham Gazette*, of 15th September, 1766, it was advertised that Joseph Green & Co, Colemore Row, Birmingham, sold brandy at 11s. per gallon.

BRISTOL GLASS. Bristol is well known today among collectors for its opaque white glass decorated in enamel colours, its famous dark blue glass—indeed, any specimen of dark blue glass is today immediately dubbed Bristol—and, to a much less extent, its bright green glass. Many other colours have been accredited from time to time to Bristol, but there is no positive evidence that glass of any other colour was made there. The Bristol glass-makers also specialised in gilding and in glass-cutting. It is probable that the popularity of Bristol glass in the eighteenth century was due more to its high quality cut and engraved crystal glass than to its coloured varieties.

The earliest record of a glasshouse occurs in 1651, and by the end of the seventeenth century there were no fewer than nine glasshouses in operation at Bristol. At that time the city ranked fourth in importance in this country in glass production. Its importance in this respect can be judged by the fact that early in the eighteenth century, when the town was honoured by a Royal visit, glass-makers took a prominent part according to the notice in the *Daily Post*, 14th November, 1738: 'Bristol, November 11th . . . Yesterday the Prince and Princess of Wales paid their promised visit to the City. . . . The Companies of the City made a magnificent appearance in their formalities, marching two by two, preceding the Corporation and the Royal Guests. The Company of glassmen went first, dressed in Holland shirts, on horseback, some with swords, others with crown and sceptres in their hands, made of glass.'

Bristol glass-makers were again accorded Royal patronage later in the century when Isaac Jacobs, a Bristol glass manufacturer, was made glass-maker to George III.

Opaque White. Of great importance to the collector today are the few specimens extant of the opaque white glass made at Bristol during the eighteenth century. Towards the close of the century, many objects were being made in opaque white in various parts of the country, but on the whole it cannot be said that the material ever reached a high standard of quality. The early types varied from dense stony white glass, which was really opaque, to a translucent, opalescent glass having the fiery characteristics of the opal when light was transmitted through it, and a milk and white appearance with reflected light.

The opaque white glass made at Bristol, however, was quite different in composition and character from that made elsewhere. It was denser in texture and more creamy white; in fact, more like fine Chinese stoneware or porcelain in appearance. The close resemblance to porcelain is not surprising when it is considered that it was developed where experiments with delft and porcelain had been conducted, and where the manufacture of these materials had become established on a commercial scale.

Bristol opaque white was a potash-lead glass, containing a higher proportion of lead, indeed, than ordinary transparent flint glass. The relatively high lead and low silica content caused it to be very soft and also gave it its high density. The glass was rendered opaque by the addition of oxide of tin to the batch.

It would appear that the first glasshouse in Bristol to make opaque white glass was the Redcliffe Backs Glasshouse adjoining a pottery. There are entries in the ledger of this glasshouse of the painter Michael Edkins concerning his work there between the years 1762 and 1787 (*see* EDKINS, MICHAEL). It is clear that Edkins and probably other enamel painters (for example, his son and his apprentices) decorated such articles as vases, quart mugs, cruets, tea-caddies, plates, candlesticks, basins and jars in both opaque white and dark blue glass.

It is recorded that candlesticks and tapersticks in opaque white were made in Bristol in 1757 (F. Buckley, *Glass*, Vol. 8, 1931, p. 278). The candlesticks are usually between nine and ten inches in height with an incised twist shaft and a multi-ring collar at each end, terminating in a domed foot. The candle-socket and foot are usually painted in enamel colours with bouquets, sprays of garden flowers and butterflies. An occasional candlestick of this style is found with a candle-socket in Battersea enamel. The tapersticks are between six and seven inches in height and are small reproductions of the candlesticks.

Other articles were made at Bristol in opaque white and decorated in enamel colours. Typical specimens are shown in Fig. 30 of a vase and two bottles. The vase, seven inches in height, has a double ogee body painted and gilded with coloured flower sprays and birds. The neck of the vase is short, terminating in a flared lip. The foot is a splayed hollow one and is folded. The bottles, just over seven inches high, are for oil and vinegar and are almost a pair; they have club-shaped bodies enamelled on one side with green wreaths in which are the words VINEGAR and OIL respectively. The necks have puce scroll work with turned wood covers surmounted by ivory knobs.

Tea-caddies are also ascribed to Bristol, typical specimens being shown in Fig. 31. The enamel painting in various colours shows exotic birds, foliage and scroll work and also labels for different kinds of tea—GREEN, HYSON (as shown on the specimens in Fig. 31), BLACK and BOHEA.

Several specimens of Bristol tea-caddies are known today and according to W. A. Thorpe, the painting on them 'may with reasonable certainty be attributed to Edkins' (*A History of English and Irish Glass*, 1929, p. 224). Two specimens are in the Victoria and Albert Museum, one which came originally from the collection of William Edkins, jnr., grandson of Michael Edkins, and a second formerly in the collection of Lady Charlotte Schreiber. Both specimens are similar to those shown in Fig. 31 and have on one side a finely painted bird and on the other a bouquet of closely painted flowers. Tea-caddies such as those described vary in height from five-and-a-half to six-and-a-quarter inches and are usually gold mounted.

Another style conceivably attributable to Edkins is the covered vase shown in Fig. 32, which is painted in enamel colours with fanciful Chinese figures. Some of these vases are uncovered and vary in height from six-and-a-half to eight-and-a-half inches.

Alternative origins have been suggested for specimens decorated in fanciful Chinese style such as the above (*see*

30. *Bristol opaque white vase painted and gilded with coloured flower sprays; also two cruet bottles painted in enamel colours, with turned wood covers surmounted by ivory knobs.*

31. *Bristol tea-caddies enamel painted in various colours and white enamel labels for different kinds of tea.* (*Messrs Cecil Davis, Ltd.*)

32. *Bristol covered white opaque vase painted in enamel colours with fanciful Chinese figures.* (*Messrs Cecil Davis, Ltd.*)

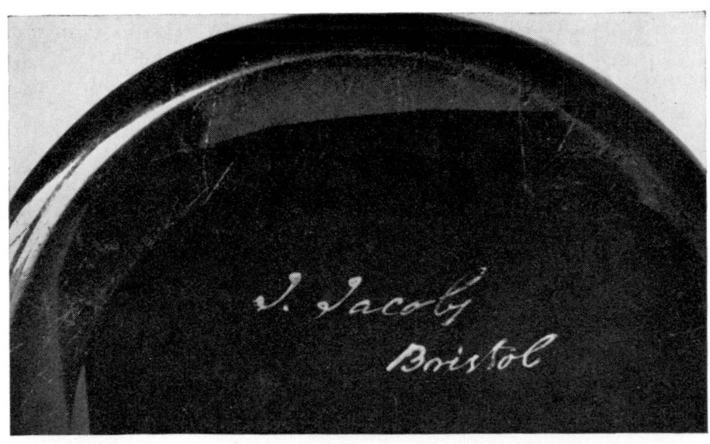

33. *Signature of I. Jacobs, found on specimens of Bristol dark blue glass. (By courtesy of the Victoria and Albert Museum)*

ENAMELLED GLASS). Beakers, somewhat taller than the vases, painted in the same manner with Chinese figures, are also known.

Blue. Articles in dark blue glass are today always assumed to have been made at Bristol. Documentary evidence, of course, proves that it was made there, but the same kind of glass was also made at other centres during the eighteenth century; indeed, its manufacture became fairly general throughout the country by the end of the century.

Only a few articles in dark blue glass can be ascribed with any certainty to Bristol. They are decanters, toilet bottles, patch boxes, wine-coolers, finger bowls and dishes. Fortunately, some of the articles in blue glass are signed 'I. Jacobs, Bristol' in gilt lettering, a specimen of the signature being shown in Fig. 33. The Jacobs, father and son, had a glasshouse in Temple Street, Bristol, and specialised in dark blue glass. An account of the family is given under JACOBS, LAZARUS AND ISAAC. The fact that many articles bear the above signature has been of great assistance in identifying the type of ware—at least in blue glass—that was made at Bristol during the eighteenth century.

The decanters, a specimen of which is shown in Fig. 34, are characterised by their long slender necks, pear-shaped bodies, and lozenge stoppers with bevelled edges. The decoration on the specimen shown is in gilt, the stopper bearing the initial R, and the bottle having a label bearing the word RUM. The base is inscribed in gilt with the signature shown above. Specimens are known similar to that shown in Fig. 34, decorated in gilt with a chain and label bearing such inscriptions as SHRUB, HOLLANDS, GIN and BRANDY.

The Jacobs also provided wineglass coolers and finger bowls in dark blue glass. Several specimens of the former are known, a typical specimen being shown in Fig. 36. It has a key-fret border and is signed on the base in gilt letters 'I. Jacobs, Bristol'.

The blue glass finger bowls, also decorated with gilt border designs (Fig. 37), have plain rims, whereas the wineglass coolers are provided with two lips to hold the wineglasses. It was customary during the eighteenth century to provide two glasses at the table for each diner. After the first glass had been emptied, it was placed upside down in the wine-cooler while the second glass was in use, preparatory to the serving of a different wine.

Blue toilet bottles can also with some certainty be ascribed to Bristol. There is a record, for example, of two blue and gold toilet bottles in a list of stolen property in the *Bristol Journal*, 15th October, 1763 (Fig. 35). The rich blue Bristol glass was also used by silversmiths for the new fashion of pierced ware, the open designs in silver being enhanced in appearance by the dark blue glass lining.

Green. Bright green glass was most probably made at Bristol;

34. *Bristol decanter in dark blue glass labelled in gilt with the word RUM. (City Art Gallery, Bristol.)* 35. *Pair of blue toilet bottles, gold mounted, decorated in enamel in fanciful Chinese design. (By courtesy of the Victoria and Albert Museum)*

36. *Dark blue wineglass cooler with gilt fret border, signed* I. Jacobs, Bristol. (*City Art Gallery, Bristol.*) 37. *Dark blue glass finger bowl, probably Bristol, decorated in gilt.*

specimens are extant of scent bottles similar in style and design to the blue ones which can with certainty be ascribed to Bristol. This green glass, of a distinctive and deep colour, was made before the Glass Excise Act of 1745; some writers, indeed, class specimens as of the seventeenth century. It was made at various centres, but it is unlikely that the Bristol variety was made before the middle of the eighteenth century. The ribbed grips of the swords in the Bristol Museum are of this dark green metal.

Early bright green drinking glasses, now rare, following the German roemer in style, cannot be described as Bristol.

Gilding. It has already been stated that decanters, finger bowls and similar articles in blue were frequently enriched with gilding. Michael Edkins and the Jacobs family both used it on blue glass. No doubt the process was developed from that employed at Bristol for firing the enamel decoration. According to Owen (*Two Centuries of Ceramic Art in Bristol*, London, 1873, p. 380), who recorded much of the work carried out by Edkins from his ledgers, the coloured enamel frit was 'vitrified in a muffler or kiln'. This method consisted in grinding gold leaf to a powder, mixing with a suitable flux, and finally with an oil medium. It was then painted upon the glass in the usual way with pencil or brush. The article was afterwards fired in a muffle until the oil medium oxidised and burned off.

Another method was used in which the gold leaf was applied to the specimen which had had its design varnished upon it. The specimen was then kept in a warm atmosphere for a few months until the varnish had become hardened. The gold was afterwards burnished in order to produce a fine lustre. The oil gilt or varnish gilt method was used in the first half of the eighteenth century to gild wheel engraving, but went out of fashion about 1770 when it was superseded by stoved gilding.

Cut and Engraved. There is no doubt that Bristol was more famous in the eighteenth century for its high quality flint glass than for its coloured variety. Many notices appeared in the second half of the century advertising glass of all descriptions. For example, one notice in the *Bristol Journal*, 12th March, 1774, included items mentioned for sale as follows: 'Wine, Beer, Jelly and a variety of plain as well as other curious cut Flint glasses, Decanters, Cans, Dobbins, Tumblers, Fruit Dishes, Candlesticks, Salts, Cruets, Castors, Mustard Pots, Patty Pans and Cream Jugs; Dram Gooseberry, Phial and neat-cut Smelling Bottles.'

The style of cutting about this period is furnished by a trade card (*Dix Collection of Newscuttings*, Bristol Library) of Wadham Ricketts & Co., who owned the Phoenix Glassworks in Bristol. The card shows a bowl with deeply scalloped rim, a band of relief diamonds on the upper part of the body and flutes on the lower half. The card also shows a candelabrum with curved arms decorated with pendent drops.

Regarding prices, opaque vases with no decoration have changed hands up to £5. Decoration, however, considerably enhances the value of such pieces. For example, an opaque white baluster vase brilliantly painted with pheasants among flowers and rockwork was sold quite recently for £520, while a pair of Bristol opaque white beakers painted with flowers and rockwork, 'famille-rose' style, fetched £340.

A pair of opaque white salt cellars on three feet, painted with pink flowers, sold for £90 and a pair of bottles, such as those shown in Fig. 30 marked oil and vinegar respectively, changed hands for £70. Opaque white tea-caddies, such as those shown in Fig. 31, have fetched as much as £190 the pair.

Blue glass is not so popular among collectors. For example, plain blue glass finger bowls have reached about the £1 mark each. On the other hand, a finger bowl with the signature 'I. Jacobs. Bristol' has changed hands for over £30. A blue decanter similar to that shown in Fig. 34 fetched around £5.

BROAD GLASS, PROCESS OF MAKING SHEETS OF.

See French Glass.

BUCKINGHAM, DUKE OF (1628-1687). George Villiers, Duke of Buckingham, is known to glass students as the owner of glassworks at Greenwich and Vauxhall. His name in political

38. *Pair of bowls in lead glass, most probably of the Ravenscroft period before the authorisation of the Raven's head seal. The bowls were no doubt in commemoration of the Buggin marriage which occurred in 1676.* (*Messrs W. T. G. Burne*)

history is rather unsavoury; he had a taste for intrigue and was imprisoned in the Tower in 1667 and again in 1677. He had also a taste for science and the arts and as he was one of the wealthiest men in the country, he could afford to experiment in glass manufacture. As a result, he succeeded in laying the foundation of the British plate-glass trade. There is evidence that he was most influential between the years 1660 and 1674; his methods and enterprise re-established the position that the trade had lost during the Civil War.

Buckingham's first glasshouse was set up at Greenwich, to which he brought over a party of Italian workmen to make glassware after the Venetian fashion. The glasshouse at Vauxhall was put into operation later, and fine crystal and looking-glass plates were successfully made there. (*See* English Glass, History of, and Soda Glasses.)

BUGGIN BOWLS. A pair of bowls discovered in 1937 at Tring. One is diamond engraved with the arms of Butler Buggin, of North Cray, Kent, and the other those of his wife, Winifred Burnett, of Leys, Aberdeen.

The bowls, of lead glass, were most probably betrothal glasses or marriage glasses. The Buggin marriage took place in 1676, the year Ravenscroft established his glass-of-lead; but as it was not until a year later that the Glass Sellers' Company 'sealed' his glasses with a raven's head, the Buggin Bowls, although undoubtedly by Ravenscroft, do not bear a seal. They are shown in Fig. 38.

BUGLES.
See Musical Glasses.

CAMEO GLASS. The type of decorated glass known today as cameo glass first made its appearance shortly after the Great Exhibition of 1851. It was due no doubt to the foreign decorative glass shown at the Great Exhibition that prompted Benjamin Richardson, a well-known flint glass-maker in the Stourbridge district, to suggest a reward of £1000 for a reproduction of the famous Portland Vase. His incentive paid handsome dividends. In the years following the Great Exhibition, up to the first quarter of the present century, many glass cameo engravers devoted their talents to this class of work, producing specimens of high artistic merit.

John Northwood (1836-1902), who had been an apprentice under Richardson, was the first to experiment on cameo carving. His first real success was a crystal vase in Grecian style after the equestrian groups of the Parthenon sculpture. This vase, known as the Elgin Vase, was completed in 1873 and is at present in the Birmingham Art Gallery. The vase took eight years to carve, but it did not deter Northwood from attempting his greatest ambition—the reproduction of the Portland Vase—and after some three years, in 1876, he eventually completed his task.

Northwood obtained permission from the British Museum authorities to take his work and place it against the original for comparison in order to create a true reproduction. The simplest tools were used for the carving process, such as rods of carefully tempered steel varying in size from $\frac{1}{16}$ to $\frac{1}{8}$ of an inch in thickness held in soft wood holders much like a pencil.

The English Portland Vase, shown in Fig. 39, is without doubt the most important piece of cameo glass of modern times; its completion by Northwood inspired many other artists of the time to undertake similar work. One of the most notable productions was by John Northwood, junr. (1870-1960), son of the original artist, who made the plaque of Aphrodite, fifteen inches in diameter, in memory of his father. The plaque, shown in Fig. 40, was finished in 1906.

The Northwood movement of cameo carving had many followers. Public interest grew as new examples of cameo work appeared, and in spite of the extreme patience required and the tedious nature of this class of work, many young artists were eager to master its technique. The most famous of them was

39. *Replica of the Portland Vase by John Northwood senior, completed in 1876.*

40. *Plaque of Aphrodite, 15 inches in diameter, by John Northwood, junior, completed in 1906.*

41. *Examples of cameo engraving by George Woodall,* (left) *a vase completed in 1923, depicting Venus coming from the sea,* (right) *a cameo vase by Alphonse Lecheveral 'Raising an Altar to Bacchus'.*

42. *Examples of cameo engraving by artists of the Northwood School.* From left to right: (*1*) *B. Fenn, 1887,* (2) *John Northwood, junior, 1887,* (*4*) *Charles Northwood, 1881* (*unfinished*) *and* (*3*) *and* (*5*) *Joshua Hodgetts, 1887 and 1888.*

John Woodall (1850-1925), who, with his brother Thomas, began his apprenticeship in Northwood's decorating works at Wordsley, although they later left his establishment to go elsewhere. George Woodall succeeded in producing some exquisite pieces of carving, an example of which is shown in Fig. 41, left.

The other artists of the Northwood school were Alphonse Lecherval (an example of his work is shown in Fig. 41, right), J. M. O'Fallan, W. Northwood, J. Hodgetts and B. Fenn. Examples of the work of some of these cameo engravers is shown in Fig. 42. Joshua Hodgetts (1858-1933), also a well-known exponent of the engraving wheel, favoured floral designs for most of his work. Examples are shown in Fig. 42.

The Northwood movement flourished until the end of the nineteenth century, but after 1890 there was a decline in the public demand for this class of work, mainly due to the cheap imitations which began to appear on the market. Much of this ware came from the Continent and some bore little or no resemblance to genuine cameo work.

Specimens of cameo engraving from the Northwood school are valuable. For example, a pair of cylindrical jars by John Northwood, cut and engraved, changed hands in 1955 for £120. A cameo vase signed by George Woodall, in ruby glass with white overlay finely engraved with a spray of convolvulus, changed hands in the same year for £40. Another example by George Woodall, of a cameo glass plaque in black glass overlaid in white and finely engraved with a sea nymph, fetched £160.

CANDELABRA. The early history of glass candelabra is obscure; practically nothing is known of them and little has been written. The earliest forms of candelabra were in brass. Ecclesiastical examples in that alloy were known long before their silver counterparts, the earliest dated specimen of which is 1714. These were a pair of silver three-light candelabra made by Robert Temple and Benjamin Bentley.

During the eighteenth century many articles in glass took their shape from vessels in silver; glass candlesticks, for example, followed much the same development in style and decoration as the silver ones, and it is to be assumed that the same reproduction followed in the case of the branched candlesticks or candelabra.

Although the silver prototype appeared as early as 1714, it was not until the middle of the century that mention is made of its counterpart in glass. It is recorded in *Chambers's Cyclopaedia* of 1753 that 'Larger and more stately candlesticks contrived for holding a great number of candles are called branches or girandoles, and when made of glass, lustres'.

The first advertisement of the branched candlestick was by Christopher Haedy, a London glass-cutter, in the Bath *Chronicle*, 20th November, 1766: 'To be sold by hand. The stock in trade of a German—consisting of a great variety of cut and engraved glasses; fine Pyramids and Girandoles; Tumblers, Cruets, Milk Ewers, Tea and other Candlesticks.' It will be noted that the terms girandole and candlestick appeared in the same notice, and as this was customary until the end of the eighteenth century, it cannot be said that the girandole or branched candlestick in any way superseded the simple candlestick.

The candlestick became somewhat more elaborate towards the end of the century and in 1777 was referred to for the first time as the 'vase candlestick' (*see* VASE CANDLESTICK). It was sometimes provided with a metal base and its single candle-socket was elaborately cut and decorated with pendent drops. The girandole, however, was distinct from the candle-

43. *One of the earliest-known specimens of glass candelabra; dating from the beginning of the eighteenth century.* 44. *Pair of candelabra,* circa *1770, when simple pendent lustres were coming into fashion.*

stick or its elaboration, the vase candlestick. Both these articles were provided with a single candle-socket, whereas the essential characteristic of the girandole was its branches for two or more candle-sockets.

The term candelabra was first used in *The Times*, 3rd March, 1792. It was an alternative to girandole, but it quickly superseded the latter term in the nineteenth century and is the popular term today for the branched candlestick.

A specimen of what must have been one of the earliest styles in glass candelabra is shown in Fig. 43. It is in lead metal and is dated *circa* 1700, although the presence of annular knops, which decorate the stem and form the finial, suggest that it might have been made any time during the first quarter of the eighteenth century. The general, close design of the candelabra is excellent. The foot is domed and terraced—that is, it rises from the rim in a series of rounded steps to the domed centre, where it joins the stem—and the terrace motif is reproduced in the annular knops of the stem and the finial. There are four plain branches carrying the grease-pans and candle-sockets, which are also plain. The specimen is unique and displays an unexpected originality in design. The glass-maker of that period usually sought inspiration in counterparts in metal or any other medium that conveniently offered ideas capable of being reproduced in glass; the specimen shown in Fig. 43, however, does not follow contemporary styles in metal and, indeed, would appear to have had no model in other media.

According to the trade notices, glass candelabra did not become fashionable until cutting was well established. From documentary evidence, it would appear that cutting was introduced into this country between the years 1709 and 1719, but there is an unaccountable hiatus between the advent of cutting and the first trade notice of glass candelabra. Early forms are known in brass; the first dated silver specimen is 1714 and the first notice of glass chandeliers occurred in the same year. Glass candelabra, however, were not mentioned in the trade notices until the end of 1766, when Christopher Haedy, who claimed he was 'the first that brought the art and cutting of Glass from Germany', proposed to sell his stock in trade at Bath. It is most probable that the candelabra (girandoles) offered for sale at Bath were decorated by cutting.

The pair of candelabra shown in Fig. 44 are of this period and convey an idea of what Haedy was most probably offering in 1766. The essential components—the foot, the shaft, and the branches carrying the candle-sockets—are the same as those of the early specimen shown in Fig. 43. The shaft, however, has been lengthened to increase the proportion of height to width, which greatly improves the general balance and effectiveness of the design. Candelabra of this period, and up to the end of the century, were more stately and dignified than those of any other, a quality achieved without elaborate or over-emphasised decoration. The grease-pans in the specimen shown in Fig. 44 are star-shaped instead of having the plain circular rim, but the candle-sockets have little relief from the original plain style.

It will be noted that the candelabra shown in Fig. 44 are decorated with simple fringes of pendent lustres, stars, crescents and other motifs. There is also a curved device, known as a 'snake', springing from the knop carrying the branches, and a canopy at the top of the shaft, both which form anchorages for additional pendent drops.

Similar ornaments began to be used on chandeliers after the turn of the half century and it can be safely assumed that the same fashion was adopted for candelabra. Indeed, candelabra followed their relatives, the suspended chandeliers, in so many respects that the two articles can be regarded as developing on

45. *Candelabra with notched shaft, branches and spires.* circa *1770.* 46. *Heavily cut candelabra blending rococo and Adam influences.* circa *1785. This specimen is 23½ inches in height.*

closely similar lines. Jerom Johnson, who had a reputation for chandeliers in the eighteenth century, and who decorated his ware in the rococo style, advertised in the *London Evening Post*, 9th November, 1756: 'Jerom Johnson, at the entire Glass Shop—is determined to sell off Lustres, High polish'd Branches, Brilliant Drops to hang on the Lustres.' This is the first notice referring to the pendent drops which later became a dominating feature of all styles of chandeliers and candelabra.

Clusters of pendent drops were sparingly applied at this early stage in the development of candelabra. In the specimens shown in Fig. 45, of the 1770 period, they are little in evidence, but cutting is somewhat heavily applied; the shaft is deeply notched and a pair of notched spires are added in keeping with the general design. A single snake, from which is suspended the crescent motif, is in this case also made part of the decoration.

Cutting became a much more important factor in the decoration of candelabra after 1777. This is shown clearly in the specimen in Fig. 46, *circa* 1785. The example has no plain sur-

47. *Candelabra with deeply incised cutting typical of the Regency period.* circa *1810.* 48. *Pair of candelabra,* circa *1800, with the plain arms that became fashionable after 1788.*

49. *Heavily cut candelabra with ornamental stands en suite. Regency style.* circa *1820.*

faces, advantage being taken by the cutter of every inch of space for embellishment by the wheel. Even the plain candle-socket has been superseded by a cut star corresponding with the grease-pans. Similar decorative devices, such as flowers, acorns and shells, became the fashion for candle-sockets and grease-pans until well into the nineteenth century. The snake motif is again in evidence in this candelabra, from which are suspended graduated pendent drops.

The Adam influence, which had begun to make itself felt at this period in every branch of art, was not without its influence on glass candelabra. The knops which had appeared on the earlier candelabra as decoration on the lower end of the shaft, together with the domed, circular foot, were now replaced with urn-like motifs above a square-cut pedestal, both acknowledgments to the Adam influence. The curves and flourish of the rococo period had not been completely abandoned, however, and the candelabra shown in Fig. 46 is an interesting example of the transition period in which the two influences attempt to merge.

Rococo is much less in evidence in the specimen shown in Fig. 48, which is of a somewhat later period—*circa* 1800. Decorative motifs, such as the snake device, had been discarded and there is now a much more symmetrical and orderly note in the general plan. Regular fringes of lustres are the dominant feature of the decoration and cutting is on a modest scale, except on the candle-sockets and grease-pans, which are exquisitely fashioned and richly cut. It will be noted also that the arms, which in the earlier examples have been an essential component of the design, now play a subservient part. In addition their importance has been diminished considerably by lack of cutting.

In some letters relating to William Parker, 69 Fleet Street, who was famous in the eighteenth century for the manufacture of chandeliers, it is stated in 1788 that 'plain arms have succeeded those cut with hollows, and are more generally approved'. Parker's letters, of course, refer to chandeliers, but the development of candelabra followed so closely that of the chandeliers that it can be regarded as applying to them also.

The disappearance of cutting on the arms of candelabra marked the beginning of their demise. By 1810—that is, the beginning of the Regency Period—the arms had degenerated into mere connecting links between the shaft and the branches. A typical specimen of candelabra of the Regency Period is shown in Fig. 47; it is much different in style from the earlier ones, the dominant feature now being the decoration. This took the form of a fringe of cut pendent drops, each unit of which consisted almost invariably of a pair of lozenge-shaped pendents, richly faceted, from which was suspended a long, slender finger or icicle, also faceted with the wheel. These fringes of sparkling lustres, hung in close formation from the rim of the candle-socket and also that of the grease-pan, succeeded in masking those parts so well as to give the appearance of almost a solid, cylindrical figure.

The fringe decoration remained a popular feature with candelabra into the second half of the nineteenth century, when they were used in various modified forms to decorate not only candelabra themselves but vases and stands *en suite* with them. An example is shown in Fig. 49, which features a candelabra with a pair of stands richly decorated by cutting.

Glass candelabra continued to be made in the second half of the nineteenth century and were displayed at the Exhibitions of 1851 and 1862. In later periods they followed no particular fashion, but were for the most part reproductions of earlier styles. Towards the end of the century, however, when cut

50. *Heavily cut candelabra of the Regency period.*

glass of all descriptions became unfashionable, glass candelabra ceased to be made and temporarily lost the popular appeal they had for so long enjoyed.

Eighteenth-century candelabra have changed hands within recent years at prices varying from £17 to £80, depending on their size and decoration. The lower prices are usually for those of about a foot in height, while those up to two feet in height are priced higher accordingly.

CANDLESTICKS. Glass candlesticks first appeared in this country during the seventeenth century. They were fairly light in construction, with hollow knopped stems and pedestal feet, but before the end of the century they began to follow their counterparts in metal, and the styles adopted were greatly influenced by them. The hollow stem gave place to a solid knopped one, in which the true and inverted baluster motifs were popular decorative features. The feet were much more practical in these later candlesticks. They added more to the stability of the article by being wider in proportion to the height and were made considerably heavier. Domed feet, both plain and terraced, were popular styles.

After the accession in 1714 of George I, candlesticks with Silesian stems made their appearance. Hence, in some specimens the Silesian stem was inverted and appeared above an annular knop. In other styles the Silesian stem is found in an upright position surmounted by one in the inverted position separated by a ball knop. At this time the foot was domed, often with radial ribs to match the candle-socket. Specimens from this period are shown in Figs. 51 and 55.

Candlesticks of the first quarter of the eighteenth century were much more useful and robust articles than those which appeared later in the century. After 1740 candlesticks began to appear with air-twist stems, and followed very much the style of the stems of drinking glasses. Some specimens are found with the plain, straight stem with air-twist and others with simple knops. Opaque twist styles are known in candlesticks, but did not remain fashionable long, being superseded by the cut variety. Opaque white candlesticks were made at Bristol, some being painted in enamel colours.

As may be expected, decoration by cutting would not have been long delayed in glass candlesticks. The properties of Ravenscroft's new glass medium were ideal for this purpose, for its transparency and powers of light dispersion caused it to be a fascinating novelty even in daylight hours; at night, the mellow glow of the candles reflected from countless gleaming facets was a spectacle of delight.

The earliest notice, however, of cut-glass candlesticks did not occur until 1742 when Jerom Johnson advertised '. . . diamond cut and scalloped candlesticks'. Scalloping was an early form of cut decoration and the candle-socket, and occasionally the rim of the foot of the candlestick, were decorated in this manner. The stem was sometimes cut in hollow diamond fashion—that is, a series of interlacing hollows whose edges intersected to form a four- or six-sided diamond motif.

Towards the end of the eighteenth century the influence of Adam's style was felt, and fluted columns, square-cut and terraced feet were acknowledgments to the classical revival. Typical examples of this period are shown in Figs. 52 and 54.

51. *Candlestick from the first quarter of the eighteenth century. The ball knop in the centre of the stem is air-beaded.* 52. *Candlestick of the Adam period with urn-shaped stem and square terraced foot.*

53. *Group of candlesticks showing development from 1780 top row left to the Regency period bottom row right. The plain moulded feet of the earlier period gave place to heavily cut ones after the turn of the eighteenth century. The candle-sockets also became much more elaborate.*

54. *Group of candlesticks of the Irish period. The bases are squat and heavy to give stability, and the candle-sockets are removable to allow for easy cleaning.* (*National Museum, Dublin.*) 55. *Group of candlesticks from the early part of the eighteenth century. Candle-sockets were at that time plain. The specimen on the right has a Silesian stem, a feature which became fashionable after 1714.*

Irish glasshouses specialised in candlesticks. The Adam influence again is shown in the square bases and urn-shaped stems. Candlesticks of this period were practical affairs; not only were they made in squat form with heavy bases to give them stability, but the candle-sockets were removable, which made the replacing of the candles a comparatively simple operation. Typical Irish specimens are shown in Fig. 54.

Eighteenth-century candlesticks of the general type, with knopped stem on a domed foot with wrythen or reticulated candle-socket, height between nine and ten inches, have changed hands recently from £4 to £14. On the other hand, a very rare candlestick, *circa* 1700, reached as much as £120 in 1955 (Illustrated in *English and Irish Glass*, W. A. Thorpe, 1927 Fig. 13).

CARAFES. A carafe is a stopperless vessel which varies in form from that of the ordinary glass bottle to one of conical or globular outline. It is used for holding water or wine and was usually referred to in the eighteenth century as a 'water craft' or a 'craft'. It was used extensively on the table. At banquets, for example, great numbers were provided, one carafe and two goblets being set in front of every two guests. One of these banqueting services of carafes and goblets, cut in the style of the early nineteenth century, is still preserved at Alnwick Castle, being brought into service on special occasions.

The carafe, cut and plain, was much advertised in the newspapers between 1758 and 1800. For example, the following notice appeared in the *Bath and Bristol Chronicle*, 20th October, 1768: 'To be sold at the Sadler's Arms in Bath, the stock in trade of a glass-cutter from London, consisting of a great variety of cut and engraved ware and gilt glasses. . . . Cut Decanters, cut Jelly Glasses, Water Crafts, Syllabubs, Sweetmeats, etc.'

The carafe of the eighteenth century was made in various sizes, but generally it appears to have been smaller in capacity than a full size decanter of the period. Often the carafe was decorated by trailing and vertical ribbing and engraved and cut with the wheel. Rarely, a specimen comes to light with a seal on which appears the crest of the owner, a feature common enough on bottles, but not often seen on carafes.

At the turn of the nineteenth century, the carafe went out of fashion in this country so far as its table use was concerned, and more often made its appearance on the wash-hand stand of the bedroom. During the last few years, however, due to the growing custom in this country of once again taking wine with meals, the carafe has made a welcome return to the table. Indeed, 'wine in carafe' is now noted on the wine-lists of many important hotels and restaurants. The modern version of the carafe follows the conventional form of the eighteenth century, but as modern taste ordains clear spaces on a glass surface, it is undecorated with either cutting or engraving.

Very few of these items have changed hands in the sale rooms during recent years. The Nailsea type of carafe, decorated with opaque white and pink festoons, has changed hands at prices ranging from £2 to £3.

CASTING BOTTLES.

See Bottles, Perfume and Smelling.

CAUDLE GLASSES.

See Posset and Caudle Glasses.

CELERY VASES. Celery vases of the late eighteenth and early nineteenth centuries were large vessels of water jug capacity, the usual style being a cylindrical bowl mounted on a rudimentary stem and spreading foot. Irish specimens have a square moulded foot, especially those from Cork and Dublin.

Most celery vases have cylindrical bowls tapering at the base to the stem and flanged slightly outwards at the rim. Alternatively, the bowl can be bucket-shaped; in some Irish specimens, the bowl is found provided with a wide turned-over rim similar to the salad bowls of the same period.

Cut decoration is usual, consisting in many specimens of vertical fluting with fan-escallops, or with a band of blazes encircling the neck. In others, the cut decoration is strawberry diamonds divided by split bands. Some excellent examples of Irish celery vases are to be found in the National Museum, Dublin.

Celery vases of the Irish type with characteristic cutting have changed hands during the last five years at prices ranging from £6 to £10 each.

CHAMPAGNE GLASSES. The sparkling, golden wine of Champagne was introduced into this country during the reign of Charles II, and from evidence available today, it was drunk more extensively than was at one time supposed. Nearly every poet and dramatist of the times sang its praises. By the end of the seventeenth century, in spite of difficulties of trade with France then existing, the London vintners and taverners had

56. *A glass which could be used for champagne but is most probably a sweetmeat.* (*Messrs Arthur Churchill, Ltd.*)

succeeded in obtaining regular supplies from Rheims and Epernay.

André Simon, in *Drink*, p. 71 (1948), explains that although at first champagne was not drunk in the taverns, 'it was the wine which every host and hostess of note tried to procure for the *petits soupers*, which were then greatly in fashion'.

Evidence of the popularity of champagne during the eighteenth century is so plentiful as to lead most modern writers to assume that the observance of its use with special glasses became a custom. In spite, however, of the controversy that has existed on the subject since the time of Hartshorne, it is doubtful whether the type of glass used for champagne in the late seventeenth and early eighteenth centuries will ever be settled with any degree of finality.

The various shapes of glasses numbered and named by Greene in his orders to Morelli at Venice, between 1667 and 1672, did not include mention of glasses for champagne; indeed, there were very few references to special glasses for champagne during the eighteenth century. Two trade bills of Thomas Betts in the Collection of the late Sir Ambrose Heal refer to glasses with ovoid bowls and champagne flutes:

1755	I.P. Neat Ice Champagne Quart Decanrs	12–0
	2.P. Waved Pints ditto	6–0
	1.P. ditto Holld.	4–0
	12 Wormd ½ Rib'd ditto Champagnes	10–6
	12 Wormd Short ditto	8–0
	12 Green ½ Mo. Egg Champagne	12–0

An explanation of the terms used in Thomas Betts's bills is given below (F. Buckley, *Glass*, Vol. V, 1928, p. 300):

Ice decanters	Decanters with pockets for ice
Holld	Hollowed at base—i.e., with pontil mark ground away and polished
Wormd	Air-twisted
½ Rib'd	Rib cresting at base of bowl
½ Mo. Egg Champagne	Half-moulded egg-shaped or ovoid bowl

Also, on 2nd February, 1773, Edward Gibbon, the historian, bought from Colebron Hancock, glass manufacturer of Cockspur Street, Charing Cross, '1 Doz. Champain Flutes, 8/-'. On the other hand, there is mention in 1781 of both flutes and champagnes in the same bill, which would appear to indicate a difference between the two styles. The bill read as follows:

Jonathan Collet, at his Glass Manufactory, The King's Arms, Cockspur St., Charing Cross. To the Rev. Thomas Moore.

2 dozen	Cut Wines engd. festoons		1–16–0
1 ,,	Champagnes	do	1– 4–0
2 ,,	Flutes		2– 8–0

It will be observed that the style of the glasses in the above bills referring to champagne glasses mentions only ovoids and flutes; there is no mention in Betts's bills or elsewhere to the tazza-shaped glass which is generally accepted as being in general use for serving champagne during the eighteenth century. On the other hand, most writers claim that glasses with shallow hemispherical bowls such as are popular today was the current style during the eighteenth century. A glass which suggests such a style is that shown in Fig. 56. It has a drinkable rim, but would be classed by many collectors as a sweetmeat.

Grant Francis, in *Old English Drinking Glasses* (1926), p. 89,

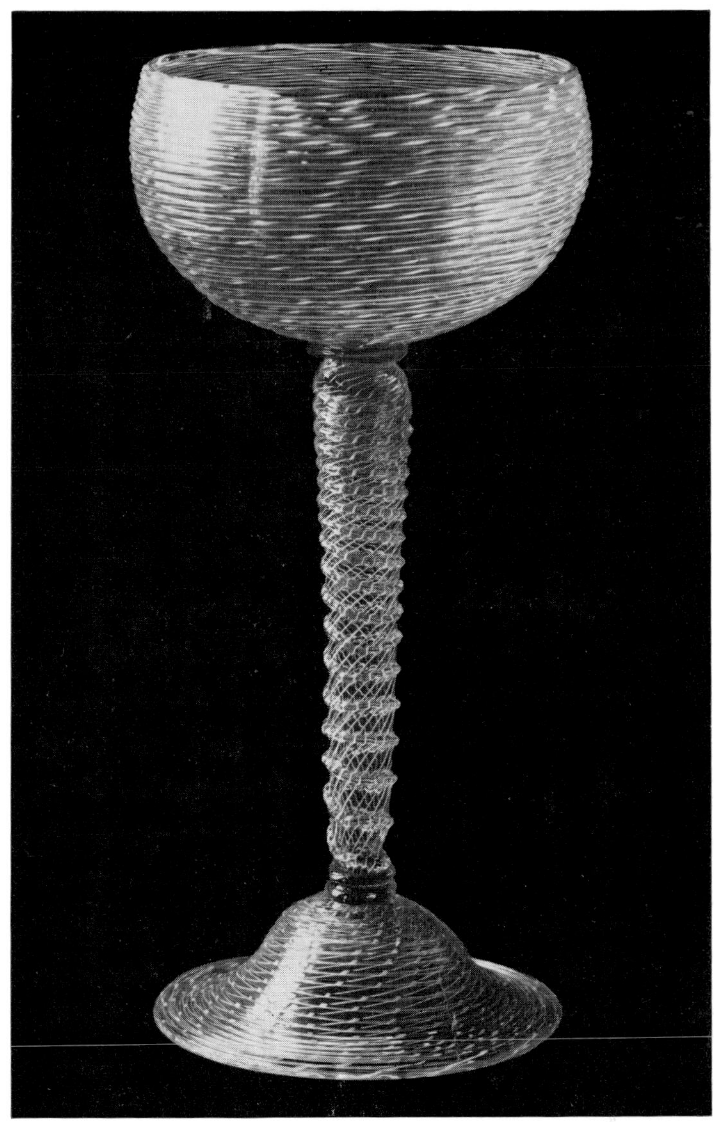

57. *Champagne glass accorded a prize by the Royal Society of Arts in 1869. (By courtesy of the Victoria and Albert Museum)*

for example, states: 'It is evident that very shortly after the English glasshouses turned their attention to the making of drinking glasses, some enterprising craftsman gave special consideration to the new wine, and realising how suitable was the tazza-shaped goblet to its sparkling richness, proceeded to adapt this shape to the current fashion.'

If, indeed, this was the case, it is more than likely that these special glasses would have been advertised and their shape described as 'new-fashioned'. Throughout the eighteenth century every conceivable type of glass for the table was advertised both in London and the Provinces, but it is significant that no mention is made to champagne glasses other than that already given in the bills mentioned above.

Both Bate and Thorpe claim that the glasses today designated champagnes were really sweetmeats, because of the rim. Thorpe states (*A History of English and Irish Glass*, Vol. 1, 1929, p. 315): 'A good many of the so-called champagnes have not a drinkable rim; the rims flare outwards as in those intolerable nineteenth-century tea-cups from which you can scarcely drink with decency.' It is significant that the so-called champagne glasses of the eighteenth century are the only type of drinking glass with the flared rim. There would appear to be no reason why glasses intended for champagne should have been given a flared rim and every other type of drinking glass allowed to retain the customary finish.

There is other evidence to support the argument in favour of sweetmeats. The practice of cutting was at first applied to the luxury glasses such as sweetmeats, cruets, candlesticks, and similar articles intended for ceremonial occasions; if there had existed that close similarity between the sweetmeats and champagnes, it is inconceivable that the latter, also being a luxury glass, would not have been given some cut decoration and advertised as such.

As already pointed out, however, not a single advertisement of this nature has come to my notice, although sweetmeats, closely corresponding in style and shape to the so-called champagnes, are advertised profusely.

I consider these few reasons—(*a*) the absence of notices, (*b*) the peculiarity of the flared rim, and (*c*) the lack of early decorative treatment to champagnes afforded to other luxury glasses—to be a convincing argument that no special glass was made for champagne, but that any elegant and moderately capacious glass available was called into service when champagne was drunk.

It is also apparent that as the popularity of champagne grew during the eighteenth century, the glasses with which it is usually identified—that is, glasses with the hemispherical or shallow double ogee bowl—became scarcer and, in the period of opaque-twists, only an occasional glass is found whose shape suggests to writers that it should be dedicated to champagne.

Some writers claim that in the mid-eighteenth century, the tall glasses, such as shown in Fig. 11, were used for it in less pretentious establishments where it would be served infrequently, and where such glasses could be also used for ale. When the tall glasses were reserved exclusively for ale, they were engraved with the familiar hops and barley motif and apparently when they were used for champagne they were left plain.

That ale and champagne should be allocated a similar glass does not appear consonant with eighteenth-century taste; moreover, the tall ale glass is not the best shape in which to serve a sparkling liquid. There is also the question of cost; plain ale glasses could be purchased at 2/- per dozen, but similar glasses engraved would cost at least twice as much. It seems unlikely, therefore, that the more expensive glass should have been reserved for the humbler beverage.

The champagne of the generous, shallow bowl so familiar today would appear to date from the early part of the nineteenth century. That it was still a novelty in 1832 is recorded in one of Disraeli's letters to his sister, in which he wrote of a dinner party: 'We drank champagne out of a saucer of ground glass mounted upon a pedestal of cut glass.' Even as late as 1869, the champagne glass had not developed entirely to the modern style judging by the design shown in Fig. 57, which is of a champagne glass accorded a prize in a competition held at that time by the Royal Society of Arts.

Glasses which have been described as champagnes have changed hands during recent years at prices up to £42. This was an early glass with shallow bowl, heavily gadrooned, supported on an incised baluster stem composed of a large knop resting on a cushion knop, and folded foot. The glass is four and a half inches high and is *circa* 1680. It is illustrated in *Rare English Glasses of the 17th and 18th Centuries*, 1926, by Joseph Bles, Plate 10, Fig. 14. On the other hand, a champagne glass with plain double ogee bowl, flared at the rim and supported on a tall Silesian stem on a domed and folded foot, changed hands recently for £6 10s.

CHANDELIERS. No article in the repertoire of the early cutter of glass is so aesthetically effective as the chandelier. The properties of transparency and light dispersion of the glass-of-lead of George Ravenscroft provided the glass-cutter with an ideal medium, and he applied himself to it with great diligence and enterprise. The more lavish the cut decoration, the more magnificent the chandeliers became, and both by day and by the flickering of the many candles at night, a thousand gleaming facets reflected and dispersed the light into every colour of the rainbow. The unwavering glare of the electric candle with which chandeliers are today provided fails to convey even a fraction of the glitter and sparkle that must have been the delight of the Georgian salons.

The idea of the chandelier, no doubt, originated from the hanging lamps decorated with glass, such as the Saracenic mosque lamps. Chandeliers were known in Venice in the seventeenth century made from both rock crystal and coloured opalescent glass, often in imitation of leaves, fruit, flowers and other naturalistic motifs. Typical specimens of Venetian

58. *Venetian chandelier of the seventeenth century with fruit and flower motifs.* (*Museo Vetrario, Murano*)

chandeliers of this period, now in the Museo Vetrario, Murano, Italy, are shown in Figs. 58 and 59.

The essential components of the Venetian chandeliers were similar to the later English versions—the central supporting shaft or shafts, the branches for holding the candle-sockets, and the decoration. Indeed, the only real difference between the Venetian and English styles was in the decorative effects.

The earliest reference to glass chandeliers in this country is in 1714, when the *London Gazette* records that John Gumley sold 'Looking Glasses, Coach Glasses and Glass Schandeliers'. It is apparent from this notice that the assembling and decorating of the chandeliers was the business of the glass grinder and not of the glass-cutter as understood today. The glass grinder was practising in this country as early as 1678, and as he bevelled and decorated the edges of looking-glasses, glass sconces, plate-glass lanterns and similar articles, it can be readily surmised that the glass chandelier came within his scope. It is quite probable, therefore, that glass chandeliers were made in this country long before 1714.

Notices were fairly frequent in the first half of the century, and in 1728 the *Daily Post* advertised 'a great quantity of Chrystal Cut-Lustres'. The term 'lustre' applied at first to the pendent drops, but later referred to the chandelier itself. For example, in the *Daily Post*, 20th July, 1739, Jerom Johnson advertised: 'Scallop'd Desart Glasses, etc., are only sold cheap by the Maker, Jerom Johnson, at the Glass Shop in Duke St., and Lustres if gentlemen please to bespeak them are done to

59. *Venetian chandelier of the seventeenth century, with fish and other naturalistic motifs.* (*Museo Vetrario, Murano*)

60. *Thornham Hall chandelier, one of the earliest known specimens.* circa *1732.*

the utmost perfection. There is likewise to be sold cheap, the most magnificent Lustre that ever was made in England.'

The earliest type of glass chandelier followed the metal ones of the period, similar to other articles made in both metal and glass. For example, the characteristics of the Palladian type of brass chandelier are comparable with the specimen in Fig. 60. This chandelier came from Thornham Hall, Suffolk, and is accredited by J. B. Perret (*Apollo*, September, 1939) a date *circa* 1732. The arms, candle-sockets and grease-pans are quite plain, and the cutting on the ball pieces constituting the shaft is in the hollow style seen on the edges of early looking-glasses, the stems of sweetmeat glasses and similar articles for display and ceremonial occasions popular in the first half of the century.

This simple style did not survive for long, however. As chandeliers were luxury pieces for the 'quality', more elaborate design and expensive workmanship could be expended on them than on the commoner drinking vessels; moreover, they gave the lead to fashion in cut ornamentation long before cut drinking vessels could compete with other styles on the market. Branches, candle-sockets and grease-pans were now all cut in the same shallow style as the shaft, but the hollow wheel had been augmented by a shallow mitre one, and simple stars set off the hollow diamonds that had been the dominant motif earlier in the century. This is plainly shown in Fig. 61, which is a six-light chandelier with the ball of the shaft cut in shallow incised mitres to form star patterns, and the arms and grease-pans cut in hollow style.

The general design still shows the Italian influence, and this fact, together with the sparse use of suspended drops as ornamentation, suggests a date a little after the mid-century.

To Jerom Johnson, an enterprising craftsman, who has

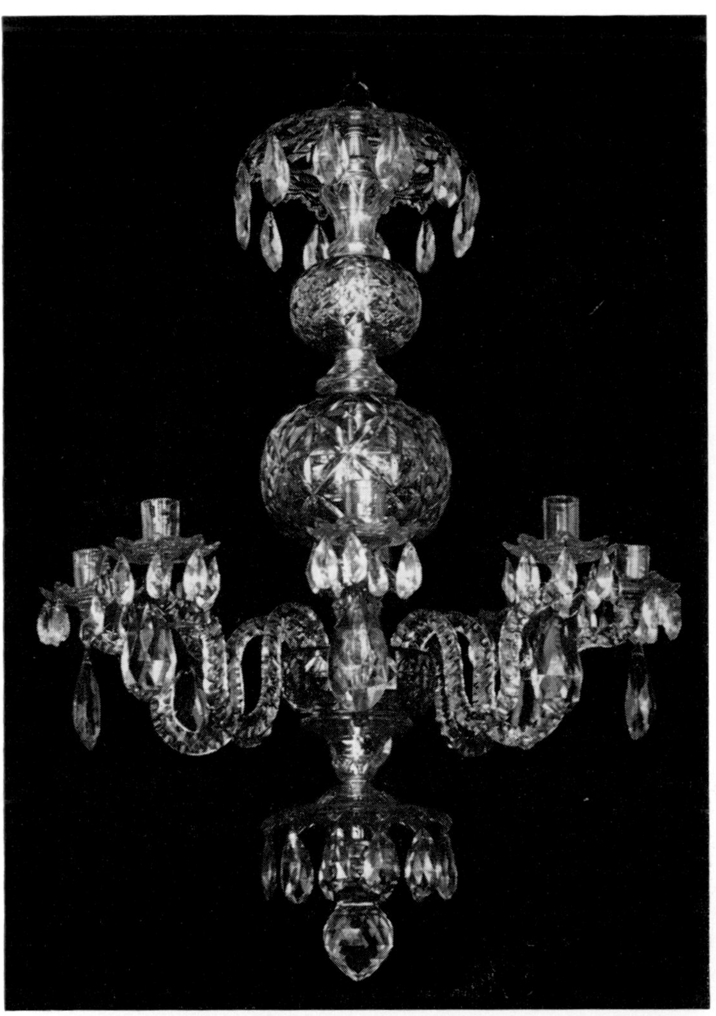

61. *Six-light chandelier showing tendency for decoration to become more emphasised.* circa *1765.* (*Messrs Delomosne & Son*)

already been mentioned in connection with his advertisement in 1739, must be credited the introduction of the incised cutting used for the ornamentation of the early chandeliers. He worked between the years 1739 and 1761 and his final occupation would appear to have concerned chandeliers in exclusion to everything else, for on 28th January, 1761, there appeared a notice in the *Daily Advertiser*: 'Chrystal Lustres only. Jerom Johnson has now made upwards of 20 and shall sell Lustres cheaper and better than any other Maker of Lustres in London, at the Star in Bow Street, Covent Garden.'

It is safe to say that up to 1750 at least, the three components of the chandelier—the shaft, the branches and the decoration—had maintained an artistic balance, no one component being more emphasised than another. This is apparent with the Thornham Hall chandelier, Fig. 60, and that shown in Fig. 61.

With later specimens, however, the tendency is apparent for the shaft to dominate the design. The centre ball developed into a series of globes and the canopy became a prominent feature. The candle-sockets and grease-pans were decorated by scalloping and hollow cutting to match the cut decoration on the arms of the branches. Still later, when the rococo influence ordained more elaborate decoration, faceted spear shafts or spires were added as ornaments to the pendants.

A chandelier typical of this period, shown in Fig. 62, is a four-light specimen. The candle-sockets and grease-pans are of more complex design and are each provided with a scalloped rim to match the lower grease-pans. There is no dominant feature, however; no undue stress has been given to the shaft, the branches or the added decoration, and the pendent drops have not yet developed into the swags which later draped the space between branches and shaft.

Shortly after 1770, the Adam influence began to make itself felt in every branch of design, including the chandelier. The series of globes constituting the shaft, which had been an established feature of the earlier chandelier, were now replaced by the classical Grecian urn, and there was a tendency for the length to become greater in proportion to the width. At the same time the pendent drops were augmented by swags made up of smaller drops of pyriform shape wired together to form chains which hung from the end of the shaft to the extremities of the branches below the grease-pans. Typical of the chandeliers of this period is the specimen illustrated in Fig. 63. The general design is now more elaborate, the graceful shaft, the six branches, and the canopy at the top of the shaft are of a more intricate pattern. Swags of pendent drops and ornaments such as stars have replaced the simple faceted drops of the earlier types.

The candle-sockets and grease-pans, exquisitely formed, mark the beginning of an exuberant vein in which their shape was inspired by naturalistic motifs such as flowers, leaves,

62. *Four-light chandelier with spear shafts and elaborate candle-sockets in response to rococo appeal.* circa *1775.*

63. *Six-light chandelier of the Adam period with elaborate cutting, and the addition of swags of pendent drops.* circa *1790.* 64. *Six-light chandelier of the early Regency period. The central shaft is almost completely submerged by concentric rings of pendent drops.* circa *1810.* (*Messrs Delomosne & Son*)

acorns and stars. The cutting of such parts especially, and, indeed, of the whole of the chandelier, was heavier and more ambitious; elaborate care was taken that each part was a match for its fellow.

The smaller ornaments were cut with the same care and precision as the larger and more conspicuous parts. Indeed, an ornament no wider than one inch would be cut with as many as thirty-two highly polished facets of almost mathematical accuracy. The ornaments themselves were often so correctly graded in size that one series constituting a swag would be indistinguishable from its fellow. Craftsmanship was of such high quality that chandeliers from this period can rightly claim to be the highest attainment of the glass cutter's art.

Probably the finest specimens from this period are the chandeliers originally in the Assembly Rooms at Bath, opened in October, 1771. In the opinion of J. B. Perret, who has given a full account of them (*Connoisseur*, 1938, CII, p. 187), they constitute what is probably the finest surviving example of the eighteenth-century glass-maker's art in the kingdom. The Bath chandeliers are in the rococo style, but it is interesting to note that the form given to the central shaft varies among the different chandeliers comprising the group. For example, the shaft of a forty-eight light chandelier is composed entirely of the earlier globe motif, while three forty-light chandeliers have both the globe and the Grecian urn motifs employed together. Another smaller eight-light chandelier has the Grecian urn only.

It is apparent that the Adam influence was just beginning to be felt at this period (1770) and the Bath chandeliers can safely be regarded as prototypes of the Adam style. J. B. Perret points out that, although in the past the Bath chandeliers have been described as 'Waterford', little knowledge is required to show that this ascription is false. The factory at Waterford was founded in 1783 and as the Assembly Rooms were opened to the public in 1771, it is obvious that the chandeliers were made elsewhere. The question of the provenance of the chandeliers was finally settled by Perret himself. When the chandeliers were being dismantled for repair in 1937, he discovered on the bowl of one chandelier the inscription PARKER, FLEET STREET, LONDON in engraved letters one and a quarter inches in height.

William Parker was as important in the second half of the eighteenth century as Jerom Johnson had been in the first. The earliest record is in 1762, which almost exactly coincides with the date of Johnson's retirement. Johnson had been anxious to retire as early as 1756 (*London Evening Post*, 9th November, 1756), but continued in business at least until 1761 when he was selling 'Crystal Lustres only'. No later record of him has so far been brought to light and it is my surmise that William Parker, with a partner, Edward Watton, took over Johnson's business connections, but I have so far been unable to find proof of this. The fact remains, however, that Johnson's flourishing business in chandeliers vanished at the same time that Parker's appeared.

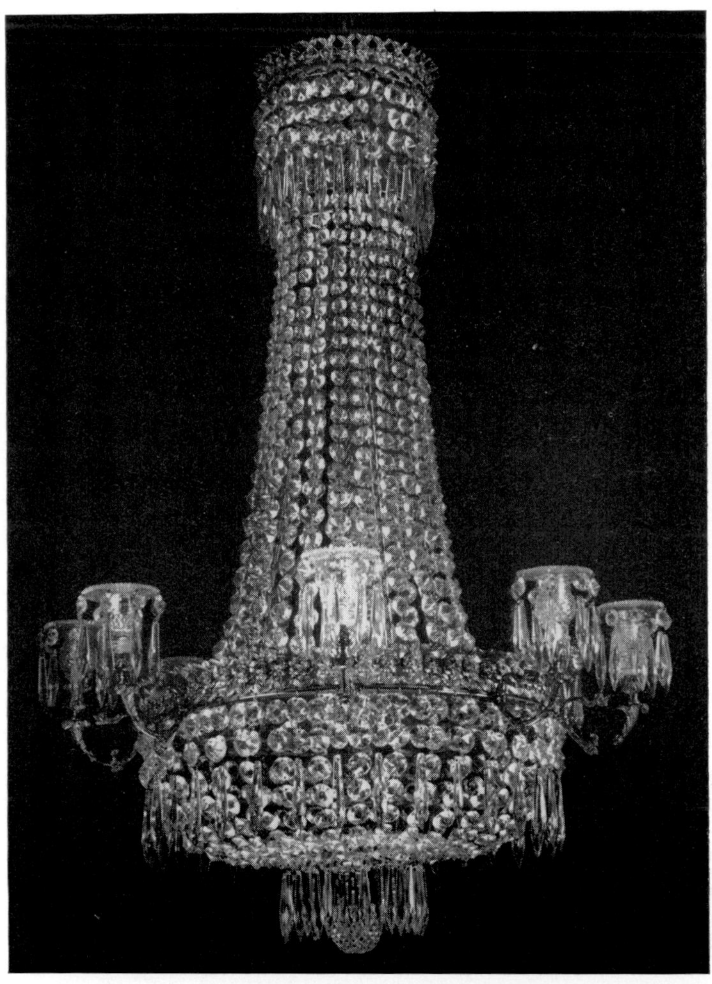

65. *Eight-light chandelier of the late Regency Period; conceived as a solid figure.* circa *1820.*

Chandeliers of the Regency Period (1810-1820) are typical of the great change in style which occurred from 1790. At first branches began to control the design and, in order to increase the lighting and to keep the general design open, they were arranged in tiers. Decoration by swags of pendent lustres, however, soon became so profuse that the branches were submerged, and it was felt (*circa* 1790) no longer necessary to decorate them by cutting. The central ornamented shaft very quickly followed the same fate, disappearing beneath a mass of swags. The elegantly curved branches which had been a prominent feature of the earlier chandeliers were now replaced by short branches which sprang from concentric metal rings situated at the base of the shaft.

A chandelier typical of this style is Fig. 64. The central shaft has not yet completely disappeared, but the closely formed chains of lustres falling from the canopy threaten to submerge it; the candle-sockets are carried by small metal branches fitted to brass rings richly ornamented with pendent icicles.

The final demise of the shaft was brought about by still closer decoration, and the chandelier was now conceived as a solid figure. A typical specimen is Fig. 65; it illustrates the general design of many famous chandeliers of the period, such as those in the Throne Room at Buckingham Palace and that from Wroxton Abbey now in the Victoria and Albert Museum.

It is recorded in H. Clifford Smith's book, *Buckingham Palace*, 1931, that Parker supplied the chandeliers for Carlton House in 1789; and up to 1826, until the final dismantling of the building, he provided a succession of elaborate and costly chandeliers for its lighting and adornment. After the dismantling of Carlton House, the original chandeliers underwent some modification before they were rehung in Buckingham Palace in 1834; they were again modified from the traditional waxen candles to electric lighting soon after the accession of King Edward VII.

By gracious permission of His Late Majesty King George VI, I was allowed to inspect the many chandeliers in Buckingham Palace. I very much doubt whether there is a finer group in existence than the seven in the Throne Room. They were supplied by Perry & Co., successors to Parker and Perry, in 1835. There are five in the Throne Room itself and two in the alcove, one each side of the Thrones. The central chandelier in the Throne Room, shown in Fig. 66, is over eight feet in diameter and eleven feet in height and is arranged for fifty-four lights, the four smaller chandeliers *en suite* having thirty-six lights each. Those in the alcove are smaller and carry eighteen lights each.

The seven chandeliers are in the Regency style and all closely follow the design of the central specimen. This is conceived as a solid figure, chains of lustres, closely formed, falling in cascades from a great corona decorated with honeysuckle in ormolu to a shallow basin about five feet in width composed of countless sparkling drops. The branches carry clusters of three lights; the glass candle-sockets and grease-pans are richly cut in relief diamonds, and ornamented with faceted icicle pendants. The seven chandeliers form a magnificent group.

The Wroxton Abbey chandelier, Fig. 67, is also an outstanding example of its type. It was made for the second Lord North and was purchased for the Victoria and Albert Museum within recent years from Wroxton Abbey, Oxfordshire. It is six feet in height and four feet in width and is dated *circa* 1815. Festoons of pendent drops, richly faceted, fall into a basin made up of eight concentric rings in ormolu, each decorated with pendent icicles. Eighteen short notched branches, springing from the widest of the eight rings, carry the grease-pans and candle-sockets, which are exquisitely formed and richly decorated with incised motifs. Each separate part of the chandelier—and there are reported to be about 4,500 pieces—is perfectly formed and cut.

The Regency Period cannot be left without mention of glass chandeliers from Ireland. It has been pointed out that J. B. Perret disposed of the theory that the chandeliers at Bath originally came from Waterford. It is a well-known fact that after the tax on the raw materials used in glass-making, first imposed in 1745, had been doubled in 1777, many English glass-makers, especially those from Stourbridge, went to Ireland. No tax had been imposed there on glass-making ingredients, and what was more important, Ireland had been granted full freedom of trade in 1780.

The Irish glass industry thus founded was immediately successful; the factories at Waterford and Cork were soon enjoying a world market which lasted until 1825, when the Glass Excise Act was extended to include Ireland, and manufacture then virtually ceased. It has therefore been assumed that as the workmen, formula, materials and even designs were all English, the products of the Irish and English factories would show some close similarity. This, of course, would include

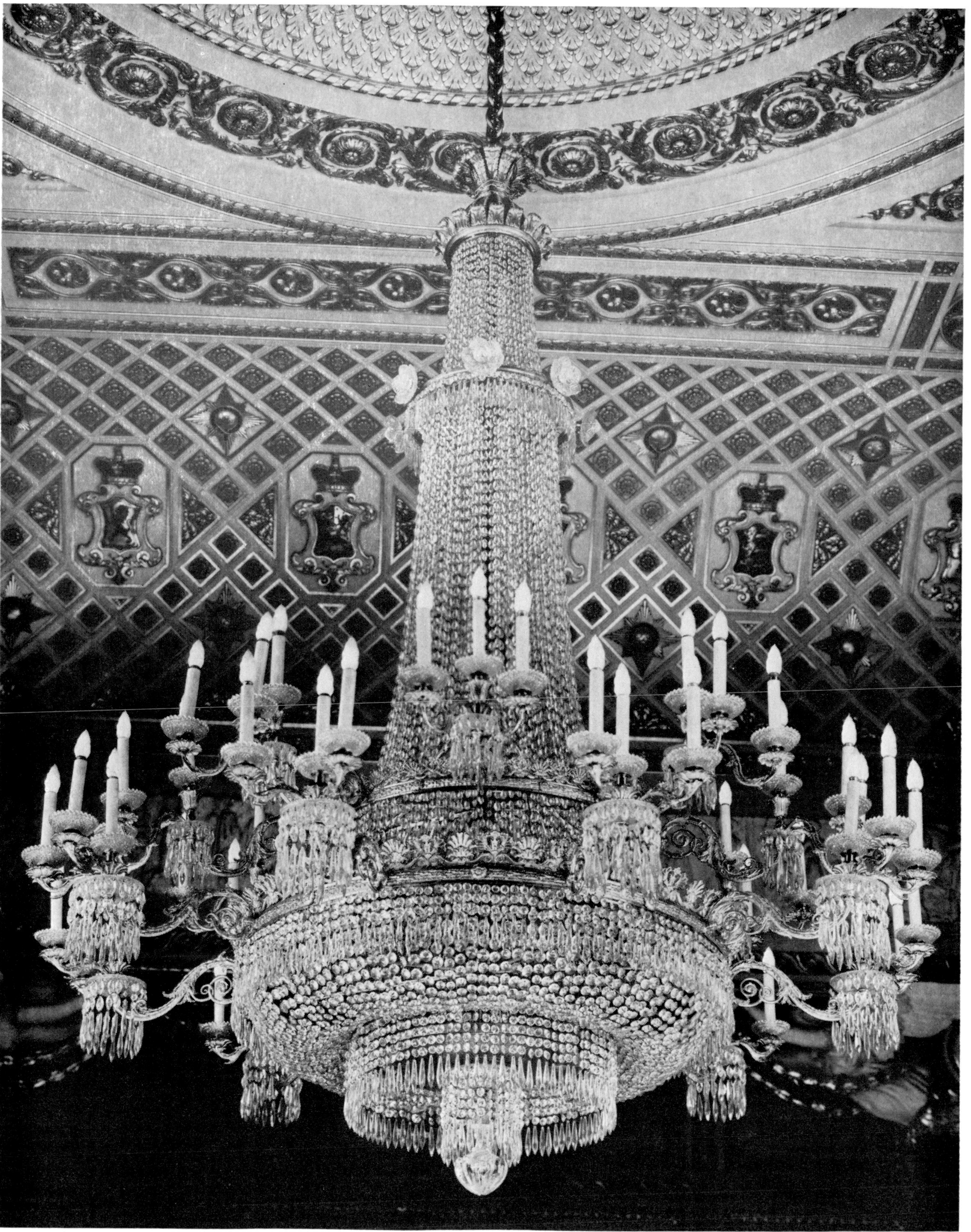

66. *Central chandelier of seven in the Throne Room of Buckingham Palace. The chandelier is in Regency style, supplied by Perry & Company in 1835.* (*Reproduced by Gracious Permission of Her Majesty the Queen*)

67. *Wroxton Abbey chandelier, 6 feet in height and composed of 4,500 pieces.* circa *1815.*
(*By courtesy of the Victoria and Albert Museum*)

chandeliers, and many specimens were at one time ascribed to Waterford.

There is no evidence, however, that glass chandeliers were made at the Irish factories on any scale. M. S. Dudley Westropp (*Irish Glass*, 1920), who examined the account books and ledgers of the Irish factories, found that pendent drops were purchased from Follet Osler of Birmingham; there is also the evidence of Martin Crean, a Dublin glass-maker, that there were no manufacturers of drops for lustres in Ireland.

There are, however, several entries in the Waterford account books of the sale of cut-glass chandeliers, the price varying from £10 to £30, which would indicate that the manufacture, if any, at the Waterford factory was on a very modest scale. As early as 1768, a large glass chandelier cost 'upwards of £100'; William Parker in 1771 charged £330 for three of the chandeliers now at Bath. W. A. Thorpe (*English Glass*, 1935, p. 228) puts the price of a large salon chandelier during the Regency Period as between £500 and £600, and although this figure may appear high, it must not be overlooked that the final increase of the Excise Duty in 1822 raised the tax on glass to the astonishing figure of £4 18s. per cwt.

The repeal of the Glass Excise Act in 1845 stimulated activity in every branch of glass production, and many firms became engaged in the manufacture of chandeliers. For example, only four years after the repeal of the Act, Apsley Pellatt & Company advertised in the *The Times*, 21st March, 1849: 'At their Glass Manufactury, Holland Street, Blackfriars—the largest and most modern collection of chandeliers (both for candles and gas) in Europe.'

Also in *The Times* on the same date appears: 'Osler's Table Glass, Chandeliers, Lustres, etc., 44 Oxford Street, London, conducted in connexion with their manufactury, Broad Street, Birmingham; established 1807. Crystal glass, drawing room chandeliers with glass arms, £5 upwards.'

Not all the productions of the times were on such a modest scale, however. A cut-glass fountain, twenty-seven feet high, was shown at the Great Exhibition in 1851, and the famous 'Alhambra' chandelier, twenty-four feet high, made of blue, white and ruby glass was regarded at the time as a masterpiece of the glassmaker's art.

Many firms in the Birmingham and Stourbridge area specialised in chandeliers; in the middle of the nineteenth century no fewer than twenty different establishments from this district devoted their energies to the production of chandelier ornaments. Towards the end of the century, however, the manufacture of cut-glass of all descriptions suffered a decline and chandeliers ceased to be made.

There are modern versions of the glass chandelier now on the market. They began to appear shortly after the second world war from south European sources. Most of the big stores today display chandeliers of various sizes suitable for rooms of modest dimensions, but larger ones in rococo style for loftier rooms and halls are obtainable. The modern versions are decorated with cut pendents similar to their originals in the eighteenth century, but it is noted that an occasional specimen is found with faceted drops made from transparent plastic material.

Original chandeliers of the eighteenth and nineteenth centuries vary considerably in price, depending, of course, on size and style of workmanship. Chandeliers of the type illustrated in Figs. 60 and 61 would today change hands in the region of £250. Small modern versions cost anything from £10 upwards, depending on size and the amount of decoration.

CHIMNEY GLASSES. Chimney glasses were popular articles in well-furnished houses during the eighteenth century. The chimney glass was fixed between the shelf above the chimney piece and the entablature, the cornice at the top of the wainscot. They were at first of horizontal shape, but as the century progressed they became squarer in design, and later tended to become vertical, more like a pier glass.

At the beginning of the century, chimney glasses were usually in three pieces, stretching across the chimney piece itself. They were designed to give the impression of spaciousness and depth to the room, by reflecting the windows and other appointments in it.

68. *Chimney glass showing centre mirror twice the width of the end pieces, an early feature.* (*Messrs Mallett & Son, Ltd.*)

69. *Chimney glass with three mirrors over which is a painting after Hondekoeter.* (*Messrs Mallett & Son, Ltd.*)

When the chimney glass is found in three parts, the central part is usually about twice the length of the two end pieces. A typical specimen is shown in Fig. 68.

Chimney glasses are also found in four pieces and have a picture above the mirror forming a sort of overmantel. The picture extends to the full length of the three mirrors, the whole being contained in a single frame. A specimen of this style of chimney glass is shown in Fig. 69. The frame is in walnut and gilt, the subject of the picture being after Hondekoeter. In some cases the mirrors were painted by artists well known at the time. The *Daily Courant* of 6th December, 1771, reported: 'Noble large Looking-Glasses, finely painted with Flowers and Ornaments by Van Zoon.' This artist had a reputation towards the end of the eighteenth century for his paintings of flowers. Another Dutch artist who painted flowers on mirror glasses was Van Huysum.

Alternative styles of painted decoration on chimney glasses of the overmantel type were landscape pictures, sporting scenes, or paintings in Chinese style. An occasional four-piece chimney glass is found with a panel in needlework in place of the picture.

The frames of chimney glasses are usually of gilt gesso or in various woods such as walnut or laburnum and in scroll giltwood. A specimen is shown in Fig. 70. Later in the century, the frames followed the classic styles dictated by the fashion set by the Adam brothers.

Chimney glasses are now comparatively rare. For example, a chimney glass contained in a rococo Gothic frame, with a three-panel plate and the sides with naturalistic trees, five foot six inches wide, changed hands quite recently for £310. Another with a central oval mirror surrounded by smaller mirrors within a rococo gilt framework with cresting in the form of a Chinese pavilion, size six feet by four feet, changed hands for £210. On the other hand, a Regency chimney glass five feet wide with an arched centre section was sold in 1957 for £14.

CIDER GLASSES. Cider glasses can be identified by such motifs as apple trees or branches engraved upon them. They date from the mid-eighteenth century onwards. They followed the ale glasses of the period very closely in form and, indeed, it is possible to identify similar specimens only

70. *Chimney glass in scroll giltwood, a popular style in the mid-eighteenth century.* (*Messrs Mallett & Son, Ltd.*)

from the subjects engraved upon them—hops and barley in the case of the ale glasses, apple blossom or apple trees upon the cider glasses.

Few notices appeared in the eighteenth century in which cider glasses are mentioned, and very little information can be gained from them. The following is a typical notice appearing in September and October, 1770, in the *Belfast News Letter* and also the *Limerick Chronicle*: 'At the Glass House on Marlborough Bank opposite the South Wall of Marlborough Bowling Green, Dublin, are now making and made by Richard Williams & Co., all the newest fashioned enamelled, flowered, cut and plain, wine, beer and cyder glasses' (M. S. Dudley Westropp, *Irish Glass*, 1920, p. 57).

The most popular style was the flute, usually with opaque-twist stem, and some are found engraved with a spray of apple blossom and leaves, or alternatively with an apple tree. One example is known with the straight-sided bowl engraved with a pastoral scene with a cow grazing between two apple trees. The opaque-twist stem has a central knop and is mounted on a high spreading foot.

Hartshorne (*Old English Glasses*, 1897, p. 312) mentions an air-twist stemmed glass engraved with an apple branch border; and another, an opaque-twist stem glass engraved with an apple tree, and on the opposite side with a large winged insect which might be a butterfly. Hartshorne refers to a third glass engraved on one side with an apple tree and on the other with two barrels and the words NO EXCISE. This glass dates *circa* 1765.

Prices have varied according to quality from £10 to £20.

CLOCK LAMPS. From various notices appearing at the time it is apparent that the glass lamp developed somewhere about 1730. At that time the only means of obtaining a light at night to tell the time was with flint and steel, and it can be well appreciated that to do this by such means in the middle of the night in a draughty chamber was no pleasant task.

The glass-maker and the tin-smith co-operated in the manufacture of glass clock lamps. The lamps, made partly of brass and partly of glass, were in great demand at the time. The oil was stored in a glass at the top of the lamp, the wick holder protruding from one side; the time was told by the sinking of the oil in the container which was marked by 'hour' degrees. A specimen is shown in Fig. 71, with an enlargement of the glass container.

This type of clock lamp was described in *The Craftsman*, 19th December, 1730, as follows: 'Ashburne's New Invented Clock-Lamp, showing the Hours of the Night exactly as they pass; far exceeding anything of this kind ever yet invented. Are sold by the Inventor and Maker, Leonard Ashburne, at the Sugar Loaf in Paternoster Row, Cheapside, at 6s. each.'

Another interesting advertisement appeared a few months later in *The Craftsman*, 27th February, 1731: 'Walker's original new-invented Clock-Lamp. Being a most compleat machine and so artfully contrived that it shows the Hours of the Night exactly as they pass; supplying at once the place of a Clock, Watch and Candle, and has been approv'd by the most Ingenious. 'Tis managed with so little trouble and so very neatly that it neither daubs the fingers nor the place where it

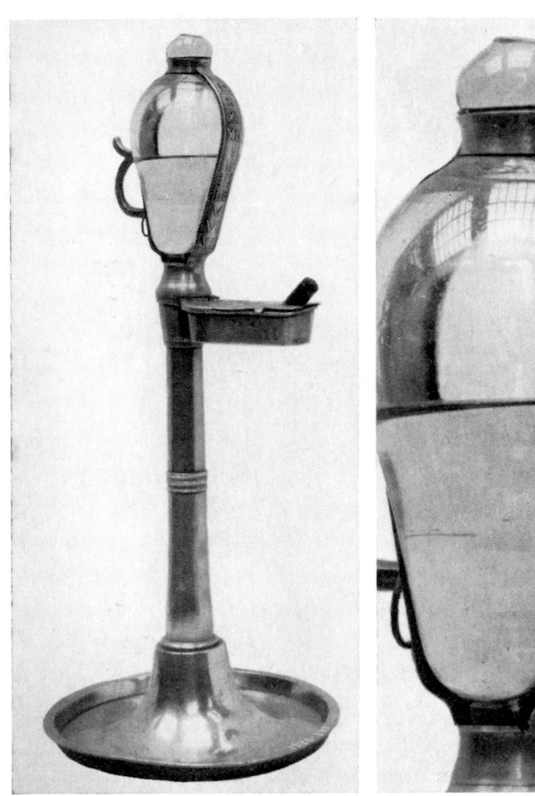

71. *Glass oil clock lamp, eighteenth century. A glass container at the top of the lamp, marked in 'hour' degrees (detail right), contained oil, the level of which sank as the lamp burned.* (*Science Museum, London*)

stands, as others do. In short, hardly any Person that has occasion to keep a light in the night, if they knew the conveniency of them would ever be without one.'

COACH HORNS.
See MUSICAL GLASSES.

COIN GLASSES. The custom of enclosing a coin in the hollow stem of a drinking glass would appear to have originated in Murano. Glasses of this type were presented to distinguished persons visiting the island. There is a specimen in the British Museum of a Venetian coin glass in which is enclosed a half sequin of Francesco Molini, who was Doge in 1647.

The fashion of enclosing a coin in the stem was probably introduced into this country about the time of Charles II, for several specimens are known containing coins of the King. The character of some of these glasses indicate that they were made during that period. It is, of course, not necessarily the case that the date of the coin is that of the glass in which it is embedded. For example, another coin glass in the British Museum contains a three-penny piece of 1679, but the glass is obviously of a very much later period, probably mid-eighteenth century.

Another specimen in the British Museum is a goblet which contains a James II coin dated 1687. The goblet is seven-and-three-quarter inches in height with the bowl 'nip't diamond waies' at the base with trailed decoration above. The stem consists of two hollow knops decorated with strawberry prunts, the upper knop enclosing the coin. W. A. Thorpe (*A History of English and Irish Glass*, 1929, p. 128) is of the opinion that the glass may well be the work of Hawley Bishopp. A further specimen is in the collection of Arthur Churchill, Ltd., the coin bearing the same date, 1687. (*See* CORONATION AND OTHER ROYAL COMMEMORATIVE GLASSES.)

It is claimed by Francis (*Old English Drinking Glasses*, 1926, p. 206) that all glasses between 1715 and 1750 which contain Charles II coins are as definitely Jacobite as if they bore the portrait of Prince Charles himself; and that glasses containing coins of William III, Anne, George I and George II, of the same period, are as much anti-Jacobite as are the glasses engraved 'To the Immortal Memory of King William'. There are specimens extant of coin glasses of Queen Anne. Some have a fourpenny piece in the stem dated 1710.

Enclosed coins are not by any means confined to the stems of drinking glasses. Tankards are known with coins of George II, and jugs with enclosed coins have always enjoyed a certain amount of popularity. They were especially in demand during the reign of Queen Victoria. Some are known with a sixpence of 1839 and others appeared on the occasion of the Great Exhibition of 1851 and of the Jubilee in 1887.

Coin glasses were re-introduced for the coronation of Her Majesty Queen Elizabeth II; goblets and other drinking vessels with a 1953 coin enclosed in the hollow stem were popular items designed to celebrate the occasion.

Two notable specimens of coin glasses have changed hands recently, one with a hollow baluster stem with a straight sided bowl and domed and folded foot. The hollow stem contained a Queen Anne shilling dated 1708. This specimen fetched £58. The other specimen was a goblet, the stem containing a Queen Anne fourpenny piece of 1706; this changed hands at £26. The straight sided bowl was 'nipt diamond waies'. (*See* NIPT DIAMOND WAIES.)

COLOUR-TWIST STEMMED GLASSES. Glasses with stems in which the spiral is one of coloured glass have always been collectors' favourites. Before the last war they fetched £20 in the sale room and today the rarer specimens realise four times that amount. They are not common glasses and do not often come up for sale.

Almost without exception the colour spiral, which can be red, blue, green, black, pink or yellow, is found in combination with white opaque. Occasionally, however, one comes to light with a colour in combination with an air-twist. Some glasses have mixed colours. The most highly prized, as will be seen from the prices given later at which they changed hands, are yellow and green, although mixed colours also appeal.

Not all the coloured spirals are opaque. Some are translucent and, on the whole, not so pleasing. Bowl forms have little bearing on the value of a colour-twist. For the most part, the wines have bowls of ogee or bell formation; ales, which are less frequent, are of trumpet form and occasionally a glass with bucket bowl comes to light. Cordials are rare and do not occur with mixed twists.

Colour-twists have changed hands during recent years up to £80. In 1959 a wine with small ovoid bowl on a shaded green corkscrew twist stem, encircled by narrow opaque white strands, five-and-a-quarter inches high, realised £80.

A few years ago a wineglass with straight sided bowl, with white corkscrew stem encircled with four yellow threads, six-and-one-eighth inches in height, fetched £75. A wineglass with ogee bowl on a red and white corkscrew twist stem, five-and-three-quarter inches high, changed hands for £48. At the same sale a wineglass with straight sided bowl with an opaque white central cable, encircled by bright blue strands, six-and-one-eighth inches high, realised £45. A mixed colour-twist wineglass with trumpet bowl on a blue, green, red, and white cable spiral, six-and-seven-eighth inches high, sold for £40.

COLOURED GLASS. The manufacture of coloured glass has always enlisted admiration and wonder from the earliest times, when the making of glass was clothed in mystery, until today, when science adds unceasingly to our knowledge of the colours and tints produced by various substances.

Colour technology in glass is a complicated science and involves many problems in furnace conditions. The colour due to nickel oxide may range from yellow to purple, depending on the nature of the glass; and according to furnace conditions, copper can impart a greenish-blue colour to the glass, a rich ruby, or remain in the glass in glistening, metallic flakes as aventurine glass.

These few examples serve to indicate that the subject is far beyond the scope of this dictionary. In general, however, the colouring agents used in glass-making fall into one of three distinct groups: (*a*) in which the substance is in true solution, (*b*) in which the substance is in the colloidal state, the colour being produced by particles of sub-microscopic size, such as the ruby tint imparted by gold, and (*c*) in which the particles are larger than in (*b*) and may themselves be coloured, such as in the example of aventurine glass given above, or colourless, as in white opal glass.

In the making of crystal glass, small quantities of the colouring agent are either added to the glass mixture—i.e., the batch—or the glass is lightly cased or flashed with a layer of coloured glass when the article is being fashioned at the furnace. The latter method was very popular during the last century; articles cased in various colours, such as ruby, green or blue, were cut and engraved in various designs to disclose the colourless glass beneath.

Some of the colouring media generally used are given in the following list:

Cobalt. This element is found in nature as arsenide, or cobalt sulphide, and is treated to give the oxide of the metal, in which form it is used by the glass-maker. Cobalt is the most powerful colouring agent used in glass-making, producing a deep blue colour. When used in any quantity in a glass, very little light penetrates through it even in thin sections; in glass of any thickness, the colour will be so dense as to give the glass the appearance of being quite black. Indeed, cobalt is used with manganese to produce black glass.

Copper. The oxide of copper imparts blue, green and also ruby to a glass according to the conditions prevailing during melting. It has already been mentioned that copper can be made to remain in the glass in glistening, metallic flakes as aventurine glass.

Chromium. The oxide of this metal gives a green or greenish-yellow colour to the glass; in some cases it is used instead of iron to produce green tints. If large amounts of chromium are used, however, crystals of chrome oxide may separate from the glass on cooling, similar to the aventurine glass of copper.

Gold. This metal is used to produce rich red tints in the glass. It is carefully mixed with the 'batch' ingredients in the form of certain salts. The intensity of the colour is such, however, that it is usual to use the glass containing gold as a thin layer over a colourless glass, a process known as 'casing' or 'flashing'.

Iron. This is generally present as an impurity in the materials used in glass-making, and according to conditions produces a green or a yellowish-green or sometimes a bluish-green in soda-lime glasses. It may be intentionally added as iron oxide to give the bottle-green colour or, in proportion with manganese, to give a deep amber, such as is found with some beer and wine bottles.

Manganese. This metal does not occur in the free state in nature, but as an oxide, pyrolusite, notably in Spain, the United States, Sweden and Brazil. It has been used as a decolouriser in glass since the time of Pliny, producing an amethyst colour which is almost complementary to the green colour produced by iron.

Nickel. This oxide, as already stated, may give two colours depending on the conditions prevailing at the time. If used in a glass containing potash, a very deep violet is obtained, but when present in a soda-lime glass, it produces a dirty yellow colour.

Selenium. When used alone, selenium metal produces a pink colour in soda-lime glasses and on this account is almost universally used in glass intended for bottles, etc., to neutralise the green tint caused by the iron impurities. With lead glass, the colour imparted by selenium is a clear amber. In combination with cadmium sulphide, selenium gives a rich sealing-wax red.

COMFIT GLASSES. A comfit glass was an alternative name for a small sweetmeat glass (*see* SWEETMEAT GLASSES), particularly those used for dry sweetmeats, chocolate, salted almonds, caraway seeds and cachous. Some writers claim that there was a distinction between 'wet sweetmeats' and 'dry sweetmeats', the latter being termed 'comfits'. (W. A. Thorpe, *A History of English and Irish Glass*, 1929, p. 321.)

The sweetmeat glass would be reserved for iced cream, sundaes, trifles, etc., and would therefore be somewhat larger than the comfit glasses. Early cookery books abound with recipes for both 'wet' and 'dry' sweetmeats. Some, richly flavoured and strongly scented, were taken after drinking or smoking, or to remove any undesired lingering taste of over-spiced food.

The sweetmeat glass and the comfit glass often appeared together in the same notice. For example, *Faulkner's Dublin Journal*, January, 1752, mentions 'comfit and sweetmeat glasses for desserts'.

Comfit glasses were small glasses with short or rudimentary stems, or they could be without any stem. This latter type is probably what is referred to in the following notice in *Notes and Queries*, 3rd September, 1725: 'Nat Barry bought for Thomas Pembrock, Mayor of Cork, in Bristol, 2 doz. glass saucers for holding sweetmeats at 4s. 4d. per doz.' Such a glass would be no more than three inches in height, the shallow bowl being from four to four-and-a-half inches in width.

More ornate comfit glasses appeared, however, and specimens such as those shown in Figs. 72 and 73 are found that can be described either as comfit glasses or sweetmeat glasses. They are both about four inches in height, and because of their small capacity were most probably employed for comfits rather than the more bulky sweetmeat delicacies.

Comfit glasses of the type described have realised up to £2 each.

72. *Comfit glass, 4 inches in height, the shallow bowl with pincered decoration. Could be described alternatively as a small sweetmeat glass.* (*Messrs Arthur Churchill, Ltd.*). 73. *Comfit glass, or alternatively small sweetmeat, with plain shallow bowl and hollow knopped rudimentary stem.* (*Messrs Arthur Churchill, Ltd.*)

COMMEMORATIVE GLASSES. Glass vessels have been employed to commemorate events, sentiments and hopes for 3,500 years. The earliest glass of this description of which the date is positively known are the three vessels with the cartouche of King Thothmes III, who reigned in the XVth Dynasty (1501-1499 B.C.). One of these vessels is preserved in the British Museum, the second in the Metropolitan Museum, New York, and the third in the Antiquarian at Munich. There is also a glass commemorative vessel of the same period in the Cairo Museum, of Queen Kamare, sister to Thothmes III.

During Roman times, a gladiatorial victory would be commemorated by a glass cup or goblet appropriately decorated. Specimens with shallow cutting executed on a wheel can be seen in several museums throughout Italy, particularly in the National Museum, Rome.

There is another group of Roman commemorative glasses, of which a score or so of specimens are preserved in the museums in Belgium, France, Germany and England, which are trophies of chariot contests. Indeed, some specimens are inscribed with the names of the contestants themselves. One, for example, bears the names of four charioteers—Pyramus, Eutichus, Hierax and the conqueror Olympus holding a wreath and palm of victory.

A chariot cup was found at Colchester also with the names of four charioteers—Antilocus, Crescens, Hierax and Olympus. In this case the victor was Crescens, for three of the names bear the inscription 'Vale', and that of the conqueror, 'Crescens Ave'. It would appear that glasses given by admirers as trophies to commemorate a victory of their favourite charioteer were quite common in Roman times.

Glasses from the fourth century are extant inscribed with such legends as 'Bibe Vivas Multis Annis'. Such specimens can be seen in the museums of Munich, Milan, Vienna, Budapest and Venice. These glasses are in various colours and are engraved by talented artists. Indeed, Roman artists of that period had complete control over their medium and made full use of its capabilities.

Among Islamic enamelled glasses of the thirteenth century are specimens bearing inscriptions including names of various Mamelukes and others. Later, in the sixteenth and seventeenth centuries, glasses were given as prizes at Venice for gondola races, and the custom grew in the Netherlands to record a marriage or betrothal. In Italy and Germany during the same period, armorial glasses became popular among the high born.

Occasional specimens of commemorative glasses from the same period are found in France and England, the most important in this country, of course, being the Verzelini group of glasses inscribed and dated between 1577 and 1602.

The eighteenth century was well advanced, however, before English craftsmen began to make full use of the medium of Ravenscroft and to express themselves by methods of engraving taught them by German engravers after the accession of George I in 1714. Indeed, it was not until 1742 that the first reference was made to 'flowered' glasses, the name given to engraved glasses. This was by Jerom Johnson in the *Daily Advertiser* of 21st December: 'At the entire Glass Shop, the corner of St Martin's Lane—all cut and scalloped and flowered Glasses, shall always be sold cheapest by the maker, Jerom Johnson.'

Johnson was one of the pioneers of English decorative glass. He practised between the years 1739 and 1761, and was the first Englishman to show that wheel decoration could be applied to glass without foreign assistance. In most of his advertisements he described himself variously as the 'inventor' or the 'maker', and because of this, claimed that he could sell more cheaply than any other engraver and cutter. He advertised almost every glass article, from a simple wineglass to the 'most magnificent lustre that ever was made in England.' It is most probable, therefore, that many of the commemorative glasses of the period can be ascribed to him.

Johnson chose designs that expressed the flourish demanded by the rococo appeal; his flowered glasses were an appropriate subscription to a taste that at the time was sweeping Europe, but he chose simple emblems to interpret it that could be easily appreciated by his public. The roses, daffodils, hops and barley, carnations, honeysuckle, and the grapes and vine leaves were in themselves sufficient to express the rococo fashion, but he freely employed curling leaves and slender twining tendrils to emphasise it.

So many glasses were made during the eighteenth and nineteenth centuries, to commemorate events of all descriptions, that a complete record of them all would most probably require a second dictionary. It is possible, however, to classify them, and to give typical examples. The following is a comprehensive grouping:

Royalty Glasses. These include glasses commemorating royal events, such as accessions, coronations, jubilees, marriages, births and deaths. They will also include the glasses made to commemorate the Restoration. (*See* ENGLISH GLASS, Royal Oak Goblet, Fig. 116, and Exeter Flute, Fig. 117, and Pretender Glasses. *See also* JACOBITE GLASSES.)

Other English Royalty glasses are discussed under CORONATION AND OTHER ROYAL COMMEMORATIVE GLASSES.

Some German enamelled glasses also come into this category. They are Reichadlerhumpen, those glasses which were decorated as a tribute to the Emperor or Elector of a German state. (*See* ENAMELLED GLASS, German Enamelling.)

Portrait Glasses. Wheel engraved portraits, usually busts, of famous people form a definite group of commemorative glasses. They cannot be said to have reached a high standard of artistic merit, but nevertheless they are collectors' favourites.

Portrait glasses appear in CORONATION AND OTHER ROYAL COMMEMORATIVE GLASSES and JACOBITE GLASSES. The latter include portraits of the Young Pretender

In addition, there are glasses with the head of a famous sailor or soldier, such as Lord Nelson, Admiral Keppel, the Duke of Wellington, Lord Roberts, or other famous men such as George Washington, Napoleon III, and Disraeli. Occasionally a glass is found with an equestrian figure such as William III, commemorating the Battle of the Boyne in 1690.

War, Battles on Sea or Land, and Peace Treaties. The battle of Waterloo was a favourite subject for engraved commemorative goblets, as was also the Peninsular Campaign. Gibraltar and Trafalgar glasses were extremely popular, and some good specimens have survived the test of time.

Privateer glasses form a section of this group, and fighting ships of the time such as the *Renown* and the *Prince George*.

Regimental glasses are numerous and include those commemorating the Irish Volunteers, the Londonderry Fusiliers, Argyllshire Militia, and many others.

Among the Peace Treaty glasses are those commemorating the Treaties of Utrecht (1713), Aix-la-Chapelle (1748), Amiens (1802) and Paris (1815).

Sport and Recreation. These glasses are numerous and include scenes depicting fishing, shooting, skating, racing and also the hunting of various animals such as deer, lion, bear and fox.

Gambling scenes are depicted on some glasses, dice games and cock-fighting being some of the subjects employed.

This group of glasses might also include equestrian scenes such as coaching, riding and steeplechasing.

Family Occasions. These occur as early as the latter part of the sixteenth century, when Verzelini made a number of betrothal glasses (*see* VERZELINI GLASSES).

The custom of recording births, christenings, betrothals or marriages on glasses was common during the eighteenth century and, indeed, is a custom which finds echo even today. There are quite a number of diamond point and wheel engravers today who have constant employment in such work.

Glasses with the monogram of the owner are common. This not only applies to glasses, but to the sealed bottles of the eighteenth century.

Glass rolling pins with a motto or message enamelled on them was another type of article which falls into this category of family glasses.

Political Glasses. This group is a large one, as politics was a favourite subject of the engraver of the time. They include the Jacobite glasses and Williamite glasses already discussed and glasses commemorating parliamentary elections and incidents of some political significance.

Miscellaneous. This group will include glasses used in Clubs and Masonic Lodges, Trade Guilds and Companies, and the 'flowered' glasses used for some specific liquor engraved with an appropriate emblem, such as the flowering vines for wineglasses, apple trees for cider glasses and hops and barley for ale glasses.

Glasses were also engraved with mottoes or words depicting hope or luck, such as 'Speed the Plough' or 'Let Farming Flourish'.

The list given above of the various groups of engraved commemorative glasses is far from complete. In many cases only one of a kind is known, and the list of such glasses is an evergrowing one.

Of all the commemorative glasses, the Royalty and Portrait glasses are the most popular of this type among collectors. For example, a portrait glass of George, Prince of Wales, engraved on the bowl with the inscription 'Long Live George Prince of Wales 1759' changed hands for £90, and a Young Pretender portrait tumbler, engraved with the full face portrait of Prince Charles Edward with various Jacobite emblems, realised £160. A Royal Armorial glass engraved with the Arms of Queen Anne fetched £62.

Those glasses commemorating war are not so popular as the portrait glasses. A rummer inscribed 'In Memory of Lord

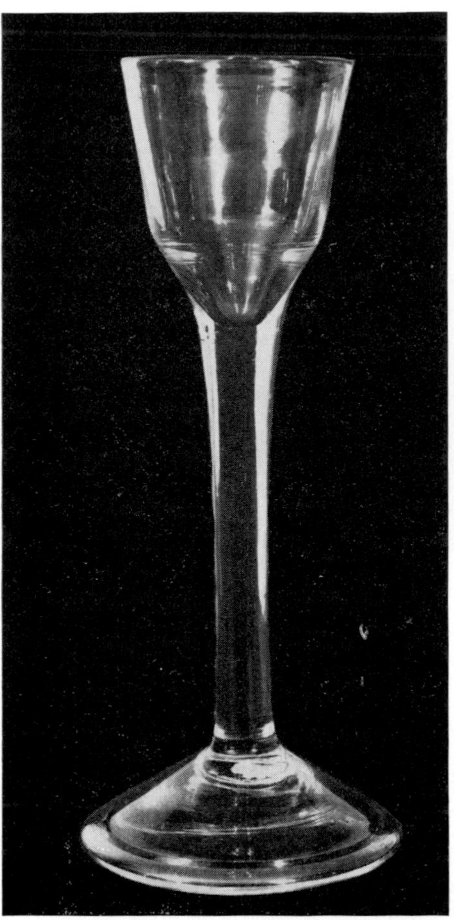

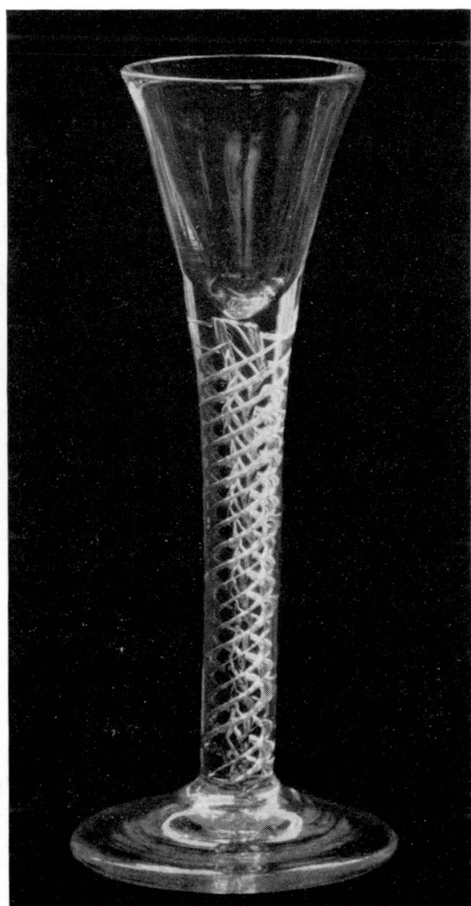

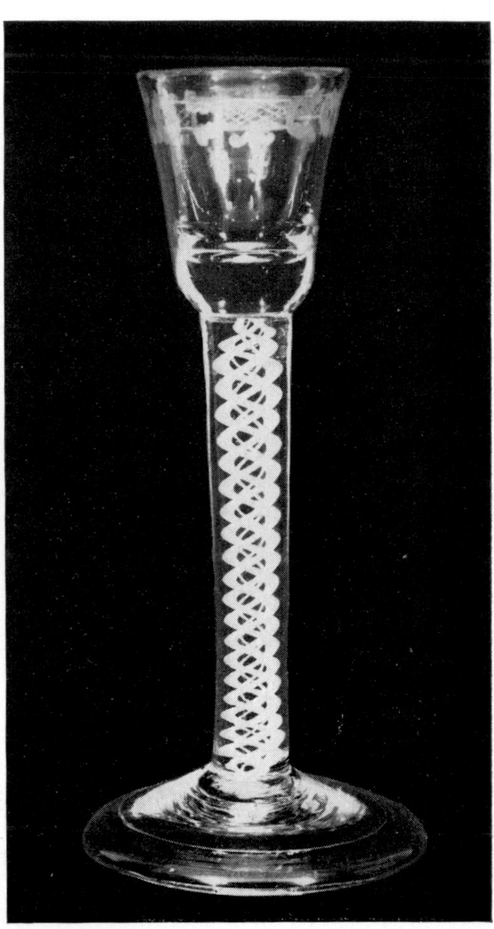

74. *Cordial glass with drawn stem; that is, the bowl and stem were made in one piece to which a foot was afterwards attached.* 75. *Cordial glass with double series air-twist stem. This is an uncommon glass. (Messrs Arthur Churchill, Ltd.).* 76. *Cordial glass with double series opaque-twist stem. The thin thread in the stem in pale pink; the heavier thread in white. The foot is folded. The combination of these features in a glass make it a rare one.*

Nelson Octr. 21 1805' and on the reverse an engraving of the *Victory* realised £24. A large Naval goblet nearly a foot high inscribed 'Howe & S.T. Vincent' fetched £26.

Sporting glasses have fetched from £8 to £46. For example, a goblet with straight sided bowl, engraved with huntsmen and fox and inscribed 'Prosperity to Fox Hunting', changed hands for £46.

Marriage glasses would appear to be comparatively rare. One changed hands, engraved with emblematic figures, at £36. Political glasses include the Jacobite glasses which are dealt with under JACOBITE GLASSES. Electioneering goblets are eagerly sought after and may fetch up to £70.

Masonic glasses vary considerably in value and during recent years have changed hands from £5 to £96. For example, a firing glass enamelled by William Beilby with the arms of the Lodge of Journeymen Masons, No. 8, fetched £85. On the other hand, a glass engraved with the usual Masonic emblems may fetch less than £5.

Glasses celebrating the opening of the Sunderland Bridge, similar to that shown in Fig. 229, have varied in price between £6 and £11.

CORDIAL GLASSES. Glasses of small capacity—that is, about one to one-and-a-half ounces—for holding cordials, strong waters, liquors or liqueurs, have been made from early times. The cordials were highly spirituous drinks, heavily sweetened and flavoured with the juices, peels and kernels of various fruits. Such drinks were very potent, indeed. John Bunyan wrote of them in 1682: 'I have a cordial of Mr. Forget-Good's making, the which, sir, if you will take a dram of, may make you bonny and blithe.'

Glasses used for cordials were referred to as drams, as the above quotation shows, and in general they were miniature versions of the ordinary wineglasses of the day, with, perhaps, a taller stem in proportion, and constructed somewhat stouter, especially in the stem, because of the greater height.

The similarity of cordial glasses to the larger glasses used for wine is not surprising, as glasses in the eighteenth century were, as they are today, often made in sets. There are, however, very few mentions of cordial glasses in the many glass-lists and bills of the English glass-sellers. On the other hand, it was not usual for them to specify the different kinds of wineglasses in their newspaper advertisements; and when, during the second half of the eighteenth century, such advertisements became rather more detailed, there existed little difference between wineglasses and cordials except in height and capacity. Throughout the eighteenth century, therefore, cordials were included under the general category of 'glasses for wine'.

In Ireland, however, it was different. Greater prominence was given to cordial glasses, and several references are to be

77. *Group of cordial glasses including air-twist, enamel-twist and cut stems.*

found in Irish newspapers to dram glasses, the popular name in Ireland as in England for cordial glasses. Thus, *Faulkner's Dublin Journal*, December, 1746, refers to 'dram and whiskey glasses at one shilling and sixpence . . . per dozen'. In 1776 there is reference to 'Wine glasses, dram and beer glasses' (M. S. Dudley Westropp, *Irish Glass*, 1920, p. 145) as having been imported to Ireland from London, and as late as 1827 there appears an entry in an account book of the Waterford Glasshouse of 'one gross of drams'.

It will be seen, therefore, from the dates of the various notices and other references, that cordial glasses enjoyed popularity for a long period. The earliest reference would appear to be in 1663 when Cowley cried 'Fetch me the Cordial glass in the Cabinet Window' (Hughes, *English, Irish and Scottish Glass*, 1956, p. 225), and the last record was a notice in the Waterloo Glass Works, Cork, in 1833.

Through the known period of 170 years, cordial glasses changed very much in style but not in design. From the baluster period at the end of the seventeenth century to the period when cutting was the vogue—that is, from the second half of the eighteenth century onwards—the design was the same, a bowl of capacity of from one to one-and-a-half ounces mounted on a tall, stout stem often on a domed, or at least a high, foot. The stem style, however, followed the popular fashions—baluster, Silesian, air-twist, opaque-twist, colour-twist and cut.

An early and popular style was a conical, slightly bell-shaped bowl set on a cylinder knop enclosed between top and bottom annular knops, the foot domed and folded. The stem and foot would be together almost twice the length of the bowl. This style, with variations in the knopping, was popular until the early part of the eighteenth century, when the Silesian stem became the vogue as a compliment to George I, who came to the throne in 1714. The bowl style changed during this period to bucket-shaped; the foot, although high, was neither domed nor folded. In the case of these Silesian stem glasses, the foot and stem together were twice the length of the bowl. On the whole they are well-proportioned and elegant glasses.

Cordial glasses with long, plain stems are known, an example being shown in Fig. 74, which is a two-piece glass—that is, the bowl and stem are in one piece.

A special flute glass was used for the cordial ratafia, a full description of which is given under RATAFIA GLASSES.

Styles changed throughout the eighteenth century, as already stated, according to the prevailing fashion. A group of specimens from the eighteenth century, from the period when air-twist stems were popular until that when cutting was the vogue, is shown in Fig. 77.

As will be seen, they are elegant and well-proportioned glasses, enhanced in some cases with applied decorative effects such as cutting and engraving. Such glasses, of course, were not found in the taverns, but were for use in well-ordered households. Tea-drinking had become popular in the middle of the eighteenth century, and the cordial glass was often found on the tea-table. It became customary to take wine, cordials or some spirituous drink after drinking tea, the notion being that the animation lost through drinking too much tea was once again restored by a spirituous drink. The high ritual of tea-drinking in the eighteenth century in England was as elaborate as its counterpart in Japan. The tea-cups and other requisites were of the best porcelain, and the cordial glasses for such occasions were the most elegant and attractive that could be obtained.

The tavern drams or cordials were by contrast simple glasses usually of the two-piece type. They were somewhat similar in shape to the firing glasses used in the clubs and societies. They had plain thick stems, but shorter than the cordial glasses already described, and the feet were of sturdy construction. The bowl forms for the most part were trumpet shape or straight sided.

In the *Belfast News Letter* of January, 1781, there is a notice about 'common dram and punch glasses', which obviously referred to the tavern variety.

There was a deceptive dram glass used by tavern keepers, but this style must not be confused with either cordial glasses or the common tavern dram. A description of the deceptive dram is given under FIRING GLASSES.

Cordial glasses are not plentiful and have varied in price during recent years from £9 to £32, depending on style and rarity. For example, a cordial glass, seven inches high with small trumpet bowl on an air-twist stem, changed hands a few years ago for £32.

CORONATION AND OTHER ROYAL COMMEMORATIVE GLASSES. In this country coronation and other Royal commemorative glasses are among the precious and significant symbols handed down from generation to generation, reminding us of the antiquity of our customs and traditions, and of the long period of growth and development which has made the British Crown the one stable element in a changing world.

English coronation history in glass, however, cannot be said to have begun much before the Restoration, and a glass engraved to celebrate the coronation of Charles II in 1660 is probably the first of what might be termed coronation glasses. This glass, termed the Exeter Flute, now in the Royal Albert Museum, Exeter, is shown in Fig. 117 and described under ENGLISH GLASS, HISTORY OF. Although the style, known as *façon de Venice*, shows strong Continental influence, the Exeter Flute was probably made by Italian craftsmen then in this country—and who no doubt would have been working for the Duke of Buckingham—and engraved by a Dutch artist. The decoration is diamond point work showing a bust of Charles II in a medallion, and the stump of an oak tree. The inscription round the rim is 'God Bless King Charles the Second'.

Another royal commemorative glass, celebrating the marriage in 1663 of Charles II, is the Royal Oak Goblet (*see* ENGLISH GLASS, HISTORY OF, Fig. 116). It is in the Venetian style also, lightly blown in greenish-brown metal, and engraved in diamond point work with a medallion portrait of Charles II framed in engraved oak branches and with the words 'Royal Oak'. On the reverse are portraits of Charles and his Queen, Catherine of Braganza, Infanta of Portugal.

78. *Glass commemorating the coronation of Queen Anne in 1702. An excellent example of baluster stemmed glass with domed and folded foot. Engraved with the Royal Arms of England as adopted by Charles II.* 79. *Light Newcastle glass engraved to celebrate the coronation of George II in 1727. This light baluster style was coming into fashion about that time.* 80. *Coronation glass of George III, who was crowned in 1760. The glass has an air-twist stem and was made by the three-piece method. The engraving is part diamond point and by the wheel.*

Following the death of Charles II in 1685, his brother, James, Duke of York, ascended the throne. His first wife bore him two daughters, Mary and Anne, both destined to become Queen. James Francis Edward, afterwards known as the 'Old Pretender', was the only issue of James's second marriage.

There are no known glasses dedicated to the coronation of James II, probably accounted for by his extreme unpopularity and his religious persuasions. There is, however, a coin glass of James II in the collection of Arthur Churchill, Ltd. It has a straight-sided bowl, on a prunted knop which contains a James II coin dated 1687. The stem has an inverted baluster with a tear. Another specimen with a coin bearing the same date is in the British Museum (*see* COIN GLASSES).

The interregnum period followed, resulting in the acceptance of the Crown in 1688 by William of Orange and Mary, daughter of James II. Again, however, there are no glasses recorded to celebrate the event.

James II had meanwhile sailed to Ireland, his Catholic stronghold, where he later took the field with Franco-Irish forces against William of Orange. The defeat of James II on 1st July, 1690, is well recorded in glasses. A usual inscription is 'To the Glorious Memory of King William III'. Other glasses are engraved with an equestrian portrait of King William and the date 'Boyne 1st July, 1690'.

Glasses celebrating the victory continued to be made well into the eighteenth century and were used, no doubt, in the Orange Lodges, founded in 1695 and which were still fashionable in the nineteenth century. It may be mentioned that there are many fraudulent versions of the Boyne glasses, and it is feared that some found their way into well-known collections. One such glass is shown under FRAUDS AND REPRODUCTIONS (Fig. 131).

William III died in 1702 and was succeeded by Anne, the second daughter of James II. Coronation glasses of Queen Anne are very scarce. One is shown in Fig. 78, an excellent example of English craftsmanship of that period. The glass shown has an inverted baluster stem, with base knop and wide folded foot. The decoration of the bowl, in diamond point and

81. *Scent or smelling bottle designed by Apsley Pellatt to commemorate the coronation of William IV. It has an excellent bust of the King and has the impressed inscription 'W IV R'.*

82. *Pressed amber glass dish commemorating the Jubilee of Queen Victoria in 1887.*

wheel engraving, depicts the Royal Arms of England as adopted by Charles II, James II and Queen Anne, until the union with Scotland in 1707.

The accession in 1714 of George I, Elector of Hanover and the great-grandson of James I, to the English throne, is well recorded in glass-ware. In spite of the fact that George I was almost unknown in this country, spoke little English, and openly preferred his native Hanover, the English nevertheless accepted him well. Indeed, so far as glass-ware is concerned, several Continental styles were adopted and became fashionable as a gesture to the new King.

Coronation drinking glasses must have been popular at the time, for several different styles are known. The more usual is that shown in Fig. 237 (*see* SILESIAN-STEMMED GLASSES). The moulded Silesian stem was a fashion introduced into this country at the time of the accession, and some specimens, such as that illustrated in Fig. 237, have sceptres or the letters GR moulded in relief on the four shoulders of the stem. Some rare examples have 'God Save King George' or 'God Save King G' impressed upon them.

There are one or two specimens engraved with the words 'God Save King George', the year of the coronation. One is illustrated in Bate's *English Tableglass*, 1905, Plate LVI, and there is another similar glass in the Victoria and Albert Museum, London.

The coronation of George II in 1727 is also recorded in glass. The specimen shown in Fig. 79 is a beautiful example of the light baluster stem with twisted bubbles of air, a style then coming into fashion. These bubbles in later specimens were elaborated into the air-twist stems, the most aesthetically effective of any kind of glass decoration.

83. *Sketches of glassware produced in Brierley crystal at the time of Queen Victoria's diamond jubilee in 1897.* (*Messrs Stevens and Williams, Ltd.*)

The coronation glass shown in Fig. 79, because of the elegance and great brilliancy of the medium, was at one time thought to have been manufactured on the Continent to the order of the English Court, but it is now fairly certain that it was of Newcastle origin, although probably engraved by a foreign hand.

George II died in 1760 and his grandson ascended the throne as George III. There are several glasses to commemorate the event. One is shown in Fig. 80, bearing the Royal Arms and the inscription 'G.III.R', the work being partly in diamond work. The air-twist stem, which had its beginnings in the previous reign, had by then been fully developed to apply to glasses made in three pieces—bowl, stem and foot.

Another style of glass celebrating the accession of George III is a goblet about eight inches high with an ogee bowl engraved with the inscription 'Success to George the III and the Queen 1761' within a circle. On the reverse is engraved a tulip and a carnation with a bird in flight. This glass has an opaque-twist stem and is in the collection of Arthur Churchill, Ltd.

Mugs celebrating the coronation of George III are also known. They are usually inscribed with 'Success to the King and Queen' and on the reverse are engraved a tulip and a carnation with a bird in flight.

Nearly sixty years elapsed before the historian in glass was again called upon to record a coronation. Owing to the mental condition of George III, his eldest son had been appointed Regent in 1811; in 1820 he succeeded to the throne. For some reason, glasses commemorating the coronation of George IV are rare.

The usual style of coronation glass at the time was a rummer, a robust and capacious goblet for general utility which became a fashionable shape towards the change of the century. The generous ovoid or bucket-shaped bowls of the rummers allowed the engraver plenty of scope, and they were chosen for commemorating all important events of the period. A typical inscription is 'G.IV.R July 1821'.

Barely a decade had passed before William, Duke of Clarence, and third son of George III, acceded to the throne as William IV, and there are many glasses extant in commemoration of the event.

The industrial revolution was then in full swing. The first application of steam power to glass-cutting had occurred at Brettle Lane, Stourbridge, in 1807, and in a remarkably short space of time power-driven cutting wheels became the standard practise at all the decorative establishments in the Stourbridge district. At the time of the coronation of William IV in 1831, glass manufacturers therefore had a wider choice of glassware with which to mark the occasion.

One of the most progressive manufacturers was Apsley Pellatt, who at the early age of thirty owned and operated the

84. *The coronation of Edward VII in 1902 was commemorated in glassware of all descriptions. A typical range in Royal Brierley Crystal is shown in the above sketches. The sugar bowl and goblet shown on the right of the illustration have a coin enclosed in the stem knop.* (*Messrs Stevens and Williams, Ltd.*)

85. *Glass articles made in 1937 for the coronation of Edward VIII. Owing to the Abdication, the glasses were never circulated. Those that are extant are today valuable pieces.* (*Messrs Stevens and Williams, Ltd.*)

86. *Goblet made to commemorate the coronation of George VI. Engraved in a medallion 'Coronation, May 12TH 1937'. On the right is a mug engraved with the Crown and the words 'The King, God bless him'.* (*Messrs Stevens and Williams, Ltd.*)

Falcon Glassworks in Southwark. He developed a process for forming cameo-incrustation in glass (*see* CRYSTALLO-CERAMIE) and another in which portraits were impressed in deep intaglio fashion on such articles as scent bottles. These articles were popular coronation mementoes. One is shown in Fig. 81, a scent bottle showing an excellent bust of William IV, with the impressed inscription 'W.IV.R.' Other popular glasses at the time of the coronation were rummers engraved with such emblems as the vine and grapes with the inscription 'King WM. 4th'. Some of these rummers, however, were but crudely engraved.

On the jubilee of Queen Victoria in 1887, many mementoes were struck in glass and other media. Glass dishes suitably decorated were extremely popular and incidentally very cheap. A typical example is shown in Fig. 82 of an amber dish impressed with the words 'Victoria Jubilee 1837-1887', with the crown and sceptre. Such articles were pressed in one piece by the process described in AMERICAN GLASS.

The diamond jubilee of Queen Victoria saw an even greater profusion of commemorative articles. The three sketches shown in Fig. 83 give an idea of the style of article and typical engraving. These articles are in Royal Brierley crystal and were made at the time by Stevens and Williams, Ltd. at their Brierley Hill Glassworks in Staffordshire. The company has a long tradition in glass-making, having been founded in 1776. The glass articles shown in Fig. 83 will now rank as collectors' pieces.

The coronation of King Edward VII in 1902 was also commemorated in glass-ware of all descriptions. A range of typical articles produced at the time by Stevens and Williams, Ltd. is shown in Fig. 84. The sugar bowl and the goblet on the right each have a coin enclosed in the knop of the stem.

Glasses were also made by Stevens and Williams, Ltd. for the coronation of Edward VIII, but, owing to his abdication, they were never in circulation. Those that are extant are therefore extremely valuable today. A group is shown in Fig. 85 of a goblet, a plaque and a two-handled bowl. They are wheel engraved with the royal coat-of-arms and the date 1937.

In the same year, 1937, glasses were made by Stevens and Williams, Ltd. for the coronation of George VI, two of which are shown in Fig. 86 of a goblet engraved in a medallion 'Coronation May 12th, 1937'. On the right of the figure is a mug engraved with the crown and 'The King, God bless him'.

Other articles made by the same company to commemorate

87. *Glasses made to commemorate the coronation of George VI. The two-handled oval flask has a coronation coin in the stopper, and is wheel engraved with the Royal Cipher and the date 1937.* (*Messrs Stevens and Williams, Ltd.*)

88. *Goblet made for the coronation of Queen Elizabeth II based on the Verzelini style popular in the reign of Queen Elizabeth I. The hollow knop contains a coin with the date 1953, the year of the coronation.* (*Messrs Stevens and Williams, Ltd.*) 89. *Glasses produced by Messrs James Powell and Sons* (*Whitefriars*), *Ltd., to mark the coronation of Elizabeth II. That on the right has a colour twist stem, in red, white and blue opaque glass. The glass on the left was the drawn stem style popular in the eighteenth century.*

90. *Range of coronation glassware produced by Messrs Stuart and Sons, Ltd., of Stourbridge. The centre specimen is a combined cigarette holder and ashtray. The goblet on the left has an air-twist stem.*

the coronation of George VI are shown in Fig. 87. The two-handled oval flask has a coronation coin in the stopper and is engraved with the royal cipher and the date 1937.

A great range of glass-ware was designed to celebrate the coronation of Elizabeth II. A very popular drinking vessel was the 'Queen's Goblet,' about six inches high, based on the style of the Verzelini glasses of the first Elizabethan era. The engraving was executed by the copper wheel and copies were numbered and signed. All pieces were conceived by craftsmen at the works of Stevens and Williams, Ltd., who have designed commemorative glasses for three generations. A typical example is shown in Fig. 88. The stem contains a hollow knop with a coin bearing the date 1953, the year of the coronation. Messrs James Powell & Sons (Whitefriars), Ltd., who have been producing drinking glasses for nearly three centuries, produced a coronation glass with colour-twist stem. Specimens are shown in Fig. 89; the drawn trumpet glass on the left was a popular style at the beginning of the eighteenth century; that on the right is a three-piece glass with colour-twist stem which has a patriotic touch in displaying the colours red, white and blue.

Another firm of Stourbridge glassmakers, Messrs Stuart and Sons, Ltd, produced some excellent glass-ware to mark the coronation of the present Queen. Three specimens are shown in Fig. 90 of a goblet with air-twist stem, a combined cigarette holder and ashtray, and a balloon brandy glass. All three specimens are engraved with the royal cipher and coronation date, June 2nd, 1953.

Not all the glass-ware commemorating the coronation took the form of drinking glasses. One Stourbridge firm supplied a wide range of ware engraved with the royal cipher and the date of the coronation, including powder bowls, vases, butter dishes and ash trays. Another company stated that they were prepared to supply any of sixty miscellaneous items of glass-ware, including cocktail shakers, engraved with suitable coronation emblems.

It was very obvious at the time of the coronation that there was a definite tendency to break from the traditional styles and forms of the past, and to favour designs more in harmony with the present age. It is, indeed, not inappropriate that modern styles should bear manifestations of the imprint of machinery, especially with articles which are more functional than decorative. As an example, a teapot stand was produced which had the advantages that, being made in heat resisting glass, it would withstand the hottest pot without fear of cracking, and because it conducted heat very slowly, would not mark highly polished tables or trays.

CRUET BOTTLES. Cruet bottles, because they are often silver mounted and therefore dated, provide invaluable evidence in tracing the development of early cutting. Strangely enough, however, silver-mounted cruet bottles are of little interest to the collector either of old silver or of antique glass. Because they have too little silver, the collector of silver articles does not consider them as falling within his province, and they have always been mistrusted by many glass collectors due to the absence of a pontil mark, regarded by some writers as the hall-mark of an eighteenth-century specimen of glass.

Cruet bottles were imported from Venice by John Greene, Ravenscroft made 'diamond cruets', which, of course, did not refer to the cut article but the style of decoration referred to as 'nipt diamond waies' (*see* NIPT DIAMOND WAIES), and 'crewit' bottles were advertised as early as 1710 at the 'flint glasshouse at White Fryars'.

The early form of mallet-shaped cruet bottle persisted up to the middle of the eighteenth century. Later, the shape changed to pyriform—that is, with a swelling body tapering towards the neck and foot—and still later this shape was provided with a pedestal foot.

During the last quarter of the eighteenth century, two new styles appeared—a cylindrical bottle with a tapering neck (1776) and, in response to the classical influence, an urn-shaped bottle mounted on a spreading foot (1778). These styles persisted up to the end of the century.

Most cruet bottles were, of course, decorated by cutting and some by engraving. (*See* CUT-GLASS and FRAUDS AND REPRODUCTIONS, Pontil Mark.)

Cruet bottles described above have very little value.

CRYSTALLO-CERAMIE. Crystallo-ceramie was the name given to a French process of glass incrustation. It consisted in enclosing the medallions and ornaments of pottery ware, metal or refractory material, in glass. The ornament itself, after preparation, was heated and, while hot, surrounded by a plastic mass of clear transparent glass.

The French method was perfected in this country by Apsley Pellatt who, at the early age of thirty, in 1821 established the Falcon Glasshouse in Southwark, London. He took out a patent for the making of glass incrustations, and his process was used for the decoration of numerous objects such as paper-weights, decanters, wineglasses, smelling bottles, girandoles and plaques. The portrait medallions, in particular, showed originality in style and finish, and although for some reason at one time they were out of fashion, today they are eagerly sought by collectors.

The process of making crystallo-ceramie would appear to have been first employed in Bohemia about 1750, being later developed by the French factories. A French glass-maker named Desprez, towards the end of the eighteenth century, was making cameos in a porcellaneous material and enclosing them in clear glass. A specimen of his work is preserved in the Sèvres Museum. In the beginning of the nineteenth century, patents were granted in France to various manufacturers, and a brisk sale of paperweights of this type was conducted in Paris, notably at the well-known establishment, *A l'Escalier de Cristal.* Specimens of this early work are preserved at the Museum at Hamburg.

Several French factories used incrustations as a form of decoration for paperweights, and many interesting specimens have changed hands recently. They are also extremely popular in America, where they are known as sulphides.

Incrustations were produced at the Baccarat factory, famous for its paperweights, in the middle of the nineteenth century. Specimens are known with cameos of Queen Victoria, the Tsar Nicholas I, and Pope Pius IX, which are quite common.

Those of Queen Victoria show a profile of the Queen's head in dexter, usually with concentric rings of millefiori florets in white, green and red, white and green, and red, white and blue canes. The ground is of clear glass. Incrustations of this description have often changed hands over the £50 mark.

Another favourite subject of Baccarat incrustation is a standing figure of Joan of Arc within oak and laurel leaves. These incrustations have a ruby ground and are faceted. Mythological figures were sometimes chosen as subjects. Another group have sporting scenes with a dog as a central subject, a man with a gun, and trees in the background. Prices of such incrustations usually fall between £30 and £40.

Incrustations were also produced by the Clichy factory much on the same lines as those of Baccarat, but they were confined to busts and portraits. Favourite subjects were again Queen Victoria, Pope Pius IX, and specimens are sometimes found with Napoleon and Frederick VII of Denmark.

The grounds of the Clichy incrustations are blue, turquoise, crimson or purple. Occasionally one with a green glass ground changes hands, such, for example, as those with an incrustation of the French poet, Alfred de Musset.

Incrustations, or sulphides as they are known in the United States, were also made there during the middle of the nineteenth century. A rare one is of General Zachary Taylor, in uniform. He was nominated by the Whig Party of America and elected President of the United States in 1848, but died in Washington sixteen months after entering office. The cameo is of excellent workmanship, with the name 'Taylor' inscribed on the back.

Incrustations are produced today at the Baccarat factory in France. They include portraits of George Washington, Thomas Jefferson, Abraham Lincoln, Robert E. Lee, Dwight D. Eisenhower, Queen Elizabeth II and Sir Winston Churchill, and are today collectors' pieces.

Specimens of incrustations from the French factories of Baccarat and Clichy have changed hands within recent years at prices between £20 and £50. Those of Queen Victoria and Napoleon fetch the best prices. Many specimens of Apsley Pellatt's work have sold recently at prices ranging from £11 to £26. These articles include vases, plaques, paperweights and scent bottles.

CULLET. The term 'cullet' is used in the trade to refer to broken glass of all descriptions. It is probably derived from the French *collet.* A certain amount of glass is always broken during manufacture, accumulated as waste, or rejected during final inspection because of some defect. This cullet is collected, cleaned and used again as an ingredient of the batch (*see* BATCH) charged to the melting furnace. It can be readily understood that cullet is a valuable material. For example, in a lead crystal batch, red lead and potash are extremely expensive materials. In addition there is the saving of fuel charges if cullet is used, as cullet always melts more easily than batch.

The term cullet was first used in the eighteenth century when it became an important consideration of the glass-maker. In 1745, Parliament passed legislation to impose a tax of one penny per pound on the materials used in the making of flint glass. This act, known as the Glass Excise Act, was to prove a great burden to English glass-makers for a full century. The Act, however, allowed the glass-maker a certain amount of cullet free of duty which he could re-melt, and many advertisements appeared after 1745 offering for broken glass articles up to one-third their original price by weight.

On the other hand, cullet had always been a valuable material, for there is evidence that even as early as 1697 cullet was collected and sold to the glass-maker. For example, the following note appears in *Tracts Relating to Trade* (Brit. Mus., 816, M 12/136): 'Many hundreds of poor families keep themselves from the parish by picking up broken glass of all sorts to sell to the Maker.'

CUT-GLASS. Decorating glass by cutting into its surface has been known from early times. Specimens of cutting survive today in various museums from the first century B.C. These vessels were prepared from multi-coloured sections of glass, heated and moulded into various shapes such as shallow bowls and trays, and afterwards cut and polished on the inside by stone wheels.

It was rock crystal, no doubt, that gave the inspiration to the glass-maker for a clear transparent glass, but it was not until the first century A.D. that anything like success attended his efforts. Vessels from this new material, both plain and decorated, soon became fashionable. Pliny (A.D. 23-78) in his books on Natural History (Pliny, *Natural History*, XXXVII, 28) has the following passage: 'It is marvellous how closely glass-wares have come to resemble those of rock crystal, but it is monstrous that they should have increased their prices without any drop in the price of rock crystal ware.'

The Romans recognised two distinct methods of decoration by cutting, both described by Pliny; they were work produced on a wheel and that of a purely sculptural nature. The first was mechanical work executed by a rotating cutting wheel, or lathe, such as was used by the lapidary craftsmen for the cutting of semi-precious stones and rock crystal. Decorative effects on the new glass medium were in shallow style, the object being to disclose and even to enhance its brilliance without in any way impairing the original contours of beauty

91. *Roman cup found at Barnwell, Cambridge, cut in interlacing grooves, second century A.D.* (*British Museum*)

92. *Hedwig glass of uncertain origin, probably Egyptian work of the eleventh or twelfth centuries. (Rijks Museum, Amsterdam)*

of outline given by the glass-maker at the furnace. The designs were built up of oval depressions and grooves. An example of this work, consisting of interlacing grooves, is shown in Fig. 91. This is a Roman cup five-and-three-eighth inches in height, probably second century A.D. It was found at Barnwell, Cambridge, and is now in the British Museum.

The second method used by the Romans, referred to by Pliny, called for a more advanced technique which might be described today as sculpturing. Simple hand tools were employed requiring the manipulation of a skilled artist. The most perfect and expressive work of this nature is without doubt the Portland Vase (Fig. 220), a two-handled urn found near Rome in 1582, dating from the first century A.D. It is constructed from two layers of glass, the under layer being of a very dark blue transparent glass, and the outer casing, or overlay, of thick white opal. The figure subjects were carved from the opal layer, and stand out in bold relief against the darker background. The almost incredible delicacy and refinement of the sculptured work make it a unique example of the glass-worker's art. This specimen is also in the British Museum.

Next in the chronological sequence to the Roman cut-glass would appear to be Islamic glass of the ninth and tenth centuries found some years ago by German archaeologists during excavations at Samarra, Iraq. Bottles, probably intended for perfume, bowls and other shapes, were cut in representation of flowers and arabesque foliage in a manner which displayed profound knowledge of the art of decorating glass by cutting. Both colourless glass, and glass cased with coloured layers, were used by the Islamic craftsmen.

A famous group of cut-glasses of uncertain origin are known as the Hedwig glasses, after a specimen, preserved in the Museum of Silesian Antiquities at Breslau, said by tradition to have been dedicated to St Hedwig, wife of a Silesian Prince, and Patroness of Silesia and Poland, who died in 1243. The Hedwig glasses, seven in number, are cylindrical cups between three and five inches in height, of thick yellowish green or brownish tinted glass, deeply incised by the wheel in cameo style in representation of animal forms. The specimen shown in Fig. 92 is in the Rijks Museum, Amsterdam, and is typical of the group; it is carved with two lions and an eagle. An inscription under the foot reads *Als dies Glas war alt tausent Jahr Es Pfalzgraf Ludwig Philipsen verehret war, 1643.* (This glass was presented to Count Palatine Ludwig Philipsen when it was one thousand years old, 1643.)

The art of cutting glass was lost for many centuries, and it was not until the beginning of the seventeenth century that a revival occurred at Prague and Nuremburg. The carving of semi-precious stones and rock crystal had been practised by Italian and German lapidary craftsmen from the fifteenth century, when the art was introduced into Italy after the taking of Constantinople by the Turks in 1453, and the transition to employing glass as a medium was a natural one. The honour of rediscovering the process fell to Caspar Lehmann of Prague, and to mark his accomplishment, he was granted special privileges by the Emperor Rudolf II and was appointed glass-cutter to his Court.

The art of glass-cutting developed very rapidly in Germany during the seventeenth and eighteenth centuries, the most flourishing period being from 1685 to the middle of the eighteenth century. High prices were paid for the finer specimens of the work. Dr R. Pococke (*Travels Through England*, Camden Society, 1888, Vol. VI, p. 231), Bishop of Meath, who travelled in Germany in 1736, stated that £100 to £150 were paid for some of the finely cut specimens, a handsome sum in those early days. The specimen shown in Fig. 93 is typical of the period. It is a beaker and cover engraved on the wheel in Bacchanalian scenes by Godfried Spiller, of Potsdam, one of the most talented artists of the time.

Little is known of the early attempts at the cutting of glass in the British Isles. Early specimens are, unfortunately, all too rare, but knowledge of them can be gained from trade notices, which indicate that little or no cutting, in a decorative sense, was attempted before the beginning of the eighteenth century. As early as 1678 attention was being paid to methods of cutting glass, but they referred more to bevelling sheets of glass than to decorative cutting.

The first notice referring to the actual cut-glass article did not appear until the turn of the century, in the *London Gazette*, 1st October, 1709: 'There is lately brought over a great parcel of very fine German Cut and Carved Glasses, viz. Jellies, Wine and Water Tumblers, Beer and Wine Glasses with Covers, and divers other sorts. The like hath not been exposed to public sale before.'

From records it would appear that cutting began to develop in this country during the ten years that followed, for a notice appeared in the *Whitehall Evening Post* and also in the *Weekly Journal* of 27th October, 1719, stating: 'John Akerman, at the Rose and Crown, Cornhill, continues to sell all sorts of tea, chinaware, plain and diamond cut flint glasses.' (*See* AKERMAN, JOHN.)

John Akerman was a member of the Glass Sellers' Company at that time and, without doubt, an important one. The Glass Sellers' Company was an influential body, its members including both manufacturers and merchants, who exercised rigid control over the industry in all its phases. Between the years 1740 and 1748 John Akerman held the mastership of the Company, the first glass-cutter to attain that honour. He was not a practical glass-cutter himself, but it is known that he employed at least one German cutter, who probably trained English apprentices.

London at that time was the most important glass-making centre in the country. At the turn of the seventeenth century there were twenty-four glasshouses in operation in London, of which nine were making the new flint glass to Ravenscroft's formula. Stourbridge was a close challenger to London, having seventeen glasshouses, but with only five producing flint. At the time of the accession of George I, in 1714, therefore, London would have set the fashion in form and decoration, and there is every indication that it continued to do so throughout the eighteenth century.

Notices appeared during the first half of the century showing that cutting was increasing in popularity. A variety of cut ware

93. *Beaker and cover with wheel engraving of Bacchanalian scenes by Gottfried Spiller of Potsdam.* circa *1700.* (*By courtesy of the Victoria and Albert Museum*)

94. *Glass-cutter smoothing an outlined pattern by means of rotating sandstone wheel.*

was advertised such as 'crystal cut lustres' (obviously referring to chandeliers), 'sweetmeat glasses', 'diamond-cut flint glasses', 'scalloped dessert glasses', 'diamond-cut candlesticks', 'plates', 'dishes', 'bowls', 'basons', and 'cups and saucers'.

It is difficult now to hazard a guess as to how this rapid development would have proceeded, for an event occurred in 1745 which was to have far-reaching effects on the industry as a whole, and which impeded its progress for a full century. This was the Glass Excise Act of 1745, when Parliament, in order to raise funds for the professional wars then being waged on the Continent, imposed a tax of one penny per pound by weight of raw materials used in the making of glass.

The tax had immediate repercussions. Drastic changes were necessary in the size and shape of vessels, and the glass-maker, in an endeavour to conserve his material, tried to make two articles from the amount of glass previously used for one. Other taxes, which followed later in the century, served even more to hamper the development of a promising native industry.

The Glass Excise Act had other repercussions. It not only delayed the development of cut-glass, but also greatly influenced the early style of cutting. The restriction of material used caused the vessels to be made much lighter. If they were capable of being cut at all, it was impossible to cut them heavily except where the glass was thick, such as on the stems of drinking glasses. The act had, therefore, a manifold effect. It delayed the free development of cutting and also had the effect of limiting the amount of cutting applied to an article, and finally of restricting such cutting to shallow styles of which flutes and hollow motifs are typical examples.

The Cutting Process. Since the advent of applied decoration to glass in this country, the most popular process has been the ancient one of cutting, in which revolving wheels are employed to grind away the surface of the glass. Annular incisions, cut into the glass surface, act as prisms with the opposite surface and reflect and refract the rays of light instead of allowing them to pass directly through it. The incisions increase the play of light and so enhance the animation and 'life' of the glass itself.

There are four distinct operations in cutting a glass vessel by this process—marking, roughing, smoothing and polishing. In the first operation, the pattern or design to be followed by the cutter is painted or drawn on the glass surface, usually with a mixture of red lead and turpentine. Next, the craftsman roughs out the pattern by means of a revolving, power-driven wheel of iron, about eighteen inches in diameter, the edge of which is flat, convex or V-shaped, according to the type of cut required. The wheel is kept coated with fine, wet sand falling upon it in a stream from a hopper suspended over the wheel. The craftsman presses the vessel against the edge of the revolving wheel, which cuts into its surface by the abrasive action of the wet sand; by varying the position of the glass, he can direct the cuts at will following the pattern painted on the glass surface.

The cuts, however, have by no means a finished appearance. The abraded surface is coarse and dull, and the cuts are shorter and shallower than required in the completed design. The roughed outline has, therefore, to be smoothed; this is accomplished by grinding on a wheel of sandstone, the edge of which is dressed flat, rounded or V-shaped, corresponding with the rough cut already made during the first operation. The surface of this stone is wetted by a trickle of water, and its smooth cutting action quickly removes the rough marks left on the glass surface by the sand. A craftsman at work on such a wheel is shown in Fig. 94.

The pattern is completed on stones of this nature, which vary in diameter from two inches to as many feet according to the pattern being followed; some of the lighter cuts are added at this stage without previous roughing. It is in the smoothing operation that the skill of the craftsman is displayed. He needs no aid other than a sure hand and a keen eye; nevertheless, designs can be cut with almost geometrical accuracy.

The final operation of polishing the dull, matt surface left by the sandstone may be accomplished by one of two methods, mechanical or chemical. In the mechanical method, polishing is carried out by means of wooden wheels and fine abrasives such as putty powder; a fine lustre is often finally applied by felt wheels and rouge. In the chemical process, which has been developed during the present century, the article is dipped for a few seconds into a mixture of hydrofluoric and sulphuric acids. The acid attacks the entire surface of the glass, removing a very thin layer from it. The result is a uniform, highly lustrous surface. Needless to say, because of the saving in time and the excellent finish obtained, the chemical process has almost completely superseded the older method.

In some cutting establishments, the roughing and smoothing processes have been combined by the use of composition wheels, which have a rapid but smooth cutting action. As in all

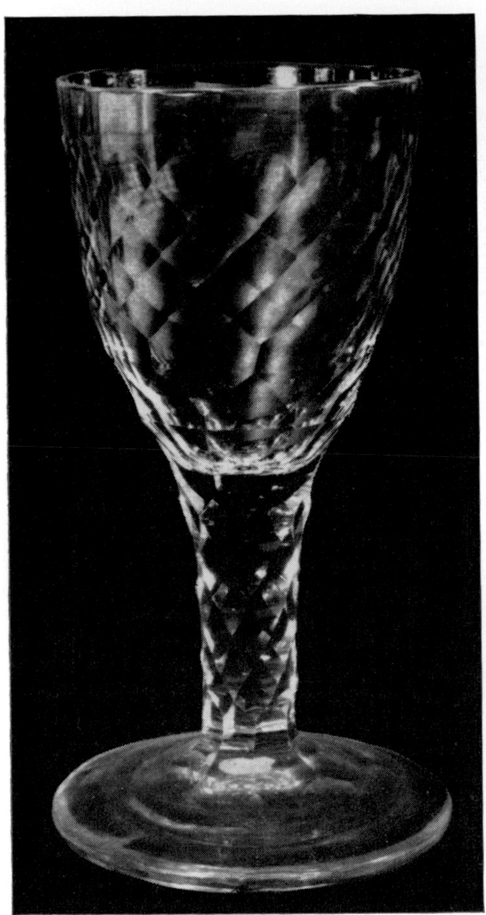

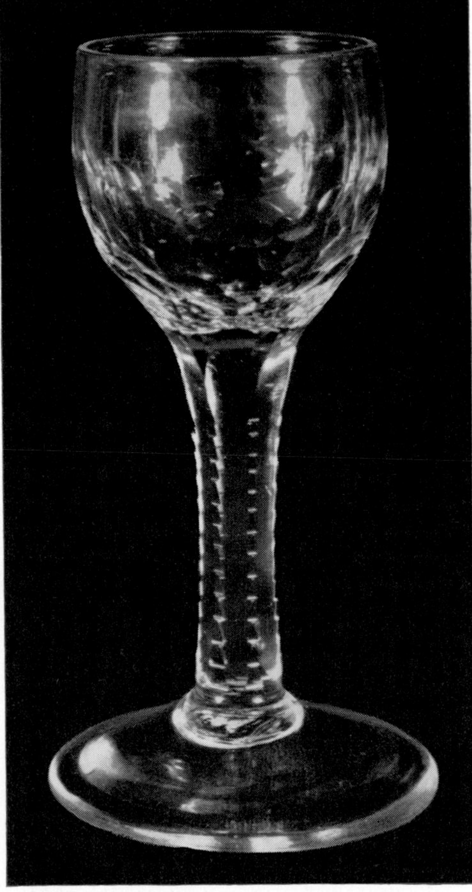

95. *Wineglass cut in shallow diamond fashion on both bowl and stem.* 96. *Wineglass with flute cresting to the base of the bowl, the stem cut in shallow diamonds.* 97. *Wineglass with fluted stem embellished by notching.*

or 'jewel'. 99. *Sugar bowl probably Waterford, the rim cut with shallow shell of strawberry diamond pattern.* 100. *Perfume bottle with alternate panel motif.*

the use of these shallow diamonds is shown in Fig. 95, of a wineglass with both bowl and stem cut in diamond pattern.

A style which appeared early in the development of cutting was the hollow flute. It was a common form of decoration on the bowls of eighteenth-century wine glasses, usually in the form of cresting at the base of the bowl. A specimen is shown in Fig. 96, with the stem cut in shallow diamonds and the bowl with flute cresting at the base.

Fluting was employed as decoration on the stems of wine-glasses during the second half of the eighteenth century. It was the simplest and easiest form of cut decoration for this part of the glass, but because of its plain appearance, it was sometimes enhanced by notching along the flutes, such as is shown in Fig. 97.

Hollow flutes were also a popular form of decoration during the Irish period and in England during the nineteenth century; the stems of sherry and port glasses were often embellished by simple fluting.

The star was an obvious choice as a motif in early cutting. Its shape lent itself to wheel technique, it was emblematic, and because it did not necessarily have to be part of a comprehensive pattern or design, it could be employed alone. Early examples are shown in Fig. 152 (IRISH GLASS), in which stars in shallow style are cut on the barrels of Waterford decanters.

The star was one of the most popular motifs employed by the English and Irish cutters. It was part of many patterns during the second half of the eighteenth century, it was also a favourite motif during the nineteenth century, and today it is almost invariably chosen as the decorative feature on the base of a cut vessel, a practice which began, mainly on cruet bottles (*see* CRUET BOTTLES), during the last quarter of the eighteenth century. It is also employed as a motif in many designs.

Its earliest form was six-pointed, but more ambitious attempts were soon made, and twenty-four pointed stars became common. As the technique of cutting developed, and

101. *Decanter, early nineteenth century, showing relief diamonds on the body and prismatic cutting on the neck and shoulder.*

where the requisite thickness of glass was available, stars were modified into more elaborate forms. A favourite pattern, for example, was the *Brunswick Star*, often referred to in the trade as a *Jewel.* A perfume bottle with this emblem is shown in Fig. 98. The jewel was based on the radiating star, a sixteen-pointed form being used as a base in the example shown. Deep cutting resulted in even more elegant and complicated forms.

The fan is used as a component of many patterns; for example, it forms the basis of the fan escallop or shell border. An example is shown in Fig. 99 of a sugar bowl, probably Waterford, with shell border and a variation of the strawberry diamond pattern.

In cutting the design, the rim of the article is 'scalloped'—that is, it is cut into the curved shape found on the upper half of a scallop shell. Lady Baillie used the term 'scalloped' as early as 1722 (*see* BAILLIE, LADY GRISELL) and it has remained an unaltered description during two centuries of cutting. A fan is then cut radiating to the scalloped edge, and finally the extremity of each mitre is notched. The resemblance to the natural shell is maintained, in that the fan has usually the same number of mitres in its formation as the shell has flutes.

There is no doubt that the most prolific of all the eighteenth-

century moti
wheel with a
parallel mitre
cut edges to t
second series
crossed, a rai
apex was for

It will be n
hollow diam
edge. The rel
style about t
on certain lu
sweetmeat g
incised form

Relief dia
For example
Waterford.
small plain s
then embelli
shown in Fi
strawberry p

A variatio
In this patte
instead of si
structure of

Hobnail
always appl
that for th
interlacing
—but in the
lished with
is no evide
cutting; ne
became pop
but it is a p
nental man

There is
erroneously
diagonal m
of single m
cuts interse
century sce

This patt
especially
easy surface
its 'tantalu
exception
mens, whic
remarkable
of the craft

The cut
introduced
eighteenth
parallel gr
decanter s
Figs. 159 a

The pris
where it w
the small r
of the neck

only possible motif that could be used, and, indeed, it is most probable that it was specially devised for the embellishments of such parts. The prism had a most effective variation in the alternate prism, which was used either horizontally or vertically. An example of the latter style is shown in Fig. 156 (IRISH GLASS).

The art of cutting cannot be left without reference to the most difficult of all types of cut motifs—the curved pattern. So far, the only patterns that have been considered are those composed of straight lines. Such motifs are executed when the article is held firmly in line with the edge of the wheel. If the article, while being cut, is deflected out of line with the edge of the wheel, however, a cut with a curved outline will be the result. Obviously, this is a much more difficult technique than the more usual straight line cutting, and is one that is attempted only by highly experienced craftsmen.

Irish manufacturers, particularly those at Waterford specialised in curved motifs. For example, the Waterford decanters shown in Fig. 152 (IRISH GLASS) and the perfume bottle shown in Fig. 98 all show curved motifs.

Faults in Workmanship. When the method of cutting a design on glass is considered, it can readily be appreciated that faults in workmanship are likely to occur. The craftsman supports the article he is cutting in his hands, and may steady his movements by resting his elbows on the bench, but no other aid is provided; his work is therefore freehand. Nevertheless, a complicated pattern can be cut with remarkable precision and accuracy.

The quality of cutting depends on the skill and conscientiousness of the craftsman; hurried and careless workmanship can sometimes be detected on close examination of some specimens. Adjacent mitre cuts may be of unequal value, one cut may be deeper or broader than another, or they may be of varying lengths; moreover, they may not be exactly parallel.

102. *A cut star twice magnified showing such imperfections as branches of unequal length and failing to meet in the middle.*

Stars may have branches of unequal length, or the points may fail to meet in the centre. An example of a star, twice magnified, showing such imperfections, may be seen in Fig. 102. Cuts intended to meet at a point often overlap. Faults of this nature can be observed on many of the early specimens produced long before cutting had advanced to the stage of a highly developed craft, and before the advantages of the power driven cutting wheel were available. Such faults are excusable and, indeed, confer the vitality of handwork on the earlier specimens. When such faults are found on vessels produced after 1830, however, the advent of the mechanical age, they can be regarded only as the outcome of carelessness or lack of skill.

DAGNIA, FAMILY OF (*c.* 1648).
See NEWCASTLE GLASSES.

DECANTERS. The term to 'decant' originally meant the pouring of a liquor from a vessel, such as a bottle or a jar, into a drinking glass. When the process of 'binning' wine was introduced, however, about the middle of the eighteenth century, the meaning of the term changed and applied to the pouring of the wine into a vessel known as a decanter, although strictly speaking the original version is still correct (W. A. Thorpe, *Connoisseur*, Vol. LXXXIII, pp. 196-271).

The early decanter, in colourless glass, was a more suitable table version of the common dark-brown or green bottle, but in no way superseded it. They existed side by side, from the middle of the eighteenth century onwards. The early eighteenth-century decanters were of the current bottle shape (*see* BOTTLES) and those that have survived from the second quarter of the eighteenth century have a projecting rim at the top for tying on a cork with string, similar to the ordinary bottle. Stoppers, however, were introduced about the middle of the century.

From 1755 decanters began to be decorated by engraved or enamelled labels. Thus the *Norwich Mercury* advertised, 26th December, 1755: 'New fashioned Decanters with inscriptions engraven upon them, viz, Port, Claret, Mountain, etc., etc., decorated with vine leaves, Grapes, etc.'

The Beilby family applied enamel decoration to the decanters of the period and an example of their work is shown in Fig. 113 (*see* ENAMELLED GLASS). This decanter also carries the spire stopper cut with the shallow diamond motif, then popular on decanters.

The barrel-shaped decanter followed a little later, its first mention being by Christopher Haedy, who advertised in *The Bath Chronicle*, 21st December, 1775: 'Curious barrel-shaped decanters cut on an entirely new pattern.' The new shape at once became popular and formed the standard shape of the Anglo-Irish period (*see* IRISH GLASS). Waterford and Cork manufacturers adopted it and cut and engraved its symmetrical curves with a variety of patterns.

Square decanters made their appearance in the second half of the century. They were known as 'squares' and retained their popularity into the last century. The 'tantalus', with its sets of three or four square decanters, could be seen on nearly every Victorian sideboard. For decanter stoppers, *see* STOPPERS.

Decanters can be purchased at fairly low prices up to £5, provided there is nothing special about them. On the other hand, a decanter from the Ravenscroft period fetched £55 and a Lynn decanter horizontally grooved realised £22 10s. Much the same can be said of the square decanters, which can be purchased between £1 and £2 when there is nothing special about them. On the other hand, a square decanter by Apsley Pellatt, with a crystallo-ceramie bust of George IV as a Roman Emperor, fetched £62 a few years ago.

Irish decanters are dealt with in IRISH GLASS.

DECOLOURISING OF GLASS. Crystal glass and good commercial 'white' flint glass should appear perfectly colourless when viewed through a thin section. Upon examination through a thicker section, however, such as through the length of a bottle instead of through its sides, a distinct tinge of colour will be discernible. Window glass, when viewed in the ordinary way, is a good example of what appears to be a colourless glass. If examined in section, however, the greenish-blue tint typical of all window glass is at once apparent. Even optical glass, prepared with extreme care and attention to detail, is not entirely colourless when viewed in comparatively large pieces. No glass is perfectly colourless, but when all conditions are under strict control, glass can be produced which for all practical purposes appears colourless when fashioned into articles of no considerable thickness.

The impurity almost wholly responsible for discolouring glass is iron, and its intense colouring action is noted under MATERIALS USED IN GLASS-MAKING and COLOURED GLASS. Practically all the materials which the glass-maker handles during the production of glass contain iron in varying amounts. The glasshouse pots used for melting crystal glass, and the fireclay linings of the larger commercial furnaces, are not entirely free from this impurity. In addition, mixing, conveying and general handling of the raw materials introduce a considerable amount of iron into the finished glass.

It is not surprising, therefore, that even under the most carefully controlled conditions, sufficient iron finds its way into the glass to impart to it a very definite green tint. The art of producing colourless glass depends upon the control of this iron; first, by reducing the amount by careful selection of the raw materials, secondly, care in handling, and finally, in neutralising chromatically the tint due to the residual iron by the addition to the glass of certain metallic oxides. These oxides are known as decolourisers, their function being to produce an absorption of the light rays penetrating the glass which the impurity present transmits. For example, iron is present in glass as a mixture of certain silicates which impart a greenish tinge to the glass. Actually, these silicates absorb some of the light penetrating the glass, mainly at the red end of the spectrum, while certain of the blue and yellow light rays are transmitted which reach the eye and cause the glass to appear green.

The action of the decolouriser is exactly the reverse. If it were present in the glass alone—that is, if the iron compounds were absent—an absorption of light would occur mainly between the blue and yellow portions of the spectrum, while light at the red end of the spectrum would be transmitted. It is apparent, therefore, that the iron compounds permit the transmission of the yellow and blue light rays while the decolouriser allows transmission of light over the remainder of the spectrum. Under these conditions, the total light transmitted is balanced along the entire spectrum, no particular light ray being in preponderance, with the result that only white light is transmitted, and the glass appears colourless. In other words, when the iron and the decolouriser are both present in the glass in balanced quantities, each absorbs light which the other transmits.

On the other hand, if insufficient decolouriser is added, the glass will still have a faint green tint, whereas a slight excess of decolouriser will result in a pinkish tint. Decolourising, therefore, is a process of pure chromatic neutralisation and one requiring very careful regulation.

In the process, however, a certain quantity of light has been absorbed by the glass, so that the total light transmitted has been diminished. With thicknesses up to half an inch, this loss of light may be as much as one-fifth of the total light falling on the glass. Under these conditions, although the glass may appear quite colourless in thin pieces, a heavy thick vessel will have a dull grey appearance. The effect is increased when the iron present in the glass is high; the amount of the decolourising material required will necessarily be greater, and a corresponding larger quantity of total light will be absorbed, resulting in a dull glass of a definite grey colour. Should the process of adding iron and decolouriser be continued, the glass will eventually become quite black—that is, no light at all will penetrate through it. This fact is made use of in the manufacture of dark-coloured beer and wine bottles for which impure sands containing a high proportion of iron are used. Manganese, a decolouriser normally producing a purple tint, is added to produce all shades from amber to rich dark brown and almost to black.

The principle of decolourising glass was known to the Roman glass-makers. Pliny, writing in the first century A.D. (*Nat. Hist.*, Lib. XXXVI, c 26), stated that 'magnes lapis' was added to the glass. This was most probably manganese, although it is generally held to mean loadstone, an iron ore. Pyrolusite, the ore of manganese, greatly resembles loadstone. From an examination of specimens of colourless glass from Roman times, it is evident that the art of decolourising had already been discovered in the time of Pliny.

Manganese dioxide, usually in the form of finely ground pyrolusite, was also the decolouriser used in the seventeenth century for decolourising Ravenscroft's glass-of-lead; it has remained the principle decolouriser for lead glasses until today.

DESSERT GLASSES.
See SWEETMEAT GLASSES.

DIAMOND ENGRAVING.
See ENGRAVING.

DICE GLASSES. It is doubtful whether dice glasses were ever popular in this country. No references to them appear in any of the seventeenth- or eighteenth-century notices. They were, however, known on the Continent.

The Germanisches Museum at Nuremberg has fluted Bohemian tumblers, three-and-a-half inches in height, which contain three ivory dice in the bottom. It is assumed that the 'call' for drinks was decided by the throw of the dice.

ᴅᴇs ᴏʀ Gʟᴀss Dᴏᴍᴇs.

N, JAMES (*c.* 1770). James Donovan was an nter who, with his son, worked in Dublin between 770 and 1829. Although they owned a glasshouse, decorated china and pottery, some specimens of signed 'Donovan, Irish manufacture'. No signed of glass, however, have so far come to light.

NOBS.
ᴠᴇʟ Pᴏsᴛs.

TOPS OR BOTTLE-GREEN PAPER-S. Popular today are the door-stops or bottle-rweights enclosing a representation of a plant grow-pot. The pale green leaves and flowers are covered of tiny bubbles, which, under the action of reflected he motif a silvery, gossamer-like appearance. They at Stourbridge and most other glass-making centres. imens of door-stops weigh several pounds, but are usually referred to as paperweights.

le-green door-stops were easily manufactured. The ites were clear green glass, such as was customarily ttle-making a century ago, and a few simple tools. lass was gathered and worked into the shape of an vas sprinkled in the required design on the marver, t glass pressed upon it. A second layer of glass was hered over the whole so that it was completely he action of the hot glass on the chalk caused f gas, which was entrapped in the mass as a film of bubbles.

men shown in Fig. 103 illustrates how a door-stop p in successive layers. There is a clear line of de-etween the first gathering of glass, which carries notif, and the second gathering, which covers it.

reen door-stop or paperweight showing how the uilt up in successive layers of glass. The motif represents a plant growing in a pot.

104. *Bottle-green door-stop in the form of fountain with sparkling cascades of water falling on all sides.*

Often the flowers were built up in tiers, one growing from the centre of another, or in the form of fountains which stream up from the base, falling in sparkling cascades on all sides, such as the specimen in Fig. 104. Others are in the form of bubbles rising to the surface from the mysterious depths of a pool. There were many such motifs employed.

As green weights of the type described above were easy to make, and were formed from the cheapest glass, most bottle factories throughout the country produced them up to comparatively recent times. It was not until hand processes of producing bottles were finally superseded by automatic ones that their manufacture ceased. It is, therefore, extremely difficult to distinguish the early specimens from those of later manufacture; nor is it possible, as some writers claim, to decide from its colour where a bottle-green weight was made.

These weights are ovoid in shape, with a flat base, and without exception have a pontil mark. The majority of specimens are between three and six inches in height.

Larger bottle green weights, usually referred to as door-stops, may be up to six pounds in weight; the smaller ones, usually described as paperweights, may be as small as an egg. The larger variety are usually decorated with bubbles and representations of plants in the manner described, but some are found with bubbles alone.

In some cases the larger door-stops had bubbles in pyriform shape with a silvery thread at the narrow end. These bubbles were formed by denting the soft glass with a sharp tool such as a large nail, to which a thin piece of wire was attached. The tool with its attachment was cooled, plunged into the glass, and sharply withdrawn. The layer of glass subsequently gathered over the indentation caused a pear-shaped bubble to form which tapered down to mere thread thickness. A number of these bubbles in a large door-stop are very effective, giving the appearance of miniature balloons floating in space.

An occasional paperweight comes to light with the words 'J. Kilner, Wakefield' impressed upon the base.

Door-stops or bottle-green paperweights naturally vary in price with size; the average size between three and four inches fetch about £2 each.

DOUBLE FLINT GLASS.
See SINGLE FLINT GLASSES.

DRAM GLASSES.
See CORDIAL GLASSES; FIRING GLASSES.

DUTCH GLASS. Many writers prefer to classify glass made in the countries now known as Holland, Belgium and the Flanders of France, as glass from the Low Countries or of the Netherlands. There was, however, such keen competition between those countries during the seventeenth and eighteenth centuries, and, indeed, such cultural differences, that there exist sharp lines of demarcation both in style and in decorative techniques. It is on this account that they should be considered separately and not as a composite group.

Dutch glass, for example, began to break away from the Venetian influence much about the same time as in this country—that is, towards the end of the seventeenth century—and for a time there existed a similarity of style between the two countries.

Early in the eighteenth century, English glass began to be imported into Holland, and this fact, coupled with the effect of the Treaty of Utrecht in 1713 which allowed the glass-makers from Central Europe to trade westwards, brought about a rapid decline in the Dutch glass-making industry.

Dutch glass produced in Holland during the eighteenth century was not distinctive. It followed English styles in the lightly knopped glasses, the air-twist and enamel-twist styles, but the potash-lime metal lacked the distinction of the glass-of-lead of the contemporary English productions. Because of this, no real Dutch style emerged apart from one or two utility types of which very few specimens have survived.

If, however, because of prevailing conditions, the Dutch glass-makers did not excel in the production of glass itself, they were supreme in the technique of engraving it. Indeed, glass vessels which, without applied decoration, would have been of no great account, became, by virtue of the engraving upon them, glasses of high artistic merit, many of which are today of great historial importance and which grace the cabinets of museums and connoisseurs alike.

The decoration of Dutch glass may be placed in three distinct categories. For a full century, from the last quarter of the sixteenth century and up to 1690 at least, engraving with the diamond point or with a steel gravure became a fashionable pastime, and because in the main it was practised by amateurs cultured in the arts, it had considerable artistic merit.

Towards the end of the seventeenth century and until the middle of the eighteenth century, diamond engrav moded by engraving with the copper wheel after th style. This was largely due to the introduction intc the English glass-of-lead, which quickly began to harder lime glass of the Continent. The wheel eng the soft nature of glass-of-lead most suitable for wheel, and because of the superior refractive p English metal, a more suitable medium to give e their artistic talents.

The third category into which Dutch engravi style of stippling, also with the diamond point, wh the middle of the eighteenth century and which s into the nineteenth century. As in the earlier style point work, it was taken up by a number of taler artists and reached a high standard of perfection

Stippling is the method of formulating the de glass surface with a countless number of tiny do the point of a diamond or hardened steel into the aid of a small hammer. Although the method was used by Anna Roemers Visscher (1583-1651) as e it did not become a popular style of diamond-poi the middle of the eighteenth century.

Anna Roemers Visscher was the first woman a of whom there is a definite record, and in some ey as the finest exponent of the so-called 'calligra (E. B. Haynes, *Glass Through the Ages*, 1948, p. the daughter of a wealthy merchant of Amsterd both a gifted scholar and poet. Her favourite the German beaker in thin green metal, but tall f and chalices with covers were also chosen for dec in naturalistic flowers, fruit and insects.

Anna Roemers Visscher possessed a complete n use of the diamond on glass. Although of the gre transparency, her work was expressive and exec utmost charm. It was mostly in linear style, but also employed in some specimens in combinatior

Fortunately, she signed some of her work, whi style easily recognisable. There are two specime in the Rijks Museum at Amsterdam. One is a r 1621, engraved with flowers and a dragonfly, exquisite taste; a second signed specimen dated 16 with fruit and insects, is executed in both dot sti as engraving with the diamond in linear style, popular in the eighteenth century.

There is a third signed specimen in the Muse und Gewerbe at Hamburg, dated 1642, with calli motto in Dutch, Latin and Greek. The Victori Museum possesses a specimen of a roemer, *cir* unsigned calligraphy, which because of the chara of Anna Roemers Visscher, has sometimes been as

Maria Tesselschade Roemers Visscher (1 younger sister of the famous artist, and Ann Schurman (1607-1678), a younger contemporary same style. Among the male members of th Willem Jacobsz van Heemskerk (1613-1692) merchant, poet and dramatist, also engraved a work, chiefly bottles, between 1648 and 169 specimens are in the Buckley Collection at the Albert Museum. One, bearing a couplet in prai signed 'Willem van Heemskerk in Leijden, 1674

Dutch engraving of this period is generally marked by its light transparent nature; heaviness of any sort was avoided and hatch work used only for the high-lights of the design. Later, however, the style changed, due no doubt to the influence of wheel engraving, which had attained great popularity in Bohemia and Silesia. Dutch engravers endeavoured to imitate, with the diamond, the light and shade so effectively produced by the wheel. This was accomplished by filling the bare spaces in the design by hatch work—that is, by narrowly joined cross strokes at various angles. In this manner much of the transparency and delicacy that had marked the earlier efforts were lost.

It was most probably the degeneration of the style that eventually caused it to be outmoded by wheel engraving after the Bohemian and Silesian fashion.

Although diamond-point work had remained almost the only style of decoration practised in Holland until the beginning of the last quarter of the seventeenth century, an occasional early specimen is found with wheel engraved decoration that can definitely be ascribed to the Dutch artists. The earliest dated specimen is a commemorative goblet dated 1659 celebrating a Dutch naval victory over the Swedes. This is preserved in the Dordrecht Museum. A second early Dutch engraved glass is in the Musée du Cinquantenaire in Brussels. This glass is somewhat similar in shape to the Royal Oak Goblet (*see* ENGLISH GLASS, Fig. 116) and has the date 1663 on the stem. The bucket-shaped bowl is engraved with *putti* among scroll work, a favourite subject with Dutch engravers.

By the turn of the seventeenth century, Dutch engravers had completely adopted the German style of wheel engraving; by the middle of the eighteenth century, work was being executed that was a fair challenge to it.

As there was a close trade between England and Holland, it is not surprising that the Dutch wheel engravers chose the English lead metal as their medium. It was softer to the wheel and of a bright and lustrous quality that displayed engraved work to better advantage than the harder potash-lime glass of Bohemia, which the Dutch artists had used as their earlier medium. Anyone who has worked the two glasses on the wheel—lead glass and lime glass—will at once testify to the advantages of working with the former metal.

Nevertheless, the Dutch style and technique were very closely related to the German, so much so that it has been suggested (W. B. Honey, *Glass*, 1946, p. 132) that much of it was the work of German craftsmen who had migrated west after the restoration of peace. The most characteristic work occurred after the middle of the eighteenth century, and portrayed domestic subjects that appealed to the Dutch sentiment. Betrothals and weddings were favourite occasions to mark the engraving of glasses, and these were given their appropriate inscriptions, but armorial and naval subjects were also very popular.

The most outstanding of the Dutch wheel engravers was Jacob Sang, who signed a number of glasses between 1752 and 1762; it is claimed (L. F. Fuchs, 15th August, 1954, 'Jacob Sang' *Weltkunst*, pp. 3-5) that he worked at Amsterdam. An advertisement in the *Amsterdam Courant*, 3rd April, 1753, stated: 'Simon Jacob Sang, Saxon artist-glass engraver, resident in the Oudebrugsteeg at the corner of the Nieuwendyk in Amsterdam, makes it known that he cuts and engraves on

105. *Wineglass with drawn trumpet bowl engraved by Frans Greenwood in diamond point work with figures, copies from engravings 'Balli di Sfessania' by Jacques Callot (1592-1635) an engraver of Nancy. The glass is signed 'Frans Greenwood pinxit 19 Jan 1720'. (By courtesy of the Victoria and Albert Museum)*

English goblets, panes, cabinet-panels and box-lids, the most fashionable curiosities known and practised in Holland, whether in large or small figures, in perspective or in relief, shallow or deep-cut, on matt or rough grounds, polished figures, coats-of-arms, names in any type of script, emblems, half-lengths or other portraits, rock- and scroll-work of the newest fashion, Ovidian and other stories.'

R. J. Charleston (*Journal of the Society of Glass Technology*, Vol. XLI, 1957, p. 242t) has the following remarks to make regarding the above notice:

'A glass dated one year before this advertisement, and signed by Sang, well illustrates this new development of his art, with an Ovidian rendering of *Diane and Callisto* (see R. Schmidt, 1914, pl. 28, 233, and L. F. Fuchs, 1954, cover) which shows him to be one of the most accomplished engravers of the eighteenth century and full worthy of the family whose name he bears. This glass is evidently a Newcastle piece, but the fashion of the cover makes one wonder whether perhaps it was not a custom to supply to the Netherlands the covers which Continental practice demanded but to which English glass-makers were not accustomed.'

The reference by Charleston to Sang's family in the above quotation is explained by him in the following passage (*loc. cit*): '. . . Jacob Sang, who worked at Amsterdam . . . was almost certainly related to Andreas Friedrich Sang, Court engraver at Weimar, whose son, Johann Heinrich Balthasar Sang, was also an accomplished artist, in his capacity of Court engraver at Brunswick. (*See* Pazaurek, *Der Kunstwanderer*, 1930, p. 1.)

There are several signed glasses by Jacob Sang in museums and private collections. The Buckley Collection at the Victoria and Albert Museum includes four glasses signed by him, the dates being 1758, 1761 and a pair with the date 1762. The first, a slender wineglass with baluster stem, is engraved with a scrolled panel with billing doves and the words 'Ons Lang Leeven' and signed 'J.Sang. Inv: et: Fec: 1758'.

The glass dated 1761 is a faceted stem wineglass engraved in commemoration of a wedding with hands clasped over an altar, with the inscription 'De Huwelyks en Handt'. The glass is signed 'Jacob Sang, Inv: et Fec: Amsterdam, 1761'.

The remaining glasses are a pair, after the Hogarth style, with glass covers. One glass is engraved with the figure of a baby and the companion glass shows the mother in bed, obviously glasses celebrating a birth. Both are signed in the same way as the glass described above, dated 1761, and both bear the date 1762.

A glass of the same Hogarth type, also at the Victoria and Albert Museum, is engraved to celebrate a wedding, with the marriage coats of members of the families of Matthes and Wernier, both of Amsterdam. It is unsigned, but from the characteristic style of the engraving, there is little doubt that it is a Sang glass.

The glass shown in Fig. 23 is also ascribed to Jacob Sang (E. Haynes, *Glass Through the Ages*, 1948, Plate 44d). The bowl is in rococo scroll work, within which is a plot of grass. On this stands a column surmounted by a pair of flaming hearts united by a true lover's knot; on each side are three trees. The inscription is IK BEMIN MAAR EEN (I love but one). The glass is typical of the betrothal glasses engraved by the Sang school and displays very careful detail work in shallow intaglio. The glass itself is in the light baluster style of Newcastle origin, a favourite medium for Dutch engravers.

Dutch decoration of English glass has been the subject of much research by R. J. Charleston (*Journal of the Society of Glass Technology*, Vol. XLI, 1957, pp. 229t-243t). Although there is strong documentary evidence that glass was made in Holland *a la façon d'Angleterre* in such centres as Ghent (1711-1715), Namur (1753), Liege (1709), Middleburg (1727), 's Hertogenbosch (1775), there is little doubt that most Dutch engravers preferred the English crystal as their medium for reasons already given—that is, the ease with which it could be worked on the wheel, and its aesthetic merits.

The third category into which Dutch engraved glass falls is the dot stippling, which became the vogue about the middle of the eighteenth century. Wheel engraving had been the popular style from the end of the seventeenth century, and it is probable that diamond engraving would have at that time been supplanted altogether had not the methods then being developed by the engravers of copper plates for printing been adapted to glass.

Thus, in the second half of the eighteenth century, stippling on glass became a vogue which lasted well into the nineteenth century. Stippling, as has been noted, is the method of formulating the design with a countless number of tiny dots by driving the point of a diamond or hardened steel into the glass by the aid of a small hammer. Although this method was undoubtedly used by Anna Roemers Visscher (*see* p. 74) as early as 1621, it did not become a popular method until the middle of the eighteenth century, when Frans Greenwood (1680-1761) gave fresh impetus to the art of engraving with the diamond.

Greenwood, as the name would suggest, was apparently of English parentage, although a native of Rotterdam. It is probable that he gained his inspiration from his association with the makers of mezzo-tints. His style, however, differed from that of Anna Roemers Visscher in that the whole design was stippled, well-defined dots representing the high-light of the subject and plain glass the shadow. Anna Roemers Visscher, on the other hand, outlined her design in linear fashion and used stippling as a means of producing light and shade.

Greenwood's earliest work was also in linear form, for he did not appear to adopt the technique of stippling until after 1720. In common with other Dutch engravers, he chose English glasses of the Newcastle type as his medium and decorated them with floral and fruit motifs, classical subjects, and subjects taken from paintings.

Many of Greenwood's glasses are preserved in museums and private collections. The Victoria and Albert Museum has several of Greenwood's glasses. One, a wineglass with drawn stem, is signed 'Frans Greenwood, pinxit 19 Jan 1720' and is engraved in linear style with figures from the Italian Comedy after Jacques Callot (Fig. 105). There are also signed specimens with dates from 1722 to 1755, including a light baluster with a half-length figure of a man holding a roemer, signed 'F. Greenwood 1728' and another, signed 'F. G. Fec[t].' engraved with two donkeys against a background of trees and flowers.

The Metropolitan Museum, New York, possesses a specimen dated 1728 stippled with a figure allegorical of the River Meuse against a landscape background.

The method of stippling introduced by Greenwood was also practised by many other Dutch artists, among whom G. H. Hoolaart and David Wolff deserve mention. Little is known of the former beyond the glasses which bear his name, although it is thought that he was a relative of Greenwood. A specimen of his work is shown in Fig. 108.

David Wolff (1732-1798) specialised on stippling with the diamond, although he occasionally employed linear work, especially in such features as in the hair of a figure. Many of the glasses ascribed to Wolff, however, are so different in technique from his signed specimens as to leave in doubt the real identity of the engraver. There are several signed specimens in various museums, such as the Rijks Museum, Amsterdam, and the Metropolitan Museum, New York. The specimens shown in Figs. 106 and 107 of glasses engraved by Wolff are in the Victoria and Albert Museum.

The Dutch artists with the diamond, of whom there were a great number, practised for two centuries until as late as the middle of the nineteenth century. The dexterity and charm of their work is unsurpassed. It shows the utmost delicacy of touch, and some specimens are of such evanescence as to be almost invisible in certain lights. Examples are highly prized

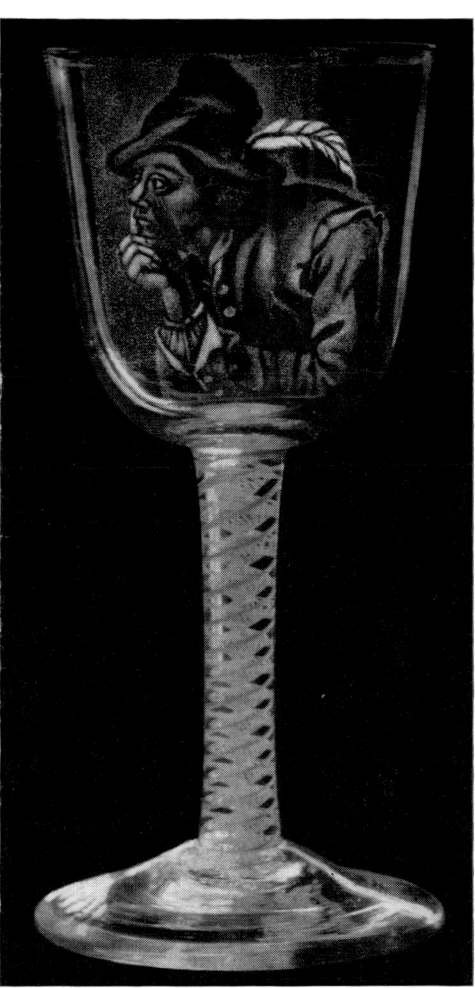

106. *Wineglass (probably English) with stipple engraving of an obelisk, two* putti *and flags. The artist was David Wolff.* circa *1780.* 107. *Wineglass, most probably Newcastle, stipple engraved by David Wolff, with two boys clasping hands, and bearing the inscription VRIENDSCHAP.* circa *1780.* 108. *Wineglass with white opaque stem stipple-engraved by the Dutch artist G. H. Hoolaart, with a man supporting his chin on his hand. The glass is initialled G.H.H.* circa *1780. (All by courtesy of the Victoria and Albert Museum)*

today and specimens signed by the better known artists are valuable.

Few glasses by famous Dutch engravers have changed hands within recent years. Probably the most important sales were of glasses engraved by David Wolff, one which fetched £52 and the other £66. The latter was a stipple engraved wineglass with the standing figure of a small boy with a bird on his wrist and another playing with his dog. The inscription reads 'Vriendschap en vryheid'.

A wineglass signed 'Jacob Sang inv; et Fec; Amsterdam 1758', and engraved with a coat-of-arms, fetched £46 a few years ago. Other glasses by less known Dutch engravers have fetched between £10 and £12.

EDKINS, MICHAEL (1734-1811). Michael Edkins is one of the few decorative glass artists in enamel of the eighteenth century of whom anything is positively known. Fortunately, Edkins kept a ledger of his business which has been preserved. It is a large volume of nearly four hundred pages and is now in the keeping of the City Art Gallery, Bristol.

Further information of the artist is obtained from Hugh Owen's work, *Two Centuries of Ceramic Art in Bristol* (1873), and finally there is a collection of glass made by William Edkins, jnr., among which are some specimens stated to have been decorated by his grandfather, Michael Edkins.

R. J. Charleston has also made an exhaustive enquiry into the career of Edkins, which was made the subject of a paper read to the *Circle of Glass Collectors* in December, 1950, and was afterwards reproduced in the *Journal of the Society of Glass Technology* in 1954, Vol. XXXVIII, pp. 3-16t.

Edkins had a colourful career. It would appear that he was born in 1734, probably in Birmingham, which he left when about twenty to try his luck in Bristol. It is known that in 1755 he married Elizabeth, daughter of William James, glass-maker, and in recognition of his marriage he was made a Burgess of the City of Bristol in the following year. He had no fewer than thirty-three children.

His first work was as a painter of delft at a pottery in Redcliffe Backs belonging to one Richard Frank. Here, apparently, he painted ornaments, plates, dishes and Flemish tiles for grates and dairies. One of the plates, bearing the initials MEB and the date 1760, was given by William Edkins, jnr., to the Museum of Practical Geology, Jermyn Street, London, and was afterwards acquired by the Victoria and Albert Museum in 1901. Its diameter is eight and seven-eighth inches.

The initials MEB stand for Michael, the first letter, Edkins, the middle letter, and Betty, the third letter, the familiar name by which Elizabeth Edkins was known. Indeed, the marriage register is signed as such.

It would appear that within a few years of his marriage, Edkins set up business on his own account, which he would have been able to do by virtue of his standing as Burgess of the City of Bristol. It is known that he took, as his first apprentice, one Benjamin Williams, in 1761, although the first entry in his ledger was not until 1762. The cover of the ledger has the motto *Veni, Vidi, Vici*, which seems to indicate that he became a free lance on or about 1761.

The first entry in his ledger, however, does not concern the painting of either delft or glass, but of coaches, a charge of three guineas being made to Mr William Powell 'for painting a post chaise with handsome gold ornaments, cyphers and crests, carriage and wheels vermillion'.

Edkins painted bas-relief work on each side of the altar piece in Redcliffe Church. It is also recorded that 'he was a very good musician and charming counter tenor singer, so much so that Mr Powell introduced him on the stage in Bristol and Covent Garden, London'. He also painted scenery property for the stage at Bristol.

His main work, however, between the years 1762 and 1787, was the painting of articles in opaque-white and blue glass. It is recorded that 'he was exceedingly clever at ornamenting enamel and blue glass-ware, then very much in vogue, at which he had no equal, which he principally did for Messrs Vigor and Stevens, successors to Messrs Little and Longman'.

The various entries in Edkins's ledger show that work was done for the following glasshouses:

1762-1767	Little & Longmans
1767-1787	Longman & Vigor
1765	William Dunbar & Co., Bristol and Chepstow
1775-1787	Vigor & Stevens, Thomas Street.
1785-1787	Lazarus Jacobs, Temple Street.

Typical entries in Edkins's ledger are:

			s.	d.
1762	July 19.	To 4 blue jars and beakers with mosaic borders to match a large set for Mr Wilson	2 .	0
1763	Sept. 30	To 18 enamel basins	1 .	6
	Oct. 28	To 13 cans and milk jugs	1 .	1
1770	Nov. 6	To 12 hyacinth glasses blue gilded	2 .	0

Descriptions of various articles attributed to Edkins are given under BRISTOL GLASS.

Edkins had a full life, as the foregoing notes disclose. He appeared to prosper in his later years, for he took an apprentice, one John Reed, in 1794, and brought his son, Joseph, into the business in 1795. Michael Edkins died in 1811. An obituary in the *Bristol Journal* records his death: 'In his 78th year at his house in Bridge Street, Mr Michael Edkins, painter, whose uniform affability and urbanity rendered him equally esteemed in his life as lamented in his death.'

EGYPTIAN GLASS.
See INTRODUCTION.

ENAMELLED GLASS. From the earliest times glass has been decorated by having enamel colours painted upon it. Broadly speaking, enamelled glasses can be divided into two categories—those in which the enamel is permanent, and those in which it is merely painted upon the surface and quickly wears off. The latter process can be considered merely as painting, although in some cases the colour was varnished in order to render it a little more permanent.

In the permanent process the enamel is made up in the form of a paste consisting of a substance intended to assist fusion, known as a flux, a finely powdered metallic colouring compound, and an oil or water medium which is added to give the paste the required consistency. The paste is applied by a brush, transfer or other means, after which the article is fired in a muffle or kiln until the flux has melted, dissolved the colouring medium, and assumed a uniform glazed finish with the glass body.

The requirements of a satisfactory enamel are many. First, in order that the article being decorated should not distort while being fired in the kiln, the enamel must obviously fuse at a lower temperature than the softening point of the article itself. Secondly, in spite of its softer nature, the enamel must be sufficiently durable to withstand the ravages of time. Finally, the enamel and glass body must have corresponding ratios of contraction, or very nearly so.

109. *Goblet painted in enamel colours by Beilby of Newcastle-on-Tyne, depicting Royal Arms and Motto as borne by George II and George III.* (*Messrs Cecil Davis, Ltd.*)

The art of enamelling was known to the Romans and it would appear that they used the same method as in the modern process just described.

The highest artistic attainment in enamelling by ancients is undoubtedly that of the Islamic craftsmen of the thirteenth and fourteenth centuries, the best known examples being the enamelled hanging lamps used for lighting mosques. Many specimens are preserved in the museums, the collection at the Victoria and Albert Museum being the finest in Europe.

Enamelling by the Venetians was applied both to coloured and colourless glasses, and the skilful use of gilding and enamels of all colours would appear to indicate that the Venetian craftsmen were familiar with the Islamic processes.

French glass-makers practised enamelling in the sixteenth century. The colours are usually red, blue, white and dull yellow and are of a distinct shade, while the execution is more delicate than that of Italian work.

German Enamelling. To the collector, however, the German enamelled glasses provide the best hunting ground. Fortunately also for the collector, the German enamellers dated their glasses. Numerous specimens bearing German coats-of-arms, with dates between 1541 and 1591, exist in museums and private collections. The style is usually beaker-shaped, broadening towards the top, and with a foot similar to the Venetian beakers or goblets.

Opinion is divided as to whether these early glasses were made in Murano and enamelled there, made in Murano and enamelled in Germany, or were entirely German in workmanship. The only means, it would appear, of determining where the glasses were made is by the dates appearing upon them, as nearly all German work is dated, whereas Italian is not. During the seventeenth century German craftsmen completely mastered the art of enamelling and produced enamelled vessels on a very large scale. The prevailing forms are the *Humpen* and *Passglaser* (banded glass). The *humpen* varied considerably in size from a few inches in height to a size that required an effort to lift. The enamelled decoration on them included coats-of-arms, representation of trades, family groups and religious subjects.

Specimens are extant with a playing card enamelled upon them, usually a Queen or Knave. Probably the best examples of enamelling are the *Reichsadlerhumpen*, which were a tribute to the Emperor, and which showed the crowned double-headed eagle, its wings bearing the names and arms of the constituent states of the Empire (*see* GERMAN AND BOHEMIAN GLASS, Fig. 144).

The Franconian and Thuringian glasses of the second half of the seventeenth century are of special notice, as lighter colours were used, the border under the rim being enamelled in white with a broad frieze formed by dots in flat entwined bows and rounded point work. Another peculiarity of the glasses from this district is that in some cases the enamel is applied on both sides of the glass, the outline of the motif appearing on the outside and the solid splashes of colour on the inside.

The most notable of the German enamellers during the seventeenth century was Johann Schaper, who usually painted in black and sepia, more rarely in transparent coloured enamels. The work was always extremely delicate, depicting ruins, battle scenes or landscapes. Schaper nearly always used the same type of vessel for his work—namely, a small cylindrical

110. *Reverse of goblet shown in Fig. 109 enamelled in colours with Prince of Wales' Feathers and signed 'Beilby Junr. NCastle invt and pinxt.'* (*Messrs Cecil Davis, Ltd.*)

cup, sometimes on three ball feet, with a domed lid surmounted by a finial. Specimens of Schaper's work are shown in Figs. 145 and 146. (*See* GERMAN AND BOHEMIAN GLASS.)

English Enamelling. The earliest mention of decorative enamelling in this country would appear to be a notice in the *Post Man*, 3rd December, 1696: 'Mr. Grillet, Enameller, makes and sells all sorts Works enamelled and of glass, different Postures of all kinds, Animals, Plants, Trees, Flowers and Fruit, together with all manner of Representations to the life. In short, whatever can be desired or thought on either in glass or enamelled in the fire, without using anything besides his hand or the matter. He lives at the sign of the Castle, St. Martin's Lane' (*Old English Glass*, Francis Buckley, 1925, p. 142).

No specimens from this worker, so far as is known, have survived the test of time.

Decoration by enamel painting was, however, not practised to the same extent in this country as on the Continent, and few English artists gained any distinction in the art of enamelling. The Beilby family of Newcastle-on-Tyne and Michael Edkins of Bristol were, without doubt, the most important

111. *Wineglasses painted in enamel colours by the Beilby family of Newcastle-on-Tyne.* (*Messrs Cecil Davis, Ltd.*)

enamel painters of the times; their decorative designs in white and coloured enamels multiplied many times the value of the glasses that they chose.

Decoration in enamel in this country was in two styles: 'thin' or 'wash' enamel, which is today very rare, and 'dense', which eventually became the more popular style. The technique of enamelling was introduced into this country by decorative artists from Germany and the Low Countries, but as the Continental metal was of a harder nature than the English glass-of-lead, early difficulties would have been experienced in attempts to emulate the Continental fashion. The harder enamels used on the Continental potash-lime glasses would have been found quite unsuitable for the softer lead glass, and modifications in the nature of the fluxes were, no doubt, found necessary.

These early difficulties may account for the fact that at first the enamel consisted of a very thin film, the necessary outlines and veinings being applied by means of a fine tool after the manner of etching. Later, when the technical difficulties had been overcome, the enamel was applied with considerable density, or body, similar to that employed by Continental craftsmen, and this eventually became the style in general use.

The decoration used by enamel painters took the form of festoons and floral emblems copied from the style of the wheel engravers. More ambitious subjects were later attempted, however, such as landscapes, pastoral scenes, figure subjects in Chinese style, and coats-of-arms.

William and Mary Beilby of Newcastle-on-Tyne were among the most famous of the enamel painters of the eighteenth century (*see* BEILBY, WILLIAM AND MARY). The glasses painted by the brother and sister are fairly numerous, but as the signature appearing on the comparative few that are signed is 'Beilby', without any initial, it is impossible to distinguish the work of one from the other.

The glasses enamelled by the Beilbys first began to make their appearance in 1762. As Mary at that time would have been only thirteen, it is most probable that these early glasses are attributable to William. Such glasses are decorated with heraldic motifs, in both white and coloured enamel, on glasses or goblets with ogee or bucket-shaped bowls.

A typical specimen of this group is shown in Figs. 109 and 110. This is a goblet painted in enamel colours on one side with the Royal Arms and Motto as borne by George II and George III, with scroll work and festoons. On the reverse is enamelled the Prince of Wales's Feathers. The style of the glass dates it about 1760, and it is probable that it commemorates the birth in 1762 of George III's eldest son, afterwards Prince Regent and George IV. The signature on this glass, seen on the illustration above the Prince of Wales's Feathers, is '*Beilby Junr. NCastle invt & pinxt*'.

There are several of these specimens known bearing similar decoration and it is probable that William Beilby painted a number of them, as they would have had a ready sale as commemorative glasses. The style of all specimens is the same, a

112. *Group of Newcastle glasses all with enamel painting by William and Mary Beilby.* (*Messrs Cecil Davis, Ltd.*)

square bucket-shaped bowl with straight double series opaque-twist stem. The style of twist, however, varies on different specimens.

Later, more ambitious subjects were attempted, such as landscapes and conventional scenes in decorative and fanciful style. Colours were not always used and much of the work was rendered in characteristic white monochrome which has a faint tint of blue and sometimes of pink.

Those glasses in white monochrome included ales and glasses with straight-sided and bucket-shaped bowls, most of which had enamel-twist stems. Some were decorated with similar motifs to those found on engraved glasses of the period, such as the flowering vine, and hops and barley, but more ambitious subjects were also chosen, such as scenes of hunting, fishing and shooting. Rarer are pastoral scenes including ruins and Chinese subjects.

Typical specimens from these groups of glasses are shown in Fig. 111. The specimen on the left shows a bird painted in white monochrome with a butterfly on the reverse. The central specimen has also a bird, but is painted in white monochrome picked out in green. On the specimen on the right is depicted an obelisk, a favourite subject of the Beilbys.

The group of five glasses in Fig. 112 also includes a glass depicting an obelisk, and another a ruin. The familiar hops and barley and flowering vine motifs are also represented. Other specimens of the work of the Beilbys are the decanters such as the specimen shown in Fig. 113. The illustration on the left shows the butterfly, a characteristic personal touch seen on many of the specimens enamelled by the Beilbys. The view on the right shows the signature '*Beilby inv & pinx*'.

Other types of vessels attributable to the Beilbys are shown in Fig. 114. The cup on the left is enamelled in white with a

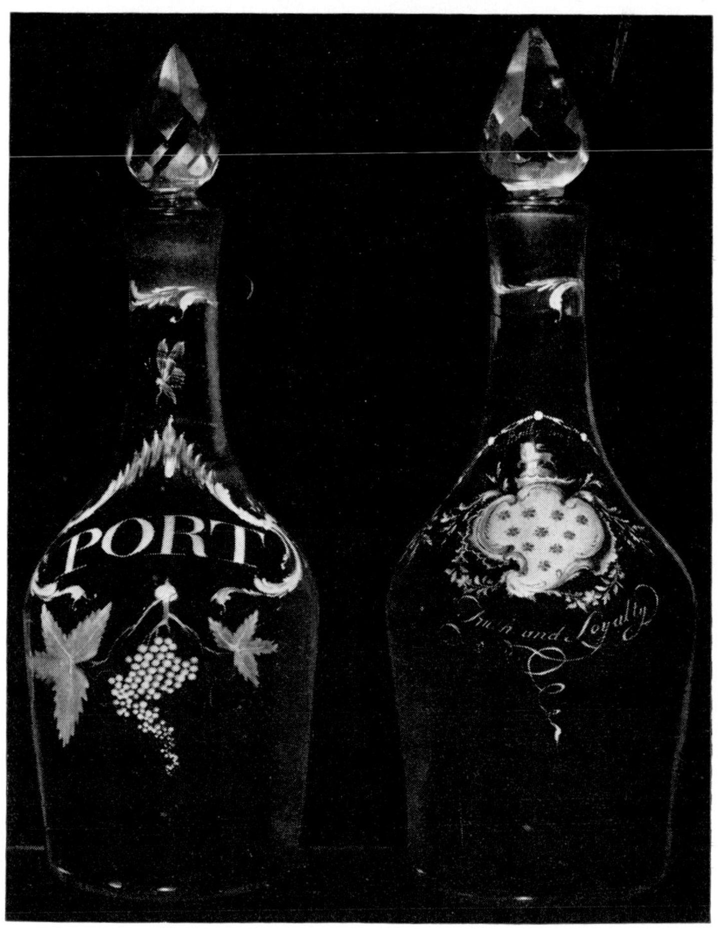

113. *Two views of decanter painted and signed by Beilby of Newcastle-on-Tyne. The view on the left shows a butterfly, a characteristic personal touch.*

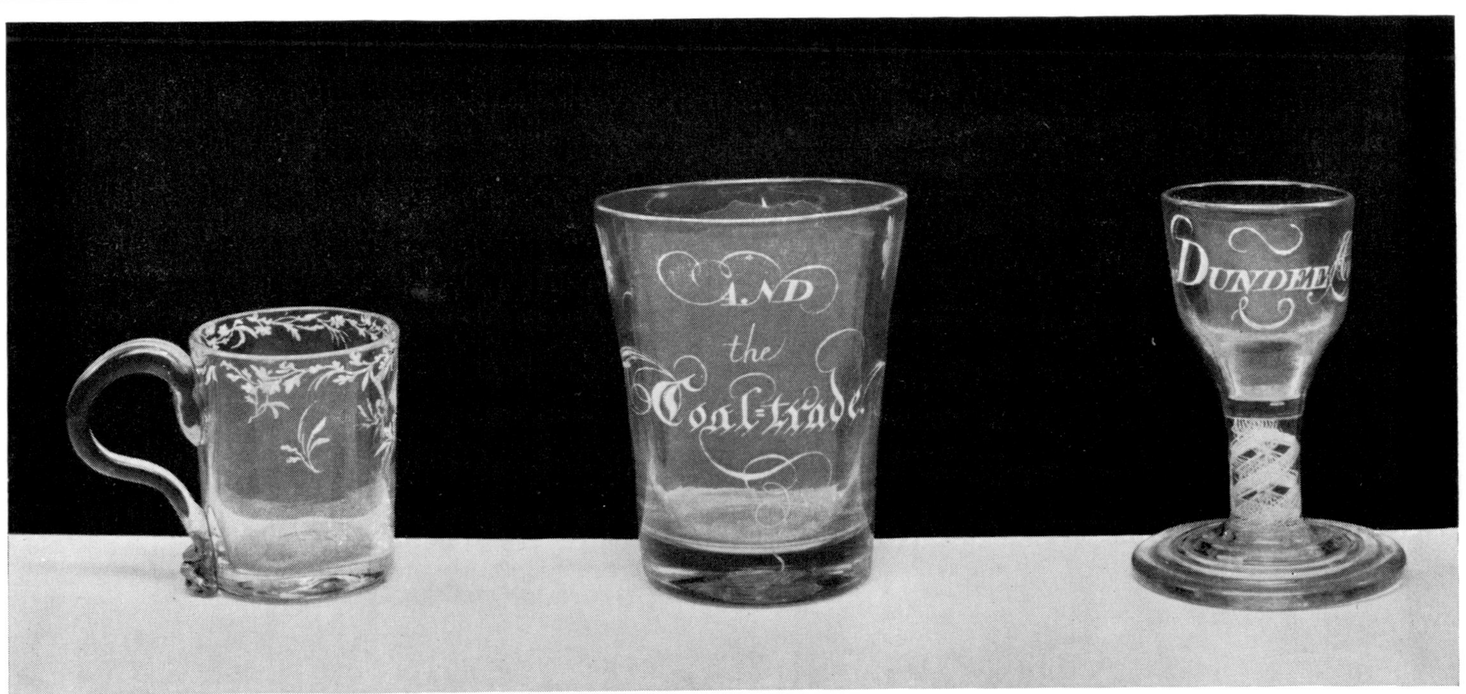

114. *Glasses attributable to the Beilby family, decorated in white monochrome. The glass on the right is a Masonic firing glass inscribed 'Dundee Ancient Operative Lodge'.*

115. *The Beilby decanter shown on the left is inscribed in white enamel 'W WINE' and is decorated with grapes and vine leaves. The wineglass is also enamelled in white. The decanter on the right is inscribed PORT and is decorated with grapes and vine leaves in white enamel similar to the decanter on the left.*

crest of two hands holding an apple; the rim has a floral border also in white enamel. The height is two-and-a-half-inches. The beaker in the centre of the illustration is also enamelled in white, and bears the inscription 'And the Coal-Trade'. The reverse shows insects and a flower. The specimen is three-and-three-quarter inches in height. The glass on the right is a Masonic Firing glass inscribed in white enamel 'Dundee Ancient, Operative Lodge'. The stem is short with double series spiral gauze in white enamel on a stepped foot. This sturdy specimen is three-and-three-quarter inches in height. Other decanters and a glass painted by the Beilbys are shown in Fig. 115.

Other enamel painters of the eighteenth century are Michael Edkins, whose work is discussed under EDKINS, MICHAEL, and BRISTOL GLASS; William Absolon, details of whom are given under ABSOLON, WILLIAM, OF GREAT YARMOUTH; and James Donovan, discussed under DONOVAN, JAMES.

There were, of course, other enamel painters in both the eighteenth and nineteenth centuries, but little has been recorded of their activities. Occasionally a specimen comes to light which suggests an exceedingly clever artist having been at work about the same time as the Beilbys and Edkins. For example, a very rare enamelled Privateer Glass is known, decorated in white and crimson enamel with a ship in full sail, with the inscription above, 'The Providence'. On the reverse is the name of the commander of the ship in white enamel, 'Jon Elliot. 1767'. The glass has a straight-sided bowl and a stem of a spiral gauze single series twist type in red, blue, green and yellow enamel. It is six-and-a-quarter inches in height. No other glass of this type has been recorded. It was formerly in the collection of the late Hamilton Clements.

The opinion is strongly held by some that most of the vessels decorated in fanciful Chinese figures in coloured enamels, usually attributed to Michael Edkins, came from Staffordshire. It is known, of course, that opaque white (enamel) glass was made there, as one of the batch formulae which John Hill took to Waterford about 1785 was for enamel glass. M. S. Dudley-Westropp (*Irish Glass*, 1920, p. 174) had the original recipe in Gatchell's hand-writing for this glass. Charleston (*Journal of the Society of Glass Technology*, Vol. XXXVIII, 1954, p. 9t) is of the opinion that the vessels with Chinese figures may have had a South Staffordshire origin or, alternatively, a London one.

Enamelling in the Nineteenth Century. The practice of enamelling grew during the nineteenth century, and a number of manufacturers from the Stourbridge district exhibited vessels, decorated in every conceivable style, at the Great Exhibition in 1851. Flowers, landscapes, marine views, Grecian figures and mythological subjects were painted in vivid colours and gilt, on both flint and coloured vessels.

Enamel painted ware continued to be popular throughout the nineteenth century and in the last quarter the fashions which had appeared at the 1851 Exhibition were reproduced in even more exaggerated style; 'Italian', 'Indian', 'Chinese', 'Arab' and numerous other descriptions were applied to them, and specimens attempting to imitate early Islamic enamelling also made their appearance. These heavily enamelled, over-emphasised styles suffered very much the same fate as the exaggerated styles in the cut article and eventually went right out of fashion.

Prices of glasses with enamelled decoration have already been discussed under ABSOLON and BRISTOL GLASS. The only other English enamellers whose glasses have changed hands within recent years are the Beilbys of Newcastle-on-Tyne. Their glasses have fetched high prices. For example, the armorial goblet shown in Figs. 109 and 110 changed hands in 1954 for £920, and another similar goblet in 1960 for £1,820.

Decanters by the Beilbys are popular among collectors, those shown in Fig. 115 are typical specimens. That on the left, sold in 1958 for £95 and that on the right for £80. The goblet in the centre of Fig. 115, enamelled in white monochrome, changed hands for £45.

Other specimens of the work of the Beilbys are shown in Fig. 114. Those on the left and in the centre sold for £30 each and that on the right for £22. Wineglasses in the characteristic style of the Beilbys have fetched anything between £26 and £82 during recent years.

ENGLISH GLASS, HISTORY OF. There is no evidence of a continuous early tradition of glass-making in this country such as occurred in the Rhineland and in Normandy, and the practice apparently died out after the withdrawal of the Roman invader early in the fifth century. Mediaeval specimens of glass found in this country indicate that they were brought by the Anglo-Saxons from the Continent in the fifth and sixth centuries (W. A. Thorpe, *English Glass*, 1935, pp. 43-74). It is known that in 676 Benedict Biscop, founder of the Abbey at Monkwearmouth, was obliged to send to Gaul for glass-makers to make windows for the Abbey.

The earliest authentic record of glass-making in this country is in 1226, when Laurence Vitrearius is mentioned as having acquired twenty acres of land at Dyers Cross, Pickhurst, near Chiddingfold (S. E. Winbolt, *Wealden Glass*, 1933). Winbolt carried out extensive excavations and research in the Chiddingfold district of Surrey, and there is evidence that glass-making was conducted there on some considerable scale. From fragments dug up at the site, it would appear that the most important product was window glass, but bottles and drinking vessels were also made. There are records that in 1240 Laurence Vitrearius provided both clear and coloured glass for King Henry III's Chapel at Westminster Abbey. Records from this time of the Wealden Industry are fairly frequent, until the proclamation of 1615, prohibiting the use of wood fuel for industrial purposes, finally caused activity in the district to cease.

During the sixteenth century, glass-makers from the Continent began to challenge the long established status of the English glass-makers. Jean Carré, a Continental merchant, introduced a number of Protestant families of glass-makers from Lorraine, of whom Hennezal, Thietry, Thisac and Houx are the best known names.

These emigrants were granted special privileges by Queen Elizabeth, and it would appear that it was the intention of the Crown to invigorate the window glass industry in this country by foreign methods of manufacture. The families first practised in the Weald, but finally settled in various other parts of the country, such as Stourbridge, because of the suitability of the clays for glasshouse pots, and Newcastle-on-Tyne, where a silicious stone from Penshaw in Durham was found suitable

116. *Royal Oak Goblet, engraved in diamond-point work with a portrait of Charles II and bearing the inscription 'Royal Oak' in a floral wreath and also a portrait of his wife Catherine of Braganza, and the Royal Coat of Arms. It is dated 1663. Height* $5\frac{5}{8}$ *inches.*

for furnace construction. In addition, coal would have been available in both these areas. The prohibition in 1615 of the use of wood fuel no doubt greatly influenced the movements of these glass-makers.

Jean Carré died at Alfold in Surrey in 1572, two years after he had set up a glasshouse in Crutched Friars in London. His work was carried on by Jacob Verzelini, whose enterprise can be justly claimed to have been the turning-point in the history of English glass.

Verzelini (1522-1606) was born in Venice and, like many Venetians of his time, sought more remunerative employment in foreign countries. For some time he worked in Antwerp, at that period the most important glass-making centre after Venice, where he married a Dutch woman in 1555. He came to England in 1571 and, on the death of Jean Carré a year later, assumed control of the glasshouse at Crutched Friars. Five years later the building was burnt down and Verzelini opened a new establishment in Broad Street, which he operated until his retirement in 1592.

In 1575, shortly after the fire at Crutched Friars, Verzelini obtained a privilege from Queen Elizabeth for a period of twenty-one years 'for the makyne of drynkynge glasses suche as be accustomablie made in the towne of Murano and hathe undertaken to teache and bringe uppe in the said Arte and knowledge of makynge the said drynkynge Glasses owre naturall Subjectes'. The privilege also allowed him sole right to make glasses after the Venetian style, and prohibited the importation of foreign glass.

Less than a dozen of the glasses which might with some certainty be attributed to Verzelini have survived the test of time. They are highly prized today. (*See* Verzelini Glasses.)

Verzelini's license of twenty-one years was apparently terminated in 1592, when at the age of seventy he retired to Downe in Kent, a rich and highly respected man. He died in 1606 at the age of eighty-four and was buried in the Parish Church at Downe, where a brass tablet, which still remains, was set up to his memory. Verzelini's business and workmen were taken over by Sir Jerome Bowes, a soldier by profession with but a poor knowledge of glass. He obtained a new license, operative for twelve years only, but it included the sole right to import Venetian and Muranese glass.

A great deal of uncertainty existed at the time in the glass industry concerning the use of wood as fuel; forest lands were being devastated at an alarming rate all over the country, and in consequence its use as an industrial fuel was finally forbidden by Royal Proclamation in 1615.

In the same year Sir Robert Mansell, a retired Admiral, with a distinguished career and a sound business head, entered the industry (*see* Mansell, Sir Robert). Within three years he gained complete control and opened an entirely new chapter in the history of English glass. In 1623 he was granted a patent by James I for sole right to 'use, exercise, practise, sett up and putt in use the arte, feate and misterie of melting and makeing of all manner of drinking glasses, broade glasses, windowe glasses, looking glasses and all other kinds of glasses, bugles, bottles, violls or vessels whatsoever made of glass of any fashion, stuff, matter or metal whatsoever with sea cole, pitt coale or any other fewell whatsoever not being tymber or wood'.

Mansell established new works or absorbed existing ones in all parts of the country. He used London as his headquarters, operating not only the glasshouse at Broad Street, established by Verzelini, but also other works in or near London, at Lambeth and Greenwich. In addition, he had glasshouses at Newcastle-on-Tyne, Swansea, Milford Haven, Newnham-on-Severn, Stourbridge, Kings Lynn, Purbeck Island, the Trent Valley, and Wemyss in Fifeshire.

Mansell successfully organised the industry and gave the public what it wanted. He prepared the way, although he was not aware of it, for the invention of lead glass which was to occur later in the century. The use of coal as a fuel necessitated the re-design of the glass furnace. In addition, to protect the glass from the sulphuric gases and dust carried over from the combustion chamber, the open pot in which the glass was melted was superseded by the covered or crowned pot. Both these improvements can be accredited to Mansell and, without them, the use of lead as a glass-making material would have met with almost insuperable difficulties.

During the Mansell period, not only the manufacture of all sorts of glass, but also its distribution to the public, began to be organised on a business-like basis; in 1635 the Glass Sellers' Company, consisting mainly of glaziers, received its Charter from Charles I. Following the Restoration in 1664, the Charter was reconstituted and the Company became much more powerful. It was able to gauge the taste of the public, and even discreetly to direct it, in order to comply with limitations of manufacture. This policy was sound and progressive, and although it tended to rob the glass-maker of his creative freedom, it did its job of supplying the multitude.

The Mansell monopoly lasted until his death in 1656, when partly due to the loss of his drive and enterprise, and partly to the unsettled state of the country politically, the industry suffered a serious decline. From records available (F. Buckley, *The Glass Trade in England in the 17th Century*, London, 1914, p. 7) it is evident that a growing export trade in fine glasses and other ware was lost. Drinking vessels, vials, water glasses, looking-glasses and window glass were some of the items mentioned in Charles I's *Book of Rates* (1642).

Mansell's successor was the Duke of Buckingham (*see* BUCKINGHAM, DUKE OF). Buckingham had a taste for art and science, and his enterprise in making fine glass in the Venetian style elicited praise from John Evelyn who wrote in his Diary: '19th September, 1676, to Lambeth . . . we also saw the Duke of Buckingham's Glasse-Worke, where they make huge vases of mettal as cleare, ponderous and thick as chrystal: also looking-glasses far larger and better than any that come from Venice.' Evelyn spoke with some authority on glass, for he had gained a personal knowledge of Venetian quality from a visit to Murano in June, 1645, when he examined the glass-houses and selected specimens of the glasses made there to be sent to England.

Few specimens which belong to this period of English glass have survived the test of time. The most important is the Royal Oak Goblet, most probably made to commemorate the marriage of Charles II and Catherine of Braganza in 1663. It is in the Venetian style, lightly blown in greenish-brown metal, and engraved in diamond-point work with a medallion portrait of Charles II framed in engraved oak branches and with the words 'Royal Oak'. On the reverse are portraits of Charles and his Queen, and the Royal Coat-of-Arms, with the date 1663. It is shown in Fig. 116.

Another is the 'Exeter Flute', seventeen inches high, with a bust portrait of Charles II and the sprouting oak stump. It is engraved in diamond-point work with 'God Bless King Charles The Second'. It is shown in Fig. 117. It was made for the coronation of Charles II probably in an English glasshouse worked by Italians and engraved by a Netherlandish hand.

Vessels such as these were probably *verres de parade* and are not representative of the popular fashions of the period. Fortunately, however, very complete records and sketches of glass vessels in general use have been preserved (Sloane MS 857, *Papers Relating to Glass-Sellers*, now in the British Museum). The records include sketches of some four hundred glass vessels of a London firm, John Greene and Michael Measey, who imported glass between the years 1667 and 1672 from Allesio Morelli, a Venetian glass-maker from Murano. A selection is shown in Fig. 118 of Greene's sketches.

Little is known of John Greene except that he was an active member of the Glass Sellers' Company. Letters show that the company had imported glasses from Venice before 1667. Greene's transactions alone give some idea of the activities of the company as a whole, for during the flourishing period following the Restoration, some two thousand dozen glasses

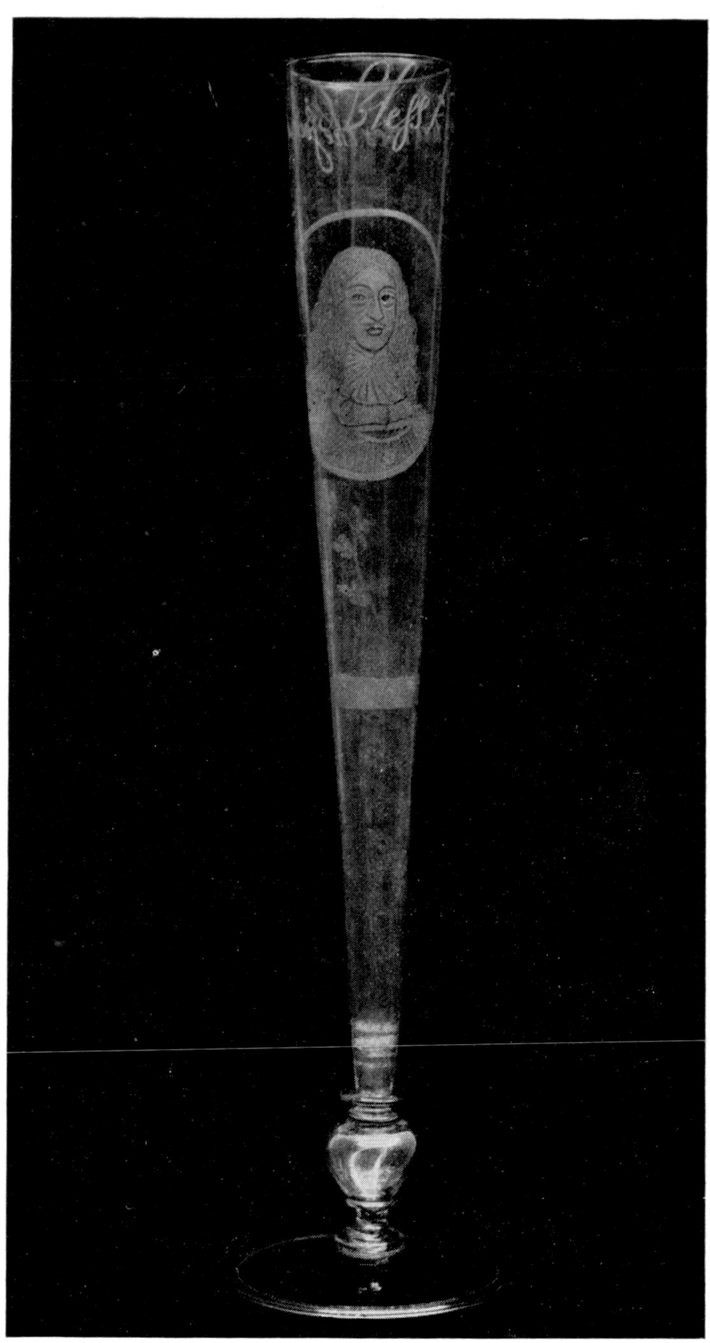

117. *Exeter Flute, engraved in diamond-point work with the portrait of Charles II and the sprouting oak stump. The glass bears the inscription 'God Bless King Charles The Second'. It is seventeen inches in height.*

and over one thousand looking-glass plates, as well as miscellaneous articles, were imported by him.

It is clear from Greene's sketches that they were not strictly in accordance with the current Venetian styles, but had obviously been designed to suit the English taste.

The quality of the glass supplied to Greene was not all that could be desired, for the records show that he complained continuously. He stated that the metal was not clear, was too thinly blown, and also that dampness had 'stained and rotted' the glass. Apparently Morelli failed to attain the quality demanded, and the increase in the standard of the English manufacture prompted a warning from Greene in 1671 that future supplies would be sought in the home market.

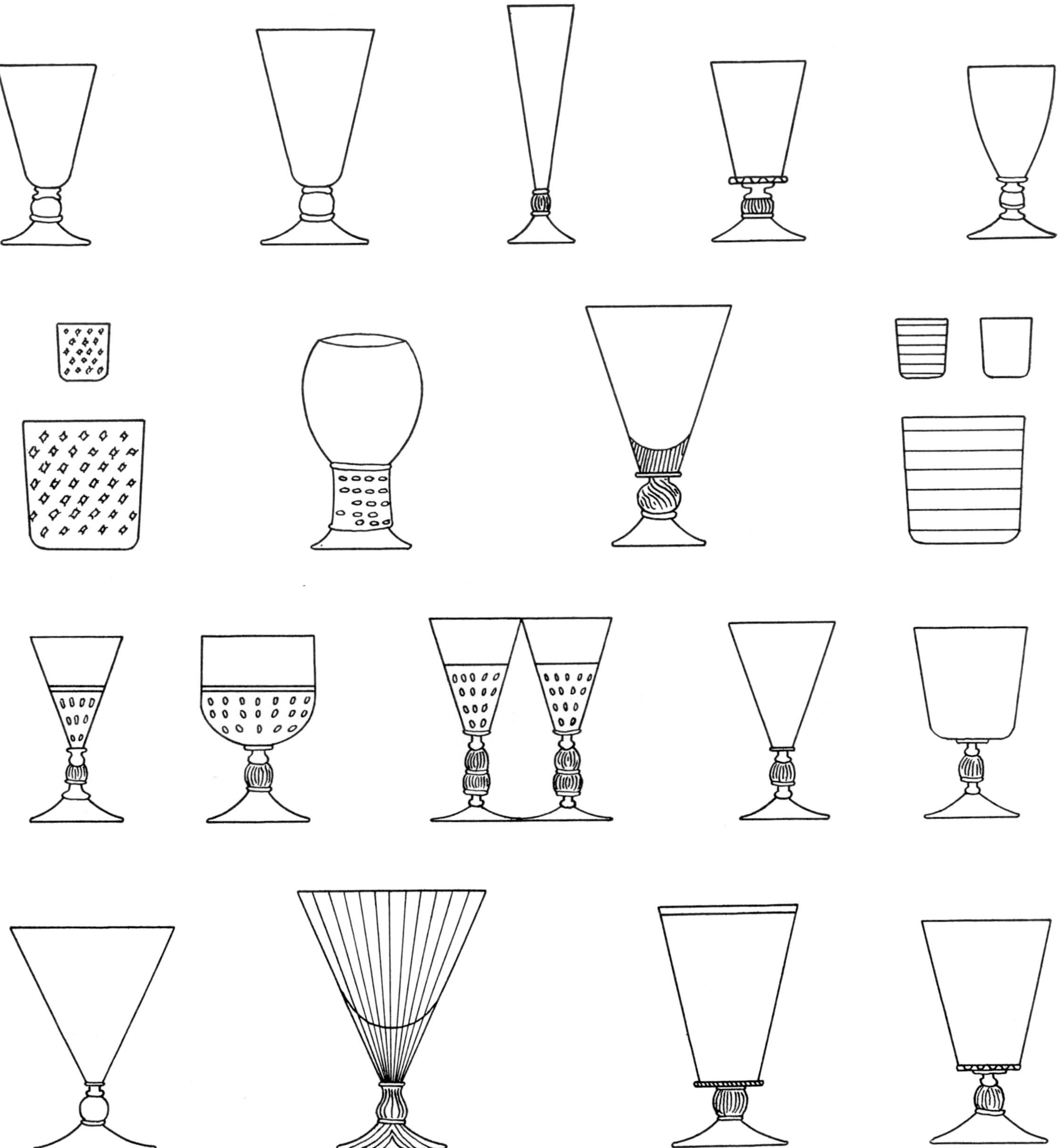

118. *Selection of the sketches of John Greene who traded between 1667 and 1672 with Allesio Morelli, a Venetian glass-maker.*

That this was no idle threat is borne out by the fact that very shortly afterwards, the Glass Sellers' Company embarked on a policy of making their glass where they made their sales. They selected George Ravenscroft, son of a prosperous shipowner who traded with Venice, to carry out research in the making of glass in this country (*see* RAVENSCROFT, GEORGE). Ravenscroft was well versed in science and he also had the advantage of having at his disposal Dr Merret's English translation in 1662 of Antonio Neri's work, *Arte Vetraria*, the standard Italian work on glass-making, first published in Florence in 1612. It was translated into English in 1662, into Latin in Amsterdam in 1668 with additions, and later translated into German by the famous German glass scientist, Kunckel. Finally, it was translated into French in 1752.

It is apparent, therefore, that Ravenscroft had the early advantage of the most important treatise on glass-making then available. Moreover, when he set up his experimental glasshouse in the Savoy, London, in 1673, he employed Italian glass-makers as his assistants, among whom da Costa, an Alturist, had a working knowledge of the use of the Italian materials. The first attempt in 1674 to make crystal glass met with some success, but it is doubtful at this stage whether lead was being used. Nevertheless, the production of this early glass enabled Ravenscroft to obtain his first patent and the Glass Sellers' Company were sufficiently impressed to instal him in a second glasshouse at Henley-on-Thames, where he could continue his experiments in comparative seclusion.

Ravenscroft continued to experiment with glass-of-lead and his efforts met with partial success. The Glass Sellers' Company distinguished the improved glass with a mark or seal in the form of a raven's head, a compliment to Ravenscroft for his accomplishment. Some of these 'sealed' glasses still survive. The specimen shown in Fig. 119 has the raven's head seal in one of the raspberry prunts which decorate the stem. The glass was not stable, however, and had the defect of 'crizzling'.

Ravenscroft unaccountably terminated his agreement with the Glass Sellers' Company in 1678, and it remained for his successor, Hawley Bishopp, to complete the work he had so successfully started.

The new glass-of-lead that was to revolutionise the production of fine glass in this country was in full production by 1682, and by the end of the seventeenth century nearly thirty glasshouses throughout the country had adopted it. It is from the period following Ravenscroft's discovery of glass-of-lead that the majority of English collections are today amassed, and there is without doubt no period in the history of English glass when so many changes occurred in the character of drinking glasses as the hundred years immediately following Ravenscroft's discovery.

119. *Ravenscroft roemer bearing the seal of the raven's head on the lowest of the raspberry prunts decorating the stem.* circa *1677.* (*By courtesy of the Victoria and Albert Museum*)

120. *Punch bowl and cover, originally in the Joseph Bles Collection. It is trailed and pincered 'nipt diamond waies'. The cover is surmounted with a cross finial.* circa *1685. Height 15½ inches. It changed hands in 1955 for £630 and is now in the Nottingham Castle Museum.*

There were many reasons for these frequent changes in style —technical, political, social and economical in character— and such influences served to keep the English style in a state of fluidity throughout the eighteenth century. At the beginning of the century glasses still showed Venetian influence; very little decoration appeared upon them and they were heavy and capacious. At that time, indeed, the value of a glass was reckoned by its mass rather than by any other characteristic and glass-ware of all descriptions was often sold by weight. Thus the *Tatler* advertised on 5th August, 1710: 'At the flint glasshouse in White Fryars, are to be sold all sorts of

121. *Drinking Glasses, nineteenth century.* (top left) *Liqueur glass with acid-embossed decoration; last quarter of the nineteenth century.* (top centre) *Glassware taken from the catalogue of the Great Exhibition.* (top right) *Wineglass; second half of the nineteenth century.* (bottom left) *Wineglass in imitation of earlier style; late nineteenth century.* (bottom centre) *Tumbler with flute decoration: late nineteenth century.* (bottom right) *Wineglass with ruby tinted bowl; second half of the nineteenth century.*

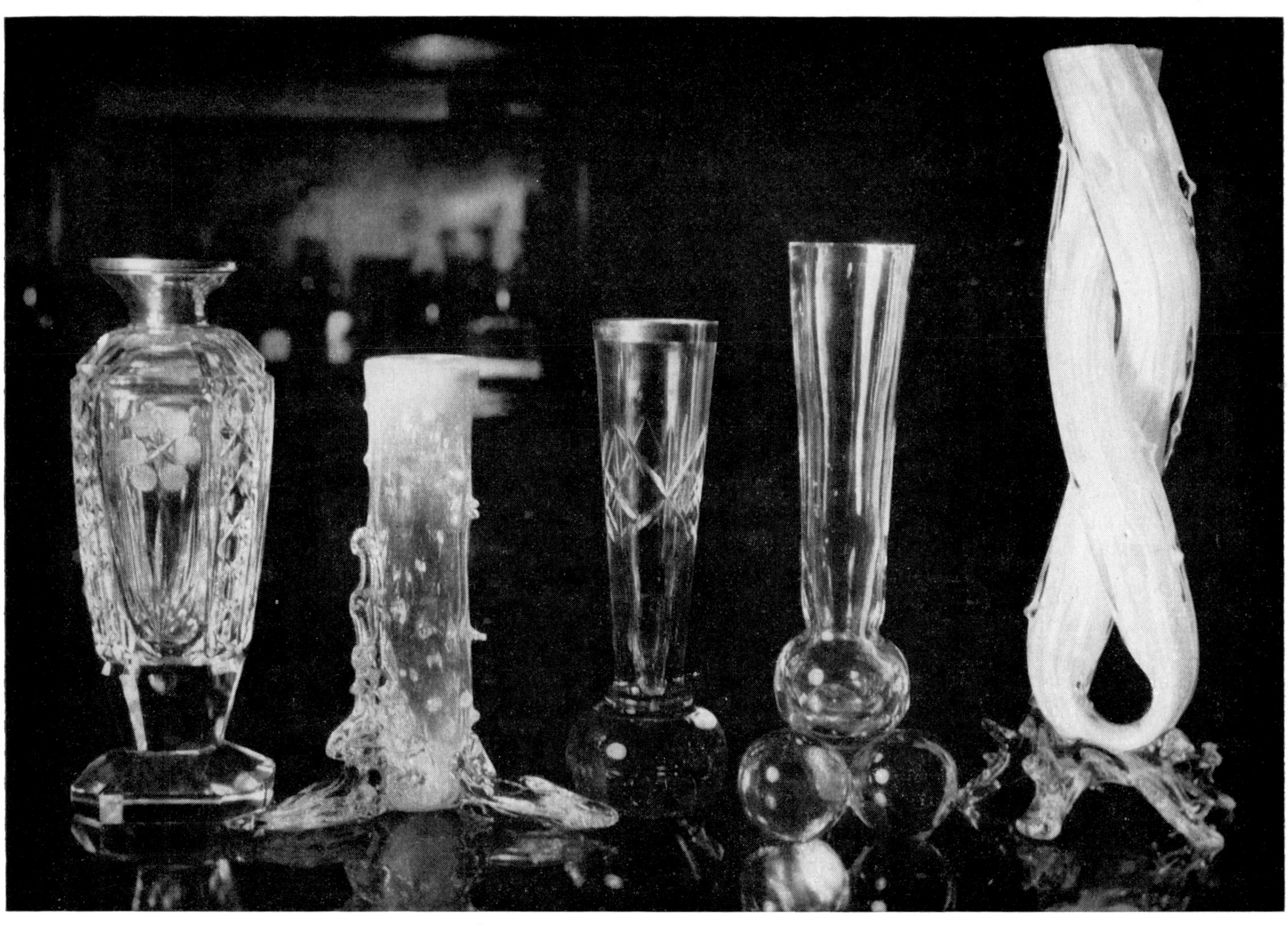

122. *Group of vases popular in the last quarter of the nineteenth century. Decorative effects such as enamelling, cutting and engraving were only sparingly applied.*

Decanthers, Drinking Glasses, Crewits, etc., or Glasses made to any pattern, of the best flint at 12d per pound.'

By the close of the century, however, glasses had undergone many distinct changes. The Venetian influence had entirely vanished or, more correctly, it had been absorbed, and glasses were smaller and much lighter in style. Decorative features appeared, such as tears, air-twists, enamel-twists; later, decoration was applied, and the practice of cutting and engraving by the wheel spread from London all over the country. Enamelling was another form of applied decoration which made a bid for popularity, but which never achieved any great success.

There were many reasons responsible for this revolution in style. First, there occurred the Treaty of Utrecht in 1713, which allowed the glass-makers of Central Europe to trade westwards. This was followed by the accession to the English throne of George I of Hanover in 1714, an event which was responsible for the infiltration of many Continental craftsmen, who brought with them new ideas in form and decoration which were to have a marked influence on the English style. There was also a national conversion to classicism in all branches of art and, finally, the very important influences of the Glass Excise Acts of 1745, 1777 and 1787.

The process of the blending of the Venetian, Continental and English forms into one of a distinctly national character continued unchecked until 1745, when Parliament, in an endeavour to raise funds for the professional wars then being waged on the Continent, passed legislation which was to prove a great burden to English glass-makers for a full century. The Act, known as the Glass Excise Act, imposed a tax of one penny per pound on the materials used in the making of flint glass; and as it was rigidly enforced. drastic changes were necessary in the style of articles in order to conserve the material. The heavy, traditional forms disappeared, light and simple vessels taking their place. Other taxes followed later in the century, which served even more to hamper English efforts, and it was not until the middle of the nineteenth century that these crippling taxes were finally abolished.

The excise Act of 1745 had not included Ireland, and no restrictions were necessary there on the weight of the materials used. On the other hand, as Ireland was not permitted to export glass, manufacture was necessarily limited to her own domestic requirements. In 1780, however, full freedom of trade was granted in Ireland and, coming at a time when the Glass Excise Tax in Great Britain had just been doubled, there at once occurred every inducement for English glass manufacturers and craftsmen to continue their art in Ireland. Many craftsmen both from the Stourbridge and Bristol districts seized the opportunities offered, and the famous period of Irish glass, which extended from 1780 to 1850, began.

The Act was finally repealed in 1845 and, as can be expected, the result was to stimulate activity in the production of glass. Unfortunately, however, the glass-maker gained his artistic freedom when the aesthetic standard in this country was of a very low order. The Victorian period was one which expressed prosperity, but it also fostered an atmosphere of over-emphasis. The tendency to display wealth was manifest in all branches of design, and there was free indulgence in all forms of decoration. The glass-maker came under the general influence and designed ugly shapes and adorned them extravagantly with prismatic cutting.

Pressed glass, then being rapidly developed in America, had begun to make its appearance on the English market, and advantage was at once taken of its capability of imitating the cut article in appearance. Indeed, a manufacturer displaying pressed glass at the Great Exhibition in 1851 recommended it because it could not be distinguished from the cut article.

The most popular styles in pressed glass were the heavily impressed articles, similar in every respect to the eye of the layman to the expensively fashioned articles cut in the traditional manner on the wheel. For this reason, and because it was cheap, pressed glass at once found a ready market, but the Victorian snobbishness which nourished the imitation also ordained the eclipse of the real; expensively cut table and ornamental glass quickly lost its appeal when an almost exact replica of it costing a shilling or so could be seen in every suburban parlour.

The Great Exhibition offered an excellent opportunity for the glass-maker to parade his unrestricted efforts, but it also exposed his lack of imagination and misuse of the materials at his command; indeed, the fall into disfavour of cut-glass in particular can be dated from the time of the Great Exhibition.

A reactionary movement against the glass-maker and cutter was strongly supported by such critics of art as John Ruskin and William Morris, and no doubt their influence greatly contributed to the new era which had its beginnings about 1860. The new movement, of which Powell and Northwood were among the best known English glass-makers, slowly grew to the modern appreciation which ordains purity of form and delicacy of applied decoration.

Drinking glasses of the last quarter of the nineteenth century are marked by their slender form and reticence in decoration; lightly constructed wineglasses with decorative borders in acid-etched patterns are typical of this transition period. The demand for the heavier decorative cutting which was popular about the middle of the nineteenth century, however, was never completely stifled, and drinking glasses and other types of tableware are still made today in which cut effects are lavishly applied.

Typical of some of the styles popular in the nineteenth century are those glasses shown in Fig. 121. The group shown in the top row centre, taken from the Catalogue of the Great Exhibition of 1851, illustrates the elaborate decorative effects such as cutting, enamelling and engraving, then employed.

In the same figure are shown drinking glasses popular in the second half of the nineteenth century. Fig. 122 gives an idea of the vases then popular. In the last quarter of the nineteenth century, much of the elaborate decoration had been discarded.

ENGRAVING. There are several methods employed today to engrave upon glass. They are: Wheel engraving, such as is used by lapidary craftsmen; Diamond engraving, in which a hand tool containing a diamond or some similar material is used to scratch a design upon the surface of the glass; Stippling, in which the point of a diamond or similar hard material is impressed upon the glass surface to produce a number of tiny dots forming a design; Acid engraving, in which hydrofluoric acid or its compounds are used to attack or obscure the glass surface; and Sand blasting, in which sand particles are directed at high velocity upon the glass surface.

Wheel Engraving. Engraving upon the surface of glass with a wheel such as used by lapidary craftsmen has long been practised. Pliny described the process in the first century A.D., and it has been employed with very little modification up to modern times.

The technique is somewhat allied to that of cutting, but the wheels used in the engraving process are of copper and much smaller than the stone wheels used by the cutter, varying in diameter from about four inches to the size of a pin's head. They are rotated in a small lathe operated by a foot treadle. The edge of the wheel is smeared with an abrasive mixture of

123. *An example of diamond-point engraving by Laurence Whistler; one of the most notable artists in the new school of glass engravers.*

124. *Sketches of cut and engraved nineteenth-century decanters and rummers taken from a catalogue of glassware produced by Messrs Stevens and Williams, Ltd.*

such materials as fine emery and oil, and the article to be engraved is pressed against the *underside* of the wheel; it requires only the slightest touch against the swiftly rotating wheel to leave a greyish-white mark on the surface of the article.

The process offers much greater scope for artistic expression than cutting; a design may vary from a simple sprig of leaves, for example, superficially engraved on the glass surface, to the deeply carved figure subjects such as those of the Portland Vase.

Wheel engraving in this country followed much the same development as cutting. There is no positive evidence that it was practised to any extent before the beginning of the eighteenth century. No doubt the silversmiths and gem engravers occasionally applied their talent to glass objects, but in the main wheel engraving as a craft in this country can be regarded as beginning after the first quarter of the eighteenth century. Work carried out during this period falls into two distinct categories: decorative work, designed to make the glass vessel more attractive, and work of a purely commemorative nature, intended to record a sentiment, event, or toast, after the prevailing custom of the eighteenth century. (*See* COMMEMORATIVE GLASSES.)

The engraving more usually attempted during the second half of the eighteenth century is typified by the emblems found on drinking glasses; those intended for wine often carried the 'grapes and vine' pattern, while some ale glasses displayed a 'hops and barley' motif. The trade name for these glasses was 'flowered' glasses.

Towards the end of the century, the capacious goblet of general utility known as the 'rummer' made its appearance, and its generous ovoid or bucket-shaped bowl allowed the engraver more scope for his work. Typical of these glasses were the English 'Volunteer' glasses following the French Revolution in 1789, 'Sunderland Bridge' rummers depicting the opening of the new bridge at Sunderland in 1796, 'Nelson' glasses which showed portraits of the Admiral and his flag-ship, and 'Wellington' glasses commemorating Waterloo in 1815.

Other well-known engraved glasses are, of course, the Jacobite glasses, on which were engraved the Heraldic and Jacobite rose and other Jacobite emblems (*see* JACOBITE GLASSES). It was about this time that the engraver began to enhance the appearance of his work by polishing certain portions of the design, roses on Jacobite glasses being typical of the style.

Diamond Engraving. Engraving with a diamond or other hard material has been practised from Roman times. The process is no more complicated than scratching the surface of the glass in the form of a design, much as an artist would sketch with pencil on paper.

125. *Sketches of rummers, wineglasses, a salad bowl and finger bowls taken from a nineteenth-century catalogue of glassware produced by Messrs Stevens and Williams, Ltd.*

Some early Venetian bowls and dishes were diamond engraved with intricate border designs. Others are found with conventional floral design and with birds or animals. An early reference to diamond engraving is made by Johannes Mathesius (1504-1565), a Bohemian priest, who in 1562 wrote on the practise of glass-making: 'Nowadays all sorts of festooning and handsome lines are drawn on the nice and bright Venetian glasses.'

The technique soon spread to Nuremburg and to Holland, and later to other parts of Europe, including this country.

The art of engraving with the diamond developed much more rapidly in Holland than in any other centre and the art flourished until well into the nineteenth century (*see* DUTCH GLASS). Engraving became a fashionable pastime and attained a high standard of artistic merit. Specimens from this period are preserved in many museums, probably the most important being the Rijks Museum in Amsterdam. Engraving of this period is marked by its light transparent nature; heaviness of any sort was avoided.

Later, however, the style changed. due no doubt to the influence of wheel engraving, which had attained great popularity at that time in Bohemia and Silesia. Dutch engravers tried to imitate, with the diamond, the light and shade so effectively produced by the wheel. This was accomplished by filling the bare spaces in the design by hatch work—that is, narrowly joined cross strokes at various angles. In this manner, much of the transparency and delicacy that had marked the earlier efforts were lost.

In England diamond engraving never approached the artistic standard attained by the Dutch artists. The earliest dated vessels are the Verzelini Goblets engraved, it is thought, by Anthony de Lysle (*see* VERZELINI GLASSES). These are sixteenth-century glasses, but very few English glasses are extant from the seventeenth century which can with certainty be identified as English engraved.

Stippling. Stippling, in which the design is impressed upon the glass by the point of a diamond or similar hard substance, was employed to a great extent in Holland as an alternative to the design being scratched upon the glass. It became a vogue during the second half of the eighteenth century and lasted well into the nineteenth. (*See* DUTCH GLASS.)

Acid Engraving. The technique employing hydrofluoric acid, the only known acid which will actively attack glass, has greatly improved during recent years and has many applications. The process, known as acid embossing, is much the same as that used by Schwanhardt, the German engraver, who is said to have discovered it about 1670 (*see* GERMAN AND BOHEMIAN GLASS). The glass surface is completely coated with a compound capable of resisting the action of the acid, such as wax, gum or varnish, the design is drawn through this thin covering with a fine steel point, and the acid allowed to attack the exposed design. After a few minutes' treatment, the glass is thoroughly washed and the resist removed.

The action of hydrofluoric acid takes many forms. The pure acid dissolves the glass, leaving the surface clear and bright; when mixed with sulphuric acid, it produces on lead crystal glass a gloss unequalled by any mechanical polishing method (*see* CUT GLASS, The Cutting Process). The addition of a neutralising agent, such as ammonia, to the acid prevents the dissolving of the glass, but the attack of the fluoride produces a frosted, obscured effect.

An infinite variety of finishes can be obtained by modifying the nature of the resist and the form of the attacking fluoride compound, from a white satin finish to a rough stippled effect. Thus, by sprinkling grains of mica evenly over the glass surface, a stippled texture is obtained, the grains of mica obscuring the surface and partially preventing the attack of the acid. Coarse and fine stippling can be achieved by varying the size of the grains of mica.

Sand-Blasting. Sand-blasting was a process invented in 1870 by Benjamin Tilghman, a Philadelphia chemist, but it has been adapted to decorative treatments only during recent years. In this process, also, a wide range of decorative effects can be achieved by slight modifications of the method.

The process consists of directing fine grains of sand by high air pressure from a portable 'gun' or tool against the glass surface, which is quickly destroyed, leaving a greyish, finely pitted finish. By altering the size of the nozzle of the gun, the air pressure of the pump and the quality of the sand, varying grades of finish can be obtained. The work can be superficial only or, by continuing the attack on any particular part of the surface, a degree of depth can be achieved, very slight relief being greatly magnified in effect by the natural refractive properties of the medium.

It is usual to mask that portion of the design not to be sand-blasted by pasting over the glass surface a specially treated paper impervious to the action of the impinging sand particles.

Sand-blasting is a method used a great deal today for the decoration of large glass panels. By combining the various processes used in engraving, the scope of the creative artist is immeasurably widened and the pleasing decorative effects so obtained open up exciting possibilities.

For prices of English engraved glasses, *see* COMMEMORATIVE GLASSES and JACOBITE GLASSES.

Decoration by the diamond and wheel is also receiving attention today, especially in this country. C. W. Yates, Helen Munro, W. J. Wilson and Laurence Whistler are among the most notable artists of the new school in this country, while the late Gertrude Bohnert of Switzerland produced work of distinction.

An example of the work of Laurence Whistler is shown in Fig. 123. In this case, the glass has been designed and made specially, but in some cases old glasses have been engraved with modern subjects. Whistler uses a steel point, and his stippling has that light touch and evanescence reminiscent of the Dutch masters of the eighteenth century. He also contrives to convey the effect of depth by ingeniously controlling the spacing of the dots to increase or decrease the play of light. This is amply displayed on the specimen shown in Fig. 123.

EPERGNE.
See SWEETMEAT GLASSES.

EXETER FLUTE.
See ENGLISH GLASS, HISTORY OF.

FAIRFAX CUP.
See VENETIAN GLASS.

FIBRE GLASS.
See SPUN GLASS.

FILIGREE or **LATTICINIO.** In the filigree glasses, white opaque, or more rarely coloured threads, were entwined and twisted throughout the mass of colourless glass to produce charming lace-like effects. This type of decoration was first used to a limited extent by the Romans, the rims of bowls of mosaic glass being a popular subject. It was not until the art was re-discovered by the Venetians during the Renaissance, however, that it was developed to a high standard. The Venetian name for this type of decoration was *latticinio*, *latticino* or *lattimo*—literally, milk-white.

The knowledge of making filigree later spread to Bohemia for we learn that Johannes Mathesius wrote in 1562: 'Formerly the churches had stained windows, but now colourless glass is common on which white threads are drawn with white enamel and which are said to be made in Silesia.'

After the Venetian decline, however, the art seems once again to have been lost, and it was not until the early nineteenth century that it was brought to perfection by French workers. George Bontemps, author of the famous *Guide du Verrier* (1868) and a director of the Choisy-le Roi Glassworks, presented specimens of filigree manufacture at the Paris Exhibition of French Industry in 1839; and, although in his opinion the specimens were far from perfect, they were of sufficient quality to inspire efforts from several other French factories to imitate them. Among such competitors were the famous works Baccarat and St Louis, which gained a high reputation shortly afterwards for the production of paperweights (*see* PAPERWEIGHTS), some of which had filigree decoration.

Bontemps showed better specimens at the later Exhibition in 1844, as well as samples of millefiori. J. Labarte (*Histoire des art Industriels du Moyen Age a l'epoque de la Renaissance*, Paris, 1864-1866; translated version by Wilfred Buckley, *European Glass*, 1926, pp. 12-14) described the methods used to produce filigree, the information being obtained from Bontemps himself. The following is Labarte's description of the method which was, no doubt, similar to that used by the glass-men of Egypt and by the Venetians:

'The vases with coloured threads and filigree ornamentation are composed of the assemblage of a certain number of small glass canes in cylindrical form, one-eighth to one-quarter of an inch in diameter, made either of opaque white glass or coloured glass, or of glass enclosing filigree patterns. These canes, prepared beforehand, are disposed in such order as the glass-maker may choose, and are often placed alternately with canes of plain white glass; they are welded together by fusion and blowing, and finally moulded, when they form a compact homogeneous paste convertible like any piece of ordinary glass into vases of every form. As many as twenty-five or thirty, or even forty, canes may enter into the composition of a Venetian vase; it is therefore indispensable, before explaining the processes of their fabrication, to describe the making of these canes of glass, which are, so to speak, the elements of their composition.

'In order to make a cane of coloured glass, the glass blower takes at the end of his blowing-iron the requisite quantity of glass from the pot in which it is fused, and rolls it upon the marver (a smooth iron slab), in order to cause the substance

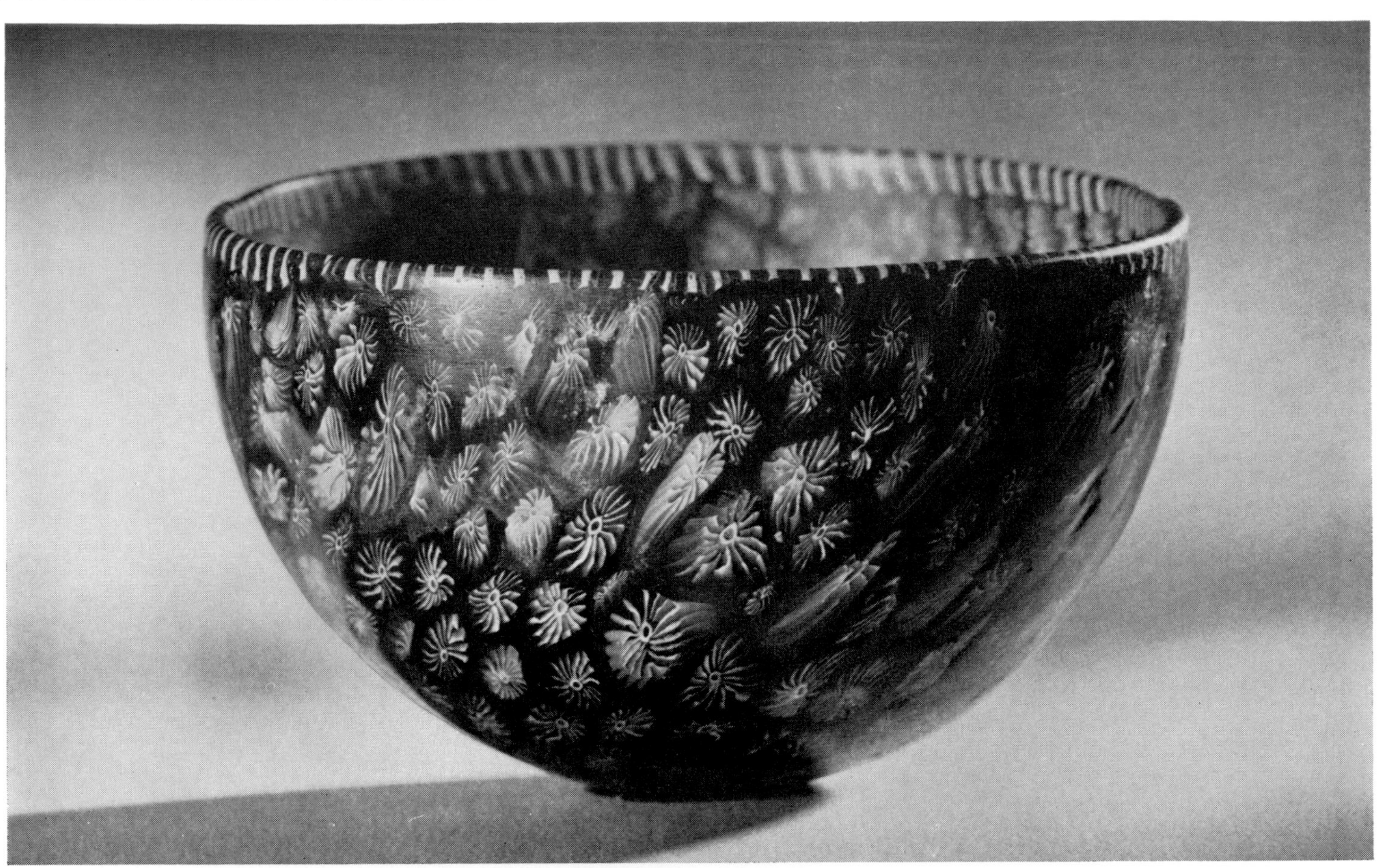

126. *Roman round-bottomed bowl in mosaic glass with filigree rim of opaque white, first century A.D. Collection of John Kalinich.*
127. *German goblet of the seventeenth century made from filigree canes.* (*By courtesy of the Victoria and Albert Museum*)

to adhere to his blowing-iron, and to make it into a cylindrical mass, of from 2½ to 3 inches long, which he allows partially to cool to give it consistency. He then dips the end of the blowing-iron, charged with the little column of coloured glass, into a melting-pot containing ordinary white (colourless) glass, in order to surround the coloured glass with a casing of white. He draws the blowing-iron from the pot and again "marvers" the lump to make the transparent glass of an even thickness round the coloured, and to form of the whole a kind of truncated column of from 2¾ to 3 inches diameter. This column is then exposed to a strong heat, to weld the layers together, and next drawn out so as to form a cane of from ⅛ to ¼ of an inch in diameter, the centre of which is coloured, surrounded by a very thin surface of white colourless glass. It is then divided into pieces of different lengths.'

The foregoing process was repeated time and time again to form canes of different coloured combinations and shapes.

Filigree work was used by the Romans, notably on the charming round bottomed bowls in mosaic with the ring decorated with opaque white twisted thread, such as the specimen in Fig. 126, probably first century B.C. or first century A.D.

It was a popular form of decoration in the Venetian period. Mention is made of it in 1540 (Biringuccio, *De la Pirotechnica*), and Guiseppe Briati, a well-known Venetian manufacturer, specialised in it as late as the middle eighteenth century. When the pattern was of an intricate nature, developed in the first

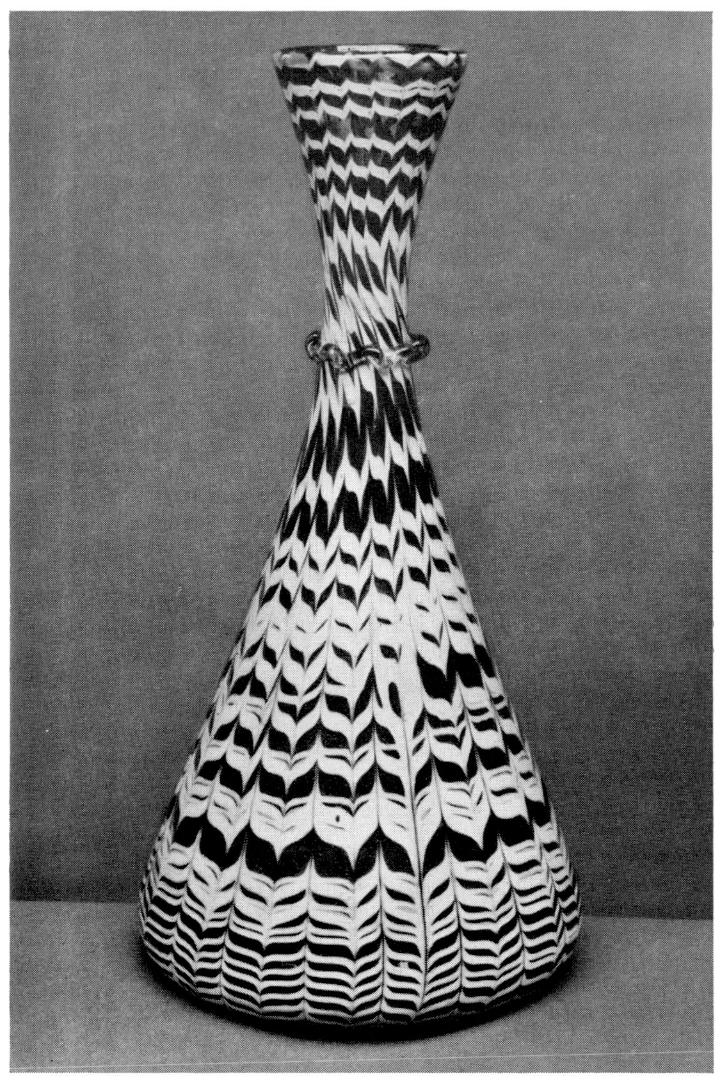

128. *Venetian ewer of the sixteenth century, in filigree glass.* (*By courtesy of the Victoria and Albert Museum*)

half of the sixteenth century, it was described by the Venetians as *Vetro de Trina*—literally, lace-glass. A typical Venetian specimen is shown in Fig. 128.

The fashion of making filigree spread northwards to the Netherlands, to Bohemia and to Germany (*see* Fig. 127). In this country, of course, its great period was from 1745 to 1780 when the stems of glasses were decorated with opaque white twist threads. (*See* OPAQUE-TWIST STEMMED GLASSES.)

FINGER BOWLS. The early form of finger bowl was a tall cylindrical vessel, resembling to some extent the modern tumbler; others are found waisted and on feet, the bowls with threaded border and patterned in the style described at the time as 'nipt diamond waies' (*q.v.*). During the first half of the eighteenth century, however, the earlier tall form, known then as a 'water glass' or a 'wash hand glass', changed to the more familiar shallow cup-shaped or straight-sided bowl.

The finger bowl or water glass of this period was sometimes provided with a glass cover, known in the eighteenth century as a 'plate'. The covers were made to match the bowls and usually terminated in a small knopped finial.

Finger bowls from the second half of the eighteenth century are fairly common and can be obtained in sets of up to half a dozen. The usual style is a straight-sided or cup-sided bowl from three and a half to five inches in width and between three to four inches in height. Those in flint are often plain, but some are found decorated with light cutting, such as stars and hollows, flat flutes and splits. Those in opaque white are sometimes painted in coloured enamels in the usual Chinese *famille rose*.

Although blue finger bowls are held by many to be a product exclusively of the Bristol glasshouses, glass bowls in various colours such as blue, green, ruby and amethyst were, of course, made at many glasshouses throughout the country. A typical Bristol finger bowl in dark blue glass with gilt decorative border is shown in Fig. 37, BRISTOL GLASS. It is signed 'I. Jacobs. Bristol'.

Early in the nineteenth century, finger bowls were blown in an open-and-shut mould, the interior surface of the mould being patterned. Geometrical designs, vertical ribbing and fluting were styles of decoration popular at the time. This type of blown finger bowl can be recognised by the light vertical seam where the halves of the mould joined.

As already stated finger bowls of the second half of the eighteenth century are fairly common and can be obtained in sets of up to half a dozen. Six changed hands five years ago for £16.

FIRING GLASSES. It became fashionable during the eighteenth century to belong to a club or a society. There were Jacobite Clubs, formed following the rising of 1715 and 1745 the Cycle Club founded in 1710 and reconstituted in 1724, the Hunt Clubs, such as the Caerwys, the Friendly and the Taporley, and a host of others. Some of the clubs were formed mainly to air political views, and although well aware of their activities, the Government of the time did nothing to discourage them. It was known that the clubs were really an excuse for riotous wining and dining.

The glasses used in such clubs were characterised by their thick stems and sturdy feet, specially designed to withstand thumping on the table during the frequent toasts or when a song was being applauded. When a number of these glasses were sharply rapped on the table during a toast, the sound emitted was for all the world like a volley of musketry, hence the term 'firing' glasses. Because of their sturdiness they are not very elegant glasses. The feet of some are as much as half an inch thick, mainly flanged, but some specimens are found of conical formation.

The bowl forms on firing glasses are for the most part trumpet or straight sided, but other forms are found such as bell, ogee and ovoid. The bowls are usually plain, but some are found engraved with the club emblems, such as the Jacobite Clubs, or Masonic glasses engraved with the appropriate emblems of the Craft (*see* Fig. 114, right).

The usual capacity of firing glasses is between two and four ounces. When hard drinking was the order of the night, the toast-master of the club had to remain reasonably clear headed in order to carry out the duties of his office. He was therefore afforded a special glass of deceptive capacity, known today as the toast-master's glass. Although to all outward appearances it was similar to an ordinary long-stemmed drinking glass, the bowl, in fact, was almost solid. It was provided with a shallow depression holding between half or three-quarters of an ounce of liquid.

Deceptive dram glasses are found which may easily be confused with the toast-master glasses. They are similar in appearance to these and were used by tavern keepers for travellers on passing coaches. When filled, they presented a normal appearance, the thick, heavy sides vanishing. At that time the usual spirit glass held between three to four ounces and it could be filled for a fourpenny piece. The deceptive dram glasses, however, only held about a quarter of their legal content.

Firing glasses such as those described, usually change hands between £3 and £5.

FLASKS.

See Nailsea Glass.

FLASKS FOR THE POCKET. After centuries of use, the pocket flask or bottle is still to be found. A typical specimen is shown in Nailsea Glass, Fig. 197. In general, they are of flat oval shape, whether single or double. The double or twin flask, for carrying two kinds of liquid, has two necks; in fact, it consists of two bottles joined together on the flat side. In this case, the sides of the flask, where the two halves join, are generally found strengthened with a thick band of trailed glass.

Although today pocket or hip flasks are made protected with a metal casing, the early flasks did not have this advantage. The protection against accidental damage was very primitive when they were first introduced about the sixteenth century. A. Hartshorne (*Old English Glasses*, 1897, p. 86) states that these articles have been found in most European countries, bearing inscriptions very much alike. He suggests that pocket flasks, filled with ardent spirits, were often given to soldiers as a parting gift on their departure for wars. An advertisement appearing in the *Advertiser*, 26th July, 1762, tends to support Hartshorne's views: 'There have been many accidents happene'd by the breaking of Glass Pocket Bottles, particularly in the military way.'

On the other hand, glass flasks were used extensively in England during coaching days. Their use for the comfort of passengers both internally and externally during night journeys must have been an important consideration, especially during the winter months.

Before the introduction of the metal casing, various methods were adopted in an endeavour to make the article as robust as possible. One obvious precaution was to make the flask from exceptionally thick glass, and this method, with the added help of strips of glass and bosses applied along the edges of the flask, was popular from the early eighteenth century. This improvement followed the introduction of gathering at the pot-mouth by the method known as 'double-flint'.

The next step was the introduction of the leather casing, and an occasional specimen of early pocket flask with the added protection comes to light, mainly in the north country.

Francis Buckley (*Glass*, Vol. VIII, 1931, p. 365) refers to a patent in connection with a protective covering for pocket flasks in August, 1709. Jane Tasker was granted a patent for making flask cases of 'flags, rushes and straw'. This was apparently a method then unknown in this country, and was most probably introduced from Florence in Italy where it was successfully applied for the protection of wine and oil bottles. Indeed, something very similar is still used for the protection of Italian wine bottles.

Later in the eighteenth century, Jackson and Sons of Clerkenwell Green (1768-1800) specialised in protective covering for bottles in general, the establishment being described as a 'case Wickered and Cut Smelling Bottle Manufactury'. Some of these old flasks may have survived, but the protective wicker casing would have perished long ago.

Buckley mentions (*Glass*, Vol. VIII, 1931, p. 366) the custom of decorating pocket flasks and refers to the following notice in the *Newcastle Courant*, 27th September, 1783: 'Stolen in Newcastle one white glass Pocket Bottle, with Barley Corns engraved upon it.' An example can be seen in the Blackgate Museum, Newcastle; it is wheel engraved on one side with a rose and bud, and on the reverse side with the initials J.S. within a wreath.

Early pocket flasks occasionally come up for sale. One with pear-shaped body, with trailing and raspberry prunts, changed hands in 1954 for £30. A second specimen of early manufacture with pincered sides realised £30 in the following year. Those of later manufacture can be obtained for a pound or so.

FLINT GLASS.

See Single Flint Glasses.

FOLDED FOOT. The folded foot was made by folding the rim of the foot under the base, forming a double layer of glass on which the glass stood. It could vary in width from a quarter of an inch up to half an inch, but on the very large baluster glasses it was even wider. The folded foot, which gave greatly increased strength to the outer rim of the fold, was a feature developed by the English glass-maker from the Venetian specimens.

Some of the Verzelini goblets have folded feet, and most seventeenth-century glasses, whether imported or manufactured at home, showed a folded foot.

The style continued in general use throughout the balustroid period up to the Excise Act of 1745, and although the rim became somewhat narrower, it was still wider than contemporary Continental specimens. After 1745, however, the folded rim rapidly disappeared, being accompanied by a reduction in the diameter of the foot itself in relation to the bowl.

The folded foot made a reappearance about 1780 for a brief period, but the foot was smaller and flatter than those of the first half of the century, and the folded rim narrower.

Folded feet are therefore rare on glasses with opaque-twist stems, and exceedingly rare on glasses with cut stems. Specimens of glasses with opaque-twist stems and folded feet are shown in Figs. 199 and 200.

FOOT-MAKER.

See Wineglass, The Making of.

FRAUDS AND REPRODUCTIONS. When it comes to frauds or fakes, glass is no different from any other commodity. Objects that are rare and demand a high price have been the subject of almost universal reproduction and imitation. There is a difference, of course, between the deliberate fake and the innocent imitation, but whether the purpose of reproduction is malicious or not makes very little difference to the collector when he finds he has not bought the genuine article.

Some experts, of course, claim that it is always possible to detect a forgery. H. J. Powell, however, who was himself a well-known glass-maker, has stated (*Glassmaking in England*, 1923, p. 148): 'A glass may be so scientifically faked that its discovery is exceedingly difficult. The workmanship, the weight, the colour, the feel, the ring and the wear of a glass are signs, but are signs which can be imitated. The only glasses about which one can be perfectly sure are those which have been handed down as heirlooms and those about which an accurate record in writing has been preserved.'

Few specimens of glass, however, are so obliging as to be accompanied by such a record, and the collector is faced with the necessity of employing his own experience and knowledge of the subject if he wishes to accumulate the genuine specimens while avoiding the imitation.

There is plenty of opportunity for him to test his skill; reproductions can be found almost anywhere, often in the most unexpected places; moreover, they have improved in quality and quantity during recent years. The following is a brief survey of the usual aids recommended for the detection of fakes.

Pontil Mark. With very few exceptions, all early glasses possess a pontil mark, but all glasses with a pontil mark are not necessarily early ones; all intentional fakes will show one.

129. *Reproduction of the Verzelini goblet shown in Fig. 269, Verzelini Glasses.*

130. *Reproduction of the Royal Oak Goblet illustrated in Fig. 116.*

Cut-stemmed glasses will also show the pontil mark on the base, because during the eighteenth century at least it was not considered necessary to remove the sharp edges resulting from the attachment of the glass to the pontil.

Probably the only articles which had the pontil mark removed during the eighteenth century were cruet bottles, and because of this, they have been mistrusted by some glass collectors. Cruet bottles were for the most part designed to come in close and continual contact with the silver or plated stand; in order that the bottles might stand firmly, and also to avoid spoiling the stand, the pontil mark obviously had to be removed.

Weight and Ring. The fact that articles in lead glass emit a ring when lightly struck is advanced in some text books as conclusive evidence that a specimen is genuine. Lead glass is not alone, however, in emitting a ring; barium glasses also give quite a resonant note. What is more important is that the ring of any glass depends entirely on whether the vessel will allow free vibration; most drinking glasses, because of their open bowls, vibrate when struck, and therefore ring easily, but a decanter in lead metal will not ring however much it is persuaded. The test based on weight and ring may be a guide, but it is by no means conclusive.

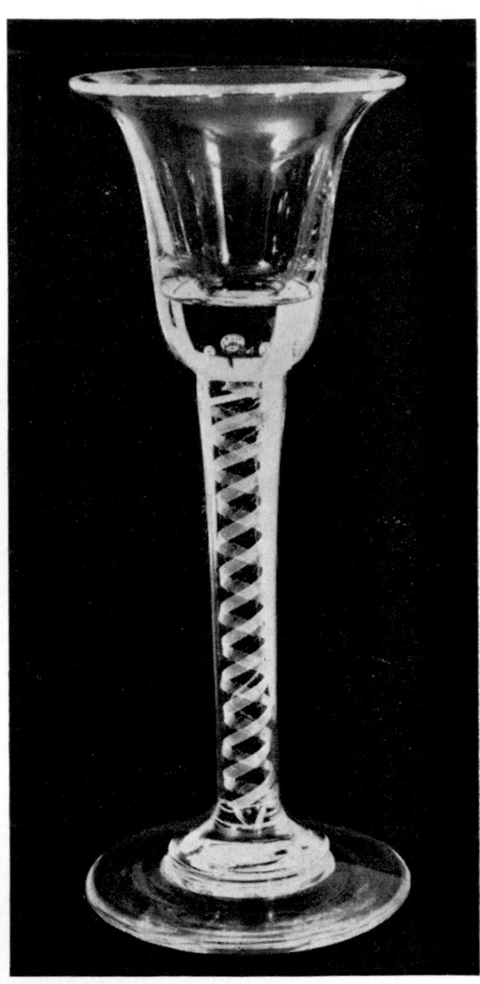

131. *Faked William III glass engraved in commemoration of the Battle of the Boyne.* 132. *Continental reproduction in soda metal of a colour-twist stem glass.* 133. *Reproduction in soda metal of a colour twist. Note the thick bottom to the bowl in order to pass off the glass as lead crystal.*

The weight of a specimen does not always indicate the nature of the metal from which it is made. Glasses made from lead are, indeed, much heavier than corresponding soda ones, but faked soda specimens are often ingeniously thickened to mislead the inexperienced or unwary. An example is shown in Fig. 133 of the bowl thickened at the base to make the glass heavier and so deceive the unwary into classing it as lead metal.

Colour. The colour of a specimen is also an unreliable indication of its age. Lead glass of modern manufacture has a much greater brilliancy than eighteenth-century metal because of the elimination of residual tints by careful decolourising and by the employment of purer raw materials. In intentional fakes, however, the colour and lack of brilliancy of some eighteenth-century glass can be exactly imitated. An example of this is the so-called 'pale blue tinge' of Waterford glass. This is discussed under IRISH GLASS.

Tests for Lead. The 'acid test' for lead glass is often recommended by authorities. A drop of hydrofluoric acid, to which a drop of ammonium sulphide is added, applied to the glass surface, preferably on the underside of the foot near the pontil mark or some inconspicuous part of the glass, will result in a black reaction if lead is present, owing to the formation of lead sulphide. Soda glasses or barium glasses will give no reaction to this test.

The question now arises as to how it is possible to detect modern forgeries made from lead metal. The fraudulent nature of such specimens is recognisable only by their faults in workmanship and form. Although the faker can reproduce exactly the more obvious characteristics of the eighteenth-century metal, and can passably imitate wear by abrasion with fine emery powder, he often fails in details of workmanship and still more frequently in the proportions given to a specimen. The flange of a bowl, the thickness of a stem, the shape of a knop, the junction of bowl to stem, and stem to foot, are details where the faker can err, quite apart from his faulty rendering of the general proportions of the specimen. The finish of modern reproductions is often too good or too crude; the happy medium attained by the eighteenth-century craftsman is rarely exactly imitated by the modern faker.

Nevertheless, the existence of clever reproductions in lead metal is well recognised by reputable authorities, and all newly-discovered specimens of old glass likely to prove important and valuable are 'vetted' by a competent committee of experts before being accepted as genuine.

The author has given an account of several new methods (*English Tableglass*, 1951, pp. 256-266) of determining distinctive differences that exist between the nature of early and modern glass, which assist in establishing whether a specimen is genuine or false. No method is infallible, however, but each test applied provides more evidence for or against the authenticity of a specimen and allows final judgment to be passed.

It has been pointed out that there is a fundamental difference between a genuine reproduction and a glass that is deliberately faked with the intent to deceive. Reproductions have been made by reputable glass-makers where it is known, for example, that only one original, most probably a museum piece, exists. An outstanding example is the Verzelini goblet shown in Fig. 269 (*see* VERZELINI GLASSES). This is known as the G. S. Goblet and is dated 1586 and engraved in diamond-point work IN: GOD: IS: AL: MI: TRVST. An expert reproduction of it is shown in Fig. 129. Another excellent reproduction is the Royal Oak Goblet shown in Fig. 130. This can be compared with the original shown in Fig. 116. (*See* ENGLISH GLASS, HISTORY OF.)

On the other hand, the engraved glass shown in Fig. 131 is a deliberate fake and should not deceive, although it is known that when a small number of these glasses were placed on the market some years ago, a few found their way into well-known collections. The specimen is a faked William III glass, the original series having been made to commemorate the Battle of the Boyne.

Portrait glasses are always popular and constitute a fruitful field for fraudulent reproduction. Jacobite portrait glasses have received a certain amount of attention in this direction, as have 'Amen' glasses. (*See* JACOBITE GLASSES.)

It has frequently been stated that reproduction of spiral stem glasses—that is, opaque-twist, air-twist and incised-twist glasses—can be detected by the direction given to the spiral itself. It has been claimed that a faked glass follows a reverse direction to that of the genuine article. Were it true, this would be a most considerate action on the part of the glass-maker responsible for the work of reproduction. The spiral in all genuine specimens should descend from right to left—that is, it should follow the spiral of a cork-screw—but the spirals in all the fakes known to the author follow precisely the same direction.

The enamel used in faked opaque-twists is often a guide. The early enamel was a dense white often with a faint cast of blue and less frequently of pink. Many fakes, on the other hand, have threads of enamel of thinner consistency, usually termed the 'milk-and-water' quality of opaque glass, which is easily detected once the layman has familiarised himself with the denser enamel used by the early glass-makers.

Examples of fraudulent reproductions of colour twist glasses are shown in Figs. 132 and 133. In this case, also, not only are the colours and thread formation quite different from genuine eighteenth-century colour twists, but the shape of the glasses themselves leaves much to be desired.

Another favourite reproduction is the paperweight, both millefiori and with a subject. Some reproductions, of course, are the result of a conscious effort to revive an old art, and there is no attempt to deceive on the part of the manufacturer; indeed, most mark their productions. On the other hand, deliberate fakes are known. According to Robert A. Elder, of the United States National Museum, Washington (*see* PAPERWEIGHTS; PAPERWEIGHTS OF MODERN MANUFACTURE) specimens of good paperweights were sent to China for reproduction purposes in the 1930s, and the faked articles so produced were of sufficient quality to deceive the collecting fraternity.

The following list gives some idea of the types of glass article which have been reproduced since glass collecting became a popular pursuit:

Air-twists	Roemers
Cameo glass.	Syrian Mosque-lamps
Colour-twists	Waterford Glass
Jacobite 'Amen' Glasses	William III Glasses (Battle of the Boyne)
Jacobite Portrait Glasses	Yards-of-Ale
Nailsea ware	Zwischenglaser
Opaque-twists	
Paperweights	

It should be noted that, in the case of zwischenglaser, some clever imitations were being made as early as the eighteenth century (Wilfred Buckley, *European Glass*, 1926, p. 21). (*See* GERMAN AND BOHEMIAN GLASS.)

FRENCH GLASS. In spite of the fact that since Roman times there has been a continuous tradition of glass-making in France, there was never any determined approach to emulate the efforts of the English or other Continental glass-makers, at least so far as domestic glass is concerned.

On the other hand, France was pre-eminently successful in the production of stained glass and window glass, and an export trade in this type of glass was established from mediaeval times.

French glass-makers also gained success in the manufacture of mirrors. Probably the most famous example is the *Galerie des Glaces* at Versailles, completed in 1682 by Charles le Brun. The sheets of glass in this famous hall measure two feet six inches by three feet six inches. They were made by the broad process, and as they were not originally ground and polished, they exhibited great distortion, held by many to be part of their beauty. Many of the original sheets have today been replaced by mirrors of modern flat glass.

The broad process for the making of sheet glass was employed extensively both in France and Germany. A cylinder of glass about five feet long by about a foot or more in diameter was blown by mouth. After being allowed to cool, the cylinder was then slit down its length, laid with its sides uppermost on a flat bed of sand in a furnace, and heated until the sides had softened and had sunk slowly to the sand bed to become a flat sheet.

The broad process had its limitations both in regards to the size of the plates that could be produced and their irregular thickness; to overcome these imperfections, a new process was invented by Louis Lucas de Nehou in 1691, which depended on the casting of sheets by pouring the liquid glass into large moulds or frames, smoothing while hot by rollers, and afterwards grinding and polishing both surfaces.

This process considerably increased the prestige and trade of the French makers of plate-glass and mirrors, especially as the process was not adopted in this country until nearly the end of the eighteenth century.

Although no great effort had been made to produce table glass after the style of the Venetian glass-makers, some distinction was gained by French glass-workers at Nevers. For something like two centuries, glass figures were produced there, decorated in colours. These figures, although described by many writers as 'enamel' figures, were really made from glass; they were 'lamp-blown'—that is, they were made by

134. *Carafe and drinking glasses produced by Cristalleries de Baccarat, France, for Louis XVIII.* circa *1800.*

working rods and tubes of coloured glass in the flame of a lamp. The coloured glass used for this decorative work was usually in characteristic shades of red, blue, white and dull yellow.

Articles of this description were made up to the eighteenth century but it is difficult to suggest, with one or two exceptions, where surviving specimens were actually made. It is known, for example, that similar articles were made at Bordeaux, Marseilles, Rouen and Paris. Jacques Raux (d. 1777) advertised in the Parisian journals: 'All sorts of grotesque figures for the decoration of cabinets and chimney pieces.' Specimens of his work are preserved in the Musée de Cluny, Paris.

As has already been stated, up to the end of the eighteenth century, France had been far behind the rest of Europe in the manufacture of table glass-ware. The only vessels produced, apart from such specialised articles as those made at Nevers and elsewhere, had been the *verre de fougère*, which for the most part was made in simple styles in the surviving Roman tradition.

Factories for the manufacture of artistic glass had, indeed, been established during the eighteenth century, but the standard was very low and most of the best glass-ware was imported from Bohemia, England and Germany. Indeed, the position gave rise to so much concern on the part of the authorities that in 1760 the Academie des Sciences offered a prize for the best suggestion to improve this branch of the French glass industry.

It was probably due to this encouragement that the factory at Baccarat, near Luneville in Lorraine, was founded in 1765 as the Verrerie de Saint-Anne, and which developed in 1800 into the famous Cristalleries de Baccarat. This establishment, still a flourishing concern today, can boast of a record for famous glass-ware from its inception.

In 1832, in association with Cristallerie de Saint Louis, a neighbouring glassworks, Cristalleries de Baccarat purchased Cristallerie du Creusot, where methods of incrustation in glass had been perfected. It was this technique which eventually led to the manufacture at Baccarat of the prized paperweights of the middle nineteenth century, and for which Cristalleries de Baccarat are world famous. (*See* PAPERWEIGHTS, BACCARAT.)

A large museum has been established in Paris by this company displaying artistic glassware that has been produced in its factories over the last one hundred and fifty years. Among the very large number of specimens preserved are table services designed for King Louis XVIII, shown in Fig. 134, a water carafe of King Charles X, Fig. 135, candelabra from the Palace of the Czars, Fig. 136, and many modern productions such as the formal dinner service for the Palais de l'Elysée, a specimen of which is shown in Fig. 137.

It was not until early in the nineteenth century, however, that French glass-makers began to interest themselves in creative work in glass. A general reaction against the over-emphasised styles which had marked the English efforts began to develop, and new styles in glass art became established.

The most notable of the glass artists of that time was Emile Gallé (1845-1904) of Nancy. His style was something entirely new and he succeeded in establishing what has become almost a renaissance in the art of glass. Gallé obtained ingenious colouring effects and original contrasts in combinations of opaque and transparent glass, and he exploited with great success the technique of delicately tinted glass from which the upper surface was removed by wheel or acid methods, to disclose some simple naturalistic motif in relief. A specimen of this work is shown in Fig. 139.

Gallé claimed that for every desired effect, there should be a specialised method. As an example, in order to reduce the time taken to carve away the background in relief work, he devised a vertical disc for engraving deep recesses into thick glass. By such methods, Gallé firmly established a new conception in glass which very quickly achieved world-wide acceptance as *L'Art Nouveau.*

Gallé had many followers. Rosseau and Léveillé were notable artists of the Gallé school; they too advanced the new technique and added to it the method of producing 'flushed' glass, in which coloured glass dusts were distributed over the glass surface and afterwards fired.

The brothers Daum, also of Nancy, were others of the new art who specialised mainly in repetition work of a similar nature (*see* Fig. 140), and because of their early experience as ceramists, their productions were largely based on processes of enamelling, and of obtaining iridescent effects.

More recently, René Lalique achieved notable success in original creations such as statuettes, chandeliers, door panels,

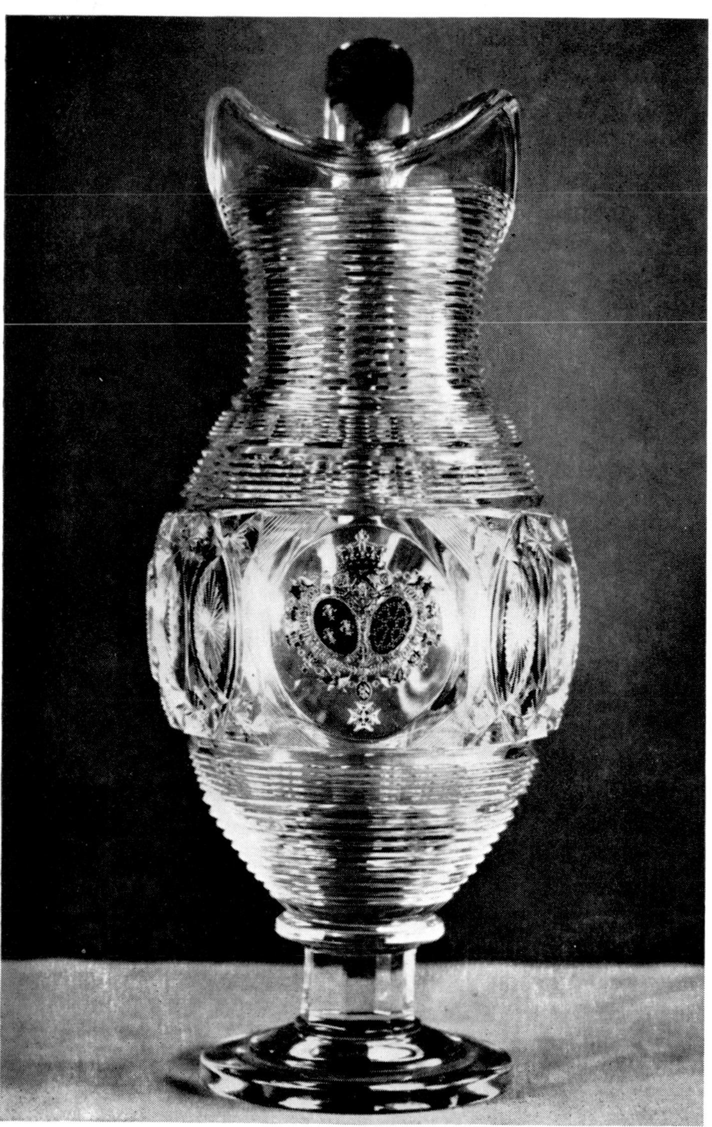

135. *Carafe produced by Cristalleries de Baccarat, France, for Charles X.* circa *1830.*

136. *Candelabra made for the Palace of the Czars by Cristalleries de Baccarat, France. The candelabra is now converted to electric light in place of candle light.*

bowls and similar articles, elegantly designed and clay moulded by blowing and pressing, and afterwards given a matt surface by acid or wheel engraving (*see* ENGRAVING). Only a certain number of pieces would be produced from a particular mould, after which it would be deliberately destroyed. An example of his work is shown in Fig. 138.

René Lalique was the first of the modern school of glass artists to use glass in association with ordinary building materials for large monumental pieces, notably in conjunction with steel. Guillaume Janneau (*Modern Glass*, 1931, p. 9) points out that 'in the framework formed by the partitions of a steel

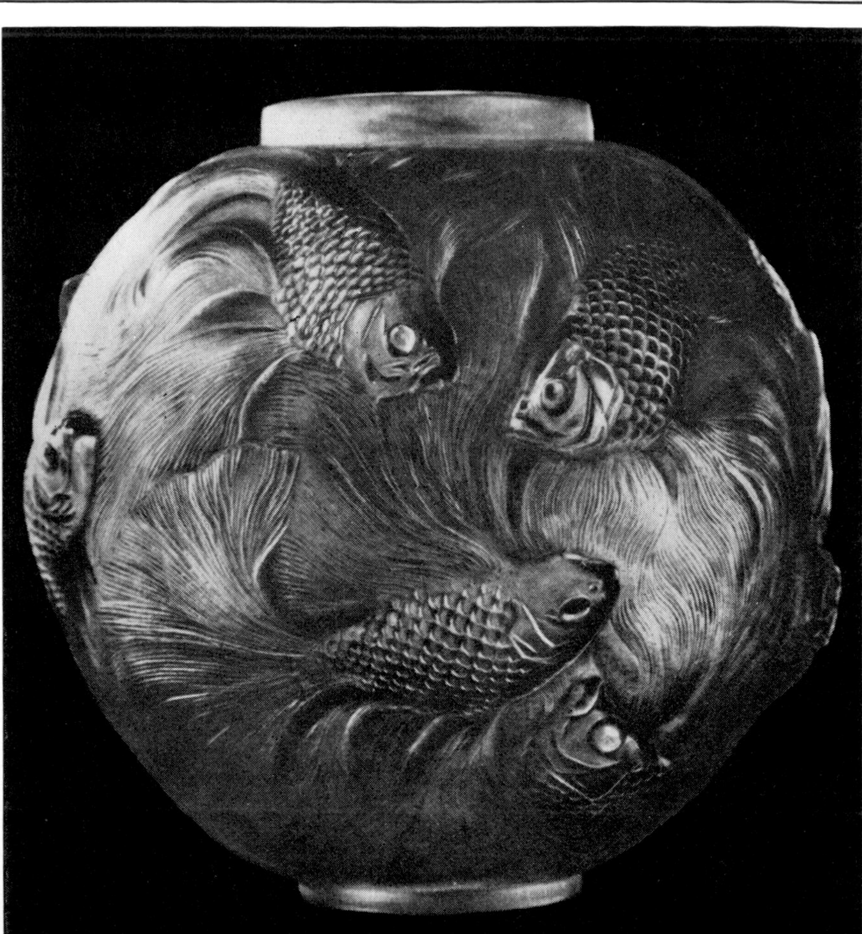

137. *Drinking glass from the formal dinner service of the French President at the Elysée Palace, Paris.* (*Cristalleries de Baccarat, France.*) 138. *Vase by René Lalique, moulded and obscured.*

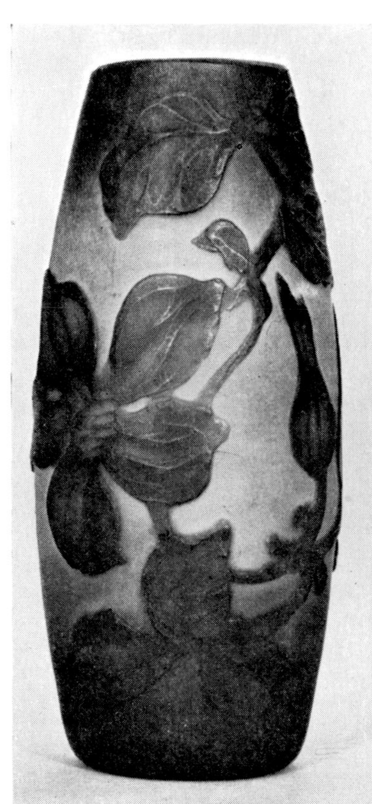

139. *Signed vase by Emile Gallé with flower motif carved in relief.* circa *1900.* 140. *Flushed glass by A. Daum of Nancy.*

door, Lalique set glass panels, whose thickness made them proof against breakage, and at the same time accentuated their luminosity. In 1930 he made the altar rail for a church, with three panels, consisting of long glass strips decorated with a design of lilies. This work will rank as one of the greatest successes, not only for the master himself, but for the whole of the French decorative glass work.'

Specimens of glass produced by the early French artists of *L'Art Nouveau* are popular today. Some are signed, but most specimens are easily recognisable by their distinctive styles.

Probably the largest collection of Emile Gallé's work to change hands during recent years was that sold in Egypt from the Farouk collection. Over one hundred vases sold for a total of £2,021 representing an average of about £20 each. The price range varied from £10 to £45. A large number of Gallé lamps from the same collection sold for an average of £15.

An occasional specimen of 'Verre de Nevers' changes hands in this country usually at prices between £20 and £40.

Glass paperweights of Baccarat, St Louis and Clichy, produced about the middle of the last century, are fully discussed under PAPERWEIGHTS.

FURNACES, TYPES OF.
See MELTING OF GLASS.

GADGET.
See WINEGLASS, THE MAKING OF.

GADROONING.
See JELLY GLASSES.

GAFFER.
See WINEGLASS, THE MAKING OF.

GALLÉ, EMILE. (1845-1904)
See AMERICAN GLASS; FRENCH GLASS; SWEDISH GLASS.

GEM STONES.
See TASSIE, JAMES AND WILLIAM.

GERMAN AND BOHEMIAN GLASS. There is strong evidence that glass has been made continuously in the Rhine district since the days of the Roman Empire, from where the knowledge spread during the middle ages to Central Europe. The centres of glass-making were naturally those in which there occurred a ready supply of raw materials, such as wood for fuel and easily procurable minerals for the manufacture of the glass itself. Such materials could be obtained in great profusion from the thickly wooded and mountainous regions which divided Bohemia from Bavaria, Saxony and Silesia.

It was not until the fourteenth century, however, that the industry began to develop on anything like a large scale, and very few vessels exist made prior to that period. The evidence, in fact, during the fourteenth century is mainly documentary.

The early German vessels were primitive, but were nonetheless of a distinct character. By far the most important forms are the basins and cylindrical vessels shaped like beakers with a high projecting 'kick' inside. They were decorated by raised spots of glass stuck on the surface known as 'nuppen' (knobs or blobs). The 'krautstrunk', so-called because of its resemblance to a cabbage stalk, was a development of this vessel.

141. *Bohemian tankard with pewter mount. The wheel engraving is in conventional form after the rococo taste.* (*By courtesy of the Victoria and Albert Museum*)

These fifteenth-century forms gave the inspiration later for the classical development during the Renaissance period. They were the precursors of the 'roemer', which the Low Countries made famous from the sixteenth century onwards, and which has been described by Hartshorne as the most popular and picturesque glass which has ever been devised (*Old English Glasses*, 1897, p. 47). Another writer, W. B. Honey (*Glass*, 1946, p. 74), has stated that the beauty of the green colour of the roemers, and their often noble proportions, entitle them to rank among the best of all vessels made in Europe. There is an exceedingly fine collection of these glasses in the Wilfred Buckley Collection at the Victoria and Albert Museum, London.

Other vessels were decorated with nuppen, and such names as 'nuppenglas' and 'nuppenbecher' are met with. The glass shown in Fig. 142 is a 'stangenglas'—literally, 'flagstaff'—and is decorated with 'warze', or knobs, for which the current English term is 'prunt' or 'raspberry prunt'. The 'stangenglas' shown in Fig. 142 is thirteen-and-three-eighths inches high and is of the sixteenth century.

It will be recalled that some of Ravenscroft's glasses were decorated in a similar manner. Fig. 226 shows a goblet with a

142. *German goblet or 'stangenglas' with a hollow stem decorated with raspberry prunts. The glass is sixteenth century.* 143. *Bohemian zwischenglaser, in which a design in gold leaf is enclosed between two layers of glass.* circa *1730.* 144. *Reichadlerhumpen, a German beaker enamelled in various colours with the escutcheons of members of the Holy Roman Empire, surmounted by a crowned double-headed eagle, on the reverse side is the date 1604.* (See ENAMELLED GLASS. German.) (*All by courtesy of the Victoria and Albert Museum*)

hollow stem decorated with raspberry prunts, the lower one carrying the raven's head seal. (*See* ROEMER AND RUMMER.)

German vessels of this period were given expressive names, such as 'maigelein' (mayflower bowl), 'scheuer' (tub), 'igel' (hedgehog), 'romer' (Roman glass), 'krug' (jug or mug) and 'humpen' (vessel).

Early in the sixteenth century, the Venetian influence began to be felt and many Italian craftsmen were at work in various glasshouses throughout Central Europe. These glasshouses were located in such famous centres as Cassel, Nuremburg, Hall-in-the-Tyrol, Munich, Langshut, Cologne and Dessau. A full list of the German glasshouses which followed Venetian practice has been given by R. Schmidt (*Das Glas*, 2nd ed., 1922, pp. 124-132).

The Italian technique was eventually mastered and by the middle of the seventeenth century Bohemian glass-makers had overcome their initial lack of knowledge of glass-making and had learnt to equal the Venetian products.

Coloured glass was one of the most notable introductions by German workers of this period, the most important of such productions being ruby glass. Johann Kunckel, a distinguished Silesian chemist, born in 1630, interested himself in various forms of coloured decoration and coloured glasses. Although he is usually credited for having discovered how to make ruby glass, Kunckel himself states (*Laboratorium Chymicum*, 2nd ed., 1722) that it was first discovered by Dr Andreas Cassius of Hamburg. Kunckel, however, was responsible for having produced it on a commercial scale about 1679, in which year he became Director of the Elector of Brandenburg's glasshouses on the Isle of Peacocks at Potsdam.

He discovered that it was necessary to reheat the glass in order to create the desired tint of ruby and that gold was required only in minute quantities. It is believed that he obtained his finest colours from gold, although he affirmed that he could produce a perfect ruby red without the use of that metal. The only other metals that can be used to tint glass red are copper and selenium, and it is to be assumed, therefore, that Kunckel had at that time mastered the difficult conditions controlling the production of ruby glass by means of copper, as selenium had not then been discovered.

Ruby glass, cut and engraved in the same way as colourless crystal glass, was highly esteemed in Germany at that time. It has been much over-rated, however, and many specimens lack both brilliancy and depth of colour.

Other coloured glasses probably initiated by Kunckel, but made after his death in 1703, are the blue and green glasses and imitation agate, made early in the eighteenth century. He also describes the making of white opaque glass, which he refers to as 'porcelain' glass.

Towards the end of the seventeenth century, the Bohemian glass-makers had developed a good crystal glass well adapted to being engraved by the diamond and the wheel. This glass now contained potash in place of the soda of the Venetian glass, with a liberal proportion of lime produced from the mountainous chalk. The potash enhanced brilliancy, but the glass had not the soft prismatic fire of the English glass-of-lead. Nevertheless, the glass was quite a satisfactory medium for the glyptic treatment, such as cutting or engraving by the wheel.

The carving of semi-precious stones and rock crystal had been practised by Italian and German lapidary craftsmen from the fifteenth century, when the art was introduced into Italy after the taking of Constantinople by the Turks in 1453. The transition to employing glass as a medium was therefore a natural one. The honour of re-discovering the process fell to Caspar Lehmann (1570-1622) of Prague, and to mark his accomplishment he was granted special privileges by Emperor Rudolf II and was appointed glass-cutter to his Court.

It is thought that Lehmann's early work was on sheets of glass in place of crystal and that later he adapted his technique to glass vessels. Only one specimen is extant, however, dated 1605, that can definitely be ascribed to Lehmann; it is cut with the wheel, but with an unpolished surface and is signed by Lehmann.

On Lehmann's death in 1622, his assistant, Georg Schwanhardt (1601-1667), obtained from the Emperor the extension of his master's patent and continued the work at Nuremburg. He advanced Lehmann's technique by polishing the cut surfaces and by enhancing the appearance of the decoration by means of the diamond point. Georg Schwanhardt fortunately left a number of signed glasses dated between 1640 and 1660. He had two sons, Georg and Heinrich, who carried on the family tradition. These two artists appeared to have worked both at the lapidary's wheel and with the diamond point, producing etchings. They were assisted by their three sisters, Sophia, Maria and Susanna.

Heinrich Schwanhardt is credited with having discovered the method of etching glass with hydrofluoric acid about 1670. He employed it to remove the background of his subject, leaving the figures with their original clear and smooth surface, which, contrasting with the dull ground, appeared in relief. He is also credited with having been even more proficient in the art of engraving than his father, but unfortunately no signed specimens remain of either his or his brother's work. Heinrich Schwanhardt died in 1693.

Several other workers carried on the Schwanhardt tradition at Nuremburg, chief among them being Hermann Schwinger (1640-1683) and Friedrich Killinger (1697-1726). There is a specimen of Schwinger's work in the Slade Collection at the Victoria and Albert Museum, London.

145. *Cylindrical cup painted in enamel colours by Johann Schaper of Nuremburg.* circa *1660.* (*By courtesy of the Victoria and Albert Museum*)

Towards the end of the seventeenth century, the quality of the glass itself was greatly improved, and the art of cutting with the wheel was so developed that, in the first half of the eighteenth century, a very high standard had been reached.

The earlier workers in Nuremburg had chosen landscapes for their subjects, but in Bohemia and Silesia conventional forms such as foliage were preferred, after the rococo taste. The style is illustrated in Fig. 141.

Potsdam also became famous for its decorated glass. As mentioned earlier, Johann Kunckel worked there in the latter part of the seventeenth century. At this time, too, the technique of deep cutting was introduced by Martin Winter (d. 1702) and both he and Gottfried Spiller produced work of the highest merit. Their designs usually contained figures and were composed to introduce the feature of deep cutting which was often covered with heavy gilding.

The German workers employed several methods for decorating glass with gold such as 'zwischenglaser' in which gold designs were enclosed between two layers of glass; Mildner glasses, in which gilt medallions were fixed to glass vessels; gold relief, where a design in gold was applied to a coloured enamel background similar to the technique employed at Meisen with porcelain; etched gold decoration, in which gold was applied first in sheet and then removed to form a design.

The use of gold foil to decorate glass was first employed by the Alexandrian Greeks in the first century. Excellent examples, taken from tombs of Canosa, are in the British Museum, London. They are decorated in gold with an exquisite design of acanthus leaves, combined with a small plant with tendrils,

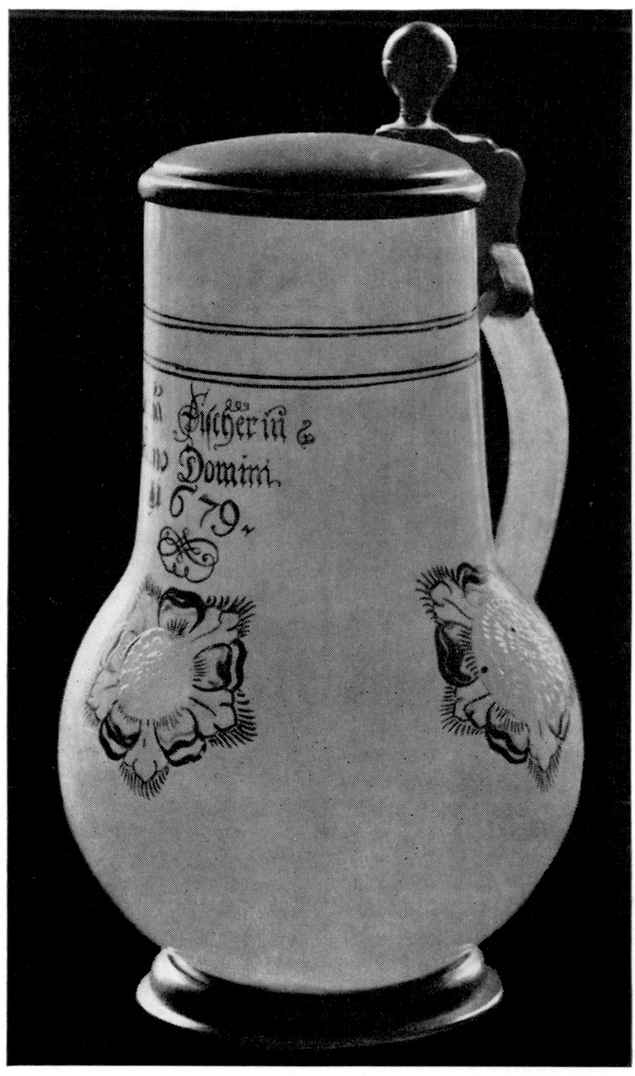

146. *Tankard painted in enamel colours by Johann Schaper with inscription 'Beata Fischerin, Anno Domini 1679'.* 147. *Beaker painted in transparent enamel by Gottlob Samuel Mohn of Vienna.* circa *1800.* (*Both by courtesy of the Victoria and Albert Museum*)

both radiating from a central flower. Even in their present condition, they compare in beauty with any other known example of ancient glass.

The following description for the making of zwischenglaser is given by Dr Schmidt in *Das Glas*, 1922, p. 352:

'Two vessels are taken, one which fits exactly into the other. The larger outer vessel is painted on the inside with oil colours, veinings and grainings being engraved on it with a needle. Gold or silver leaf is then fixed over the painting with linseed oil.

'The outside of the smaller vessel is also coated with gold or silver leaf in a similar manner. One vessel is then fitted into the other, and the upper rims cemented together with a mixture of powdered chalk and lacquer.'

Most of the zwischenglaser made in the manner described are of the eighteenth century, usually ascribed to the Bohemian and Silesian districts.

The specimen of zwischenglaser shown in Fig. 143 is a Bohemian goblet and cover, *circa* 1730. The design is in engraved gold leaf and the two layers of glass are distinctly shown in the illustration. The specimen is about ten inches in height.

Some clever imitations of zwischenglaser were made during the eighteenth century. Zwischenglaser of ruby glass in the form of round bottom cups are also known. They do not have the quality, however, of the earlier specimens; they are too harsh and mechanical for any claim to high artistic merit.

The Mildner glasses have been described in detail by Wilfred Buckley (*The Art of Glass*, 1939, p. 63). Johann Mildner (1764-1808) was employed in the Guttenbrunn in the lower Austrian district of Ottenschlag. He decorated glasses in a special way and, fortunately, he had the habit of signing his work. He did not favour the earlier form of zwischenglaser, his peculiar form of decoration being to enrich the sides of the glass with medallions. He first cut out medallions from the example he intended to decorate and then fitted in other medallions curved in the form of the example itself. In some cases narrow friezes were added at the top and bottom and a medallion was added at the bottom. The medallions on some specimens show pictures of holy subjects, portraits and initials on the outside and usually an inscription on the inside.

The Venetian craftsmen had used the method of decorating glass by painting in oil colours, particularly on its under surface, and this art was also practised in Germany during the sixteenth century. One method was to paint on the underside and to cover the work with a protective material; another was to paint the subject on the outside of the glass on a backing of gold or silver. This latter style is referred to by Dr Schmidt, who suggests Nuremberg as their place of origin. He mentions a number of pieces decorated with gold lace border and arms, dated from 1603 and 1615.

Glasses were also decorated in oil painting in combination with gilding and diamond engraving. The engraving was in the style of a repeated design, such as lace, the object being to form a border. W. Buckley mentions a record of 1614 that there were made at Wilhamsburg Works, in south-west Bohemia, 'great glasses with oil colours, scratched and engraved glasses with mastic colours'.

The art of enamelling was quickly mastered by the German workers. (*See* ENAMELLED GLASS, *German Enamelling*.) The most notable of the German enamellers was Johann Schaper, a specimen of whose work is shown in Fig. 145. Most of Schaper's work was in monochrome such as black or sepia, but the specimen shown in Fig. 145 is in coloured enamel and is therefore rare. A further specimen of Schaper's work is shown in Fig. 146 of an opaque white glass tankard painted in red, blue, black and gold, and inscribed 'Beata Fischerin Anno Domini 1679'.

A beaker painted in transparent enamel is shown in Fig. 147. The artist was Gottlob Samuel Mohn of Vienna, who worked about the end of the eighteenth century.

148. *Group of Bohemian cased glass, cut and engraved to disclose the opal underlayer. Taken from the Catalogue of the Great Exhibition of 1851.*

At the time of the Great Exhibition of 1851, Bohemian glass had gained for itself a wide reputation. *The Times*, 7th June, 1851, reporting on the glass-ware shown at the Exhibition stated: 'In glass, we cannot equal the ornamental manufactures of Bohemia.' The *Birmingham Journal*, 31st May, 1851, was not flattering in its report of products shown from the glass-makers of neighbouring Stourbridge and suggested 'the purchase of a collection of Bohemian glass which will be accessible to the workmen'.

A group of Bohemian glass-ware taken from the Catalogue of the Great Exhibition is shown in Fig. 148. The specimens shown are opaque white cased in coloured glass which has been cut away to disclose the lighter underlayer. This type of ware is popular among collectors today.

German glasses vary considerably in value. Humpen, for example, of plain cylindrical form with light enamelling and dated as early as 1680, have changed hands for as little as £7. On the other hand, a humpen and cover enamelled with the arms of Schwachheim and inscribed 'Anno Domini 1662', realised £78 a few years ago. Another humpen enamelled with the arms of Prince Johann George III, also of the seventeenth century, fetched £58.

Zwischenglaser change hands for unexpectedly low prices considering the specialised technique employed in their manufacture. During recent years prices have varied between £7 and £19.

Roemers in characteristic green glass with hollow stems, embellished with raspberry prunts, have been purchased for as little as a £1.

GLASS EXCISE ACT.

See AIR-TWIST STEMMED GLASSES; BRISTOL GLASS; CHANDELIERS; CULLET; CUT-GLASS; ENGLISH GLASS, HISTORY OF; FOLDED FOOT; INCISED-TWIST STEMMED GLASSES; JELLY GLASSES; LYNN OR NORWICH GLASSES; NAILSEA GLASS; OPAQUE-TWIST STEMMED GLASSES.

GLASS SELLERS' COMPANY.

See AKERMAN, JOHN; BOTTLES; BUGGIN BOWLS; CUT-GLASS; ENGLISH GLASS, HISTORY OF; RAVENSCROFT, GEORGE.

GREENE, JOHN (*c.* 1667).

See BALUSTER STEMMED GLASSES; BRANDY TUMBLERS; ENGLISH GLASS, HISTORY OF; SODA GLASSES.

GREENWOOD, FRANS (1680-1761).

See DUTCH GLASS; NEWCASTLE GLASSES.

GUMLEY, JOHN. John Gumley gained prominence towards the end of the seventeenth century and early in the eighteenth century for the making of mirrors. The earliest notice of him is in the *London Gazette*, 21st June, 1694, referring to a sale which included 'Looking Glasses'.

Gumley set up a glasshouse at Lambeth in 1705 and his products were still much in demand during the reign of George I. Richard Steele, who wrote for the *Spectator*, the *Tatler* and the *Lover*, wrote in the latter, 13th May, 1715, when describing Gumley's new premises in the New Exchange: 'A place where people may go and be very well entertained . . . we have arrived at such perfection of this ware . . . that it is not in the power of any Potentate in Europe to have so beautiful a mirror as he may purchase here for a trifle.'

Records show that Gumley was a Royal tradesman and supplied in that capacity mirrors for Hampton Court and elsewhere. (*See* CHANDELIERS and MIRRORS.)

HAEDY, FAMILY OF. The Haedy family had a glass-cutting business in London and are referred to in the London Directories as follows:

Cut Glass Manufactory, 287, Strand.
1778 C. & D. Haedy.
1788 C. Haedy & Son.
1792 Joseph Haedy.
1801-1810 Haedy & Lafount.

Haedy senior was a Bohemian and according to F. Buckley (*A History of Old English Glass*, 1925, pp. 34-5) was probably the man referred to in the advertisements in the *Bath Chronicle*, 20th November, 1766, and the *Birmingham Gazette*, 11th May, 1767, both of which stated: 'To be sold by Hand . . . The Stock in trade of a German, who was the first that brought the Art of Cutting and Engraving Glass from Germany. The above named German having met unforeseen losses and Misfortunes in Trade is obliged to sell his Stock for the Benefit of his Creditors.'

Buckley is of the opinion that the German referred to was either Christopher Haedy or more probably his father, and is the one who was employed by John Akerman after 1719 (*see* AKERMAN, JOHN).

Following the sales in 1766-7, the fortunes of the Haedy family appeared to have improved considerably. Notices appeared in the newspapers of sales, particularly at Bath, up to the end of the eighteenth century (*see* CANDELABRA).

HAND COOLERS OR MINIATURE PAPERWEIGHTS.
See PAPERWEIGHTS, BACCARAT MAGNUMS AND MINIATURES.

HATS.
See NAILSEA GLASS.

HEDWIG GLASSES.
See CUT-GLASS.

HILL, JOHN (*c.* 1785).
See IRISH GLASS; ENAMELLED GLASS.

HOGARTH GLASSES. William Hogarth (1697-1764), the celebrated painter and engraver, began to work about 1720. The glasses shown in several of his pictures, such as 'Rake's Progress', the four 'Election Pictures' and 'A Modern Midnight Conversation', must have been typical of tavern glasses of the time. They are known today as Hogarth glasses. They are plain stemmed, but there would appear to be a tendency to abolish the stem altogether.

The feet of the Hogarth glasses were usually of stout build, sometimes half an inch in thickness, while others appeared thicker than they actually were by virtue of a downward-flanged rim; folded feet and terraced feet were also known. These glasses have been given various names; 'firing glasses' (*see* FIRING GLASSES), because of their particular use in rapping the table during the toasting ceremony in Masonic Lodges; 'Hogarth glasses', from their appearance in that artist's pictures; and 'drams', a term still in use in Scotland today for a small quantity of liquor.

The great robustness of the glasses made them much less liable to damage than contemporary styles; the heavy, thick feet and rudimentary stem gave them such a low centre of gravity that the risk of their being knocked over was exceedingly small. For these reasons they were no doubt originally devised for use in taverns and on board ship and it is therefore only those glasses engraved with Masonic emblems that can definitely be ascribed to the Craft.

For prices of these glasses see FIRING GLASSES.

HOOLAART, G. H.
See DUTCH GLASS.

HOUR GLASS.
See SAND GLASSES.

HUMPEN.
See ENAMELLED GLASS, German Enamelling; GERMAN AND BOHEMIAN GLASS.

INCISED TWIST STEMMED GLASSES. For the origin of the incised twist it is necessary to turn to Venice. It was a form of decorating the stem of a glass externally by a series of closely formed, twisted ribs. Specimens of seventeenth-century glass of Venetian origin with this type of decoration are still preserved and, from fragments discovered in London and other centres, it would appear probable that the style was also made in this country by the early glass-makers.

149. *Glass with incised twist stem, the round funnel bowl decorated at the base with honeycomb moulding, a usual feature with this style of glass.* circa *1760.*

Support is lent to this view from the fact that many specimens with straight unknopped stems are in soda metal mainly of drawn stem manufacture, and as they are not found with a folded foot and are of poor workmanship, it is most probable that they were made outside the general run of known glasshouses. Some are found in bright green glass.

The revival of the incised twist for a short period does not appear to have occurred until the second half of the eighteenth century. The absence of the folded foot on all specimens is significant, knopping is rare and, in addition, the glasses are usually of the light construction which followed the Excise Act. Honeycomb moulding of the bowl is a common feature and faint moulded fluting also occurs, such as in the specimen shown in Fig. 149. The common bowl form is the round funnel, but waisted and ogee types also appear. F. Buckley (*A History of Old English Glass*, 1925), is inclined to give the origin of incised twists as Stourbridge or farther north, but there is no positive evidence, either documentary or from the style of the glasses, as to their provenance.

Glasses with incised twist stems have fetched up to £10. Those with knops have realised a little more.

INCRUSTATIONS.
See CRYSTALLO-CERAMIE.

INKWELLS. Inkwells are a favourite article for the glass-maker. They are usually made in pairs from white transparent glass, with flat highly polished sides, and repose on a wooden stand which also serves as a pen rest.

150. *Inkwell made at Stourbridge at the time of the Great Exhibition in 1851. The base of the stopper and of the inkwell itself is decorated with concentric rings of red, white and blue millefiori canes.*

The Stourbridge glass-makers of the last century produced stoppered ink bottles or inkwells of the type shown in Fig. 150. They were made from white transparent glass, but the base of the bottle and also that of the stopper were in millefiori pattern similar to the paperweights made at Stourbridge. There are usually five concentric rings of pastry mould florets in blue, red and white, and sometimes with lilac, yellow and green, with a central star-shaped cluster.

The height of the specimen shown in Fig. 150 is six and a quarter inches, but specimens are known about seven inches.

Stourbridge ink bottles with millefiori have changed hands within recent years for between £9 and £21.

IRISH GLASS. The early stages of the development of glass-making in Ireland were very much the same as in England over the same period. Probably the earliest record is of a grant of land in St Brigid, Dublin, to William the Glassmaker in 1258. There is reason to assume that he was a Frenchman and may have worked in Sussex before he migrated to Ireland. Records of other glass-makers occur in the fourteenth and fifteenth centuries.

Much the same as in England, however, no serious enterprise occurred in Ireland until the sixteenth century, when Thomas Woodhouse, a retired army officer, received a patent from Queen Elizabeth in 1586 granting him a monopoly in Ireland for glass-making for a period of eight years. The patent states: 'Her Majesty considering that the making of glass might prove commodious to both realms and that Woodhouse was the first that with any success had begun the art in Ireland is pleased to condescend to his petition and therefore orders that a grant be made to him of the privilege of making glass for glazing and drinking or otherwise, and to build convenient houses, for the term of eight years, the glass to be sold as cheepe or rather better cheepe than the similar glass in foreign parts' (State Papers, Ireland).

In 1589, however, three years after the granting of the patent, Woodhouse sold his monopoly to George Longe, an Englishman with a good business sense and a sound knowledge of glass-making. Longe made both common drinking glasses and window glass, and established a good business which thrived for at least eight years.

There were several attempts to establish glasshouses during the seventeenth century, but none appeared to have enjoyed the earlier prosperity of George Longe.

In 1639 a proclamation was issued forbidding the manufacture of glass in Ireland owing to the use of wood as fuel for the furnaces, and following this restriction, glass-making was carried on only in a small way in the towns, where coal was more easily procurable. A glasshouse of this nature was taken over by Philip Roche about 1690, and it is probable that Ravenscroft's glass-of-lead was for the first time used in an Irish glasshouse. About the time of Ravenscroft's invention, James II had granted to the Lord-Lieutenant of Ireland a warrant for fourteen years for 'a sort of crystalline glass resembling rock crystal'.

The business that Philip Roche established thrived rapidly. The glasshouse, known as the Round Glasshouse in St Mary's Lane, Dublin, advertised its products in the Irish newspapers

151. *Impressed marks on the base of some Irish decanters.* (*National Museum, Dublin*)

until 1759. The glass lists were much the same as those appearing in the English newspapers of the period and included all types of drinking glasses, decanters, jugs, jelly glasses, syllabub glasses, comfit and sweetmeat glasses, lanthornes and candelabra.

A notice in *Faulkner's Dublin Journal*, January, 1752, quoted in full by Westropp (*Irish Glass*, 1920, p. 43), claimed that 'no pains or expense have been spared by the proprietor to procure the best workmen and newest patterns from London . . . the above goods at much cheaper rates from him than those imported from England or elsewhere can be sold'.

Philip Roche had died in 1713 and the flourishing business he had established had been carried on by a partner, Fitzsimons, but towards the middle of the eighteenth century the business began to deteriorate and, about 1760, the glasshouse was closed down.

Very little activity occurred in glass-making after the closing down of the Round House, until 1780, when Free Trade was finally granted to Ireland. Glasshouses that eventually made Irish glass famous throughout the world then began to be established at Waterford, Cork and Belfast.

Throughout the long history of glass, it is doubtful whether any single glasshouse has gained such world-wide distinction as that which functioned at Waterford between the years 1783 and 1851. As a measure of its popularity, it can truthfully be said that more so-called 'genuine Waterford' glass has changed hands than could possibly have been produced during the years the factory functioned. Until quite recently, indeed, a decanter was dubbed 'Waterford' provided it had three rings round the neck, a mushroom stopper and, of course, the distinctive 'blue tint'. The controversy regarding the colour of Waterford glass still rages today and writers still persist in ascribing a 'characteristic blue tint' to Waterford glass, and in presenting new theories as to how it occurred.

The earliest mention of the Waterford factory occurred on 4th October, 1783, in the *Dublin Evening Post*: 'Waterford Glass House. George and William Penrose have established an extensive glass manufacture in this city; their friends and the public may be supplied with all kinds of plain and flint glass, useful and ornamental.'

The history of Waterford, however, can be traced back to earlier beginnings. George and William Penrose were businessmen, but there is no evidence that they knew anything about the manufacture of glass. On the other hand, they obviously would not have embarked on a chance venture. They had no doubt observed the crippling effect on English manufacturers caused by the doubling of the Glass Excise duties in 1777. This tax had not included Ireland, but Ireland was not permitted to export glass, manufacture being limited to her own domestic requirements. In 1780, however, full freedom of trade was granted to Ireland and the possibilities of a big export business became at once apparent.

On the other hand, the heavy duty on glass in England, and the poor prospects of trade there, forced many glass-workers to leave the country, some migrating to France and many to Ireland. In the evidence given before the Committee appointed in 1785 to enquire into the commercial relations between Great Britain and Ireland, it was stated that a 'Mr Hill, a great manufacturer at Stourbridge, had lately gone to Waterford and taken the best set of workmen that he could get in the county of Worcester'.

On 24th January, 1786, the Penroses petitioned Parliament for aid, the following request being recorded in the *Irish House of Commons Journal*: 'Petition of George and William Penrose of Waterford stating that they had with great difficulty, and at the expense of nearly £10,000, established a complete flint glass manufactury. The works employ from fifty to seventy manufacturers, who have mostly been brought from England at heavy expense. Since the factory was erected, the imports of flint glass into that part of the kingdom had entirely ceased, and therefore ask for aid to carry on the manufacture.'

Little is known of John Hill before he went to Ireland. He was undoubtedly an accomplished glass-maker and it is to be assumed that he was employed by the Penroses to recruit the necessary craftsmen, to furnish the glass formulae and designs, and to direct and control the entire process. Hill remained at the Waterford factory for only three years, when he left through a misunderstanding, but during that short period of time he succeeded in establishing a flourishing and prosperous business.

His successor was Jonathan Gatchell, an English Quaker employed as a clerk by the Penroses, and to whom Hill handed his glass formulae on his departure. Gatchell was eminently successful and although he had no previous experience of glass-making, he eventually acquired the business for himself in 1810, retaining it until his death in 1825. After Gatchell's death, little development occurred at the Waterford factory and in 1851 it ceased to function.

From the outset, the factory was noted for its variety of ware, its originality of form and decoration, but above all for its quality. The Waterford lists included everything known in table and ornamental glass in flint: decanters, claret-jugs, water-jugs, pickle-urns, butter-coolers, custard- and jelly-glasses, wineglasses, goblets, tumblers, salt-cellars, various kinds of bowls and dishes, bottles for smelling-salts, candlesticks, lustres and chandeliers; some of these articles were marked PENROSE WATERFORD.

Other factories were established in Ireland about the same time as that at Waterford. Benjamin Edwards, a Bristol glass manufacturer, set up a glasshouse at Belfast in 1776, and in

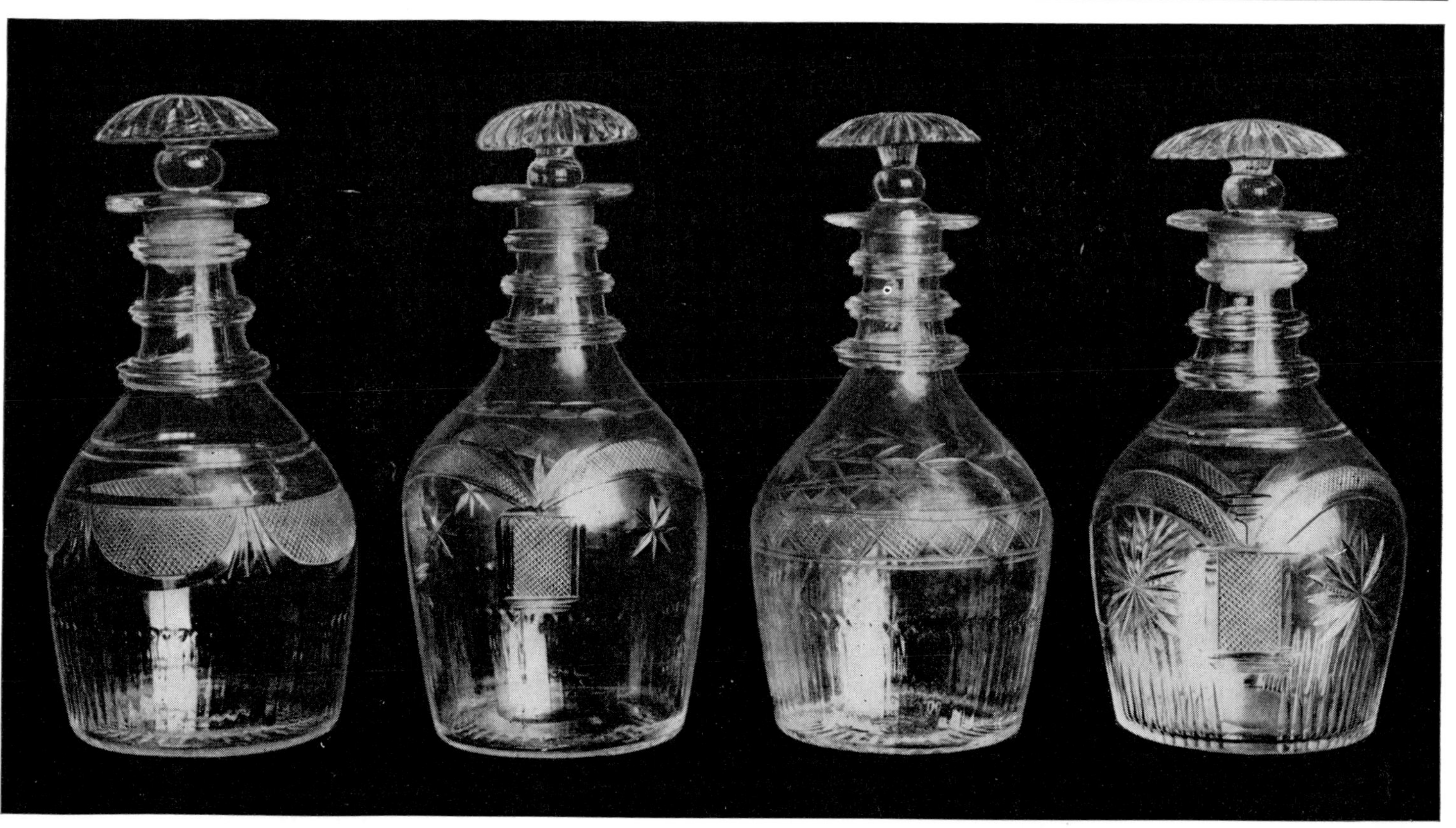

152. *Examples of Waterford decanters.* (*National Museum, Dublin*)

153. *Examples of decanters from Cork Glass Co.* (*National Museum, Dublin*)

154. *Examples of Waterloo Co., Cork, decanters.* (*National Museum, Dublin*)

155. *Examples of decanters from the Belfast factory, marked B. Edwards, Belfast.* (*National Museum, Dublin*)

156. *Typical Irish salad bowl with square moulded base and bowl with turned-over rim.* 157. *Irish boat-shaped salad bowl and solid moulded foot.*

1781 advertised that he was making cut and plain decanters, punch glasses, cruets, salts, goblets, and that he had brought a glass-cutter from England.

A glasshouse was erected in Cork in 1783 by Atwell Hayes, Thomas Burnett and Francis Rowe, who, in a petition to Parliament for financial aid, stated that they had sent an agent to England to study the process, to procure the best materials, and to employ experienced hands. The factory changed hands several times, but appears to have been in continuous operation until 1818, when it was closed. At that time the products included cut lustres, lamps, lighting-globes, candlesticks, glasses for dessert and jellies, butter-coolers, salt-cellars, wineglasses and wine-coolers, decanters, water-jugs and various other sorts of tableware both in the plain and the cut variety. Some articles such as decanters were marked CORK GLASS CO. in raised letters on the base.

A second company had been formed in Cork a few years before the Cork Glass Company ceased; the proprietor, Daniel Foley, built a new glasshouse in 1815, calling the establishment the Waterloo Glass House Company, advertising that it employed over one hundred persons and that its products were of the most superior quality flint. It made a variety of ware; in 1833, three years after Daniel Foley had retired from the business, the company was producing decanters, claret-jugs, tumblers, butter-coolers, chandeliers, pickle-urns, dessert services, jelly-glasses, drinking-glasses of various kinds, and other tableware, some of which were marked WATERLOO CO CORK. Two years later the factory appears to have ceased operation.

A third works was established in Cork in 1818 by two brothers, Edward and Richard Ronayne, and was known as the Terrace Glass Works. The products were lustres, lamps and tableware of all descriptions. After 1838 Edward Ronayne carried on the business alone, giving employment to about forty cutters, but three years later the factory closed its doors, the last factory in Cork to do so.

Other glasshouses producing tableware operated during the same period as the Cork glasshouses, at such places as Dublin (Charles Mulvany & Co.) and Newry, but their products are not so well authenticated as those of Waterford and Cork. In addition, cutting establishments were set up at various centres, notably Cork, the cutters obtaining blanks from the local glasshouses.

In some cases, however, it is impossible to distinguish Waterford glass from the products of other contemporary undertakings such as those mentioned or, indeed, from the glass produced in the English factories. It is known that designs were borrowed freely from the Waterford factory, but, on the other hand, there is no doubt that a successful design created by a competitor would be quickly reproduced at Waterford.

In some cases, however, identification is made fairly positive by a trade mark impressed on the base of the vessel. Only some items were marked, such as decanters, jugs and finger bowls, but then not by any means all of them. The following trade marks used by the Irish factories are known: PENROSE WATERFORD; CORK GLASS CO; WATERFORD CO CORK; FRANCIS COLLINS DUBLIN; J. D. AYCKBOWN DUBLIN; B. EDWARDS, BELFAST; C. M. CO (Charles Mulvany of Dublin); and ARMSTRONG ORMOND QUAY. Impressed marks on the bases of some decanters are shown in Fig. 151.

Irish decanters have a wide appeal and probably have more distinguishing features than any other type of tableware produced during the Irish period. For example, the decanters made at Waterford were distinguished by their style of cutting; a popular motif was a field of fine diamonds in arches resting on rectangular panels or in pendent semi-circles. Examples of Waterford decanters are shown in Fig. 152. All but the decanter on the right are marked PENROSE WATERFORD. The base of a Waterford decanter was decorated with moulded flutes, although this feature occurred on specimens from other factories. The general type of bowl was round, barrel-shaped—that is, with a wider diameter at the shoulder than at the base—usually with three triple rings round the neck. The lip of the

158. *Specimens of Irish salt-cellars.*

neck of a Waterford decanter is somewhat wider and flatter than those from other factories.

Waterford stoppers were almost invariably of the mushroom type, sometimes cut, but more usually with radial flutes, with a rounded knop immediately below the neck of the stopper. It is sometimes stated that the knop was a characteristic feature of the Waterford decanters, but this is not the case; it also appeared on decanters from the Waterloo factory, Cork.

Decanters from the Cork factory were usually mallet-shaped, although sometimes specimens are found of the barrel form and also straight sided. The rings on the neck were two or three of the double feathered type, but three rings cut in flat facets, three plain triple rings and square sectioned rings are sometimes found. The stopper was the usual mushroom shape with a tendency to be flat across the top.

The characteristic feature of the decoration is a vesica pattern, which takes the form of a plain incised oval, pointed at the narrow ends. There are usually six round the widest part of the barrel of the decanter, often containing an eight-pointed star. The four decanters shown in Fig. 153 illustrate these various features; each is marked CORK GLASS CO.

Decanters from the Waterloo factory closely follow the Waterford styles. The body form is mainly barrel-shaped, the neck having three plain triple rings. The usual stopper is the mushroom type, with moulded radial flutes, and some are provided with a knop immediately below the neck of the stopper similar to the Waterford style.

Decoration follows many styles, some being borrowed from other factories. Probably the most characteristic decorative feature of the Waterloo factory is engraved patterns in circles and loops. The usual moulded flutes appear round the base of the body.

Typical specimens of decanters from the Waterloo factory are shown in Fig. 154. Each decanter has WATERLOO CO CORK impressed on the base.

Decanters from the Belfast factory differ from those of either Waterford or Cork. They are mainly pyriform in shape, much after the style of the Bristol decanters. It will be recalled that Benjamin Edwards, who founded the Belfast factory, originally came from Bristol.

The necks of the decanters are usually encircled with three plain rings of triangular section. An important feature, as compared with decanters from Waterford and Cork, is the narrowness of the rim at the top of the neck. The stoppers are also different; they are usually upright, plain and flat, with a bevelled edge or narrow border of moulded flutes radiating

159. *Irish jugs of the early nineteenth century.* (*National Museum, Dublin*)

160. *Typical styles of late eighteenth-century Irish jugs.* (*National Museum, Dublin*)

from a plain centre, often referred to as the target stopper. Alternatively, the plain centre of a target stopper is cut with a six-pointed star.

Decoration is usually not so much in evidence as with specimens from other factories. A characteristic feature is flat vertical fluting, extending from the lower ring on the neck, well down the shoulder of the decanter. Simple incised pendents around the body, with stars and shallow hollows in scale pattern on the shoulder are alternative styles of cutting.

The four specimens shown in Fig. 155 are characteristic of the decanters from the Belfast factory; each is marked on the base B. EDWARDS. BELFAST.

Salad Bowls. Most Irish factories manufactured large boat-shaped and circular bowls, often referred to today as 'salad' bowls, and these items are still popular with collectors. They were made in various styles, one of the earliest being to provide the bowl with three supporting feet suggested, no doubt, by the style of articles in silver which made their appearance about the middle of the eighteenth century.

Bowls with tripedal support usually displayed the deeply flanged or turned-over rims, and were often decorated with plain or alternate prisms round the rim with long horizontal hollows in chain fashion round the body of the bowl. Bowls which appeared later in the century were provided with moulded stands, some hollow and others solid, in such shapes as square, diamond, round or oval. A typical specimen is shown in Fig. 156. An occasional specimen is found with a bowl and stand in separate pieces.

Salad bowls were decorated with cutting on a more ambitious scale than on other articles from the Irish factories and included some of the less common motifs; the sunburst, the fan escallop or shell border, and various curved designs were some of the better known styles.

Salad bowls did not appear in the earlier Waterford lists but they are mentioned fairly frequently in the nineteenth century.

It is difficult to distinguish Irish salad bowls from those made by the English manufacturers in the early part of the nineteenth century. Bowls with deeply flanged rims were popular with English manufacturers at that time. What is no doubt an Irish style is the specimen shown in Fig. 157, a large boat-shaped bowl decorated with edge flute motifs and a solid pressed foot.

Salt Cellars. In many respects, the Irish salt cellars are smaller versions of the salad bowls, resembling them in such features as the deeply flanged rim of the circular variety or the boat-shaped bowl. Specimens are shown in Fig. 158.

Salts were made at most Irish factories and it is almost impossible to assert with any degree of finality the origin of a particular specimen. Occasionally it is possible to recognise a Waterford specimen by the style of cutting; this particularly applies to specimens without feet on which the cutting was lavishly applied. The less pretentious varieties of salts, however, were probably of Cork origin or even Dublin.

Some specimens were in plain undecorated style with moulded patterns on the bowls, but the plain, boat-shaped salts without feet offered great scope for the cutter. Specimens

161. *Irish mirror with small chandelier suspended in front.*

are found with strawberry diamonds and relief diamonds on the bowl with escalloping and notching to the rims, very similar to the salad bowls of the same period.

Water Jugs. Water jugs appeared throughout the Irish period and were in most Irish cutters' lists. As they were made in a great variety of shapes, they constitute a fascinating group for the collector. As in other items made in the Irish period, however, there was such similarity of form among them that it is difficult to state at which factory a particular specimen was made. There are, however, characteristics which assist in dating them.

Jugs from the late eighteenth century were, in general, taller in form and of a greater variety of shapes. Some were urn-shaped or pyriform, mounted on a spreading foot; those with the barrel-shaped body were usually provided with a pedestal foot. These earlier styles of jugs were sometimes provided with hollow spreading feet, but those with pedestal support were ground and polished and carried the basal star. Typical specimens are shown in Fig. 160.

Cutting was more profusely applied than on the later specimens; rims were deeply scalloped or notched, and notching appeared also on the handles of some examples.

Irish jugs made in the early part of the nineteenth century somewhat resemble the barrel-shaped decanter in form. They are low and squat, the lower part of the body being of conical shape, finishing square at the base with a shoulder rounded inwards to a constricted neck below the flared rim and the spout. Typical specimens are shown in Fig. 159.

The type of handle is often useful in identifying the period in which a jug was made. For example, jugs from the early nineteenth century had handles which decreased in thickness from the junction of the flared rim to the point where it joined the shoulder of the body; in many cases it was finished at the lower end in a curled knob, and was invariably undecorated. The earlier jugs did not show these characteristics, the handles being of a uniform thickness throughout their length and the curled knob did not appear.

Mirrors. Irish glasshouses were beginning to produce mirrors towards the end of the eighteenth century, notably in Dublin and the south of Ireland. They were oval in shape with frames made up of facets of coloured glass; the facets were dark blue, green and opaque white, and others had rows of clear glass. For example, a specimen in the National Museum, Dublin, has the outer row of clear glass and the inner of alternate pieces of dark blue and opaque white with gold flutes. In some cases, there is a small chandelier suspended in front of the mirror, such as shown in Fig. 161. This specimen is four feet in height.

Other Irish specimens have a scroll base, such as that shown in Fig. 162. This example, about two feet six in height, also has the double faceted border, one of clear glass, the other of blue facets alternating with white opaque with gilt flutes. The specimens shown in Figs. 161 and 162 were probably made in the last quarter of the eighteenth century.

Colour. Some writers still persist today in ascribing a 'characteristic blue tint' to Waterford glass and in presenting new theories as to how it occurred. This fallacy, however, was exposed by the late Dudley Westropp in his book, *Irish Glass* (1920), in which he stated: 'I have never seen a marked Waterford piece with a blue tint.' Westropp was Curator of the National Museum, Dublin, for a number of years, where there is a very extensive collection of Irish glass from all the factories operating during the Irish period, 1780-1850.

Westropp's authoritative statement was supported by W. A. Thorpe of the Victoria and Albert Museum, who said in his book, *A History of English and Irish Glass* (1929), p. 277: 'Marked pieces of Waterford are very rare, and no other pieces whatever afford material for judgment. The metal of Waterford glass is extremely clear and white in colour, and in this respect nearer than any other to realising the general aim of the eighteenth-century glass-maker.'

If further evidence is required of the absence of colour in Waterford glass, a few final words may be quoted from the foreword of the catalogue of an exhibition of Waterford glass held a few years ago at Waterford by members of the Old Waterford Society. The foreword stated: 'The statement that Waterford glass has a distinct bluish tinge has been disproved by experts. Waterford glass, certainly, is lovely and has many wonderful qualities, but a bluish colour is not amongst them.'

Some specimens of glass, however, which can definitely be ascribed to Cork have a blue cast and are, in the main, duller than authentic Waterford specimens. It is conceivable, therefore, that due to the fact that the styles from different factories were in some cases very similar, a confusion has arisen over the blue cast, Cork specimens having been wrongly identified as Waterford.

166. *Examples of Jacobite glasses engraved with heraldic rose.* (*Messrs Cecil Davis, Ltd.*)

eighteenth century, during which there was an overlapping of the various stem styles.

The analysis of the glasses indicates that the Rose with the single bud made its appearance before the Rose with two buds. Also, a comparison of the various emblems shows that, on glasses bearing no further devices, the Rose appears with one bud on fifty-three glasses and with only two buds on twenty-one; on glasses which carry only the emblem star, oak-leaf and the word FIAT, either alone or in combination, eighty-nine have two buds and there is no single example with one bud only.

From these significant basic facts and other inferences, Horridge established his theory that the Heraldic Jacobite Rose (or its Scottish counterpart, the Thistle, as in Fig. 168) represents the triple Crown, that of Britain, France and Ireland; the small or Sinister Bud (that on the right) represents the Old Pretender, and the large or Dexter Bud (that on the left) represents Prince Charles Edward.

Haynes (*Glass Through the Ages*, 1948, pp. 133-141) who, like Horridge, had a large range of Jacobite glasses on which to base his deductions, agrees with Horridge that the Rose represents the Crown of England. Indeed, he points out that the traditional connection needs no stressing when there is a 'Rose and Crown' inn in half the villages in England.

Early Jacobite glasses show the Rose with a single unopened bud on the sinister side, and for a short time this represented the Old Pretender. Up to this point Horridge and Haynes agree. Haynes, however, suggests that probably when Charles Edward became of age (1741), the emblems changed, the Old Pretender being represented by an expectant opening bud on the senior dexter side and his son by a bud on the sinister side. It merely meant an additional bud, which the engraver could easily have added to earlier glasses in some cases.

There have been two earlier theories; the first, that the Rose represents James II, and the larger and smaller buds the Old Pretender and the Young Pretender respectively, and the second theory, that the Rose represents the Old Pretender, and the two buds his two sons. In the light of the evidence produced by Horridge and also by Haynes in support of their respective theories, the earlier ones now appear untenable.

Examples of Jacobite Rose glasses are shown in Fig. 165. The glass shown on the right in Fig. 165 has the word FIAT and the star engraved near the rim. Many Jacobite glasses carry the former inscription, which, according to modern Jacobite theories, means 'May it come to Pass', or 'Let it be so'. It constitutes a prayer that the hopes emblematically expressed will be fulfilled.

The Star has always been regarded as having special signi-

167. *Jacobite glass engraved with heraldic rose on the bowl, and a spray of rose leaves on the foot.* 168. *Jacobite glasses showing the thistle, the Scottish counterpart of the English heraldic rose.*

ficance in connection with Prince Charles; indeed, it is held to represent him. Specimens are shown in Fig. 169.

The glass shown in Fig. 170 is one of a small group of about a score of glasses engraved in diamond-point with a Crown, the Cipher IR and RI entwined, and the figure 8. There are usually two or four verses of the Jacobite hymn on the bowl, concluding with the word AMEN, from which this group of glasses get the designation 'Amen' glasses. The following are the verses in full:

God Save the King, I pray.
God Bliss the King—I pray.
God Save the King.

Send Him Victorious.
Happy and Glorious.
Soon to reign over us.
God Save the King.

God Bliss the subjects all,
And save both great and small
in every station.
That will bring home the King,
Who has best right to reign,
It is the only thing
Can save the Nation.

God Bliss the Prince of Wales.
The true born Prince of Wales.
Sent us by Thee.

Grant us one favour more.
The King for to restore.
As Thou has done before.
The Familie.

God Save the Church, I pray,
And Bliss the Church, I pray,
Pure to remain.
Against all Heresie
And Whigs Hypocrisie,
Who strive maliciously
Her to defame.

The 'Amen' glasses were previously considered as being made in the first quarter of the eighteenth century to commemorate the birth of one or the other of the two princes, but from recent evidence it is probable that they are contemporaneous with other Jacobite glasses.

The 'Amen' group of glasses are essentially private glasses. A few are found with a date, such as the Dunvegan Castle glass, 1747, and the Mesham and the Drummond Castle glasses both dated 1749. Fraudulent reproductions of the

169. *Group of Jacobite glasses engraved with the star and the word FIAT.*

170. *Two views of an 'Amen' glass engraved in diamond point work with a Crown, the Cipher IR and RI entwined and the figure 8. (By courtesy of the Victoria and Albert Museum)*

'Amen' glasses are known, probably put into circulation in the 1930s (Haynes, *Glass Through the Ages*, 1948, p. 135).

Because Jacobite glasses are collectors' favourites, they are expensive. In addition to the 'Amen' glasses, there are a number of forgeries and reproductions of all types.

Portrait glasses are the most popular type of Jacobite glass with collectors and during recent years prices have fluctuated between £80 and £170 for the engraved variety, while an enamelled portrait glass changed hands for £330.

Jacobite glasses with the usual emblems such as the rose and buds, Fiat, Redeat, Audentior Ibo, Thistle, etc., fetch lower prices than the portrait variety and have changed hands between £13 and £60.

Authentic Jacobite glasses often have a history and in many cases their record can be traced through various owners. For example, the well-known Horridge Collection of drinking glasses was sold in 1959, when some rare Jacobite glasses changed hands. The Keith-Douglas 'Amen' glass, with drawn trumpet-bowl on drawn air-twist stem with verses of the Jacobite hymn in diamond-point work, fetched £275, while the Burn-Murdock 'Amen' Glass, similar to the Keith-Douglas glass but the bowl lacking the Jacobite toast, realised £750, a record for a glass of this type.

A Jacobite decanter of globular shape engraved with the bust portrait of the Young Pretender, with the motto AUDENTIOR IBO in scroll engraving above, changed hands for £200 at the same sale.

Portrait glasses engraved with AUDENTIOR IBO fetched between £125 and £170. A rare Macdonald portrait glass changed hands at the Horridge sale in 1959 for £660. This glass has a knopped air-twist stem with round funnel bowl engraved with a three-quarter length of Flora Macdonald facing right holding a spray of flowers. A similar glass is illustrated in *Old English Drinking Glasses*, 1926, by G. R. Francis, Plate LXIV.

JACOBS, LAZARUS AND ISAAC. The Jacobs, Lazarus (d. 1796) and his son Isaac, had their glasshouse in Temple Street, Bristol, where Lazarus senior had established a good business. Both father and son are mentioned in the Bristol Directory as being in business there between the years 1775 and 1800. That they were prominent glass merchants is borne out by the fact that Isaac was made glass-maker to George III.

The Jacobs specialised in dark blue glass (*see* BRISTOL GLASS), and according to the ledger of Michael Edkins, they employed him between the years 1785 and 1787 to decorate their blue glass in gilt work. Indeed, it has been suggested by R. J. Charleston (*Journal of the Society of Glass Technology*, Vol. XXXVIII, 1954, pp. 10-11t), who has carried out an exhaustive research on the career of Michael Edkins, that the gilt labelling on a class of decanters signed 'I. Jacobs, Bristol' may be identified as the work of Edkins. There is a record in Edkins's ledger: '2 Gold Decanters and Glasses decorated for Lazarus Jacobs,' and 'To 6 five-Galln jars Blue a Gold Scroll and Wrote.' There is drawn in the margin of the ledger a simple scrolled label enclosing the word RUM.

Specimens signed 'I. Jacobs, Bristol' include wine-coolers, decanters and finger bowls. (*See* FINGER BOWLS.)

It is recorded in the *Bristol Gazette*, 21st April, 1796: 'Died in the Great Garden, Mr Lazarus Jacobs, a Jew and eminent glass-merchant.'

JELLY GLASSES. Jelly glasses have been much neglected by the collector in spite of the fact that, although simple in form, they are excellent examples of the craftsmanship of the early eighteenth-century glass-maker. The early styles were well designed and finely made vessels, shaped and decorated at the furnace mouth by the few simple tools at the command of the glass-maker, and displaying, without the necessity of applied decorative effects, all the inherent beauty and charm of the medium.

Because of their beauty, they were among those glasses used for display at fashionable dinner parties and *les petits soupers*. From records, such as those kept by Lady Baillie (*see* BAILLIE, LADY GRISELL), it is clear that after the various courses were served, the table was finally cleared for dessert and various delicacies, which were served in dishes or stands in as attractive a manner as possible. At the time of Lady Baillie—the first quarter of the eighteenth century—glass vessels were clearly playing an ever-increasing part in such displays. Lady Baillie remarks in her diary, for example: 'Milk in a China bowl, but I think glass as good.'

Jelly glasses appeared throughout the eighteenth century in a variety of shapes and sizes. The earliest type was a small, straight-sided bowl, conical in shape, set directly on a foot,

171. (Extreme left) *Jelly glass in style of the early eighteenth century. Straight sided bowl set on a conical foot with collar.* (Right) *Bell-shaped bowl set on a wide conical foot surmounted by small knop.* circa *1720.*

172. *Jelly glass with double swan neck handles, annulated knop set on domed foot. Could also be styled posset glass.* circa *1740.*

plain or with some sort of gadrooning, or a collar containing air beads at the junction of the bowl to the foot. A typical specimen is shown on the left of Fig. 171. The foot itself could be plain, folded or domed and folded. This style persisted until 1710, when the fashion changed to a bell-shaped bowl, also set directly on a foot, which could be a high conical shape, such as Fig. 171 right, or in some cases, domed.

These glasses were still small—between four and five inches in height—and were attractively decorated in a variety of ways. Some were ribbed with a knop above the lobe of the foot; others were ribbed or gadrooned or decorated with fine spiral or twisted reeding.

Most jelly glasses were provided with a single handle or with a pair, one on each side, in the swan-neck style, which could be plain or alternatively double looped—that is, the usual swan-neck with a bottom curled and elaborated into a definite loop. A typical specimen of this latter style, which could also be termed a posset glass, is shown in Fig. 172.

These styles persisted up to 1745, the year of the Glass Excise Act, after which jelly glasses were made lighter and smaller, and such features as handles were dispensed with. The shape of the bowl was retained, but the moulded patterns were replaced by cut motifs. Although an occasional glass is found with hollow diamonds cut in shallow form, the most popular pattern was vertical fluting, each alternate flute enriched along its edge by a series of continuous hollows. Often the rim of the bowl was scalloped to correspond with the radial flutes, a style which came into fashion about 1760. The feet were sometimes cut with radial flutes.

Jelly glasses are comparatively common and because they are not considered as important glasses by the keen collector, they can be purchased relatively cheaply. They are often sold in sets of half a dozen. For example, seventeen jelly glasses changed hands a few years ago for as little as £4 10s. They were the usual type with bell bowls and some of almost bucket shape.

JOHNSON, JEROM. He was one of the first of the English cutters and engravers and most probably the first to practise without foreign assistance. He worked between the years 1739 and 1761 and advertised systematically in the London newspapers, declaring himself as the 'workman', 'the first inventor', the 'maker', and 'the real workman for many years, and shall be sold no where cheaper'.

It is obvious from his many advertisements that there was a market abroad for English cut-glass probably as early as 1749, but most certainly a few years later. The following notices give a clue to this development. *London Evening Post*, 18th February, 1749: 'For all manner of Cut-Glass. This is to inform the Nobility, Gentry, Merchants, Captains and Others, That Jerom Johnson is removed opposite the New Exchange in the Strand; where he continues to sell the finest Cut Lustres, Candlesticks, Salts, Desarts, all brilliant pollish'd, better and cheaper than has hitherto been done.'

Whitehall Evening Post, 19th November, 1757: 'At the Intire Glass Shop, Strand, Glasses are to be sold at the very lowest rates. All foreign Commissions will be executed with the utmost care and perfection—all other Sort of Glasses for Exportation.' Francis Buckley, *Glass*, Vol. V, 1928, p. 393. *See* Candelabra, Candlesticks, Chandeliers, Commemorative Glasses and Sweetmeat Glasses.

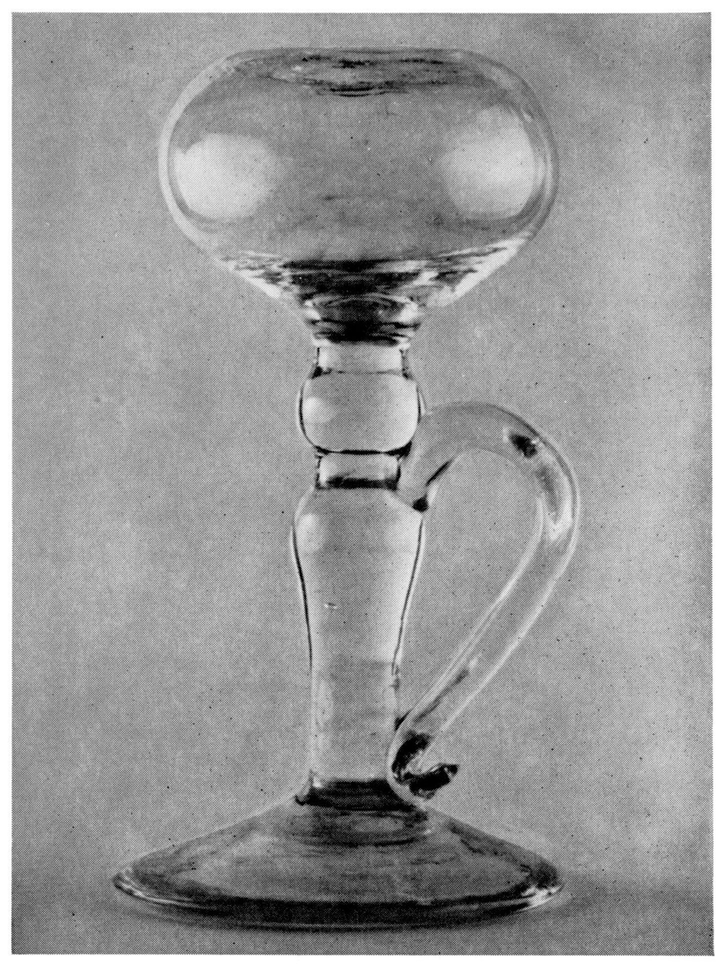

173. *Glass oil-lamp, early eighteenth century.* (*Tolson Memorial Museum, Huddersfield*)

JUGS.
See Irish Glass; Nailsea Glass.

KIT-KAT GLASSES.
See Balustroids.

KNIFE RESTS. Glass knife rests are not common. They are usually in cut crystal glass of a shape something like a dumb-bell, about three to four inches in length. Stourbridge glass-makers of the last century made them from millefiori or filigree cane with coloured twists usually in red, white and blue glass.

The usual sale room price has been about £1 each.

KUNCKEL, JOHANN (1630-1703).
See German and Bohemian Glass.

LACE-MAKERS' LAMPS.
See Lanthorns and Glass Lamps.

LALIQUE, RENÉ.
See French Glass.

LAMPS, GLASS.
See Lanthorns and Glass Lamps.

LANTHORNS AND GLASS LAMPS. It was not until the end of the seventeenth century that lamps with glass sides began to replace the earlier rush lamps and metal holders for candles.

174. *Glass oil-lamp with multiple wick holders; first half of the eighteenth century.* (*Messrs Cecil Davis Ltd.*)

One of the earliest forms of the new glass lamps was the 'lanthorn', a chamber lamp with glass sides and holding a candle. The great advantage, of course, of the lanthorn was that it could be used out of doors and was very much safer than the open candlestick. Its use was different from that of the candlestick, for whereas the candlestick was mainly used in one position such as on a table, the lanthorn could be carried about the house, and used in a manner for which an expensive candlestick was clearly out of place.

After Ravenscroft's discovery of glass-of-lead in 1676, the early lanthorns, which had their sides of light green window glass, were now provided with glass plates, some of which were ground and polished. Hanging lamps of this style with polished plate glass were soon being used in the halls and passages of the best houses.

The earliest notice of glass chamber lamps occurs just before the end of the seventeenth century. *London Gazette*, 30th October, 1693: 'Glass lanthorns, finely painted to burn candles in, for Halls, etc., from 4s. to £10. William Fells, Tinman, in King Street.'

The lanthorn with its candle was soon replaced by the use of glass oil lamps. Their development must have been exceedingly rapid, for in 1735 they were advertised as being able to burn for 40 hours without refilling.

The original glass lamp was a flattened glass globe, provided

175. *Glass hanging lantern for oil or candles used from the Adam to the Regency period. The specimen is nineteen inches high and is decorated with cutting.* 176. *Lamp used by lace makers. The beam of light was concentrated through a glass globe filled with water, which condensed the light on the pillow of lace.* (*Crown Copyright, Science Museum, London.*) 177. *The globe used by lacemakers. It was filled with water which condensed the light from a lamp on the pillow of lace.* (*By courtesy of the Victoria and Albert Museum.*)

with an aperture at the top through which was inserted a wick; it was mounted on a stem and foot, and was usually provided with a handle on the stem. A typical early eighteenth-century glass lamp is shown in Fig. 173.

Later the idea occurred to increase the lighting power by providing the vessel with more than one wick holder; for this purpose the stem of the earlier simple type was discarded and the body was modified to vase form and provided with several branches. A specimen is shown in Fig. 174. They were usually about three to three and a half inches in height.

The multiple glass lamp remained popular until the second half of the century and some specimens are extant cut and engraved, but, unfortunately, very few specimens have survived the test of time.

During the eighteenth century, chandeliers and candelabra became the popular lighting vehicle, but there also appeared a hanging lantern after the style shown in Fig. 175, which enjoyed a certain amount of popularity into the Regency period. The specimen shown in Fig. 175 is nineteen inches in height.

Robert Adam designed a similar lantern for burning oil, for Osterley Park, hung above the landing at the top of the main staircase. It has a plain glass bowl with an upper frieze of honeysuckle ornament in brass openwork, and a brass heat and smoke disc above.

Another form of glass lamp was that used by the lace-makers. The light from such a lamp—one is shown in Fig. 176—or from a candle or rush was concentrated through a glass globe (Fig. 177) filled with water which acted as a condensing lens for concentrating the beam of light on the pillow of lace.

Glass lamps such as used by lace-makers illustrated in Fig. 176 have been purchased relatively cheaply, between £2 and £3.

LATTICINIO.
See FILIGREE OR LATTICINIO.

LEAD OXIDE.
See MATERIALS USED IN GLASS-MAKING.

LEHMANN, CASPAR (1570-1622).
See CUT-GLASS; GERMAN AND BOHEMIAN GLASS.

LIMESTONE.
See MATERIALS USED IN GLASS-MAKING.

LINEN-SMOOTHERS. Glass linen-smoothers were made in the Stourbridge district early in the eighteenth century. They had a solid base, with an attached handle about five inches long regularly knopped to ensure a firm grip. They had the appearance of an inverted mushroom and were usually made in ordinary bottle glass. They were known as 'slickers' or 'slick stones'.

Glass linen-smoothers were used, as the term suggests, for the smoothing of linen, and they were also used for rubbing floors to give them a glossy appearance.

About the middle of the nineteenth century the Stourbridge glass-men found the heavy base of the linen-smoother a convenient subject for millefiori decoration. It is most probable, however, that the millefiori linen-smoothers were not part of the recognised production of the glass factories at the time, but were made by the workmen for their own use. This may account for the fact that they are comparatively rare and that in many specimens the millefiori decoration is of scattered rather than of regular formation.

LOG GLASSES.
See SAND GLASSES.

LUSTRES.
See CANDELABRA; CHANDELIERS.

LYNN OR NORWICH GLASSES. Hartshorne (*Old English Glass*, 1897, pp. 251-278) stated that there were reasons for assigning horizontally ribbed glasses to a glass house at Lynn or Norwich, but unfortunately did not say what the reasons were; it was probably because the glasses were found in Norfolk.

For example, Bate (*English Tableglass*, 1905, p. 52), referring to the style of glass with horizontal grooves, says: 'It has been suggested that it emanates from a glasshouse at Lynn or Norwich; and as both Mrs Rees Price's example and my own (each, by the way, showing the *folded* foot) came from that district the conjecture may reasonably be accepted.'

According to F. Buckley (*History of Old English Glass*, 1925, p. 8), no record of glass-making during the eighteenth century at Norwich has yet been found in any old history, map or newspaper. Sand was obtained for glass-making from the Lynn area in the eighteenth century and, as a point of interest, is still supplied today to many glasshouses throughout the country; glass-making in the vicinity was, therefore, not an unlikely occurrence. Indeed, it is known that a glasshouse was functioning at Lynn in 1693, by the following notice in the *London Gazette*, 27th February, 1693: 'To be sold all sorts of the best and finest Drinking-Glasses, and curious Glasses for Ornament, and likewise all sorts of Glass Bottles, by Francis Jackson, and John Straw, Glass-makers, at their warehouse in Worcester-Court near the Fountain Tavern in the Strand, or at their Glass-Houses near the Faulkon in Southwark, and at Lynn in Norfolk; where all Persons may be furnished at reasonable rates.'

It appeared in Houghton's list of glasshouses in 1696 and was still in production in 1747, as the following notice in the *Ipswich Journal*, 28th November, 1747, shows: 'To be sold by the glass-house in Lynn, a large quantity of fine Flint-Glass both figured and plain, well sorted, the stock consisting of a great Variety of the most Valuable sorts of drinking Glasses, Decanters, Salvers and other glassware.'

After that, however, it would appear that the restrictions of the Glass Excise Act had caused the glasshouse to cease production (as, indeed, had occurred temporarily in 1696 when a tax was first imposed for five years), for from 1754 the trade notices refer only to a 'warehouse' which had been opened, and which also stocked 'a great variety of German Glass'.

There was also a glasshouse at Yarmouth, given in Houghton's list of glasshouses in 1696, and in 1728 there is mention of a number of glass-makers who left Southwark and are supposed to have gone to a glasshouse near Yarmouth, which, according to a notice in a Norwich paper, had been in production for some time.

A pair of so-called Lynn or Norwich glasses is shown in Figs. 178 and 179. Most glasses of the Lynn group are of exceptionally fine quality, simple and admirably proportioned, and are distinguished by their horizontally ribbed bowls. The

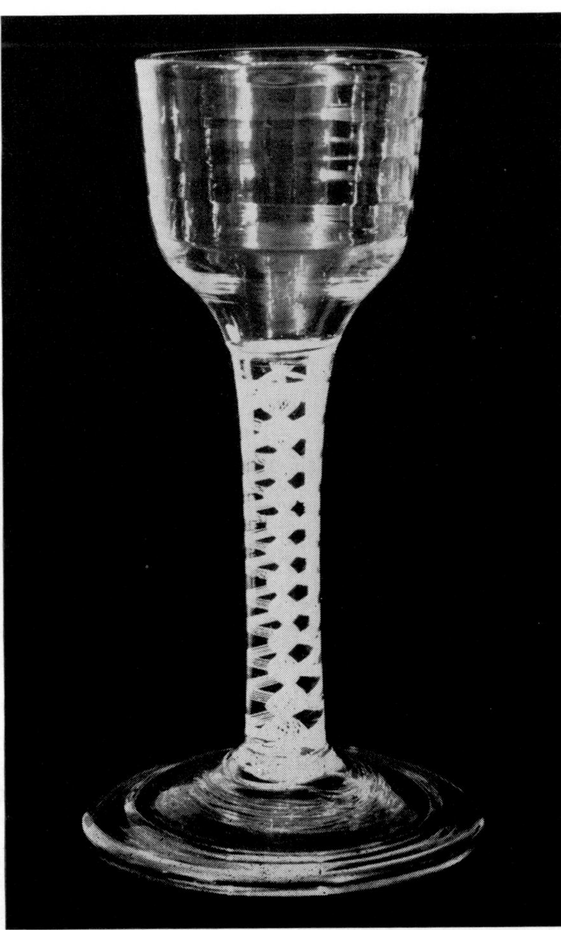

178. (Extreme left) *Lynn or Norwich wineglass with opaque-twist stem of the single series multiple spiral type, folded foot and bowl with two horizontal ribs.*

179. *Lynn or Norwich glass with opaque-twist stem of the double series type, folded foot and bowl with six horizontal ribs.*

ribs or grooves vary from two to seven lines, the specimens shown having two and six grooves respectively. Both specimens possess the folded foot, a feature commoner with Lynn glasses than with any other of the opaque-twist style, but only relatively so.

Tumblers with the body encircled with six to eight horizontal grooves are also accredited to Lynn or Norwich.

Lynn glasses have been sold in recent years for up to £20 each. In 1955 two changed hands in the same lot for £40. One was an ale glass with horizontally grooved funnel bowl and the other was a wineglass with ogee bowl. Both have a corkscrew opaque-twist stem and folded foot.

For prices of Lynn decanters *see* DECANTERS.

MANSELL, SIR ROBERT (1573-1656). Robert Mansell was a wealthy man of a good Welsh family and an Admiral of the British Fleet. His interest in glass-making can be traced from 1608 until his death in 1656. He came to the front as a glass-maker at a critical time when the making of flint glass and window glass was conducted under a system of monopolies—that is, the whole business was placed in the hands of one man, who, in return for the privilege, agreed to pay a rental or royalty to the Crown.

That at least was the theory, but bands of glass-makers who wandered up and down the country were producing common green glass for windows and household purposes, and it was no easy matter to locate them and to suppress their activities.

The story of Mansell's struggles with these rival and contumacious glass-makers, his heavy losses initially, and his ultimate success, have been fully narrated by Hartshorne in *Old English Glasses* (1897), Chapter VII, p. 179, *et seq.* (*See* BOTTLES; ENGLISH GLASS, HISTORY OF; MIRRORS; and SCOTTISH GLASS.)

MARBLES OF GLASS. The glass marble no doubt originated from the *margaritai* and *perlai*, the Venetian craftsmen who made glass beads. (*See* VENETIAN GLASS.) The making of marbles and beads of glass commercially dates from the early sixteenth century. The process consisted of breaking a glass rod, which had a small hole through its entire length, into short sections. The pieces were then mixed with sand and charcoal and placed in an iron vessel which was rotated and, at the same time, heated. As the glass slowly softened under the heat, the sharp edges became removed by the rotary motion of the furnace, until the beads were completely round. They were then allowed to cool, shaken in bags to remove the sand and charcoal, and finally polished.

Glass marbles were made in much the same manner, with the difference that it was only necessary to use solid glass rod, as the central hole was not required. The rods were made from coloured enamel twists, prepared in the manner described for the making of latticinio (*see* FILIGREE OR LATTICINIO) or for the making of stems for opaque-twist glasses. (*See* OPAQUE-TWIST STEMMED-GLASSES.)

Glass marbles have an important industrial application today. They are used in the production of glass fibre (*see* SPUN GLASS) on a large scale, and are produced in a high-speed machine very much on the hand principle used by the Venetians in the sixteenth century. The rate of production is something like 500,000 marbles every twenty-four hours.

180. *Glass marbles with coloured glass twists, popular in the nineteenth century, and again coming on the market today.* (*Mr J. H. Edwards*)

At the end of a production run for colourless glass marbles for glass fibres, coloured glasses are introduced into the process, which assures a constant supply of gaily coloured marbles for the amusement of children. An assortment is shown in Fig. 180.

MARVER.

See WINEGLASS, THE MAKING OF.

MATERIALS USED IN GLASS-MAKING. It is one of the unfathomable mysteries of nature that such commonplace materials as sand, soda and limestone can be made to combine by heat in producing such a remarkable medium as glass.

Technically speaking, glass can be considered as a mixture of acidic and basic oxides, the acidic oxides being silica (sand) and boric oxide, and the basic oxides, lead oxide, calcium oxide, sodium oxide and potassium oxide. The function of the basic oxides is to lower the melting temperature of the silica so that glass can be produced at temperatures that are commercially possible.

Sand, by itself, can be persuaded by very high temperatures to fuse into a clear crystal substance. This product—fused silica—has very useful thermal properties and is employed extensively today in science and in industrial processes. But when a basic oxide, such as soda, is made to combine chemically with the silica, introduced as sodium carbonate or sodium sulphate, the temperature required for the melting process is lowered some hundreds of degrees. The resultant glass, however, is a simple one and is soluble in water, and in this condition is employed as 'water-glass' for many purposes—for example, for colour making, artificial stone, in soaps, and for the preservation of eggs.

When carbonate of lime, such as limestone or chalk, is added to the sand and soda, and the mixture fused in the furnace, a glass is formed which for all practical purposes is *insoluble* in water. It is now a more stable glass and is used on an enormous scale for the manufacture of such articles as bottles and jars, window glass and electric light bulbs.

At the other end of the scale of glass-making, there are the luxury glasses, imitating natural crystal, that fascinate by their sparkle and brilliancy. The basis of this crystal glass is still sand, but of a much purer quality and in a more carefully prepared condition than that used for the manufacture of the commercial soda-lime glasses. In addition, the soda and lime are replaced by potash and lead, which enhance the properties of transparency, purity and lustre.

The three main types of glass manufactured today are as follows:

1. Soda-lime glasses for bottles, window glass, etc.
2. Lead-potash-silica glasses for tableware, etc.
3. Boro-silicate glasses for laboratory and oven-ware.

The following is a brief description of the principal raw materials used for the manufacture of the glasses given above:

Silica. This material is the base of all common glasses and is found universally in great abundance, as sand, sandstone, quartz rock and, combined with alumina and other metallic oxides, as felspars.

Although sand is so abundant, the supplies for the making of colourless glass are limited owing to contamination of small quantities of iron. Indeed, all sands contain this impurity, and their suitability for the making of colourless glass is determined very much by the amount of iron present. As little as one part of iron oxide in 5,000 parts of sand is sufficient to impart a pale sea-green tint to the finished article.

The sand used for making the best colourless glass is of a special kind. It is carefully selected, first, to have as low an iron content as possible, secondly, to have grains as uniform in size as possible and angular in shape, and thirdly, to be free from impurities such as carbonaceous matter which would tend to discolour the glass. To achieve these conditions, the sand is well washed, then heated to a dull red heat to remove the carbonaceous matter, and finally passed through a screen to remove coarse grains and lumps.

In this country the main sources of supply for commercial colourless glasses are Reigate, Kings Lynn and some Welsh quartzite rocks. The purest deposit, however, is at Loch Aline in Scotland. Similar pure deposits occur at Fontainebleau, near Paris, New Jersey and Pennsylvania in America.

In the seventeenth and eighteenth centuries, the source of silica for glass-making was not sand but flint stones, which were burnt and then ground to a fine powder. It was from this early practice that the term 'flint' glass was derived, a term still used in the glass trade today to describe a colourless glass. Later, towards the close of the eighteenth century nearly all the flint glasshouses obtained their supplies of sand from Alum Bay, in the Isle of Wight, the Lynn river and Aylesbury. Sand used in the Irish factories during the period 1780-1850 was also obtained from Alum Bay and Lynn.

Soda. The everyday compound of soda used for household purposes is common salt, which also forms the basis for the manufacture of the soda compound used by the glass-maker—that is, soda-ash or sodium carbonate. In a somewhat similar form, the carbonate is used in the house as washing soda and forms the base of some detergents.

In the manufacture of soda-ash, common salt (sodium chloride) is converted into crystalline soda-ash by carbonating a solution of brine. The crystalline product is then heated to drive off the water of crystallisation, leaving the anhydrous soda-ash as used by the glass-maker.

Other materials containing soda are used in glass-making, such as Chilean saltpetre and borax.

Soda considerably lowers the melting temperature at which glass forms. It acts as a good flux, but has the disadvantage of lowering the durability of the glass. It has already been stated that silica and sand fused together (in roughly equal proportions) produce a glass which is readily soluble in water. Hence, glass contains only from twelve to fifteen per cent soda.

Potash. In all glasses where the cost of the raw materials is of secondary importance, such as the crystal glass used for tableware, potash is used in preference to soda, experience having shown that potash glass is less subject to discoloration during melting than corresponding glass containing soda as the fluxing agent. This is particularly the case with a glass containing lead, and it is therefore found in practice that potash and lead are invariably used in combination for glasses where clearness is essential, such as optical glass and the best tableware.

Potash is a well-known material, being used extensively as a fertiliser and as an ingredient of gun-powder. It is found naturally in South America and also in Germany. The modern method of manufacture is similar to that for the conversion of common salt into soda-ash—that is, a solution of potassium chloride, or sylvine, as it is termed, is carbonated, resulting in the formation of potassium carbonate.

From the early days of glass manufacture in this country up to the middle of the last century, carbonate of potash was produced from the ashes of wood. Most plants, shrubs and trees when burnt leave an ash containing potassium carbonate. Thus, the ash formed by burning such substances as straw or the bark of certain trees, like the oak or the lime, contains between six and seven per cent of carbonate of potash. The salt is extracted by leaching with water.

Lime. This well-known material is used both for household purposes and on the land; before the days of distempering, the hydrated form of lime was used as ceiling white.

Lime occurs naturally as marble, limestone and chalk, in such places in this country as the Dover cliffs, the Cheddar Gorge and the Derbyshire hills. Like most other materials used for glass-making, however, the quality required must be good and the iron content must be low, as in the case of sand. Fortunately, the deposits in Derbyshire are remarkably good in this respect. The limestone rock is quarried and crushed until almost powder form, of similar grain size to that of sand.

Lime added to a glass gives increased stability and weathering properties. It is an ingredient of the commoner glasses used in the production of bottles, window glass and electric light bulbs, but is not an ingredient of the lead crystal glasses.

Lead Oxide. The metal lead has been known from ancient times. Egyptians employed lead for water conduits as far back as 3000 B.C. It is mined in the form of Galena, a lead sulphide found extensively in America, from which lead is easily extracted by roasting. If, however, air is blown over the surface of the molten metal, litharge is formed, from which red lead is produced by further oxidation. Litharge was the oxide first used when Ravenscroft discovered glass-of-lead in the seventeenth century, but today glass-makers prefer to employ red lead.

Lead crystal glass is produced from the fusion of sand, red lead and potash. As the lead ingredient is a heavy substance, it considerably increases the density of the glass, enhancing its power to refract and disperse the light transmitted through it more than any other glass-making material. It is this property of density and corresponding power to disperse light that gives to lead crystal glass its unrivalled sparkle and brilliancy when cut, and its bell-like note when sharply struck. Special optical lenses are made from lead glass because of its superior refractive power.

Lead glasses differ from others in their technique of melting. The furnace condition under which the melting is conducted must necessarily be of an oxidising nature in order to prevent the reduction of the lead compounds to a metallic condition. The presence of metallic lead may cause not only the discolouring of the glass, but may result in severe attack upon the fireclay from which the melting crucibles are formed.

Borax. Boric oxide is a substance which has many domestic and industrial uses. It occurs naturally as many minerals, the most well known of which is Tincal, found in Tibet, India, China and other countries, but now almost entirely mined in California, where enormous deposits have been found in recent years. The mineral is purified chemically, and as borax, its most well-known form, consists of a crystalline product of boric oxide, soda and water of crystallisation.

Borax is used in glass for many reasons, but there is no doubt that in the early days of lead crystal glass it was employed solely for its fluxing properties—that is, its readiness to dissolve other glass-making materials. It becomes a mobile fluid at about 1550°F. and under certain conditions exerts a greater fluxing action than either soda or potash.

Boric oxide has other uses as a glass-making material, however, the most important being its property in imparting to the glass increased resistance against various kinds of shock, such as sharp blows or sudden changes of temperature. Boric oxide in a glass also helps to increase its chemical durability, and for this reason is used in the production of laboratory ware.

Arsenic. There are very few colourless glasses used for tableware that do not contain arsenic. It is usually introduced into the glass as the white oxide of arsenic, and is a valuable constituent from many points of view; colour, transparency and brilliancy of the glass are all enhanced by the presence of arsenic. Although, during the melting process, it is to some extent transformed into a vapour, quite a large proportion of the arsenic remains dissolved in the glass, but in the long history of glass, there is no case on record of any catastrophe having resulted from it.

White oxide of arsenic is manufactured from minerals containing the metal, such as the tin ores in Cornwall, by heating them in a current of air. The oxide is given off as a vapour which is carried into flues where it condenses into a white powder very much of the appearance of flour.

The amount of arsenic used in glass is comparatively small, usually of the order of one part to one thousand parts sand.

Decolourisers. Small quantities of certain substances are added to a glass batch in order to improve its clarity, and to counteract the effect of impurities which would otherwise colour or tint the glass. These ingredients are termed decolourisers and are dealt with under DECOLOURISING OF GLASS.

181. *Fireclay for pot-making being won by open-cast working in a deposit in Yorkshire. An entrance to a mine is shown in the bank in the background.* (*Messrs Parkinson & Spencer, Ltd.*)

MEAD GLASSES. Mead is an old-world drink, dating back to the time of our Saxon ancestors, when it was a potent brew prepared from honey and seasoned with herbs. It is said to have been 'woundily strong' and needed only a small glass. It was an exceedingly popular drink in the seventeenth and eighteenth centuries and, indeed, mead drinking was a custom that lingered in some country districts until the last century. There have been revivals among mead enthusiasts even in recent times. Many varieties of mead were known such as Sack Mead, Walnut Mead, Cowslip Mead and Small Mead, the varieties taking their names from the character of the main seasoning ingredients.

The particular type of glass used for mead has, like the champagne glass, always been a controversial matter. Tradition claims that mead glasses were of low or tumbler form. There is no doubt that they must have been easy glasses to manufacture and therefore of simple design, for, owing to the great popularity of mead, they would have been required in quantity. It is likely, of course, that any small bowl capable of being used as a drinking vessel would have been called into service.

Some writers claim, however, that like many other drinks in the eighteenth century, mead had its special glass, the popular style being a shallow bowl, usually about three inches in height, often incurved, with a lip finish. An alternative style was a low, tumbler-shaped vessel, waisted in the middle and provided with a 'kick-bottom'—that is, indented at the base similar to the champagne bottle.

Haynes (*Glass Through the Ages*, 1948, p. 162) describes a mead glass as a goblet with stem rudimentary or absent. They were not made after 1760.

A mead glass of rummer shape with cup bowl and plain stem with wide folded foot changed hands in 1936 for £31. Another with cup bowl and an opaque-twist stem with wide conical foot fetched £17 in the same year.

MELTING OF GLASS. The melting of glass for tableware and articles of similar quality is conducted in what is described as a pot furnace. The term 'pot' refers to the actual melting crucible housed in the furnace itself. Furnaces used in the production of glass for such articles as bottles and window glass are, however, of an entirely different construction. They are known as tank furnaces, because the glass is melted in a shallow tank or basin, the larger types often containing several hundred tons of molten glass.

A pot furnace, on the other hand, contains from one to

twenty fireclay pots. Glasshouse pots vary in size according to the requirements. An assortment (Fig. 182) shows the larger pots, three feet six inches high and four feet six inches long, typical of those used for colourless crystal, and a smaller kind, or 'skittle-pot', usually employed for the coloured glasses.

The preparation of the fireclay pots used for tableware and fancy articles is an important phase of crystal glass-making. They are the largest known example of the potter's art; as they are fashioned entirely by hand, they constitute an interesting study for the student of ceramics. They are prepared from special clays selected for their purity, plastic nature and property of withstanding intense heat. Such clays are very scarce, but English glass-makers are fortunate in that two of the best European deposits occur in the Stourbridge district, Worcestershire, and at Halifax, Yorkshire. The latter is an extensive deposit dating back to the late eighteenth century, from which time it has been continuously mined until today, when its products are exported to almost every corner of the globe.

The clay is won by mining or open-cast working (Fig. 181); first, the over-burden of soil, ganister and coal is removed, after which the clay is carefully cut from the seam by hand, examined for any foreign matter, and finally allowed to remain in the open to 'weather' for several months.

The raw clay is then ground, any iron present being removed magnetically, and afterwards mixed with a proportion of burnt clay to increase its refractory properties. Water is added to the mixture, which is then pressed under heavy rollers until a plasticity is reached so that the clay may easily be fashioned by hand.

The first stage in the making of a pot from the prepared clay is the preparation of its bottom, usually four or five inches thick; for this a wooden ring mould is used, oval in shape, set upon a flat wooden base. The pot-maker uses rolls of clay about seven inches long and up to three inches in thickness, shown ready for use in Fig. 183 (left), which he presses down by hand into the ring mould. When the bottom is complete, the ring mould is removed, and the sides of the pot are then built up by hand, a few inches each day, after the manner shown in Fig. 183; the diameter is gradually decreased until the pot, except for an opening in the side, is completely covered.

In crystal glass-making, the pots are covered or crowned, as the process is called, to prevent the gases and impurities from the combustion chamber of the furnace coming into contact with the molten glass and so discolouring it.

The final stage in the making of a glasshouse pot is the addition of the 'mouth', an opening just above the level of the glass it will later contain. A period of several weeks' drying is then allowed in special chambers where the temperature conditions and humidity are under careful control.

The process of slowly heating the empty pot to red heat, and transferring it to the glass furnace while hot, is, perhaps, the most critical period in the life of the pot. A sudden change in its temperature due to a draught of cold air, or too long exposure during transfer from one furnace to another, may ruin the patient work of weeks.

Much of the success of crystal glass-making depends upon the subsequent behaviour of the pots, for, in addition to the properties of purity and heat resistance already mentioned, they must also survive a number of successive melts without cracking or collapsing. When a failure occurs, not only are the costly materials lost, but the molten glass flows into other parts of the furnace causing damage and delay.

The melting of best crystal glass is always conducted in pot-furnaces, housing from one to twenty of the glass-maker's pots just described. A model of the type of furnace in general use today is shown in Fig. 184. It consists of an upper chamber above floor level, usually circular in shape, containing the pots, and a lower chamber consisting of recuperators. Hot gases from a gas-producer pass through an opening, known as the 'eye' of the furnace, sweep over the pots, escape downwards through ports or openings, to the recuperator tubes, and thence to the stack.

Air required for combustion of the gas is drawn from the atmosphere and preheated by being passed through sets of tubes adjacent to the recuperators where the waste heat of the outgoing gases is absorbed.

The melting of glass is usually conducted during the night. The mixture of batch and cullet is shovelled into the pot through its mouth until nearly filled to this level. The mouth of the pot is then 'stoppered' with a fireclay slab, and the melting commences. Shrinkage in bulk occurs as the glass is formed, and large bubbles of gas are evolved due to the decomposition of the raw materials. Further quantities of batch and cullet may now be added. The temperature of the furnace is raised as high as possible during this process in order to increase the fluidity of the molten glass mass to allow the escape of the residual specks of gas known as 'seed', some of which are only of pin-point size.

After a period of several hours the glass becomes a quiescent, intensely brilliant mass with such a highly reflecting surface that it is difficult to distinguish its level from the gleaming walls of the pot itself. In this condition the 'metal', as it is termed, is judged ready for 'working', and the temperature is then lowered until the glass attains the correct consistency for the glass-maker to gather and fashion it into the shape he requires.

The furnaces used in early times were not essentially different from those of modern construction, except that the pots were heated by the direct application of the burning fuel; the principle of recuperation of waste heat was, of course, not established until the last century, when F. & W. Siemens brought about notable improvements in furnace design.

A description (S. E. Winbolt, *Wealden Glass*, Hove, 1933; p. 75) of a glasshouse furnace is given by Theophilus, a priest, probably German, who wrote in the tenth or eleventh century; some writers place him, however, as late as the thirteenth century. A model built to the following description is shown in Fig. 185:

'The furnace is made of stones and clay 15 feet by 10 feet, the foundation walls one foot thick. A firm and level hearth for the fire box is made of stones and clay, and divided by a wall breadth-wise, so that the two compartments are two-thirds and one third. Stoke holes are at both ends. Build the enclosing walls nearly 4 feet high. Now make a hearth above the fire box and throughout the length. In the hearth of the larger chamber make four holes along each of the long sides for the working pots, and two holes in the centre through which the flames may ascend. In each side opposite the holes make windows, one hand (about 8 inches) square. In the smaller chamber must be a hollow in the hearth near the dividing wall, and a window one hand square near the outer wall of the front.'

182. *Assortment of fireclay melting pots used in crystal glass-making. The smaller pots in the foreground are 'skittle' pots used for coloured glass. The larger pots in the background hold about one ton of molten glass. (Messrs Parkinson & Spencer, Ltd.)*

183. *Pot-maker constructing a glasshouse pot from prepared clay. The process occupies several weeks of patient work. (Messrs Parkinson & Spencer, Ltd.)*

184. *Model of a modern recuperative gas-fired pot furnace. A glass melting pot is shown in position at floor level.* (*Lent to Science Museum, London, by Messrs Stein and Atkinson, Ltd.*)

185. *Model of a glass-melting furnace constructed from a description by Theophilus, probably twelfth century. An idea of size can be judged from the walls, which are 1 foot in thickness.* (*Crown Copyright, Science Museum, London*)

A model of a glass-melting furnace, built to the description of Georgii Agricola (*De Re Metallica*, published by Froben at Bale in 1556), of the type in vogue in the sixteenth century, is shown in Fig. 186. According to this writer, the glass-making materials were often partially melted together before being placed in the melting pots, a method employed by the Roman glass-makers. The glassy frit was then broken up in small pieces and given a final melting in a second furnace, such as that shown in the illustration. A translation is as follows:

'The second furnace is round, eight feet wide and twelve feet high, strengthened on the outside with ribs, 1½ feet thick, and is composed of three chambers, the lowest having a narrow opening for stoking the logs on the ground-level hearth. In the wall of the middle chamber are six arched openings which, when the heated pots are put in, are blocked up with clay, only small openings being left. The thickness of the pot should be two fingers, their height two feet, the breadth of bulge 1½ feet, and of mouth and base, one foot.

'In the centre of the roof of the middle chamber is a square opening, a palm (about four inches square) long and broad, through which the heat penetrates into the topmost compartment. At the back of the compartment is an opening, so that in the oblong pottery tunnel placed in it, the glass articles may be cooled off gradually. If they were not thus gradually cooled, they would crack. These tunnels are then taken out of the upper compartment and replaced in their chambers.'

Although easy of accomplishment today, the complete elimination of seed was rarely obtained by the early glass-makers. The fuel for heating the furnaces was wood, and although the glasshouse pots were very much smaller and not covered as they are today, the glass-maker was unable to raise sufficient heat to remove all the seed. Many early specimens of glass are extant which contain hundreds of these tiny specks of seed.

MILDNER, JOHANN (1764-1808).
See GERMAN AND BOHEMIAN GLASS.

MILLEFIORI. The process for making millefiori was very similar to that used for the making of filigree. (*See* FILIGREE.) Blobs of glass of different colours were placed together and heated until they became welded into a whole, but not to a point at which the colours would mix. The hot, plastic mass would then be drawn into a long cane, the pattern or mosaic formed by the original colours being perfectly retained in the reduced section of the cane. The process has a modern counterpart in the production of the sticks of 'rock', which advertise with every succulent mouthful the name of the seaside town in which they were made. Sections of the mosaic canes, cut either square or obliquely, were then placed together, reheated, and finally moulded into the shape required.

The name millefiori is not an ancient one. It is an Italian word meaning a thousand flowers—a truly descriptive word for these delightful pieces of mosaic in which the rich and subtle tones of the colours blend as naturally as the flowers in an old English garden.

The art of making millefiori has been known for centuries. Whole rods of millefiori have been found in Thebes dating from the eighteenth dynasty onwards; they were probably manufactured there and sold to glass-makers. Similar rods have been found in Palestine (F. Neuburg, *Glass in Antiquity*, 1949).

186. *Model of a glass-melting furnace according to the description of Agricola in the sixteenth century. Height of melting pots about 2 feet.* (*Crown Copyright, Science Museum, London*)

In the Roman period, beads manufactured from millefiori were very popular. Many specimens of bowls in millefiori, remarkable for their beauty of outline and harmony of colour, exist today. Those in the Victoria and Albert Museum, London, and in the Metropolitan Museum of Art, New York, are from Rome or Alexandria, from the period 100 B.C.-A.D. 100.

There is evidence that millefiori vessels were made in Silesia and other parts of Central Europe in the eighteenth century. Gustav Pazaurek (*Gläser der Empire-und Biedermeierzeit*, Leipzig, 1923) states that millefiori vessels were produced at the Hoffnungstal Works in Silesia in 1833 and later at Schonebeck near Magdeburg, specimens from the latter factory being shown at an exhibition at Mainz in 1842.

It is true, of course, that the Venetians mastered the art of making millefiori, but the technique differed somewhat from the Roman in that the coloured motifs were embedded in clear glass, whereas in all Roman specimens the coloured sections are assembled in either translucent or opaque mosaic.

The French craftsmen of Baccarat, St Louis and Clichy excelled in the manufacture of millefiori. Articles such as paperweights, inkstands, pen-rests, rulers, wafer-stands and other table requisites are fascinating masterpieces; they excel in the quality of their workmanship, harmony of colour and beauty of design.

English efforts in the manufacture of millefiori occurred soon after the Exhibition at Vienna in 1845. At that time the Stourbridge glass-makers, having been given their industrial freedom by the repeal of the Glass Excise Act in 1845, were experimenting with colour, and it is not unreasonable to assume that the first millefiori articles made in this country came from Stourbridge, being based on French models. There is, indeed, a marked similarity between paperweights known to have been made at Stourbridge and, for example, some Clichy millefiori paperweights of the 1849 period.

According to some French writers, English factories were at the time engaging workmen from the Clichy factory for the making of millefiori articles such as paperweights. Many articles were made at Stourbridge similar to the French factories, such as ink-stands, rulers, pen-rests, wafer-stands and other writing table requisites already mentioned, and which were for the most part flagrant imitations of the French models.

Other articles in millefiori made by English factories, either copies of French models or created by Stourbridge glass-makers, were door-knobs, newel posts, linen smoothers, drinking vessels, candlesticks, lamps, knife-rests and seals.

MIRRORS. Glass mirrors have been known for many centuries. They were not unknown in Roman times, although polished metal mirrors were then more generally used. In the twelfth century in Germany and Lorraine, glass mirrors were made with the reflecting surface prepared from tin, lead or other metal, and by the fifteenth century improvements in

187. *Mirror signed by John Gumley and dated 1715. It has a separate frame of glass and is surmounted by glass cresting. (Hampton Court Palace. By Gracious Permission of her Majesty the Queen.)* 188. *Mirror from Chippendale period,* circa *1763. (Messrs Mallett & Son)*

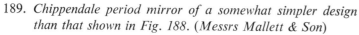

189. *Chippendale period mirror of a somewhat simpler design than that shown in Fig. 188.* (*Messrs Mallett & Son*)

190. *Mirror in carved giltwood frame after Chinese taste, nearly 5 feet in height.* (*Messrs Mallett & Son*)

preparing sheet glass enabled glass-makers to bring about considerable improvement in the quality of mirrors.

The glass-makers of Nuremburg during the fifteenth century earned fame by manufacturing convex mirrors by a process of blowing a glass globe, and while it was still hot, blowing into it a metallic mixture with a little resin or salt of tartar. The globe, when cold, was cut into small mirrors which reflected a reduced image of the object.

During the sixteenth century, manufacturers of glass mirrors in Venice had so improved in technique that they formed themselves into a Corporation. According to the regulations controlling this body, everyone claiming to be admitted had to prove his ability to flatten and polish a piece of glass and to apply the metal leaf backing.

The process used for making sheets of glass at the time was the blowing of large cylinders, which were split along their length and flattened on a heated stone. This was later known in this country as the 'broad' process.

Sir Robert Mansell, the Elizabethan glass-maker (*see* MANSELL, SIR ROBERT), imported the Venetian process into this country in 1623, and during the following years much progress was made. Indeed, in 1676, John Evelyn, after a visit to the Duke of Buckingham's glasshouse at Lambeth made the following entry in his diary: 'To Lambeth—where they make huge vessels of mettal as cleare, ponderous and thick as chrystal; also looking glasses far larger and better than any that come from Venice.'

Mirrors began to grow in popularity very quickly, for it was soon realised that the mirror was decorative as well as functional; it was used in architecture, for furnishing cabinets, and for use in coaches. The earliest mention in this country of polishing mirrors was in 1678 when there was reference to a new process, dated 15th May, 1678: 'Patent for 14 years to John Roberts for his invention of grinding, polishing and diamonding glass plates for looking glasses, etc., by the motion of water and wheels.' (S. P. Dom, 15th May, 1678, Entry Book, 51, p. 21.)

By 'diamonding' was meant a form of bevelling in which

191. *Mirror in classic style in response to Adam influence with decorative motifs such as urns and acanthus foliage.* (*Messrs Mallett & Son.*) 192. *Oval mirror of the Adam period with classic urn and acanthus foliage.* (*Messrs Mallett & Son*)

hollows cut into the glass surface were made to intersect forming the outline of a diamond along the edge of the mirror.

About this time mirrors were supplied ground and polished, and very much larger than those supplied from Venice, notices showing that they were from the smallest size up to six feet in length.

The increase in popularity of the mirror can be judged from the report in 1705 by John Gumley, a prominent glass manufacturer, that: 'The trade of looking glass plates is so considerably improved that they serve not only for Furniture and Ornament, in Her Majesty's Dominions at Home, but are likewise in great Esteem in Foreign Parts; the *Venetians* themselves buying of the *Plates*, and preferring them before their own.'

The broad process of manufacturing glass sheets had its limitations. It was a difficult matter to obtain large plates of even thickness and, after grinding and polishing, a large plate often had to be rejected or cut down in size, because of thickness along the edges.

To overcome these difficulties a new process was perfected in 1691 in France, which depended on the casting of sheets by pouring the liquid glass into large moulds or frames, smoothed while hot by rollers, and afterwards ground and polished on both surfaces. This process was, however, not taken up in this country until much later. See this section under PROGRESS IN MAKING PLATE-GLASS.

During the reign of Queen Anne and George I, John Gumley carried out an extensive business in plate-glass, and in 1714 was selling 'Looking Glasses in Frames, and out of Frames, Coach-Glasses, Chimney-Glasses, Sconces, Dressing Glasses, Union Suits, Dressing Boxes, Swinging Glasses, Glass Schandeliers, Lanthorns, Gilt-Brockets, and the like.'

Pier-glasses, designed to hang on the pier wall between two windows, were also becoming popular about this time. (*See* PIER GLASSES.)

Early mirrors, such as the plates made by John Roberts in 1676, and those supplied by John Gumley about the turn of the seventeenth century, had decorative cut borders in the style then known as 'diamonding', but this simple motif became elaborated about the turn of the century into a separate frame of glass mitred at the corners and often surmounted by glass cresting.

Some of John Gumley's mirrors are still preserved today. One at Hampton Court Palace, signed by him and dated 1715, has a separate frame of glass and is surmounted by glass cresting. It is shown in Fig. 187. A pair of mirrors, signed by Gumley and dated 1703, were made for the first Duke of Devonshire. They have cut borders and the coat-of-arms in applied decoration on the cresting. An interesting feature concerning these mirrors is that their reflecting properties are still perfect. They each measure sixty-eight inches by thirty-nine inches. They are now at Chatsworth, Derbyshire.

The decoration changed as the eighteenth century advanced, and glass frames for mirrors were superseded by richly carved wood frames or those decorated by gesso work. Soon cabinet makers were supplying mirrors in plain, moulded frames of veneered walnut with cresting or hoods in pierced styles, which competed with the simple gesso frames.

Gesso was popular until 1730 or thereabouts, but was superseded in its turn again by frames of carved giltwood with wave moulding which, in various styles dictated by fashion, held the popular market throughout the century. Architectural designs were in demand after gesso had lost its appeal, and this style in its turn was succeeded by the rococo, Chinese and Gothic as the popular taste changed.

Mirrors from this period are probably the most interesting to the collector today. A specimen shown in Fig. 188 is one of a pair of carved and giltwood Chippendale mirrors designed by William Ince (William Ince and Thomas Mayhew, *Universal System of Household Furniture*, 1763, Plate LXXX). Another specimen from the same period is shown in Fig. 189, but it is somewhat less ornate than that shown in Fig. 188.

The mirror shown in Fig. 190 is in carved giltwood and is after the Chinese taste. This specimen, nearly five feet in height, has a pagoda top with a Chinese figure and a swan motif at the base.

Towards the end of the century, frames in the so-called classic style, with arch cresting and decorative motifs such as urns and acanthus foliage, appeared in response to the influence of the Adam brothers. Specimens from this period are shown in Figs. 191 and 192.

Regency or Empire styles followed in the nineteenth century, but the mirrors of this period are without any great merit. In the main they are rather coarse, much too ornate and of poor quality, and the early individual craftsmanship had begun to give place to the mass produced article of the factory.

Mirrors, Convex. There has already been reference to the convex mirrors made during the fifteenth century by the glass-makers of Nuremburg. It was not until the end of the eighteenth century, however, that the convex mirror was manufactured in this country. Sheraton described the new type of looking-glass (Thomas Sheraton, *Cabinet Dictionary*, London, 1803) in this way: 'An article of furniture, a circular convex mirror in a gilt frame, silvered on the concave side, by which the reflection of the rays of the light are produced. The properties of such mirrors consist in their collecting the reflected rays into a point, by which the perspective of the room in which they are suspended presents itself in the surface of the mirror, and produces an agreeable effect. On this account, as well as for the convenience of holding lights, they are now become universally in fashion and are considered both as a useful and ornamental piece of furniture.'

193. *Convex mirror with decorative effects typical of the Sheraton style at the turn of the eighteenth century.*

Convex mirrors were usually given frames of carved wood and were ornamented in gilt often with a single row of small gilt balls in a channel in the frame. There was usually an acanthus leaf or laurel leaf cresting, but in some cases the cresting was of a figure subject, such as an eagle, a sea-horse, or more complex designs. A specimen with this style of decoration is shown in Fig. 193.

As two walls of a room in the Regency period were often already occupied by mirrors—that is, the pier wall and the facing chimney wall—the circular concave mirrors usually occupied a position on an end wall, which enabled them to reflect the entire contents of the room.

Mirrors, Irish. *See* IRISH GLASS.

Progress in Making Plate-Glass. The French method of casting glass sheets was taken up in this country towards the end of the eighteenth century. A company known as the British Cast Plate Glass Company was formed in 1773, with the object of competing with the French manufacturers, who at that time had what amounted to almost a monopoly in the mirror trade throughout Europe. The new company was entirely successful; indeed, in 1842 it is recorded that it had thrived beyond all expectations. The company was in existence until 1901, when it was acquired by Pilkington Brothers, the famous company who in 1959 introduced a new process known as the Float Process, for eliminating the grinding and polishing of plate-glass.

Glass mirrors with giltwood frames or gilt gesso vary in price according to their decorative effect. For example, a wall mirror with a rectangular plate in a carved giltwood frame in Restoration style about four feet high by three feet wide changed hands for £16, while a small Chippendale wall mirror in a carved giltwood frame of much the same size realised £66 in the same sale.

MONTEIGH or **MONTITH.**
See WINEGLASS COOLERS.

MUSICAL GLASSES. Because of their ability to emit a musical note when sharply struck, certain glass vessels have from time to time been used as musical instruments. The 'ring', as it is termed, is a test for a glass containing a high percentage of lead, and glasses of this nature, because of their greater density, emit a more resonant note than glasses of different composition.

Caruso, the great Italian tenor, could shatter a glass vessel by singing into it; the vibration set up by the high quality of his voice caused the glass to exceed its elastic limit and so break.

The sound emitted by rubbing a wetted finger round the rim of a thin wineglass has often been a source of amusement and at times, it must be admitted, of annoyance, in restaurants.

It was at one time popular in Germany to indulge in this sort of music. Hassdorfer (*Mathematische und Philosphische Erquickungen*, Nuremburg, 1677) refers to 'gay wine music', in which he claimed that it was a well-known after dinner occurrence to play on wineglasses. The required notes were obtained by filling suitable sizes of wineglasses or tumblers with water, and adjusting their level to get the correct pitch. This seventeenth-century entertainment has often been re-introduced in modern times by stage entertainers.

There is a notice in the *General Advertiser*, 23rd April, 1746, which reads as follows:

'At the Desire of several persons of quality. At the New Theatre in Haymarket, this Day, will be performed a Concert of Vocal and Instrumental

MUSICK

By the principal performers from the opera, particularly Signor Gluck, composer of the Opera, will play a Concerto, and a song to be sung by Signora Frazi, upon a new instrument of 26 Glasses, and thereby hopes to satisfy the curious, as well as the Lovers of Musick.

'Pit and boxes to be put together at half a guinea each, galery 5 shillings.

'To begin at half an hour after six.

'Ticket to be had at the Prince of Orange coffee house in the Haymarket.'

It is recorded that Gluck played this 'Concerto on 26 drinking glasses tuned with spring water, accompanied with the whole band, being a new instrument of his own invention, upon which he performs whatever may be done on a violin or harpsichord'.

Whether or not Gluck can claim credit for his range of drinking glasses being a new invention and equivalent in quality to the violin remains a source of doubt, but it is certain that this form of entertainment enjoyed much popularity at the time.

A book was published in 1762 by Anne Ford on *Instruction for Playing on Musical Glasses with such directions that any persons of a musical turn may learn in a few days, if not in a few hours.*

Dr Paul Lynton and K. L. Loewenstein (*Journal of the Society of Glass Technology*, Vol. XXXV, 1951, p. 17) have given an account of the experience of Benjamin Franklin in London in connection with musical glasses. When about to leave Europe in 1762, he wrote to Baccaria of Turin thanking him for his support, and regretting that he had nothing new to erport. He continued: 'Perhaps, however, it may be agreeable to you, as you live in a musical country, to have an account of the new instrument lately added to the great number that charming science was possessed of. As it is an instrument that seems peculiarly adapted to Italian music, especially that of the soft and plaintive kind, I will endeavour to give such description of it, that you or any of your friends may be enabled to imitate it, if you incline to do so, without being at the expense and trouble of the many experiments I have made in endeavouring to bring it to its present perfection.'

At this point Franklin described an instrument that had been brought to the notice of the Royal Society invented by Richard Pockrich, an Irishman, who used tuned wineglasses which were fixed in position on a table. Pockrich played this instrument in Dublin in 1743 and toured England with it in the following year. The 'Musical Glasses' as they were known became very popular, but Pockrich's success was cut very short, for in 1759 he was killed in a fire which also destroyed his instrument.

The account of Benjamin Franklin then continues: 'Mr E. Delaval, a most ingenious member of the Royal Society, made an imitation of it with a better choice and form of glasses, which was the first I saw or heard. Being charmed by the sweetness of its tones and the music he produced from it, I wished only to see the glasses disposed of in a more convenient form, and brought together in a narrower compass, so as to admit of a greater number of tunes and all within reach of hand to a person sitting before the instrument.'

Franklin experimented in Philadelphia on an instrument using thirty-seven specially made glasses which were mounted on a spindle, the glasses being ground to the required size and tested for pitch against a well-tuned harpsichord. The instrument was sufficient to produce three octaves, including all the semi-tones.

To operate the instrument, the glasses themselves were rotated in a trough of water by means of a foot treadle connected to the spindle. The desired tune was produced by applying the tips of the fingers to the edges of the glasses while they were rotating. If necessary, all ten fingers could be used as on a keyboard instrument.

Franklin wrote of this ingenious device: 'The advantages of this instrument are that its tones are incomparably sweet beyond those of any other; that they can be swelled and softened at pleasure by stronger or weaker pressure of the fingers, and continued at any length, and that the instrument, being once well tuned, never again wants tuning.'

lin named the instrument the Armonica, but it later known as the Harmonica. Copies made to Franklin's tion sold for forty guineas. Many famous musicians s instrument in tours of Europe and America between s 1764 and 1823. In the latter year, a Scotsman named s gave performances in Scotland on 120 glasses varying om three gallon capacity to one the size of a thimble, e set providing a scale of six octaves.

n and Loewenstein give a most interesting account of ılarity enjoyed by the harmonica, but these writers t that by 1780 its most serious defect became known. t of the vibrations of the glasses on the very sensitive s of the performers produced nervous disorders of erious nature that several performers had to retire ir profession.

attempts to overcome the trouble failed. Special pads plied by the makers, violin bows were used instead of rs, and in Germany an instrument was developed with ammers operated by a lever system somewhat on the piano.

n and Loewenstein say in their concluding remarks, that 'all efforts were in vain. The musical beauty of Harmonica lay in the sensitive touch of the fingers, nad gone. All forms of the Harmonica were eventually ıt by the cheaper, easier and less fragile instruments w Harmonica family, although the sound of the latter le relation to that of the glass Harmonica'.

gh now mainly of historical interest, the glass har- s still used occasionally. As recently as 1938 it was a concert in the London Museum. The music critic *mes*, 11th March, 1938, remarked at the time on the one of extraordinary charm, and it seems that for tone, musical glasses have never been surpassed.

ıss harmonica of Benjamin Franklin is preserved in ches Museum in Munich, Germany.

the harmonica, there were other musical instruments n glass. Dulcimers, consisting of glass strips mounted t side on a horizontal resonance box, were known in uring the eighteenth and nineteenth centuries. They lly a little more than an octave and were played with nmers, very much like the modern xylophone.

and Nailsea have been accredited with producing , bugles, coach horns and similar articles. They are found, but are more decorative than functional. They bably originated from either Birmingham or the area.

ls vary considerably. They are usually from six to es in height of heavy metal in different colours. A ndle is formed from an inverted baluster between . Some are found with clappers and some without. er may be of a different colour from that of the bell pecimen in the Taunton Museum has a ruby bell, a clear white glass, the handle a greenish opaque white p peacock blue. Another specimen has a bell of clear s with latticinio work in opaque white, the clapper , and the handle cobalt blue. Another large bell is ass with pale blue streaks, the handle clear white, nother is opaque white with pink loops, the handle nt green.

les may be a foot in length and are usually in clear glass, sometimes wrythen. There is a mention of a glass bugle from South Shields (W. A. Thorpe, *A History of English and Irish Glass*, 1929, Vol 1, p. 333).

Coach horns are usually similar in shape and size to their metal counterparts and are found up to three feet in length. They may be in colourless glass or coloured, such as deep blue.

NAILSEA GLASS. The glassworks from which the well-known style has taken its name functioned at Nailsea, seven or so miles from Bristol between 1788 and 1873, but from documentary records and an examination of the debris at the factory site, it is apparent that only window glass was made there; no evidence at all has been found of coloured glass or even bottle glass.

Nevertheless, Nailsea has given its name to a fascinating group of ware such as jugs, long-necked bottles, and two-handled vessels in smoky-green bottle glass, flecked with coloured enamel or bold looped and striped decoration in white enamel, such as is shown in Fig. 194.

It is quite evident that much of the ware now accredited to Nailsea was made at Bristol and Stourbridge, but there were so many centres in which similar styles were current, such as Wrockwardine in Shropshire, Yorkshire, the Newcastle district, Warrington, St Helen's, and Alloa in Scotland, that it is an extremely difficult matter to claim with any certainty that a specimen is 'Nailsea'. On the other hand, it is doubtful whether any evidence, however positive, that the articles were made elsewhere, will have any influence today on the designation 'Nailsea'.

Nailsea glass, then, must be regarded as a style, and it is possible today to recognise it from the several collections throughout the country, notably at Taunton and Bristol Museums, and in private collections. From a study of such

194. *Group of articles in the so-called Nailsea style with striped decoration in white enamel.*

195. *Nailsea jug in mottled or flecked style, in which chips of different coloured enamels are splashed over the glass surface.* sea jug (left) *with broad encircling bands in white enamel and* (right) *jug in smoky-green glass with white opal rim.* (*Sir Hug*

specimens, it is evident that three styles are represented (*a*) mottled or flecked ware as shown in Fig. 195; (*b*) ware crudely decorated in bold white festoons, such as the example shown in Fig. 196; this group is in smoky-green bottle glass and comprises jugs, two-handled vessels, long-necked bottles, mugs and other useful articles; and (*c*) vessels quite different from those in the other groups, more sophisticated in style, with well-formed latticinio decoration in milky-white and pale pink on a flint or pale green glass, examples of which are shown in Fig. 197. This group comprises articles more ornamental than functional, and includes flasks, large pipes, hats, bells, shoes and bellows. They were often decorated with ruby, blue and green glass, but other colours are known, although much rarer, such as yellow and dark red.

Some writers claim that the ornamental ware was made by some French glass-makers, who resided permanently at Nailsea; a row of cottages was built for their special colony, the block of buildings being known as 'French Rank'.

Tradition and superstition have both added their quota to the popularity of Nailsea glass. Witch balls, the inner surface smeared and daubed with a variety of colours, are accredited to the Nailsea workmen. They hung in their cottages, so the legend claims, to ward off the evil eye. Modern imitations, in various colours silvered on the inner surface, are not unknown.

Then there was the twisted glass rod, in the form of a walking stick, which may have been anything from four to eight feet in length. The rod was hung in a conspicuous position in the dwelling and was carefully cleaned every morning to create a spell against certain diseases, such as malaria. This superstition was so deeply rooted that the owner could seldom be persuaded to sell one (George Soane, *Curiosities of Literature*, 1847, Vol. 1, p. 206). If the rod unfortunately became broken, it was said that some dire misfortune would soon be the lot of a member of the household.

Also described as 'Nailsea' are the peculiar love-tokens which were, indeed, made at all glassworks near coastal towns —i.e., Nailsea, Bristol, London, Sunderland and Newcastle. They were mainly useful articles such as rolling p bottles and drinking vessels, and had inscribed initials and dates, or an amorous verse or motto. Fo there are scent bottles inscribed: ML 1822; SR 1822; and rolling pins inscribed with such words as 'May the Lord watch over you', and 'Be true to me'. A t called Nailsea rolling pin is shown in Fig. 198.

From a careful examination of specimens of the r flecked ware, it is easy to hazard a guess as to why a came to be manufactured. First, the duty imposed by Excise Act of 1745 of one penny per pound by wei raw materials used in the making of flint glass, doubled in 1777 and again increased ten years later. Nailsea works began operation, the tax was nearly pound by weight on flint glass. The duty on green b however, was only roughly one fifth of this amount to avoid the tax, therefore, it is likely that some of domestic ware was made in bottle glass, but to give drab nature an appeal, mottled decoration in th enamel flecks of colour was liberally splashed surface.

It is known that enamel glass was made at Bris would have been an easy matter for the workme neighbouring factories, such as at Nailsea, or Sta (six miles from Bristol), to have obtained discarde the enamel glass and to have crushed it ready for

In the making of an article with flecked decora enamel chips were sprinkled over the surface of plate', and the hot glass attached to a gathering over them, to which they would have adhered. T glass was reheated and finally blown into the requ the enamel chips being firmly welded to the surf vessel.

H. St George Gray (*Connoisseur*, June 1911, pp. 85-98) states that jugs of this type with splashe as well as white were also made at Sunderland and wardine Wood and Hopton Wafers, both in Shro also stated that excellent imitations specially prepa

197. *Gimmel flask* (left) *with white enamel festoons,* (centre) *cup and covering with latticinio decoration, and* (right) *bellows flask in typical 'Nailsea' style.*

198. *Typical inscribed rolling pin of the Nailsea style.*

unwary collector were on the market, in particular long-necked bottles with splashed decoration.

Thorpe (*A History of English and Irish Glass*, London, 1929, Vol. 1, p. 287) mentions that the yellow mottling found on some specimens of flecked ware seems to distinguish Wrockwardine glass from that of the Nailsea style.

The jug shown in Fig. 196 (left) in the collection of Sir Hugh Chance, whose ancestor, Robert Lucas Chance, controlled for a time the factory at Nailsea, can definitely be ascribed to Nailsea. It is four and a half inches in height, and is in the similar smoky-green glass to specimens found at Nailsea, and is encircled with broad bands in white opal.

It is conceivable, therefore, that authentic articles of this type have given their name to the Nailsea style. Such ornamental glass may have been made by the workmen in their spare time as *tours de force*, which was a usual practice permitted in most glassworks after the day's work had been done.

The third style of Nailsea has been already mentioned as including articles more decorative than functional, large pipes, shoes, bells and bellows, etc., being typical; examples are shown in Fig. 197.

The flasks vary from three and a half to ten and a half inches in height, and some have separate compartments and two necks, making them suitable for different liquids. They vary in colour from a transparent body with regular loops and festoons in white opaque glass, to flasks with blue or white opaque bodies with festoons in pink. The rarer colours are yellow and dark red.

The stopper decanters in latticinio were obviously not made at Nailsea; neither were the glass bells in various colours, although specimens were found in the Nailsea district. One specimen in the Taunton Museum has a ruby bell, a clapper in clear white glass, the handle in greenish opaque white and the top peacock blue. Such articles were much more likely to have been made at some other centre such as Stourbridge or Birmingham.

Articles of the so-called Nailsea type have realised comparatively low prices in the sale rooms. Rolling pins, gimmel flasks and walking sticks have fetched up to £2 each, while jugs, trumpets and swords realised about twice as much.

NEVERS GLASS.

See FRENCH GLASS.

NEWCASTLE GLASSES. Newcastle-on-Tyne had a much greater influence on English glass-making than is generally supposed. Indeed, during the first half of the eighteenth century, Newcastle led the country in glass production of all types, with no fewer than twenty-two glasshouses, one-third of which were producing flint glass. Its fame spread abroad and in countries such as Holland and Norway, it had a marked influence on style and form.

There is no doubt that the main impulse in Newcastle, so far as the production of domestic glass-ware was concerned, came from the Dagnias, an Italian family of glass-makers, who established their first glasshouse there in 1648. A member of the Dagnia family owned a glasshouse in Bristol in the middle of the seventeenth century, and it was from this centre that the Dagnia family migrated to the Tyne. There are three brothers mentioned in the Newcastle records—Onesiphorus, Edward and John—and there is little doubt that they introduced lead glass to the Newcastle district, based on the Ravenscroft formula. It would appear also that it was the Dagnias who were responsible for the development of that distinctive style of drinking glasses known today among collectors as 'Newcastle'.

The brothers Dagnia had every opportunity for establishing themselves firmly in the business of glass-making. They came from a glass-making family; they had the Italian tradition in the art and an inherited flair for style and form. Moreover, the family had an almost uninterrupted monopoly in the north for nearly half a century so far as the production of the best flint glass was concerned. Another generation of the Dagnia family inherited the business established by the three brothers, and new blood was infused from Stourbridge, as the widow of one of the sons married, in 1731, John Williams, an iron-founder from Stourbridge. It would appear that Williams's knowledge of furnace work served him in good stead, for the business in Newcastle continued to thrive and expand, and the quality of the glass itself greatly improved.

Newcastle glass is sufficiently brilliant, colour-free and homogeneous to suggest that the technique of melting was well understood, and that the use of decolourisers had been thoroughly mastered. Some writers have described the metal as 'thin', but there is no evidence whatsoever that it differed in composition from the generally accepted standard of flint, which was then, and, indeed, is today, one containing one-third of its weight as lead. Manufacture was also of a high order, the glasses themselves being delicately fashioned and of elegant form. There is nothing crude about a true Newcastle glass, as every detail of its construction was given expert care and attention.

Drinking glasses were at that time undergoing constant modification. After the invention of Ravenscroft's glass-of-lead in 1676, the baluster style of glass rapidly became the vogue, but the heavy knopping of the late seventeenth century soon gave place to a lighter variety known today as balustroids (*see* BALUSTROIDS.) With the transition of the heavier forms to the lighter style, there was also a tendency for the stems to lengthen at the expense of the bowl and thus to provide more scope for the glass-maker to employ simple stem motifs.

The Newcastle glass-makers were much alive to the change in style that was occurring and in this respect their superior skill and technique served them well. So that full expression could be given to the development of the stem, they chose what was known in the trade as the 'stuck shank' method of making a drinking glass—that is, the glass was made in three pieces, bowl, stem and foot. This allowed the glass-maker a much wider choice of stem motifs, for obviously elaboration of the stem was considerably limited by the alternative method of making a drinking glass—that is, the so-called 'drawn shank' method used in other parts of the country, in which the bowl and the stem were made in one piece, the foot being added afterwards. These alternative methods are sometimes referred to today as the 'two-piece' glass (drawn shank) and the 'three-piece' glass (stuck shank).

The variation on the stem formation of the Newcastle Balustroids is discussed under BALUSTROIDS.

There is no shadow of doubt that the Newcastle style was popular abroad. Frans Greenwood, the Dutch engraver, was using Newcastle glasses of the type described as early as 1728. Jacob Sang was also engraving them in Holland during the middle of the eighteenth century. He was probably the most outstanding of the wheel engravers, and always chose the Newcastle style of glass, a number of which he signed between the years 1752 and 1762.

It is, of course, not surprising that the Dutch wheel engravers chose the English lead metal as their medium, for it was softer to the wheel, and of a bright and lustrous quality that displayed engraved motifs to better advantage than the harder and less refractive potash-lime glasses of Continental manufacture. Modern wheel engravers who have used the two glass media, lead glass and potash-lime glass, will at once testify as to the advantages of the lead medium.

It is, of course, not unreasonable to assume that the lead glass from Newcastle was also preferable to that from other English glass-making centres, because of its superfine quality and style.

At the close of the eighteenth century, Newcastle glass was still the popular choice of the Dutch engravers. David Wolff, for example, employed a very similar style of Newcastle glass as late as the final decade of the eighteenth century.

In Norway, too, Newcastle glass was well known, and several collections today contain specimens of its eighteenth-century productions. There is a record that in 1746, a consignment of several dozen drinking glasses was sent from Newcastle-on-Tyne to Alexander Wallace, the British Consul-General in Bergen (*Gammelt Norsk Glass*, Oslo, 1953, p. 222, Ada Buch Polak).

About the middle of the eighteenth century, a company was formed in Norway which had for its object the full utilisation of Norway's natural resources, to include glass-making. For a few years the main technicians of this enterprise were Germans, but later an English glass-maker from the Newcastle district, James Keith, was employed by the company to introduce to the Norwegian factories the artistic developments then occurring in England.

Although Keith was a young man when he went to Nøstetangen, his first glass-works in Norway, he was nevertheless a fully qualified glass-blower. That his influence was quickly felt is shown by the marked similarity between glass from Nøstetangen after his arrival and eighteenth-century Newcastle glass. Keith was by far the most inventive and able of the workers at Nøstetangen, and he was induced to stay in the Norwegian factories until 1787, when he retired after over thirty years' service, a highly respected man.

Many of the Nøstetangen glasses extant today are of the style described as Newcastle—that is, glasses with round funnel bowls, knopped stems with inverted balusters and annular knops which were both plain or with small tears. The feet were folded, and most specimens are of the three-piece construction similar to the Newcastle balustroids.

Newcastle glasses were also the choice of the Beilbys for their enamel painting. (*See* ENAMELLED GLASS.) It might be reasonable to assume that they chose Newcastle glasses because they worked there, and would have had no other choice. This is not true, however, for glasses were being sent to Newcastle from London glasshouses long before the Beilby family went to live there. There are notices from 1750 onwards of consignments of glass 'of the newest fashion and best London Polish' in the Newcastle newspapers.

The prices fetched by Newcastle glasses are given under BALUSTROIDS.

NEWEL POSTS. Glass newel posts were usually ball-shaped, three to four inches in diameter, and were metal-mounted for attaching to doors, to be used as handles, or for attaching to the newel or upright post at the head of a flight of stairs. For this reason, they are mostly found in pairs.

Some newel posts in glass are decorated with millefiori in concentric rings of florettes such as red, white and blue; other specimens have red shading to white at the edges.

A pair of Stourbridge newel posts of the type described, three and three quarter inches in diameter, changed hands a few years ago for £15. Another pair of newel posts of similar design eight and three quarter inches high realised £75.

NIPT DIAMOND WAIES. A style of ornament probably referred to in Ravenscroft's price list of 1677 as 'extraordinary work' (S. Young, *History of the Worshipful Company of Glass-sellers of London*, 1913, p. 68).

Thick evenly spaced vertical ribs round the sides of a vessel were pincered together into a diamond-shaped network. Ravenscroft's price list describes beer glasses and quart bottles as being all over 'nipt diamond waies'. Pint bottles, half-pint bottles, quartern bottles, claret glasses and sack glasses are also described 'of the same sort'. (For example, *see* Fig. 120.)

NORTHWOOD, JOHN, Sen. (1836-1902); **JOHN, Jun.** (1870-1960).

See CAMEO GLASS.

NORWEGIAN GLASS.

See NEWCASTLE GLASSES.

NORWICH GLASSES.

See LYNN OR NORWICH GLASSES.

OPAQUE-TWIST STEMMED GLASSES. Glasses with opaque-twist stems have a peculiar attraction. The dazzling whiteness of the stems with their infinite variety of lace-like patterns, and the clear, lustrous metal of the bowls and feet, give them everlasting vitality and freshness. It is remarkable, too, that although they passed through a period when the form of most other vessels was influenced by the economies enforced by the Glass Excise Act, they still retained their excellent proportions.

Few collectors can resist them, which perhaps is the reason why there are probably more modern reproductions of the opaque-twist stem than of any other style.

The art of making vessels with threads of white opaque glass has been known from the very early times. It was known to the Romans, was rediscovered early in the sixteenth century by the Venetians, and was employed in this country in the sixteenth century. There is a Verzelini goblet preserved in the British Museum encircled on the bowl with two white enamel threads. (*See* VERZELINI GLASSES, Fig. 269.)

Following the glass-maker's success with air-twist stems, it did not require a great deal of imagination to apply enamel threads to the stems of drinking vessels, and this new fashion began to replace the popularity of the earlier air-twist stems. The method of preparing the glass for an opaque-twist stem was very similar to that described for the manufacture of filigree. (*See* FILIGREE OR LATTICINIO.)

It is safe to assume that the earliest efforts of the glass-maker to form opaque-twist stems followed very much on the lines of the air-twist, the tiny canes of white opaque glass taking the place of the air threads to form a simple multiple spiral design.

At the beginning of the period, the opaque-twist stems were somewhat crude. An early example, shown in Fig. 199, has a heavy and irregular opaque thread of the single series type, a wide folded foot and central swelling knop, all features of an early glass.

Later, as he grew more proficient, the glass-maker elaborated the stems into a countless variety of patterns. He found that by

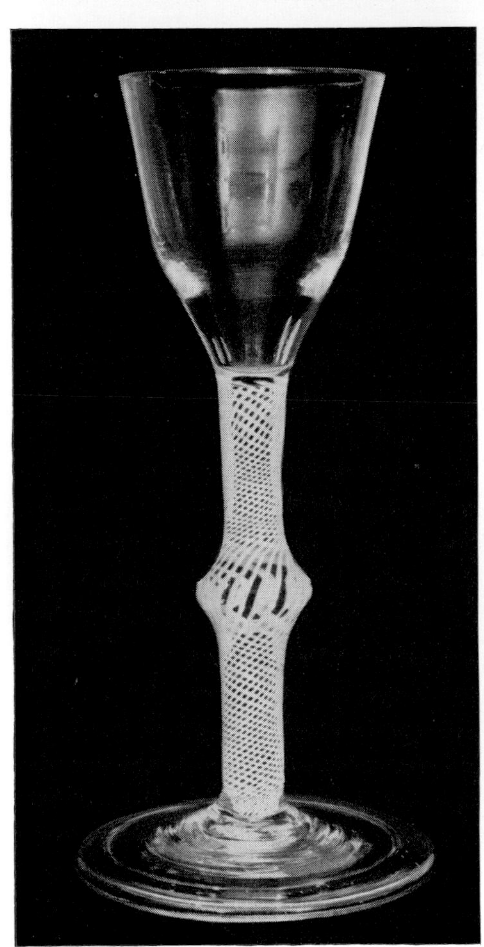

199. *An early example of opaque-twist stem; heavy irregular multiple spiral of the single series type, folded foot and central swelling knop.* circa *1745.*

200. *Goblet with bucket bowl with opaque-twist stem spiral gauze.*

201. *Corkscrew pattern opaque-twist, in which the enamel canes were flattened to obtain the effect of bands, which were then twisted. The bowl in this specimen is eight-sided, an unusual style.*

202. *Glass with knopped stem, single series opaque-twist, and folded foot.*

203. *Very rare glass made in five pieces, i.e. bowl, and foot, with stem in three pieces, i.e. with an air-twist, plain and annulated knop, and opaque-twist section below, double series twist with knopped extremities. Height 7⅝ inches.* circa *1760.*

gathering a larger quantity of glass to cover the canes, so that they were more deeply embedded in the glass, he could obtain the effect of a gauze tube running through the core of the stem. When the canes were placed in circular form, but in an eccentric manner in the mould, they formed a gauze as before but in spiral form, the pattern being referred to as a spiral gauze, such as shown in Fig. 200. By grouping the threads, the glass-maker could obtain the effect of bands, and by flattening the enamel canes in the first part of the process, strips or tapes were formed, from which the well-known corkscrew pattern was made, as in Fig. 201.

By modifying the arrangement, number, shape and size of the original canes in the mould, any number of intricate patterns could be produced.

Although the opaque-twist stems were fashionable only for a short period, over one hundred varieties have been recorded, of which about seventy consist of double series twists. Almost without exception, the glasses were constructed by the three-piece method, and, as they began to make their appearance shortly after the Excise Act of 1745, such features as knopping, folded and domed feet are, therefore, not to be expected. Specimens where such features do occur, therefore, are rare and collectors' pieces.

The classification given by Haynes (*Glass Through the Ages*, 1948, pp. 212-217), is a very safe guide. He has divided the glasses with opaque-twists into five sections:

1. Knopped glasses with a single series twist.
2. Knopped glasses with a double series twist.
3. Unknopped glasses with a single series twist.
4. Unknopped glasses with a double series twist.
5. Unknopped glasses with a triple series twist. This type is very rare.

Nine out of every ten glasses with opaque-twist stems will show an unknopped stem, while the proportion of folded feet is much rarer. Examples of folded feet are shown on Figs. 199, 200 and 202. Domed and folded feet are still rarer. An example is shown in SWEETMEAT GLASSES, Fig. 254.

Glasses with opaque-twist stems have varied considerably in price, depending not so much on the type of stem but on other features. A Lynn glass with opaque-twist stem has realised £20, whereas a glass with a similar stem but with no other distinguishing feature might fetch only a tenth of that amount.

A good idea of the value of these glasses can be gained from a sale in 1947, when a series of 93 straight-stemmed glasses, each with a different formation of white opaque-twist, changed hands for £280.

PAINTED PICTURES ON GLASS.
See PICTURES PAINTED ON GLASS.

PAPERWEIGHTS. The French glasshouses of Baccarat and St Louis, both situated in the Vosges mountains, and that at Clichy, a suburb of Paris, began to produce glass paperweights in the middle of the nineteenth century.

No greater proof is required of the appreciation of the workmanship and beauty of the products of these three factories than the meteoric rise in the prices at which they change hands today. In 1912 they could be purchased for a matter of shillings, by 1920 those that could be purchased for ten shillings had risen to five or six pounds, and between the wars the figure for the same paperweights was doubled.

During recent years, the popularity of and demand for French paperweights have increased enormously. Large and valuable collections, dispersed at sales, have stimulated world-wide interest, and rarities have changed hands at ever-increasing figures. In 1952 a salamander weight changed hands for £1,300 and was later sold at approximately £1,400. It was then thought that the record figure for a glass paperweight had been reached. In 1957, however, Sotheby's electrified the paperweight market by announcing the sale of a St Louis overlay encased in yellow, a hitherto unrecorded colour. This specimen changed hands at the record figure of £2,700.

Baccarat. In the main, Baccarat weights can be divided into two main groups—millefiori, which form roughly two-thirds of all Baccarat weights, and flowers, which comprise a little less than one-third. In addition, there is a small group, which in all does not amount to five per cent, with a subject, such as reptiles or butterflies; from the point of value, this is by far the most important group.

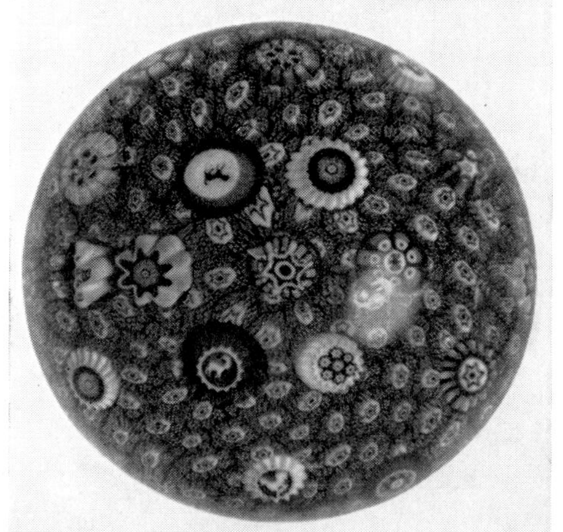
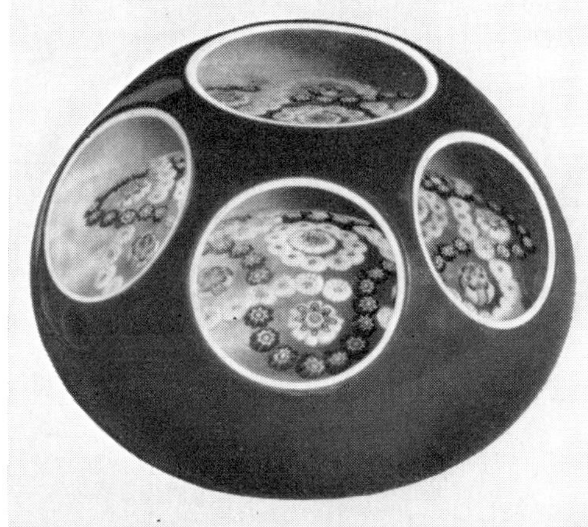
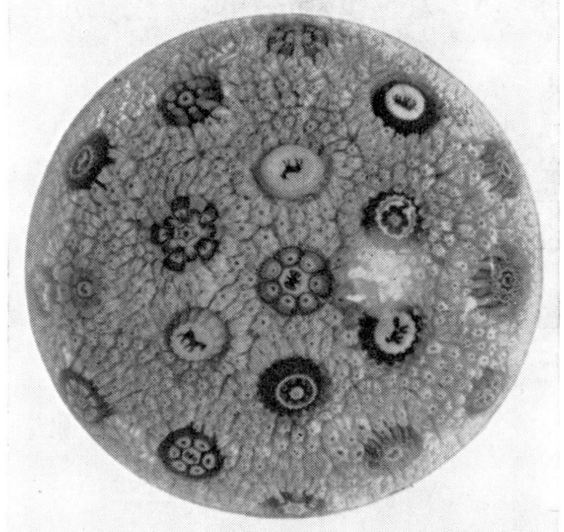

204. *Baccarat millefiori paperweight with coloured floral and animal canes on a blue carpet ground; dated B 1848.* (*Messrs Delomosne & Son.*) 205. *Baccarat dark blue overlay paperweight with entwined florets in red and white. Six windows are cut in the sides and one on the top to disclose the set-up; 3⅛ inches in diameter.* 206. *Baccarat millefiori weight with coloured floral and animal canes on white 'star dust' ground; dated B 1848.* (*Messrs Delomosne & Son*)

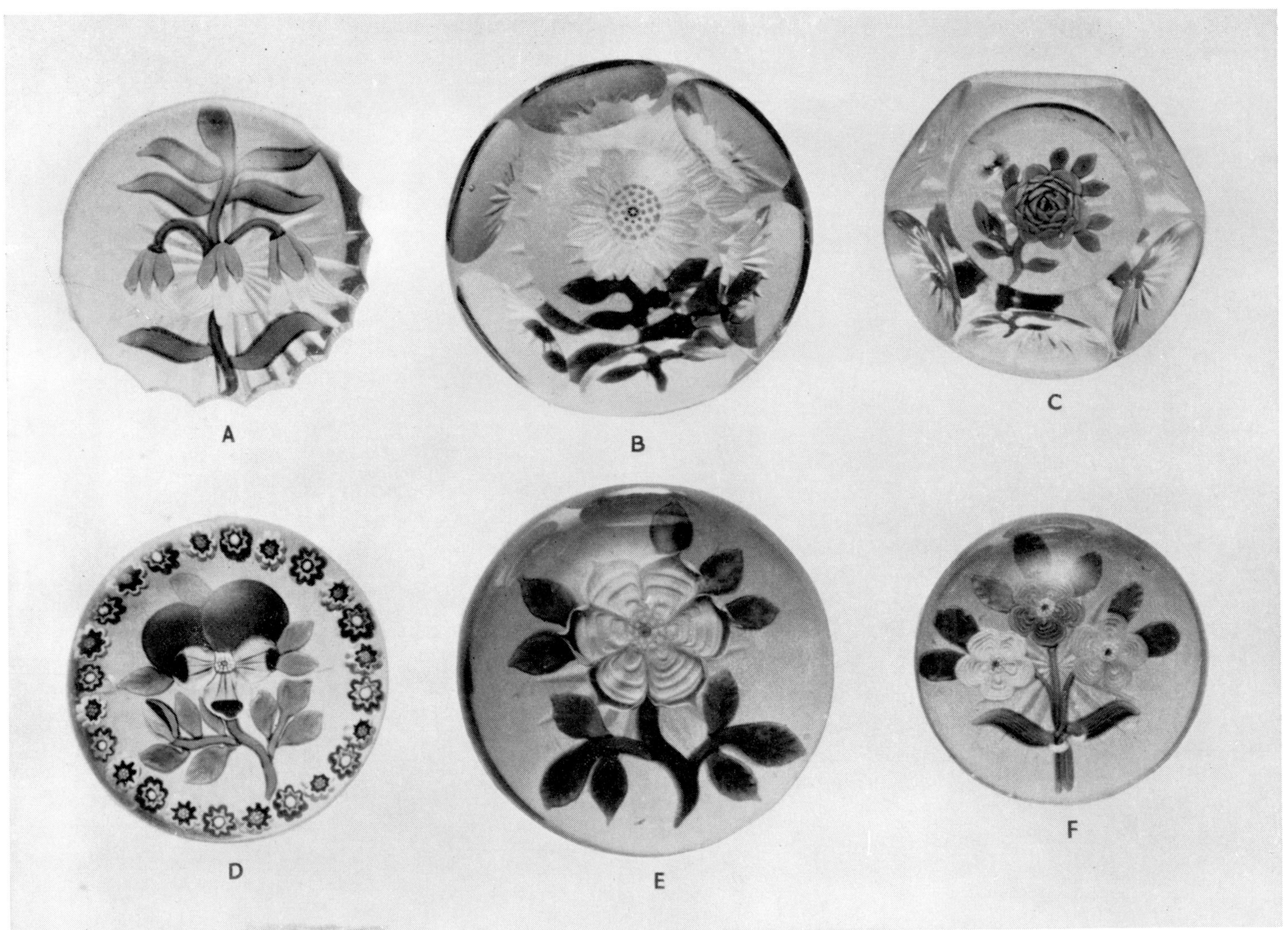

207. *Baccarat flower weights. A. Bell flowers with white petals and green foliage. B. Unusual Baccarat flower, possibly a marguerite. C. Pink rose, a rare Baccarat flower. The sides are faceted and cut with stars. D. Pansy with mauve and yellow petals enclosed in a garland of green and white canes. E. Unusual Baccarat flower with six white petals tipped pinkish-red, and bright green foliage. F. Rare bouquet 'tricolore' weight with three buttercups, pink, white and pale blue with bright green foliage.* (*All from Messrs Delomosne & Son*)

Baccarat Millefiori. This would appear a difficult group to classify. Actually, however, there are well defined lines of demarcation which make grouping fairly easy. First, the figures in dated millefiori weights are all much of the same pattern. An examination of a very large number of Baccarat weights shows that very approximately half the millefiori type are dated. The dates are from 1846 to 1849 inclusive, the most common being 1848 and the rarest 1849. About seven out of every ten dated Baccarat weights will bear the date 1848, one in five will be dated 1847, and one in ten 1846. The date 1849 is exceedingly rare.

An occasional weight is found with the letter B, J or F alone. These are probably workmen's initials.

The figures are usually in separate canes of red, blue or green against a white background. The order of the colours varies and appears to follow no definite sequence. In many cases the dates are initialled by a tiny letter B in one of the canes.

Many of the millefiori weights have rods showing silhouettes. In the Bulletin of the Paperweight Collectors' Association, of 1957, a list was given including monkey, squirrel, spaniel dog, horse, goat, elephant, pigeon, pelican, butterfly, hunter, stork, black rooster, dove, pair of tiny birds, swan, jumping man, red and white daisy, pheasant, green shamrock surround, stylised rose, chicken, multi-coloured pansy, and a dated cane.

Examples of Baccarat millefiori weights with coloured floral and animal canes are shown in Figs. 204 and 206. That in Fig. 204 is dated B 1848 and has a carpet ground; the weight shown in Fig. 206 is also dated B 1848, but has a white 'star dust' ground. Both are in the rarer class of millefiori weights because of their grounds.

P. Jokelson (*Antique French Paperweights*, 1955, pp. 14-15), in discussing the main characteristics of Baccarat weights, has followed the classification given by Imbert and Amic. (R. Imbert and Y. Amic. *Les Presse-Papiers Français*, France, 1948.) He shows the following list:

Red trefoils—seven or eight small white rods with a red trefoil set in one of the centre, the other around it. This cane is sometimes put inside a yellow tube presenting a white cross section, which is in turn put inside a red tube.

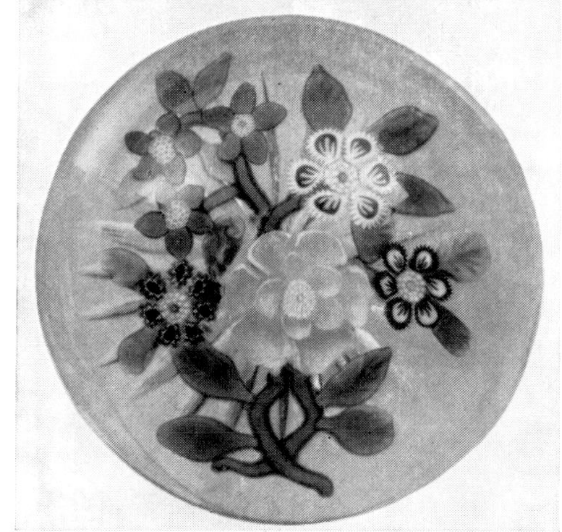

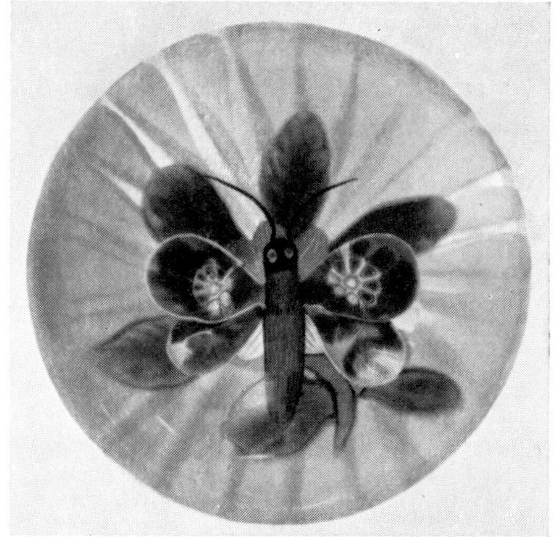

208. *Rare Baccarat bouquet weight composed of central yellow primrose flanked by three stylised flowers and a spray of blue forget-me-nots.* 209. *Rare Baccarat bouquet weight, composed of pink rose and bud, yellow and amethystine blue pansy, blue primrose with bud and unusual yellow flower of the double clematis type.* 210. *Baccarat butterfly hovering over a white flower with green leaf spray.* (*Messrs Delomosne & Son*)

Red quatrefoils—same as above, but the centre is a yellow twist.

Turquoise blue quadrifoils—four canes similar to those described above, but turquoise blue and set crosswise.

Turquoise blue dots—seven or eight tiny white hollow tubes lined with turquoise blue, set in the same manner as the red trefoils.

Turquoise blue honeycomb—the same tubes in undetermined number side by side, but not in a circle.

Stars—of different kinds; star-shaped canes, monochrome or marked with a differently coloured dot; cylindrical rods with a star-shaped hollow centre; white canes with a star in green, red or blue enamel.

Green leaves—small white rods carrying emerald green leaves, these pointed leaves being perpendicular to the millefiori centre or stemmed trefoils. The leaves are set in a circle and alternate with canes of red design, such as trefoils or semi-circles.

Arrows—five to eight triangular rods in white or with an outside coating of red, green or blue, set with points towards the centre to form a cylindrical cane. Each rod carries an arrow also pointing towards the centre. These are all of a single colour, or of two alternating shades.

Few of the ordinary Baccarat millefiori weights are of any great value. During recent years a large number of millefiori weights have changed hands and more than eighty per cent have realised less than £50.

An initial and date do not necessarily enhance the value of a paperweight, though the date may be a rare one; for example, two Baccarat weights marked with the rare date 1849 changed hands in a London Sale Room recently, one at £38 and the other at £240. The difference in value was due entirely to the rarity of design. The first had the usual tightly packed brightly coloured florets and animal silhouette canes; the other had a rare chequered design of turquoise rods in a latticinio gauze ground, each square containing a different floret or silhouette cane.

Much the same applies to paperweights of the commoner dates. As an example, in the sales room recently two adjacent lots were Baccarat weights both dated 1848; one sold at £45 and the other at £275; the difference again being due to the rarity of the set-up.

Baccarat Overlays. Highly prized by connoisseurs are the Baccarat overlay paperweights. Overlays were usually made with the millefiori mushroom in a crystal globe, which was given a thin coating of white opaque glass and a final coating of colour such as red, blue or green; often, there was also a final coating of transparent glass in order to protect the more fragile coloured layer. Windows were cut by grinding and polishing on the top and sides to expose the millefiori centre. The cutting process exposed a very thin lining of the white opaque underlayer, which greatly enhanced the general effect of the overlays.

Baccarat overlay weights are uncommon, amounting to less than two per cent of all Baccarat weights. They are all fairly similar in design, the mushroom or tuft of millefiori being encased in a faceted casing of colour over white. The usual overlay colour is turquoise or bright blue, but occasionally an emerald green overlay comes to light. A few of the overlays have traces of the original gilt scroll decoration over the overlay colour.

The tuft is composed of the usual coloured florets in red, white and blue and other colours, and are typical of the Baccarat design. Usually there are five windows cut in the side in order to expose the tuft motif with a larger one at the top, but six-sided specimens are known.

An example of a Baccarat double overlay is shown in Fig. 205. This is a dark blue overlay with two entwined trefoils of canes, one red and the other white, with larger canes of arrow and pastry mould type interspersed. There are six windows at the sides and one at the top.

This is a rare weight, three and one eighth inches in diameter, and is from the Maurice Lindon Collection; it sold in 1957 at Sotheby's for £290.

Prices of Baccarat overlay weights vary considerably according to rarity of design. During recent years the price range has been between £105 and £290.

Baccarat Flower Weights. The flower weights form an interesting group, and those with natural colouring and excellent

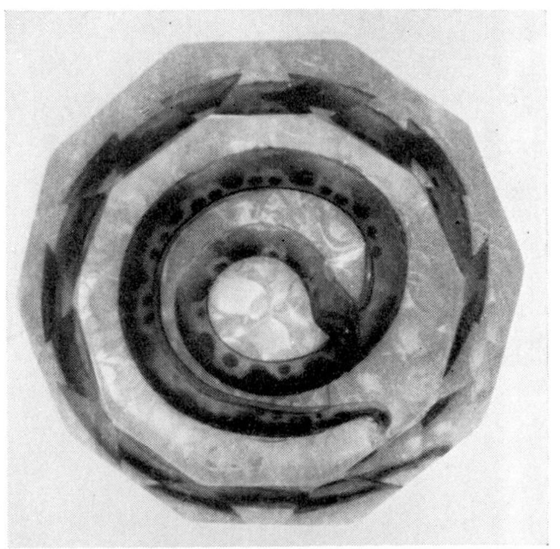

211. *Typical Baccarat strawberry weight with two green and one red fruit and two green leaves. The base is cut with a star. (Messrs Delomosne & Son).* 212. *St Louis encased yellow overlay weight which changed hands in 1957 for the record sum of £2,700. It has an upstanding bouquet of blue, yellow, red and white flowers and florette canes with long green leaves. It is 3 inches in diameter.* 213. *A rare St Louis paperweight featuring a red snake with green markings coiled on an upset muslin ground. The weight, formerly in the Maurice Lindon Collection, changed hands in 1957 for £480.*

craftsmanship are collectors' favourites. Some have individual flowers, but others with garlands and posies of mixed blooms are classed as 'bouquets'.

The most common individual flowers are primroses, pansies and clematis, which, in equal proportions, comprise together roughly two-thirds of the flower weights. Then come buttercups, camomiles, tulip-buds, and undefined flowers, which account for nearly one-third. The more uncommon varieties are narcissus, anemones, bell-flowers, daffodils and roses, but the fact that they are scarce does not necessarily enhance their value. Indeed, individual flower weights, with few exceptions, are comparable in price with the commoner millefiori weights. A group of Baccarat flower weights is shown in Fig. 207.

The rarest of all Baccarat flowers is the rose. A particularly beautiful specimen is shown in Fig. 207 C, of a pink rose of natural formation and green foliage. The weight is faceted with stars cut on the sides. Roses vary in colour from light pink to deep red and prices have approached the £100 mark.

Prices of Baccarat flower weights have varied, according to rarity and colouring, between £20 and £115.

Baccarat Bouquets. Although nearly one-third of all Baccarat weights are flower weights, very few have a bouquet of flowers for a subject; certainly less than three per cent. A common style of bouquet is the so-called 'tricolore', in which a central motif, such as a buttercup or blue flax flowers with light green foliage and stems, are flanked left and right by red and white primroses or white clematis, all on a clear glass ground.

A feature of the foliage of Baccarat bouquets is crossed stalks. This is shown in Figs. 208 and 209, of two rare bouquet weights which were originally in the Maurice Lindon Collection. The bouquet shown in Fig. 208 is composed of a central yellow primrose with two concentric rows of petals, flanked by three stylised flowers. The two flowers seen on the right of the illustration have typical Baccarat arrow canes in the petals. A spray of blue forget-me-nots completes the bouquet set-up. The bouquet is set in clear glass, three and a quarter inches in diameter, with a large star cut in the base. This weight changed hands in 1957 for £460.

Another rare Baccarat bouquet weight is that shown in Fig. 209, consisting of a pink rose and bud, a pansy with yellow and amethystine petals, blue primrose with bud and an unusual yellow flower of double clematis type. In this specimen also, the green stalks are crossed. This specimen, three and one eighth inches in diameter, changed hands in 1957 for £420.

Baccarat Subject Weights. The Baccarat factory produced a number of weights with subjects such as caterpillars, snakes, ducks and butterflies, and these are among the most valued of all Baccarat weights. A caterpillar weight changed hands in London in 1952 for £1,200. These weights are exceedingly rare, only two or three specimens being known.

Weights featuring a snake are not so rare, probably comprising about one per cent of all Baccarat weights. The snake is usually in bright colours such as green with darker green or brown markings, or pale green with dark green or reddish brown markings. The snake is usually coiled on a muslin ground or on a buff or green rockwork base. Prices have varied from £90 to £350.

Four per cent of all Baccarat weights feature a butterfly. They can be divided into two main classes—the butterfly alone, or with a single flower, as in Fig. 210.

In both cases the butterfly has a body of a bluish tint, such as deep lilac, translucent amethyst, violet, purple or mauve, usually with a black head and antennae. Blue antennae are known. The wings are multi-coloured, usually described as 'marbled', the motif being set in garlands of alternate millefiori canes in red or white or blue and white, but in some rare cases in alternate florettes of red and white and green and white.

The individual flower in butterfly weights is almost invariably white, of the clematis or daffodil type with green foliage. The motifs are so arranged that the flower occupies a central position with the butterfly hovering above, its head and antennae falling across the flower. The dark colour of the wings, body and antennae of the insect contrast well against the light background of the flower. The green leaves are placed above the flower to complete a symmetrical balance.

The ground of most Baccarat butterfly weights is of clear

214. *Group of typical St Louis paperweights. A. Fruit weight featuring a lemon. B. Rare fruit weight with strawberries. C. Two pears, an apple and four red cherries set in a white lattice basket. D. White flower and green leaves. E. Tuft with millefiori cluster dated S L 1848. F. Dahlia with pink petals. G. Millefiori with carpet ground. H. Millefiori in scrambled or macedoine formation. I. Crown weight with ribbons in latticinio.*

glass, but latticinio grounds are known. Prices vary considerably, depending on design and workmanship. Butterfly weights with a flower have fetched from £60 to £290 and the individual butterfly type from £40 to £145.

Imbert and Amic (*Les Presse-Papiers Français*, 1948). point out the poor quality of some of the individual butterfly weights, and suggest that they may have been manufactured up to a late period. It is, of course, also well known that butterfly weights are a popular subject with glass-makers producing paperweights today.

Baccarat did not make a feature of fruit weights. Nevertheless, an occasional strawberry weight is met with which shows characteristics of Baccarat. One changing hands recently had two pink and two green strawberries with dark green foliage and stem. Other specimens show two red strawberries with a single green one. The fruit has coloured dots for the seed, bluish dots for the red berries, and red dots on the green fruit. A typical specimen is shown in Fig. 211. Baccarat strawberry weights are rare; prices have varied between £70 and £80.

Baccarat Magnums and Miniatures. As the name implies, a magnum is an extra large paperweight. Specimens are usually about four inches in width and of the millefiori type. Specimens are known dated 1848 and occasionally 1847. The canes are in silhouette, geometrical and floral design.

The bases are covered with a star, raised diamonds or occasionally with strawberry diamonds. These large specimens are valued more highly than corresponding weights of the normal three inch size, prices varying between £50 and £180.

Miniature paperweights are sometimes described as hand-coolers. Balls of cool glass held in their hands in the summer weather by Roman ladies may have been solid spheres of glass, like the spheres of rock crystal put to a similar use by Japanese ladies.

About five per cent of millefiori weights are of miniature size, varying between one and three quarter inches to two inches in width. Baccarat miniatures are replicas of the normal three-inch millefiori weights with dated, animal silhouette and floral canes. The usual dates are 1847 and 1848, and most have the star cut base. They are low in price.

Miniatures are also found with floral design, the flowers being of the white double clematis type with green leaves and foliage, some with a garland of alternate coloured and white canes. Other flowers are anemone, primrose and six petalled flower. A salmon-pink clematis sold in 1961 for £130.

St Louis. St Louis had a somewhat wider range of subjects than Baccarat. The latter factory, for example, concentrated two-thirds of its output on millefiori; St Louis, on the other hand, not only employed millefiori less extensively, but combined it in floret form with green foliage in weights with bouquet motifs. St Louis also devoted a considerable portion of its output to flower weights, fruit, vegetables and reptiles.

There are many distinguishing characteristics of St Louis weights. The colours are more delicate and in some specimens pale by comparison with either Baccarat or Clichy. Characteristic colours are gentian blue, pink, bright yellow, red and pale and bright green. Soft combinations are often featured in a specimen, such as pink, pale blue, white and yellow flowers or florettes.

The proportion of signed and dated St Louis weights is much smaller than in the case of Baccarat. The usual dates are 1847 and 1848, but occasional specimens are found with the date 1849, and one specimen at least bears the date 1845. An occasional specimen is found with the letter SL and no date, and a few others have a date and no initials, but it is more usual for the initials SL to accompany a date.

Paul Jokelson (*Antique French Paperweights*, 1955, p. 135) gives characteristics of canes which help to identify a St Louis product from those of other factories. The characteristics tabulated by him are as follows:

(*a*) Plaited hollow tubes of one, two or three colours—i.e., cobalt blue or white, lined with red and coated with blue.

(*b*) Stars, in white with white and blue centre. A cane made of coloured twists surrounded by two rows of white stars is also found, although only in millefiori weights. A large white star serves as florettes in bouquet weights or as a centre part of flowers. A finely plaited ochre cane with a white cross section bearing a cobalt blue star is also used in the same manner.

(*c*) Arrows, which are similar to the Baccarat ones, but which are not so precise. These point in all directions and come in any colour.

(*d*) Figured canes, which may represent either a dog and a camel, both silhouetted inside a hollow cane, or a couple of dancers. Of the dancers, the man wears a long bonnet and his arms are raised crosswise; his head is thrown backwards. The woman, shorter, has her arms stretched forward.

There are nine known silhouettes in the St Louis group; they are a dancing couple, duck, man dancing alone, woman dancing alone, a flower with two leaves and a stem, a turkey, a camel, a dog, and dancing devil with arms outstretched entwined around the lance.

The millefiori group, comprising millefiori alone, constitutes about twenty-five per cent of all St Louis weights. There are several styles, such as the usual or tufted variety or in the so-called scrambled or pell mell (macedoine) formation.

St Louis Overlays. St Louis overlay weights are highly prized by connoisseurs. The general pattern is much the same in all the overlays, the central motif being usually a bouquet of flowers with green leaves. The flowers are mostly of imaginative design with floret canes in the various colours popular with St Louis, such as blue, yellow, red and white. There is often a central bloom, such as a many-petalled white flower, or one with deep blue petals and yellow stamens.

The usual overlay colours are deep blue, emerald green or pink, with white opaque lining, or the colour may be opaque white alone. All St Louis overlays have a further casing of clear glass to protect the fragile casing of colour underneath.

The most famous of all St Louis overlays, formerly in the Maurice Lindon Collection, changed hands in 1957 for the record sum of £2,700. The weight, shown in Fig. 212, is encased in yellow, a colour hitherto unrecorded in overlay weights. It has a central bouquet of blue, yellow, red and white flowers and the florette canes with long green leaves. The overlay is cut with six windows at the sides and another larger on the top.

Apple-green overlays are also highly prized. One, which changed hands recently at £900, shows the usual coloured flowers, with green leaves, encased in apple green lined with white. There are three windows, one on the top and two on the sides, one of which is engraved with a fox and hound.

215. *Clichy paperweights. A. Typical loop formation of millefiori florettes. B. Millefiori florettes on muslin ground with Clichy roses. C. Pink and white millefiori garland on opaque turquoise ground. D. Millefiori, signed with the letter C in a cane. E. Turquoise blue and white double overlay, with millefiori centre tuft with circles of Clichy roses. F. Swirl weight in red and white. G. Garland of pink and white canes arranged in loop design. H. White muslin ground, with garland of pink florettes. I. White muslin ground with entwined garland in brick-red and green.*

St Louis Flower Weights. The true flowers constitute an equal group with millefiori floret bouquets, and consist of a dahlia, clematis, camomile, fuschia, rare flowers such as the primrose, convolvulus and jasmine, and those of imaginative design.

Dahlia weights are sought after by collectors and have changed hands for between £40 and £80, but occasional specimens have fetched much higher prices up to £330. A typical specimen is shown in Fig. 214 F.

The convolvulus is also fairly rare in the St Louis flowers, the flower being a pale pink with white inner petals on an emerald green stem and leaves. The ground is white latticinio in regular trellis formation. These weights have changed hands round about the £150 mark.

There are several St Louis flowers of imaginative design, such as pink or blue flowers with a single or double row of petals. Pink flower sprays are also known. All specimens have the usual green leaves, the ground being latticinio or clear glass.

Some St Louis weights have a fruit motif such as pears, cherries, apples, etc., flanked with green leaves usually resting in a white latticinio basket. A specimen illustrating this general pattern is shown in Fig. 214 C; it has two pears, an apple and four red cherries with green leaves on an opaque white lattice basket.

Most fruit weights have two or three pears with three cherries, but some have only one pear and others have four cherries. Five cherries are known. The pears may be green, yellow or red, and the cherries are invariably red.

Other fruit is sometimes found in combination with pears and cherries, such as apples, plums and rarely an orange or a lemon. The specimen shown in Fig. 214 A features a lemon. The apples are most valued when they are of pink and yellow stripes. Plums are coloured bright blue.

A rare St Louis fruit weight is one featuring strawberries, a typical specimen being shown in Fig. 214 B.

Although only three per cent of all St Louis weights have vegetables as a motif, they are not highly prized specimens. The normal pattern is five, six or seven turnips set in a white latticinio basket with their points turned inwards. The colours are light purple, white and yellow. Some specimens, in red and white, are claimed to be radishes. There are usually green stalks; prices have varied from £20 to £80.

The St Louis factory produced some excellent snake weights. In most specimens, the reptile lies coiled on a white latticinio gauze ground. The usual colours are pink with green markings, but a specimen is known of pale green colour with darker green markings, the reptile having red eyes.

One formerly in the Maurice Lindon Collection, shown in Fig. 213, changed hands in 1957 for £480. The reptile is red with green markings and lies coiled on an upset muslin ground. The top of this weight is flat and the sides faceted. Prices are usually high for St Louis snake weights, varying between £125-£480.

St Louis Magnums and Miniatures. As in the case of Baccarat, a magnum St Louis is rare. They are about the same size as Baccarat magnums—i.e., four inches in width—and are composed of concentric rows of millefiori florets in characteristic colour. Only one dated magnum weight is recorded. Prices have varied between £100 and £200.

Miniature weights are not so frequent as in the case of Baccarat. They are replicas of the larger millefiori in both style and colouring. The size varies between one and a half inches to two inches in width. A miniature crown weight occasionally comes to light; prices are low.

Clichy. Less is known about the Clichy factory than of either Baccarat or St Louis, and few records exist from which to build up authentic information. Fortunately, there are a few signed specimens, which make the general style of the factory recognisable. The signatures are the letter C or the word Clichy in full. The colours are brighter than those of Baccarat, which is probably accounted for by the fact that the glass was of different composition from either Baccarat or St Louis.

Jokelson (*Antique French Paperweights*, 1955, p. 91) gives the following characteristic features of Clichy weights:

(*a*) Roses. A weight containing the Clichy rose is like a signed Clichy product. The rose appears in white or pink, with or without green. It also comes in yellow or red, often with a purple coating. A specimen featuring both white and pink roses is shown in Fig. 215 B.

(*b*) Twists. These are threaded through one another, the centre part being filled by a tiny stubby cane.

(*c*) Stars. These come in one colour or with a dot of another colour in the centre.

(*d*) Mould shaped canes. These resemble children's pie moulds. The centre part of these canes is occupied by a tiny round rod, usually yellow, raised like the stamens of a flower.

Clichy Millefiori. The Clichy factory specialised in millefiori and conformed more to a standard pattern than other factories; millefiori, indeed, constitute the largest group in Clichy weights, no fewer than eight out of every ten being of this type. Because of this, they are the least valued of the Clichy weights. A typical specimen is shown in Fig. 215 D. One cane has the letter C.

Clichy Overlays. The most sought after Clichy weights are the overlays, which comprise less than two per cent of all types of Clichy weights. Several beautiful specimens changed hands in the London Sales in 1951-1953 at prices varying between £125 and £400.

Most Clichy overlays have a rich turquoise casing. A typical paperweight of this type is shown in Fig. 215 E, of a turquoise blue and white double overlay now in the Corning Glass Museum, New York. It has a green and white rodded mushroom stem and mushroom centre with a circle of Clichy roses. Specimens in deep pink are also known, with the usual white lining.

Clichy Bouquets. Next to the overlays in importance are the weights with the central motif of a bunch of flowers, in some cases tied at the base with ribbon, hence the term bouquet weights. Many have changed hands recently between £100 and £200.

Some of the flowers in the bouquets are obvious, such as the pansy or the Clichy rose with bud; many are fanciful but nonetheless attractive designs. Typical is a bunch of three flowers of double clematis and dahlia type in such colours as blue, lilac, striped pink, mauve, dark violet, pale blue and white.

Clichy Swirls. These are fairly common, constituting about ten per cent of all types of Clichy weights. The spirals are made up of a single colour alternating with white, the most common colours being green, purple, turquoise, pink, blue and lilac. The usual ones are pale blue and rose pink. A typical specimen is shown in Fig. 215 F.

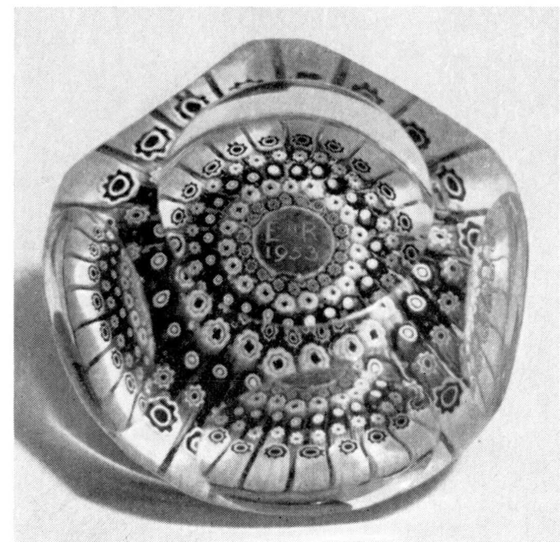

216. *Paperweight made at Wealdstone, England, commemorating the coronation of Queen Elizabeth II, with concentric rings of red, white and blue millefiori canes with the cipher E II R 1953 as the central motif.* (*Messrs James Powell & Son* (*Whitefriars*), *Ltd.*)

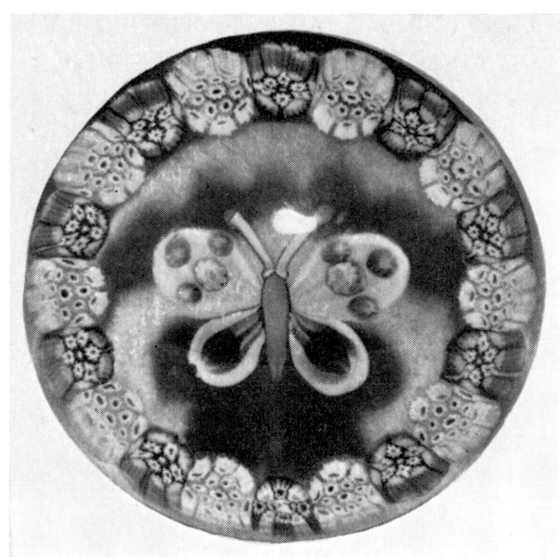

217. (Extreme right) *Paperweight made by Ysart of Scotland featuring a butterfly circled by millefiori canes, one of which is signed P Y.*

The central motif may be a millefiori rosette or floral of pastry moulded canes or occasionally a Clichy rose. There is only one silhouette which can be safely ascribed to the Clichy factory. This is a running hare found in a floret cane on the top of a Clichy swirl.

Clichy Miniatures. Miniature Clichy weights occur rather more frequently than either Baccarat or St Louis, roughly about ten per cent of all Clichy weights being of this size. They are small replicas of the larger weights, two-thirds of them being of the millefiori type. A large proportion have the Clichy rose similar in pattern and arrangement to the larger weights. An occasional miniature weight has a bouquet of roses and florets with green leaves. Sizes vary between one and five-eighths to two and one-eighth inches in width, and as in the case of miniature weights from other factories, prices are low.

English. Paperweights and other articles in millefiori were made in this country about the time of the Great Exhibition of 1851. Specimens are known from Stourbridge, from the Bacchus Works at Birmingham, and from the Islington Glass Works, London.

It is thought that some of the Clichy workmen were attracted to Stourbridge; indeed, it is quite true that some of the Stourbridge styles were not unlike those favoured by Clichy both in pattern and the form of the ground. Typical are the turquoise grounds and yellow baskets set with coloured florets. Another pattern is a heart-shaped, tartan-twist ribbon.

On the whole, the colours of the Stourbridge and Bacchus weights were more pastel than those made at Clichy. On the other hand, the paperweights made at Islington were brighter in colour, but were for the most part uninspired. An occasional specimen is found with a cane marked with the initials I G W (Islington Glass Works) and a cane with the silhouette of a horse.

Paperweights of the style described above have generally changed hands for between £5 and £10.

Most of the English factories making paperweights also made ink-wells with stoppers, scent-bottles, door-knobs, newel-posts, rulers, knife-rests, seals and similar objects.

Modern Manufacturers. Paperweights are made today in America, England, Scotland and China. In America probably the best known manufacturer of paperweights today is Charles Kazrun, American-born son of Lithuanian immigrants. Many of his millefiori weights are signed with the letter K in the centre of the base. His subjects are flowers or millefiori similar to the French weights, overlays, and his speciality, a tinted rose.

Paperweights are also made at the Wealdstone works of James Powell & Sons (Whitefriars), Ltd., formerly a company at Whitefriars in the City of London. The example shown in Fig. 216 is one made at Wealdstone for the Coronation of Queen Elizabeth II. It is in millefiori style similiar in design to the Stourbridge weights of the nineteenth century. There are five concentric rings of red, white and blue canes, with the cipher E II R 1953 as the central motif. The Wealdstone factory also produces overlay weights and other styles.

In Scotland paperweights are produced by the Ysart family, who migrated from Barcelona, Spain, in 1904. Glass blowing has been practised in the family for several generations. Some of the paperweights are signed PY in one of the canes, the initials standing for that of a son, Paul. The signed specimen in Fig. 217 features a butterfly, the red initials against a white background appearing in one of the canes below the butterfly.

According to an article by R. A. Elder, jnr., assistant Curator of Ethnology, U.S. National Museum, Washington, D.C. (*Bulletin of the Paperweight Collectors' Association*, Vol. III, June, 1958), Chinese paperweights began appearing on the American market about 1930 or slightly earlier.

Though the Chinese glass-maker had no previous experience in the detailed millefiori work, he was able to produce casts of the floral weights by lamp-blown methods. According to this writer, several American import dealers, who had direct contact with Chinese sources, sent good specimens of paperweights to China for the express purpose of having them copied when the authentic Western items were becoming more scarce.

The writer says that, though the total qualitative features of the Chinese in this branch of art may leave a good deal to be desired, they produce a sufficient quantity of paperweights to confuse the collecting fraternity. The Chinese weights can be identified by the nature of the glass, which is a soda-lime relatively light in weight. As it is frequently high in alkali it is greasy to the touch, and usually of greenish or yellow tint instead of being of water white clarity.

PAPERWEIGHTS, BOTTLE GREEN.

See DOOR-STOPS OR BOTTLE-GREEN PAPERWEIGHTS.

PARKER, WILLIAM.
See Candelabra; Chandeliers.

PASSGLASER.
See Enamelled Glass, German Enamelling.

'PÂTE-de-VERRE'.
See Tassie, James and William.

PELLATT, APSLEY (1791-1863). A glass-maker of the nineteenth century, who succeeded in gaining a high reputation for himself in his business as a glass-maker, as an inventor, a writer, and in his later life in public life and politics.

Pellatt's father had a glass warehouse in Holborn, which was subsequently moved to St Paul's Churchyard, but his son, Apsley, before he had reached the age of 30, established a glasshouse in Falcon Street, Southwark. Apsley Pellatt was associated with French glass-makers and through them he perfected a method of glass decoration known as incrustation or Crystallo-Ceramie. (*See* Crystallo-Ceramie.)

Pellatt wrote two books on glass-making, published respectively in 1821 and 1849, which considerably enhanced his reputation. In later life he became much interested in public life and from 1852 to 1857 sat as a Member of Parliament for Southwark.

PENROSE, GEORGE AND WILLIAM.
See Irish Glass.

PICTURES PAINTED ON GLASS. An occasional mirror comes to light with a picture painted upon it. The fashion would appear to have started during the seventeenth century, and although a few artists continued to use mirrors as a medium during the eighteenth century, it never gained any great popularity.

The first notice appeared in 1688 (*London Gazette*, 8th July, 1688): 'Isaac Becket, so eminent for working in mezotinto, being lately deceased, his widow doth continue in the Trade at the Golden Head in the Old Baily, where all persons may be furnished with all the newest and best sorts of mezotinto printing, likewise all other things appertaining to the painting them on glass.'

During the eighteenth century, there is mention of Van Zoon and Van Huysum, both Dutch artists who specialised in the painting of flowers on glass. For example, the following notice appeared in the *Daily Courant*, 6th December, 1771: 'Noble large Looking-Glasses, finely painted with flowers and Ornaments painted by Van Zoon.'

A favourite medium for these artists was the chimney glass. These articles were often made in four pieces assembled in a arge rectangular frame, three mirrors being below and a long one across the top. This mirror was often painted, an example being shown in Fig. 69. (*See* Chimney Glasses.)

A pair of mirror pictures painted in the style of Van Huysum, with vases of flowers, thirty-one inches high, changed hands a few years ago for £40.

PIER GLASSES. (*See also* Mirrors for illustrations.) Mirrors began to play an important part in wall decoration and in furniture during the early part of the eighteenth century, and the upright mirror, known as the pier glass, designed to hang on the pier wall between two windows, was becoming a popular decorative feature for those who could afford such luxuries.

Most eighteenth-century houses were built with the windows of the principal rooms on one side only, which caused the pier wall between the windows to be dark and obscure. A long, upright mirror on the pier wall at once illuminated the shadow by light reflected from brighter parts of the room. It not only occupied a place which could serve no other useful purpose, but it also gave the illusion of space and height, an important consideration in the early part of the eighteenth century when most rooms were small and narrow.

For this reason, pier glasses of the Queen Anne period are narrower than those of the later Georgian styles, when the houses were built loftier, and the pier walls were correspondingly wider.

Because of their length and the cost of making large plates, early pier glasses had to be made in two pieces; indeed, some of the longer pier glasses, up to ten feet in length, are found made in three pieces.

The English glass-maker at that time had not adopted the French process of casting which enabled much larger plates to be produced, but he was able to meet the demand so far as size was concerned by building up large mirrors from sections of smaller ones. Indeed, the English glass-maker was not unaware of the advantage of this method and applied the same process to small mirrors in an endeavour to enhance their decorative value.

The decoration of pier glasses changed as the century advanced. The early ones had decorative borders of glass, but this quickly became elaborated into a separate frame of glass made up of sections mitred at the corners and enhanced by cut motifs.

This style was superseded in the early years of the eighteenth century by richly carved wooden frames or those decorated by gilt gesso work. Such elaborately decorated mirrors, however, were within reach only of the most wealthy; the cabinet makers, quickly realising the potential market for such a useful article as a pier glass, were, by 1720, supplying them at a cost within reach of the more modest purses. Plain, moulded frames or veneered walnut, with crestings for hoods in pierced styles, competed in this new market with simple gilt gesso frames.

Gesso was popular until 1730 or thereabouts, and, again, no doubt, because of the cost, was superseded by frames of carved giltwood with wave moulding, which, in various styles dictated by fashion, held the popular market throughout the century. Architectural designs were in demand after gesso had lost its appeal, and this style in its turn was succeeded by rococo, Chinese and Gothic as the popular taste changed.

Towards the end of the century, frames in the so-called classic styles, with arch cresting, sides of balustrading, and decorative motifs such as urns and acanthus foliage, appeared in response to the influence of the Adam brothers.

Regency or Empire styles followed in the nineteenth century. The tendency for the height to be greater in proportion to the width was much less evident and, in the later Victorian period, the pier glass as such ceased to be made.

Pier glasses have changed hands at prices ranging up to £40, depending on size and style. A Louis XV pier glass in a rococo giltwood frame, five feet by three feet, changed hands recently for £36. A Queen Anne pier glass about six feet by three feet, in a giltwood frame, realised £30. On the other hand, a Queen Anne pier glass in a narrow walnut frame, about half the size of the former, changed hands a few years ago for £19.

PIPES.
See Nailsea Glass.

PLAIN, STRAIGHT-STEMMED GLASSES. Glasses with plain, straight stems constitute by far the largest group of eighteenth-century drinking glasses, representing something like a quarter of the glasses of the century.

Glasses with plain stems are usually regarded as representing the cheap tavern and domestic variety in vogue during the eighteenth century, and probably for this reason do not interest collectors to the same extent as glasses in other groups. It is only when they carry some engraved motif that they excite any particular attention. No doubt, most eighteenth-century glasses could claim to have had tavern and domestic use, but the plain-stemmed glasses, because of their simplicity and, therefore, cheapness, can be regarded as the utility article of the time.

They were cheap, first, because in nearly all cases they were made by the easiest and quickest method of manufacture; the bowl and the stem were made in one operation—in other words they were two-piece glasses. Secondly, they were devoid of any embellishments such as knopping, which enabled them to be turned out rapidly and to a pattern. That does not necessarily mean that there was no great variation among them; most types of bowl were employed, and the differing outlines of the glasses themselves were infinite. (*See* Bowl Forms, Fig. 274.)

The earliest style was the drawn trumpet, represented in Figs. 1 and 218. They were almost invariably made with a tear in the stem, graduated in shape from globular form (Fig. 1), or drawn into almost thread formation (Fig. 218). The tear, however, later disappeared from this type of glass, when air-twists became the popular fashion. The bowls were both straight sided (Fig. 74) and flared (Fig. 218), and the feet of these early glasses were more often folded than plain.

Contemporaneous with the trumpet glasses were those with a waisted bowl, also made by the two-piece method and of the same heavy build, a feature which did not detract in any way from their pleasing outline. For example, the specimen shown in Fig. 219 is eight inches in height, weighs a pound, and has a stem nearly an inch in thickness; it is nonetheless an elegant glass.

These early trumpet and waisted glasses are usually thought to have first appeared at about the turn of the century, although one or two writers show a preference for a somewhat later date. There is much about these glasses, however, to suggest that they were contemporaneous with the early balusters. For example, engraving is rare, although the ale-glasses of the series are occasionally found engraved with the conventional hops and barley emblems. The solidity and massiveness so reminiscent of the baluster period is characteristic and the metal itself is of the same nature; it has not the brilliance and lustre noticeable even with some of the early balusters.

The plain-stemmed glasses became smaller about 1745, and new bowl forms were introduced such as the ogee, round-funnel and bucket shapes. Whether this transition in style was the result of the Excise Act of that year is impossible to say,

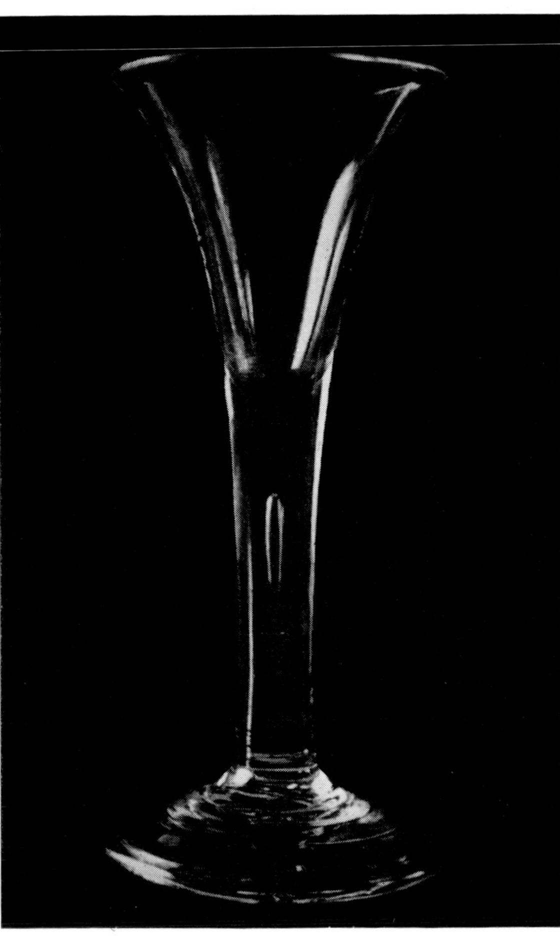

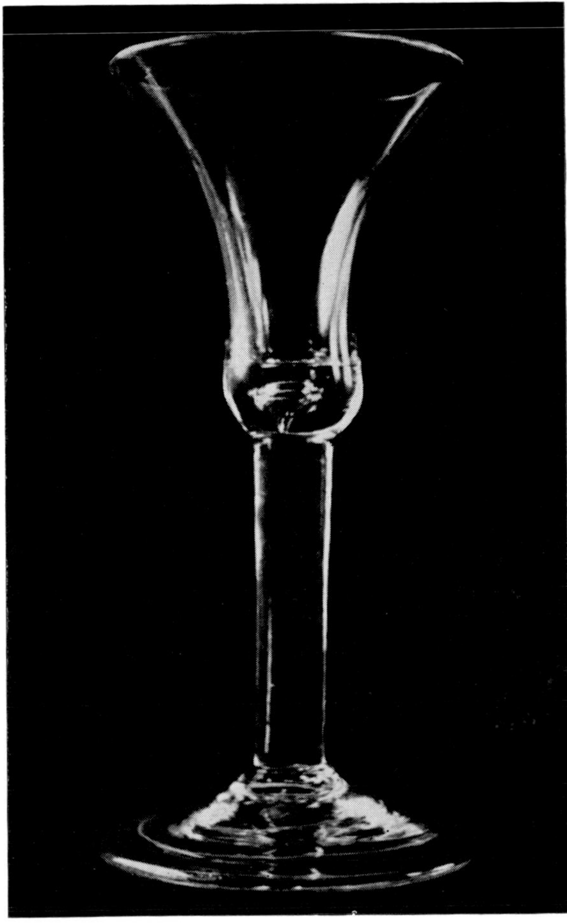

218. *Plain straight-stemmed glass with trumpet bowl, the stem has a tear enclosed.*

219. (Extreme right) *Plain straight-stemmed glass with waisted bowl. This specimen is 8 inches in height and weighs one pound. The stem is nearly an inch in thickness. It is an early eighteenth-century glass.*

220. *The Portland or Berberini Vase, a two-handled glass urn made from an underlayer of dark blue glass over which was superimposed a layer of opaque white glass. Grecian figures have been carved from the outer casing so that they stand out in bold relief against the dark background of blue glass. Probably first century A.D. Now in the British Museum, London.*

but it is to be observed that the same reduced dimensions occurred with the air-twists—the fashionable glasses of the time. Typical glasses of this period are the cordial (Fig. 74), with ogee bowl and folded foot, and the ale (Fig. 13), with round-funnel bowl engraved with the hops and barley motif.

Although the general dimensions of the glasses were reduced after 1745, it was at first a general diminution, and the stem did not lose its lengthy proportion in relation to the bowl. This was most noticeable in such smaller glasses as cordials (Fig. 77), where the stem was especially long.

Plain-stemmed glasses, provided the glass has no distinguishing feature, have been sold for a pound or so.

PONTIL MARK.

See FRAUDS AND REPRODUCTIONS, Pontil Mark; WINE-GLASS, THE MAKING OF.

PORTLAND OR BERBERINI VASE. The vase (Fig. 220) is a two-handled glass urn and is, without doubt, the most famous example of its class in the world. It was found near Rome in 1582 in a sarcophagus dedicated, it is claimed, to the Emperor Alexander Severus, who was killed in A.D. 225. The vase itself, however, is of an earlier date. There is some evidence that it may have been made in the first century A.D. (Edward Dillion, *Glass*, 1907, p. 69), possibly about the time of the invention of the blow-pipe.

The vase, at one time in the Berberini Palace, later belonged to the Duke of Portland. In 1809 the vase was deposited with the British Museum, where it was exhibited as the gem of the Greco-Roman Department. In 1845, however, it was maliciously shattered by an Irishman in a moment of aberration. The fragments were later skilfully assembled, in which condition it is still exhibited today in the British Museum.

In 1929 it was offered for sale at Christies when it failed to find a purchaser. The reserve at the time was said to be about £30,000. In 1945 the vase was bought by the Nation, but the purchase price has never been disclosed.

The Portland Vase is about ten inches in height and six inches in width and has an underlayer of dark blue glass over which has been superimposed a layer of white opaque glass. Grecian figures have been carved from the outer casing so that they stand out in bold relief against the darker background. The almost incredible delicacy and refinement of the sculptured work alone make it a unique example of the glass-maker's art, but the unknown artist used the properties of his medium to achieve extraordinary effect. Where shading was required, the white outer layer was cut away nearer the dark background, often to the thinness of paper, so that the dense whiteness of the opal was softened by the partial penetration through it of the darker glass. Shading ingeniously contrived in this manner was made to blend with the true perspective of the figure subjects, conferring upon them the effect of painting as well as sculpture. It is to this feature that the work owes no small part of its beauty.

Other famous vases in the same style, and of the same technique as the Portland Vase, have been found in Rome and Pompeii. The Aldjo Vase, also in the British Museum, was assembled from fragments found in the ruins of Pompeii, destroyed by fire in A.D. 79; another is the Vendange Vase, now in the Museum at Naples. Fragments of other vessels following the same technique are known to exist in other collections.

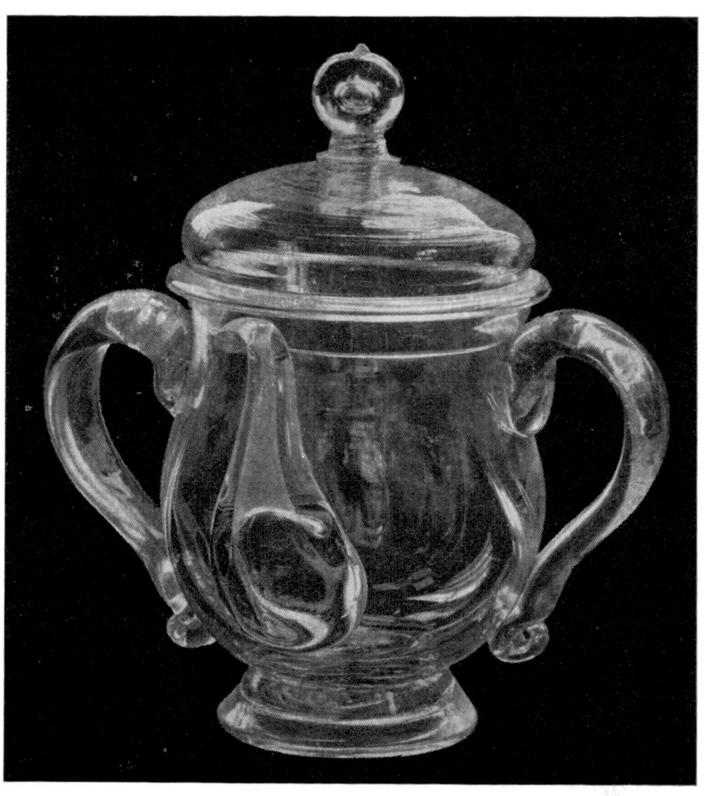

221. *Posset cup and cover. They were made in the time of Ravenscroft, and some have his seal; others are of earlier soda metal.*

POSSET AND CAUDLE GLASSES. Posset was a drink made of curdled milk with ale or wine, to which were added fine breadcrumbs. It was used on social and convivial occasions, much the same as caudle, a curious hot drink prepared from mulled wine or ale, thickened with bread and sugar, and seasoned with various spices.

Posset and caudle cups were similar in form, the general type being a squat- or round-sided vessel provided with two handles and a spout. Some of them, indeed, have the appearance of a modern teapot, and are provided with covers, such as the specimen in Fig. 221.

Posset pots date from the seventeenth century and continued to be used for various drinks well into the eighteenth century. They are found both in soda metal and later in glass-of-lead.

The posset pots which changed hands at Sotheby's in 1947 are definitely glass-of-lead. Three uncrizzled posset pots were discovered with the 'Raven's Head' seal (*Glass Notes*, Arthur Churchill, Ltd., No. 9, December, 1949, pp. 11-18). This seal, it will be recalled, was a mark in the form of a raven's head, given to George Ravenscroft as a compliment for his work on glass-of-lead in 1676-1678. These glasses are made of perfect uncrizzled metal, water-white and lustrous. The bowls are all cylindrical, the handles solid.

Posset glasses were advertised as late as 1758 in a Liverpool List (*Liverpool Chronicle*, 24th March, 1758): 'To be sold by auction in the Town's Hall, Liverpool, A quantity of Glass Salvors, Salts, Cruets, Sweetmeat Glasses, Jelly Glasses, Glass Baskets, Comfit Glasses, Flower Bottles, Glass Plates, Glass Basons, Posset Glasses.'

Posset pots were used for serving syllabub as late as 1769 (Raffald, *Experienced English Housekeeper*, 1769, p. 184), but,

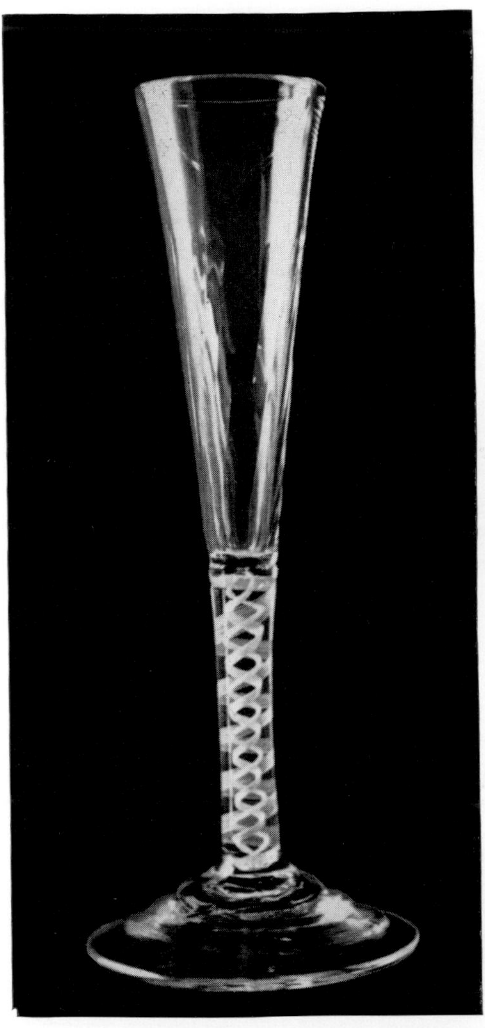

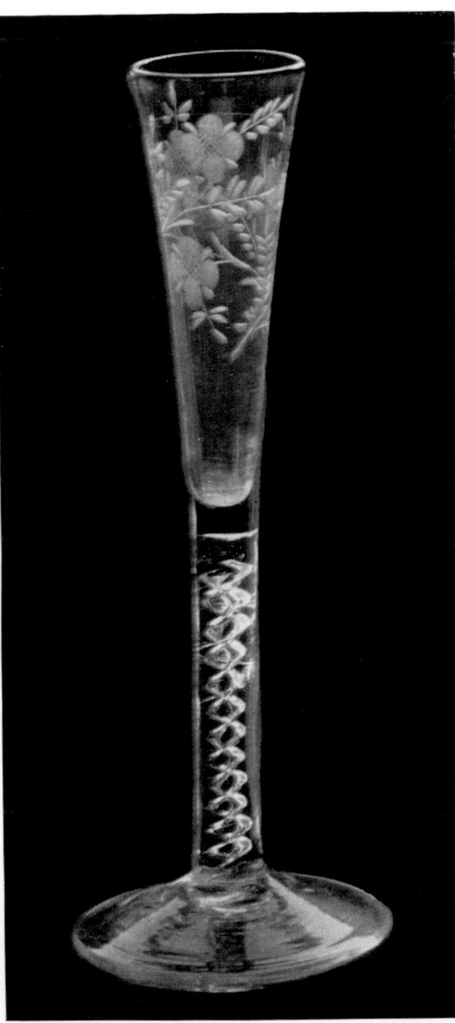

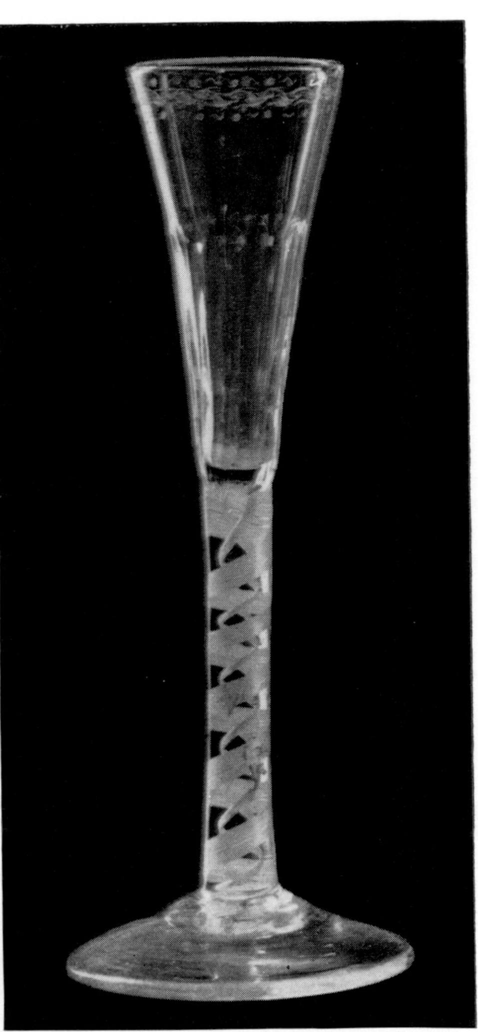

222. *Flute glass used for ratafia or similar cordial. The bowl is moulded with light flutes from the base to about two-thirds of its height. The stem is an opaque-twist of the double series type.* circa *1750/60.* 223. *Flute glass similar to that shown in Fig. 222 but with air-twist stem. The bowl is wheel engraved with floral designs.* 224. *Flute glass similar to those shown in Figs. 222 and 223. The stem is an opaque-twist of the double series type, and the bowl engraved by the wheel with a formal border.*

no doubt, the style resembled the jelly glass of the 1740-1750 period such as that shown under JELLY GLASSES, Fig. 172.

Sealed Ravenscroft posset pots of the style shown in Fig. 221 change hands at high figures. One from the Horridge Collection fetched £880 in 1959. Two other sealed Ravenscroft posset pots changed hands in 1952 for £820 and £870, respectively.

POTASH.

See MATERIALS USED IN GLASS-MAKING.

PRESSED GLASS.

See AMERICAN GLASS.

PUNCH BOWLS.

See TODDY LIFTERS.

PYRAMIDS.

See SWEETMEAT GLASSES.

RATAFIA GLASSES. The eighteenth-century equivalent of the modern cocktail and liqueur were the so-called 'cordials', spirituous drinks prepared from the juice and kernels of fruits such as apricots, cherries and peaches, and from the peel of the citron, orange and lemon. Recipes for cordials may be found in eighteenth-century books such as Mrs Raffald's *English Housekeeper* (1769), Moxon's *English Housewifry* and the *Compleat Family Piece* (1741). Special glasses were devised for the consumption of cordials, the usual style being a glass with a small bowl of capacity about one ounce on a rather tall and extra stout stem.

A fashionable cordial was ratafia, a drink introduced about the end of the seventeenth century; it was flavoured with the kernels of almonds and either peaches or cherries. Ratafia had its own special glass, a long very narrow tapering funnel bowl of capacity between one and one and a half ounces, with drawn stem of similar length to the bowl. A typical specimen is shown in Fig. 222. This ratafia glass has a slender funnel bowl moulded with light flutes from the base to about two-thirds of its height; it is mounted on a white opaque-twist stem of the double series type. The specimen is seven and a quarter inches in height, *circa* 1750-1760.

Although the more usual style is clear glass with fluting, such as on the specimen illustrated in Fig. 222, some specimens are found with the bowl engraved with floral designs or with a formal border. Specimens with such engraved emblems are shown in Figs. 223 and 224.

Ratafia glasses of the type described have changed hands up to £5.

RAVENSCROFT, GEORGE. George Ravenscroft (1618-1681) was the man selected by the Glass Sellers' Company to establish a suitable glass medium, and who eventually succeeded in perfecting glass-of-lead.

He set up his glasshouse in the Savoy in July, 1673, and about a year later, obtained his first patent. An agreement was made with the Glass Sellers' Company, whereby they offered to find a market for his output and to establish him in a glass-house at Henley-on-Thames, where he could continue his work in comparative seclusion.

In 1676 he was granted a certificate for his glass-of-lead; in 1677 his earlier agreement was renewed, and the raven's head seal authorised by the Glass Sellers. In 1678, however, Ravenscroft unaccountably gave six months' notice to the Glass Sellers, following which Hawley Bishopp took over the control of the glasshouses.

George Ravenscroft died in 1681 and, appropriately enough, was buried at the Savoy Chapel.

The following are the glasses or fragments extant with the raven's head seal; four posset pots, three roemers (one is shown in Fig. 226), a jug, a bowl, a decanter, a tankard and broken stems of two drinking glasses. (*See* BALUSTER STEMMED GLASSES; BUGGIN BOWLS; CANDLESTICKS; CUT-GLASS; DECOLOURISING OF GLASS; ENGLISH GLASS, HISTORY OF; IRISH GLASS; LANTHORNS AND GLASS LAMPS; MATERIALS USED IN GLASS-MAKING; NEWCASTLE GLASSES; NIPT DIAMOND WAIES; POSSET AND CAUDLE GLASSES; ROEMER AND RUMMER; SALT-CELLARS; SINGLE FLINT GLASSES; SODA GLASSES; SWEETMEAT GLASSES and SYLLABUB GLASSES.)

ROEMER AND RUMMER. The roemer was a form of glass vessel made in the Rhine areas, in the Low countries, in Central Europe and, to a much less extent, in Sweden from the sixteenth century onwards. Its origin is most probably to be found in the knobbed beakers (*Warzenbecher*) of the fifteenth century, but the roemer did not appear in its better known form until the sixteenth century.

The early roemer was of colourless glass or pale to deep green. It had a relatively short foot with up to six spirals, but as the seventeenth century developed, the height of the foot was increased and the bowl became proportionately shorter. The lower part of the bowl is always decorated with blobs (*warze*) or 'prunts', as they are known in this country. They are not always of the raspberry formation, but may be flat and smooth or finished with a short projection where the hot glass has been drawn off. This latter style was probably from Roman influence.

The roemer has been described as one of the most popular and picturesque glasses which has ever been devised. The beauty of the green colour of the glasses themselves and their often noble proportions entitle them to rank among the best of all vessels made in Europe.

The roemer soon became popular in this country. Merrett (*The Art of Glass*, 1662, pp. 225-226) speaks of the 'Romer for Rheinish wine, for Sack, Claret, Beer'. It is generally accepted today that the English word rummer is a corruption of the German *roemer*, and that it had no significance in its conception with the spirit rum. Typical seventeenth-century English versions of the outmoded roemer are shown in Figs. 225 and 226.

225. *Roemer in soda metal engraved on the bowl in diamond work with four medallions containing figure subjects representing the four seasons. The stem has a number of raspberry prunts, and is also diamond engraved with a windmill and the inscription 'August the 18th 1663 and WHE'. It is most probably a marriage cup.* (*British Museum*)

There is no mention of the rummer in English newspaper notices until 1751, and only after 1772 do they become at all common. There is no doubt that the rummer did not become a fashionable glass in this country until it had evolved into something like its now familiar form, and this was a slow process. The German form was absorbed and reproduced with such strong native flavour that the original roemer and the nineteenth-century rummer have no points in common.

Thorpe (*A History of English and Irish Glass*, 1929, p. 327) has traced the evolution of the rummer through a number of stages, beginning with the English version of the German roemer made by George Ravenscroft and given his seal of the Raven's Head. This specimen is shown in Fig. 226

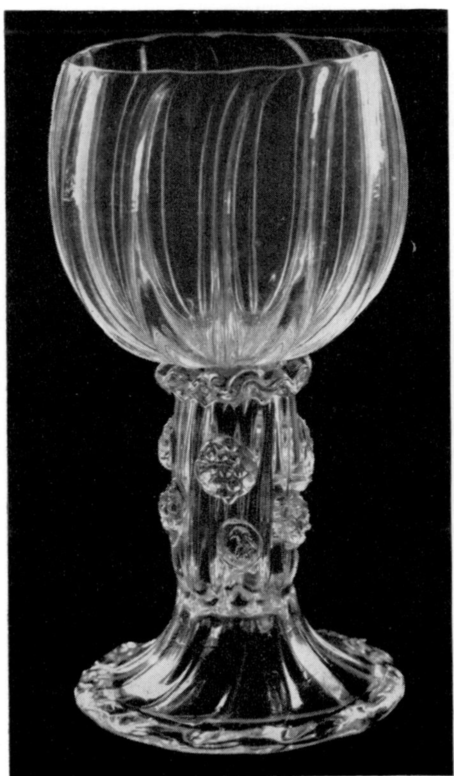

226. *Roemer sealed with the raven's head on the lowest of the prunts on the hollow stem. Made at the Savoy or Henley glasshouse by George Ravenscroft.* circa *1677.* 227. *Rummer engraved with the bust of Nelson and the Victory celebrating Trafalgar. The style is typical of that period.* 228. *Goblet after the style of the roemer. The hollow stem has raspberry prunts. At the junction of the stem and bowl there is a narrow trailed collar.* circa *1680.* (*All by courtesy of the Victoria and Albert Museum*)

229. *Rummer engraved with Sunderland Bridge opened in 1796. A number of these glasses were made for some years after the opening of the bridge.* (*By courtesy of the Victoria and Albert Museum.*) 230. *Popular style of rummer of the middle nineteenth century.* 231. *Style of rummer still popular at the time of the Great Exhibition in 1851.*

and would have been made during the period of the Savoy and Henley glasshouses between 1676 and 1678.

After a period of three or four years, the style had become slightly modified. The bowl was now changed to a wide, incurved style with gadrooned base, the stem hollow with attached prunts, and the foot plain as the specimen shown in Fig. 228. The tendency to follow this style was maintained until the end of the seventeenth century; about this time the hollow stem was replaced by a solid knopped one, a popular knop form being the ordinary baluster.

The German ancestry of the rummer was now no longer in evidence. The German form had followed a proportionate balance between bowl, stem and foot; the English version by comparison always gives the impression of being unsymmetrical, the bowl being too large for its insignificant stem and foot.

From 1700 onwards the progress to the style which was still popular a century later is not easy to follow. New styles were introduced in response to the influence of the Adam brothers, and the bowls of these glasses were often decorated by engraving in simple border styles. Commemorative engraving appeared on some glasses, most bowl forms being popular with the exception of the round funnel style. Such glasses maintained their popularity until the time of the Great Exhibition in 1851. The usual form at that period was a generous bowl on a short stem, sometimes embellished with simple knops mounted on a plain spreading foot. The bowl forms were numerous—ovoid, bucket-shaped, round funnel, ogee and double ogee. A square cut base, which could be terraced or ridged, was also fashionable. These styles were in vogue up to the end of the last century. Typical specimens are shown in Figs. 227, 229-231.

Rummers of the late eighteenth century have not fetched high prices. Quite recently eleven sold for £12. The style was as shown in Fig. 231. On the other hand a rummer with large bucket bowl, engraved on one side with a windmill and on the other with the initials T.M.W., above hops and barley, sold for £14. Rummers commemorating the opening of Sunderland Bridge in 1796 and engraved with a picture of the bridge with a boat passing underneath it, such as is shown in Fig. 229, have changed hands between £6 and £11.

ROLLING PINS.
See NAILSEA GLASS; SCOTTISH GLASS.

ROYAL OAK GOBLET.
See ENGLISH GLASS, HISTORY OF.

RUBY GLASS.
See GERMAN AND BOHEMIAN GLASS.

RUMMER.
See ROEMER AND RUMMER.

SALT-CELLARS. Glass salt-cellars have not such a well-defined course of evolution as those in silver or even pewter. Unlike silver and pewter, glass vessels of the eighteenth century had no distinguishing marks, and few early notices occur that give a clue as to their early form. Probably the earliest notice of salt-cellars, and one conceivably providing a pointer as to form, occurred in the *Stamford Mercury*, 21st March, 1724: 'S. Houghton, goldsmith from London, designs to be at Stamford Fair . . . with Wine-glasses, Ale-glasses and Glass Salts.'

It is most probable, therefore, that as the metal-smiths of the times were interested in glass salt-cellars, the early forms followed the lines of their metal counterparts. There is no doubt that the glass-maker turned to the metal-smith for inspiration for many of the vessels he formed. The new medium, Ravenscroft's glass-of-lead, had no Continental counterpart. Indeed, there was a marked difference between the working properties of the Venetian soda-lime glass and glass-of-lead. The Venetian *cristallo* was a quick-setting medium which required speedy and dexterous manipulation. Glass-of-lead, on the other hand, was a slow-setting one.

The English glass-maker could not emulate the Venetian craftsmen who fashioned their delicate vessels to any whimsical

232. *Pair of plain salt-cellars, with the three supporting feet surmounted by lion masks, 2¼ inches high.* circa *1735.*

233. *Pair of reeded salt-cellars with three supporting feet surmounted by gargoyles, 2½ inches high.* circa *1740.*

or fleeting fancy that occurred to them, and he found the long working range of the lead medium particularly suited to his easy-going style. Once the sober properties of the new crystal glass were understood, he became adept in its manipulation, but when it came to creating form and style, his efforts were not nearly so successful. In many cases he borrowed ideas from the metal-smiths, with the result that a close similarity can be traced between some glass vessels and similar objects in metal. Chandeliers, candlesticks and cream jugs are outstanding examples of this parallel development, and much the same similarity can be traced between the metal salt-cellars and those of glass.

During the seventeenth century the custom was introduced of providing each diner with a small salt-cellar called a 'trencher' or 'small' salt. They were small vessels when compared with the 'standing' or 'great' salts of earlier times, which were often a foot in height. The trencher salt was usually only an inch in height and between two and three inches in width, and was of either silver or pewter. These early seventeenth-century metal trencher salts were circular in form, but later in the century, triangular and octagonal styles were introduced.

The glass trencher salt of the late seventeenth and early eighteenth centuries followed its silver counterpart. Thorpe (*A History of English and Irish Glass*, 1929, p. 328) points out that when the new glass-of-lead 'was struggling for social recognition, the glass-makers were apt to copy silver, which had an older tradition and better prestige. The glass trencher, a good example of this, is derived from a silver trencher, which goes back to 1680'.

These early trencher salts had simple hemi-spherical bowls, plain surfaced, mounted on a pedestal base. They were about two inches in height and width. An example is shown in Thorpe's *A History of English and Irish Glass*, 1929, Vol. II, Plate CLII, No. 4. There are a few examples known of this early type of glass trencher, but they appear to have gone out of fashion rather quickly, which may account for their scarcity.

A notice in *Faulkner's Dublin Journal*, November, 1729, stated: 'At the Round Glasshouse in St Mary's Lane, Dublin, the fire being in, are made all sorts of fine Drinking Glasses . . . Fine Salts, Ground and Polished . . . and for the encouragement to dealers, 'tis proposed to sell them much cheaper than they can import them from England, or elsewhere.'

It is not clear whether the salt-cellars being 'finely ground and polished' referred to the article decorated with a cut pattern, or whether it meant a ground and polished base. It is probable that the latter was true, as it was not until 1752 that the same Journal advertised of the Round Glasshouse: 'All sorts of cut and flowered glasses may be had of any kind to any pattern . . . as no pains or expense have been spared by

234. *Salt-cellar with boat-shaped bowl and oval foot with shallow cutting to the bowl. The rim is notched on the inside.* circa *1765.*

the proprietor to procure the best workmen and newest patterns from London.'

During the first half of the century, salt-cellars with tri-pedal support made their appearance. An example is shown in Fig. 232. The fashion of balancing all sorts of tableware on three legs was popular about this time and, indeed, one which lasted until nearly the close of the eighteenth century. This fashion applied equally well to salt-cellars in other media, such as silver, Britannia alloy and porcelain. The style of the vessel itself was the same to all media also—that is, a shallow cup-shaped bowl supported by three clawed feet surmounted by lion masks. The embellishment given to the legs and feet in glass attempted to follow those in metal, but, as may be expected, what could be executed in great detail in metal could not be copied in glass. Pincer moulds were used to fashion the feet and the lion masks or gargoyles in glass, but the joining of the legs to the bowl was an operation which necessarily had to be carried out during the short period of time that the glass remained sufficiently hot to make a satisfactory weld. After the glass had set, no other fashioning work could be done on it, such as would be the case with the malleable metals, silver and Britannia alloy. A pair of reeded salt-cellars with three supporting feet surmounted by gargoyles is shown in Fig. 233.

Cutting and engraving were not attempted on the style of salt-cellars just described, but it was used on other styles such as those with double-ogee, round and boat-shaped bowls. These were especially popular during the Irish period, 1780-1850 (*see* IRISH GLASS). Glass salts of this description were of the period when cutting was the most popular form of decoration, and specimens can be found cut with festoons, or in relief diamond patterns, and with scalloped rims.

A typical salt-cellar from this period is shown in Fig. 234, with boat-shaped bowl and oval foot. The cut decoration is in shallow style, the rim notched on the inside.

Many of these salt-cellars had moulded feet in square or octagonal form similar to the candle-sticks and salad bowls of the period. They displayed the Adam influence and remained popular until well into the nineteenth century especially in Ireland.

Some glass salt-cellars have the rim turned over outwards in a graceful flange. The flange was sometimes left plain or it could be cut in alternate prism pattern. These salt-cellars have short rudimentary stems and square or oval feet, which were cut smooth and polished on the wheel. Parallel forms in silver of the period are occasionally found. The glass salt with plain boat-shaped bowl, short stem and oval foot, has an exact counterpart in English silver of the 1799 period.

Examples of Irish salt-cellars are shown under IRISH GLASS, Fig. 158. These are low in price and have sold at between £1 and £2.

SALVER.

See SWEETMEAT GLASSES.

SAND GLASSES. The sand or hour glass has a long history. It would appear to have been invented during the eighth century by Liutprand, a monk at Chartres.

Sand glasses require little description, as most people have seen them in some form or another. Twin, pear-shaped bulbs with a tiny connecting hole allowing the passage of fine sand, were familiar objects a few years ago for timing the cooking of eggs.

A more established form—a two-minute sand glass—has a place on the Speaker's Table in the House of Commons. When the bells begin to sound for a division, the sand glass is reversed and the bells continue to sound their warning ring until the sand has run out.

The custom of timing with a sand glass was, until recent years, common in the home, in churches, ships, schools, or wherever time had to be taken into account. For example, it is recorded by Cocke Lorelle in *Cocke Lorelles bote* (1518), that on board ship 'one man kepte ye compas, and watched ye our glasse'.

After the Reformation, all Scottish churches used sand glasses to time the length of the sermon, usually half an hour. The custom was continued in some Scottish churches until the present century. The sand glasses at Rothesay, for example, continued to be used until 1911.

It is probable that sand glasses were introduced into Scotland by Flemish glass-makers, for the Table of Customs at Leith contains the entry 'Hour-Glasses (Horloges de Sable) fra Flanders' (A. Fleming, *Scottish and Jacobite Glass*, 1938, p. 19).

The early sand glass was sturdily constructed from heavy bottle glass, protected by a wrought iron casting. The pear-shaped bulbs used in the making of a sand glass had a well-flaired neck at the narrow extremity. Two such bulbs would be used, one with the neck at the top and the other inverted, so that the two flaired necks met. Between the flaired portions was placed a thin metal disc provided with a central hole, the size of which regulated the flow of the fine dried sand to the required time.

The necks of the two bulbs at their junction were given an adhesive coating of putty and then bound into position with a coarse linen wrapping. Some specimens are found with an additional binding of leather strips over the linen joint.

In the early eighteenth century, when the English glass-maker had attained efficiency in the manipulation of his medium, sand glasses were made by welding two pear-shaped bulbs together at the furnace mouth, at the same time inserting a metal bead drilled with the required hole. The leather binding at the joint, however, still continued to be used.

As the century progressed, it became possible to dispense with the metal bead and to make the glass in one piece, the narrow constriction through which the sand passed being part of the glass vessel itself. After the glass had set and while it was still hot, dried sand previously well heated would be introduced into an opening at the wide extremity of one bulb, which was at once sealed.

The sand used in a sand glass had obviously to be specially prepared. It was essential that it should be perfectly dry, but in addition, the grains of sand had to be regularly and uniformly shaped. One coarse grain could cause a stoppage at the constricted neck. Careful grinding and sieving of the sand was therefore essential to ensure reliability and correctness. Alternative materials were used, but in the large majority of sand glasses extant today, the medium used was sand.

The frames used to encase the sand glass were many and varied. Wrought iron has already been mentioned, but wooden frames of oak were a popular alternative. Some are found in silver frames and also in frames of ivory and bone. The oak

235. *Ship's four-hour sand glass.* 236. *Set of four sand glasses set in a wooden frame. The usual timing of such a set is fifteen minutes, thirty minutes, forty-five minutes and one hour.* (*Both Crown Copyright, Science Museum, London*)

frame consisted of circular top and bottom plates joined together in cage formation by four uprights which could be plain cylindrical oak rods or decorated with knops.

The most usual timing found on old sand glasses is the hour and half-hour. Specimens timed for three-quarters of an hour are uncommon. A ship's four-hour sand glass is shown in Fig. 235. Some specimens are found with four glasses encased in a single frame, timed to one-quarter hour, half-hour, three-quarters of an hour and one hour respectively (Fig. 236).

The Science Museum, Kensington, has specimens of Admiralty sand glasses as used in the Royal Navy and Mercantile Marine. Every ship carried a fourteen second and twenty-eight second sand glass. They were known as log-glasses and were used in timing the sailing speed by the quantity of line paid out against the timing of the sand glass.

Marine sand glasses are sometimes found encased in square wooden boxes with open sides fitted with glass or horn windows. These are most probably early nineteenth-century specimens.

SANG, JACOB (*c.* 1752-1762).
See DUTCH GLASS; NEWCASTLE GLASSES.

SCHWANHARDT, GEORG (1601-1667).
See GERMAN AND BOHEMIAN GLASS.

SCOTTISH GLASS. The first mention of glass-making in Scotland was in 1610, when James I granted to George Hay, later created Lord Hay of Kinfauns, a patent for the exclusive right of making glass at Wemyss, in Fife, for forty-one years. The monopoly enjoyed by Lord Hay, however, was subsequently transferred to Sir Robert Mansell in 1627 (*see* MANSELL, SIR ROBERT). The glasshouse at Wemyss was not a very profitable one and was eventually closed down.

It is doubtful whether glass was made in Scotland in any quantity until after 1615, in which year the use of coal for glass-making was enforced and the use of wood for fuel prohibited.

Glasshouses were in operation in the Edinburgh district shortly afterwards, notably at Leith, where in 1628 a glasshouse was established for the manufacture of black and green bottles of all kinds.

After the Restoration in 1664, the Privy Council, in order to compete with foreign glass then being imported from the Low Countries, issued an order forbidding the public from buying bottles other than those made locally.

Records of glass-making in Scotland are scanty, however, until the end of the seventeenth century, but it is clear that by that time the industry in bottles had gradually become established. In 1682, Charles Hay, a relative of Lord Hay of Kinfauns, opened a glasshouse in Leith, the port to Edinburgh, which was to supply 'A superior metal to that of bottles suitable for ale, and clear wine glasses' (A. Fleming, *Scottish and Jacobite Glass*, 1938, p. 111). The business evidently prospered, for some years later 'clear chemistry and apothecary ware' were being supplied at prices competitive with similar wares from the London and Newcastle glasshouses.

Other glasshouses were established in the Leith district; Dr Merret, translator of *L'Arte Vetraria*, was appointed London representative of one of them. In 1696, the Leith glasshouses were reported as employing 122 glass-blowers, not counting their various assistants.

The beginning of the eighteenth century saw the expansion

of the Leith glasshouses, and all types of bottles and glasses for beer and wine were being produced. Large bottles appeared to be a speciality of the Scottish glass-makers, for there is a record in the *Manchester Magazine* of the 15th January, 1751: 'Leith, December 28th, 1750. A globular bottle has been lately blown here by Thomas Symmer, a principal director of the glassworks, South Leith, at the desire of several gentlemen, undertakers of a private work at Prestonpans, containing two hogsheads, and being measured, the dimensions are 40 inches by 42 inches. This piece of curiosity is not yet removed from Symmer's House and is reckoned by all who have seen it to be completely blown to exceed in capacity anything ever done in any glasshouse in Britain.'

Arnold Fleming explains how these large bottles with a capacity of over one hundred gallons were made. 'In these pioneer days the sole aid available in making such a capacious hollow vessel was a method of injecting some spirit which evaporated at once through the heat of the glass and by the operative pressing his thumb tightly over the end of the blow-pipe; the force generated by the vapourised alcohol was sufficient to expand the bulb to the required capacity.'

In 1777 there were seven glasshouses in operation in the Leith district, the wares mainly being bottles and glasses for beer and wine. Fancy articles were probably made in the workmen's spare time, as there is an account which refers to the making of 'birds and beasts' in glass, and of a 'swan with divers coloured threads of glass' (A. Fleming, *Scottish and Jacobite Glass*, 1938, p. 114).

A new factory was established at Leith in 1864, which later became Webbs Crystal Glass Company, famous then, as it is today, for its excellent tableware.

About the same time, a factory was erected at Perth, destined to share the fame of its Leith competitor for artistic tableware. This was the North British Glass Works, established by John Moncrieff. Bottles and gauge glasses were at first the main productions, but later chemical ware was made. The works, now known as John Moncrieff, Ltd., however, has gained a great reputation for its Monart Ware, produced by a novel process of making glass bowls and other vessels in which various colours are blended harmoniously.

Scottish glass cannot be left without mention of the factory at Alloa. This was erected in 1750 and during its long history has mainly dealt in glass bottles. As is the case with most such factories, however, fancy ware was made. Ware similar to that reputed to have been made at Nailsea, such as rolling pins and flasks, can certainly be accredited to Alloa.

There is a record of Timothy Warren, who served his apprenticeship in glass-making at Nailsea, and who later travelled north, first to Newcastle-on-Tyne, where he owned a glasshouse in St Thomas Street, and later to Alloa, where he finally settled with his wife and family. It is known that Alloa glassworks produced articles of the type shown in Fig. 197 (*left*), the thin white opaque streaks being known in Scotland as 'quillings'. The double-necked flasks of this type were claimed to be used for oil and vinegar.

Warren considerably widened the scope of the Alloa Works and at one time Alloa table glass was declared to be 'Equal to the goods made in Newcastle' (John L. Carvel, *The Alloa Glass Works*, privately printed, 1953, p. 16).

The Alloa craftsmen also engraved seals, coats-of-arms and other emblems on various types of vessels, examples of which can be seen in the Scottish Museums, notably Smith's Institute, Stirling.

The method of engraving was stippling with a sharp-pointed hammer, various designs and inscriptions being employed. For example, a large globular bottle in Smith's Institute has engraved upon it a digging fork, spade, two reaper's hooks, and a whetstone, a scythe and a festoon of flowers. Another specimen has the words 'Speed the Plough' stippled upon it. The collection at Smith's Institute also includes a rolling pin claimed to have been made at Alloa. It is in white opaque glass with the motto 'Forget me Not'.

SEALS. Coloured glass seals came greatly into fashion during the second half of the eighteenth century. It was found that for cheap seals, glass had one positive advantage over stone or crystal. To engrave stone or crystal by hand was a costly business, whereas designs on glass could be obtained easily by moulding. The bottle-makers had long made their seals in this manner. Thus, moulded glass fob-seals became common after 1750; they were made in various colours and in imitation of stone, such as cornelian.

Towards the end of the eighteenth century, when colour twists were used to decorate the stems of drinking glasses, the shaft of the seal was embellished in a similar manner, and occasional specimens are today found with a twin multiple corkscrew with dark blue entwined threads.

With the introduction of millefiori into this country in the middle of the nineteenth century, however, glass seals were made with the shafts decorated with millefiori florettes. They were about three inches in length and were apparently supplied with plain ends, for an occasional unengraved seal is met with.

Glass seals rarely change hands; those that have are decorated with colour twists or millefiori florettes. A St Louis hand seal with a spray of pink, white and blue florettes sold some years ago for £12. Another with millefiori canes, including one with a silhouette of a gondola, the initials A.G., and the date 1847, sold for £20. Other glass seals have changed hands between £2 10s. and £3 during recent years.

SERVITOR.
See Wineglass, The Making of.

SHADES OR GLASS DOMES. The mantelshelf of the Victorian parlour usually sported a pair of coloured glass vase lustres (*see* Vase Lustres), but in addition or as an alternative there would in most cases be some article under a large glass dome.

The idea probably developed from the clocks which were provided with glass covers as a protection against the dust and dampness of the atmosphere, which could affect efficient working. Later the idea extended to wax reproductions of flowers and fruit and to religious and sporting subjects.

The early name for these glass domes was 'shade'. Arthur Morrison, in his *Tales of Mean Streets*, wrote a story around a shade of waxen fruit, with the title, *Behind The Shade*. The word 'embellishment' was sometimes used as an alternative to shade.

These shades were made by the glass-makers who made window glass by the broad method. A mass of glass would be gathered on the blowing-iron and blown into spherical shape. After allowing it to cool, the workman would cut it away from the blow pipe, grip the rounded end with a spring clip, known as the gadget, and reheat and shape the severed end to a neat smooth finish.

When the broad method of making window glass was replaced by mechanical methods of manufacture, glass shades ceased to be made. The last to be made were probably those used as covers for white posies of waxen flowers used to adorn graves.

SHOES.

See Nailsea Glass.

SILESIAN-STEMMED GLASSES. The baluster period of glasses extended from Ravenscroft's time to 1730, but there had been a tendency towards the end of the first quarter of the eighteenth century for transition to a lighter style, which later developed into what is today known as the Balustroid Group of glasses. (*See* Balustroids.)

In 1714, however, when George I ascended the English throne, a style of stem was introduced and named in his honour the 'Silesian Stem'. This stem style was quite different in every way from the baluster style which preceded it. The baluster stem was fashioned 'free-hand' at the furnace and its development into its various styles can be traced back to Venetian influence. The Silesian stem, on the other hand, was moulded into shape. Because of this fact, it is known to collectors today under various titles—moulded, pedestal, shouldered and, of course, Silesian.

The term Silesian implies that this particular style originated in Silesia. It was certainly made in Hesse, a neighbouring glass-making district to Silesia, but it is today thought that the style was imported into this country from Lauenstein, in Hanover, where a glasshouse was founded in 1701. It must also not be overlooked that George himself came from Hanover to this country, and the Silesian stem was regarded as a compliment to him.

On the other hand, it is claimed that the shouldered stem style was known in Venice in the seventeenth century. In the collection of Venetian glass in the Museo Vetrario in Murano, Venice, there is a glass with a six-sided pedestal stem with an eight-pointed star on each shoulder. This specimen, shown in Fig. 238, is claimed by the Museum authorities in Murano to be of Venetian origin of the seventeenth century.

237. *Silesian-stemmed glass moulded on the four shoulders with G R in relief, in honour of George I of Hanover who ascended the English throne in 1714.* 238. *Glass with moulded pedestal stem in the Museo Vetrario at Murano, near Venice. Claimed by Museum authorities to be seventeenth century.* 239. *Specimen with eight-sided Silesian stem without the usual collaring at the base of the bowl.* circa *1720.*

240. *Sweetmeat glass with moulded Silesian stem vertically ribbed or reeded.* circa *1745.*

In this country, the early style of Silesian stem was a four-sided pedestal with a crown, sceptres, or the letters G R moulded in relief on the four shoulders, such as the specimen shown in Fig. 237. Some rare examples have 'God Save King George' or 'God Save King G' impressed upon them.

The four-sided stem variety was quickly replaced by polygonal styles, six- and eight-sided examples being known. A specimen with an eight-sided stem is shown in Fig. 239. This is an unusual glass, in that the waisted bowl is set directly on the stem, the usual collaring at the base of the bowl being absent. In this specimen, each rib terminates at the top of the stem with an impressed four-sided relief diamond. This particular style appeared until 1735.

Later forms became twisted and vertically ribbed or reeded, such as the example of a sweetmeat glass shown in Fig. 240.

The Silesian stem began to lose its popularity after the death of George I in 1727, but its manufacture did not cease as abruptly as it had begun when he ascended the throne in 1714. It continued mainly in combination with simple knopping to the middle of the century; glasses with a single knop, two knops, one of which might be angular, and a single annular knop, are known.

In certain glasses, however, the Silesian stem was often used alone, such as with salvers and sweetmeat glasses, and these appeared well into the second half of the eighteenth century.

The price of glasses with Silesian stems depends very much on other distinguishing features. For example, sweetmeats with Silesian stems have been purchased up to £10, and wines up to £15, depending on their rarity.

SILICA.

See MATERIALS USED IN GLASS-MAKING.

SINGLE FLINT GLASSES. Although the baluster style had its beginnings in John Greene's time, and to some extent developed during the experimental period through which the English metal was passing, it did not emerge as the style with which we are so familiar until the so-called 'double-flint' stage had been reached.

It is now generally accepted that Ravenscroft's lead glass was perfected about 1676, but the period occupied with its teething troubles, and the experience required by the glass-maker to adapt himself to its peculiarities, was a lengthy one. The following notes from the Glass Sellers' Bills found a few years ago in Woburn Abbey tell an interesting story (W. A. Thorpe, *Transactions of the Society of Glass Technology*, Vol. XXII, 1938, pp. 165-203):

Dec. 6th, 1671	12: Large English christall tumblers	£0. 7 . 0
April 25th, 1674	2: dozen and 2 fine flint Christalline glasses	£2. 9 . 0
Nov. 30th, 1675	6: flint Ribd beer glasses 18s.	£0. 9 . 0
Mar. 27th, 1676	12: new flintt wine Glasses mrd.	£0. 16 . 0
May 9th, 1682	12: Thicke ffint Glases	£0. 12 . 0
June 23rd, 1682	1: doz of thine flintt Glases	£0. 6 . 0
May 16th, 1685	6: duble flintt Glases	£0. 5 . 0
June 23rd, 1686	12: Single fflint Glasses	£0. 4 . 0

It is to be assumed that the thick flint and the double flint glasses referred to the same method of manufacture adopted by the glass-maker—that is, a second gathering of metal to remedy the tendency for lightness, a characteristic fault of the imported Venetian glasses. Thin flint and single flint were also, doubtless, synonymous terms used to describe vessels made from a single gathering of metal.

There is no evidence whatsoever that single flint indicates a glass composition with a lower proportion of lead. Scientific research has shown that following the perfecting of glass-of-lead by Bishopp in 1678, the composition has remained unvaried. This applies to single flint glasses in lead metal (E. M. Elville, *English Tableglass*, 1951, p. 256).

Single flint glasses are now rare. They followed Greene's designs more closely in form than the heavier balusters, and are marked by conical or round funnel bowls on an inverted baluster stem or one with a wide angular knop. The folded foot is common and the glasses are without exception very thinly made. A typical specimen is shown in Fig. 241, which is of yellowish-green metal rather seedy in nature.

From the records of the Bills found at Woburn Abbey, it is evident that single and double flint glasses made their appearance about the same time—that is, in 1682. Until recent years, the earliest known mention of double flint was in 1710, which led writers to assume that single flint glasses preceded the double variety by about a quarter of a century. It is unlikely, however, that the term 'single flint' would have been employed had the necessity not arisen to distinguish it from some other kind of flint.

It is fairly safe to assume, therefore, that immediately after

241. *Single flint glass of light construction made from one gathering of metal; straw-coloured glass filled with countless specks of 'seed'.* circa *1690.*

Ravenscroft's discovery, the new flint-glass was offered to the public in two styles, light and heavy, at the same time. The matter of choice was not settled at once, for after a substantial reduction in cost, the two styles were still competing at the turn of the century. Eventually, as is known, the heavier style —that is, 'double flint'—despite the fact that it was twice the cost of the lighter, proved to be the more acceptable variety for use both in the taverns and in the noble households alike. The greater robustness of the glasses was, no doubt, a strong point in their favour, but there was also the fact that massiveness was more fitting to the forms evolved by the glass-maker from an artistic point of view.

Single flint glasses are rare. One with rounded funnel bowl on a swelling knopped baluster stem and folded foot, six and five-eighth inches high, *circa* 1700, similar to that shown in Fig. 241, changed hands for £12 in 1960.

SLICKERS or **SLICK STONES.**
See LINEN-SMOOTHERS.

SMELLING BOTTLES.
See BOTTLES, PERFUME AND SMELLING.

SODA.
See MATERIALS USED IN GLASS-MAKING.

SODA GLASSES. Up to the time of Ravenscroft's glass-of-lead in 1676, the composition of English glass had been essentially what is known as soda-lime. Soon after the Restoration, experiments had been conducted in an effort to improve the English glass. For example, Clifford and Powlden had obtained a licence for 'christall glass' in 1661, Thomas Tilson was granted a similar licence in 1662, and from 1660 to 1668, John

242. *Group of soda glasses popular following the Restoration in 1660 up to the Ravenscroft period.*

243. *Typical glasses in soda metal popular at the time of John Greene.*

de la Cam was working with the Duke of Buckingham in efforts to perfect 'rock-crystal glass'.

Soda glasses from this period are difficult to distinguish. Glass from the Low Countries and from Venice were at that time very similar both in style and composition. Continental glass was made *façon de Venise*, and the English version existed also.

The glasses shown in Figs. 242 and 243 give some indication of what styles were popular from the Restoration up to the time of Ravenscroft's glass-of-lead. Such glasses were made by the licensees mentioned above, by Morelli for John Greene's English market, or by the provincial glass-makers after Ravenscroft's glass-of-lead was established.

To distinguish definite English specimens of pre-Ravenscroft glass is, therefore, an extremely difficult matter.

Soda glasses such as those shown in Figs. 242 and 243 in *façon de Venise* style have fetched small prices in the sale rooms, usually between £2 and £4.

SPRINGEL GLASSES.
See BOTTLES, PERFUME AND SMELLING.

SPUN GLASS. Spun glass or glass fibre, in spite of its many recent industrial applications, is not a new product. It was made two thousand years ago in Egypt and Rome. There is a specimen in the British Museum of a small glass representation of a human bust and head with a lock of hair hanging over the forehead. The hair is no thicker than a horse hair, yet under magnification its section is found to consist of nine alternate layers of transparent and opaque glass.

After Egyptian and Roman times, glass fibres were made by Arabs, Syrians, Venetians and Germans; indeed, it became part of the glass-maker's technique wherever glass was made,

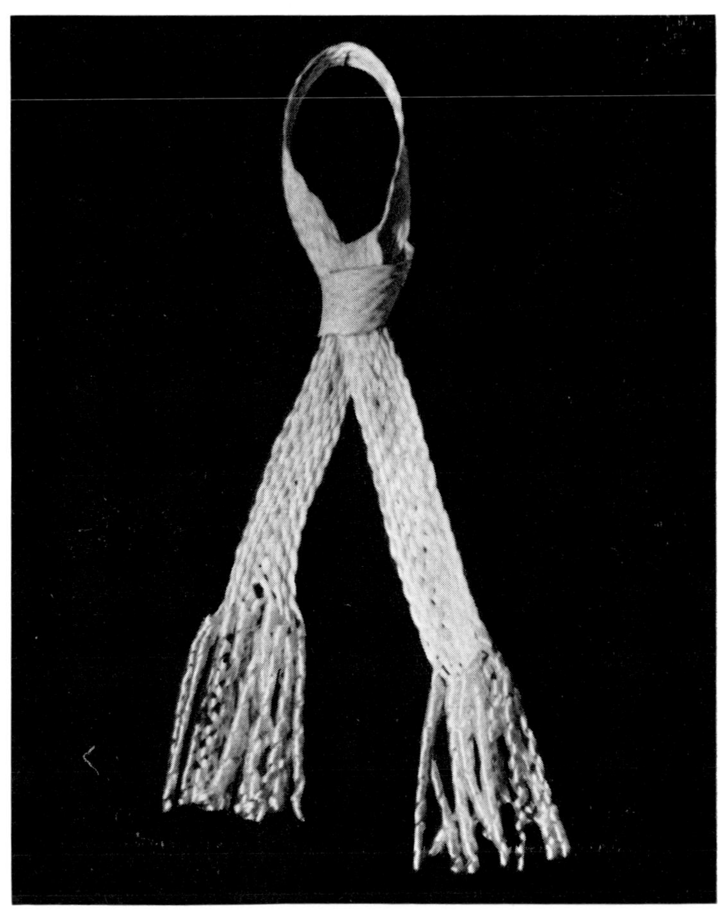

244. *Glass tie woven from fine glass threads in blue and white, nineteenth century from Lancashire district.*

and in the nineteenth century it became quite a familiar curiosity.

It is impossible to say when spun glass was first made in this country. Animals and exotic flowers, glass ships being tossed on a foaming sea of glass wool, and many other such novelties, have come to us from the last century, being much in vogue at the time of the Great Exhibition. A glass tie made about this period, woven from fine glass threads, is shown in Fig. 244. It is made from blue and white strands, composed of threads less than a thousandth of an inch in thickness, of opaque blue and white glass.

The process then used was to spin the glass by heating a glass rod under a flame. A thread was continuously drawn from the soft glass, and wound round a large wooden wheel. By carefully synchronising the speed of the wheel and the movement of the rod into the flame, it was possible to draw a thread of even thickness until all the rod was used. Many miles of continuous thread was drawn in this manner at a speed of something between fifty and one hundred feet each second. The threads were then treated in much the same manner as cotton or silk and made into novelties such as the glass tie illustrated. Such articles are rare, but are occasionally found in the Stourbridge district and in Lancashire.

In St Helen's, Lancashire, an important town in the glass-making industry, glass ties were woven in the colours of the St Helen's Football Club.

Around Bristol also, in the middle of the nineteenth century, mantelpiece ornaments were made in which spun glass was an important decorative feature—such, for example, as the drooping tails of birds in coloured glass. These items were no doubt intended as toys, but there was a delicate craftsmanship, and almost classical feeling, in some of the best examples (A. Hudson Davies, 'The Development and Use of Glass Fibres', *Glass*, Vol. XXXIV, 1957, pp. 403-410).

Spun glass today is even finer than that produced by the ancients. The individual threads can be as small in diameter as a three-hundred-thousandth part of an inch. Threads of this type are used inside the skin of air liners as protection against cold and noise.

Much of the spun glass of today is produced from marbles (*see* MARBLES OF GLASS), re-melted and drawn through a group of two hundred and four openings at the rate of one hundred feet per second and combined into a single strand. So fine is a single filament of the strand that a hundredweight of it would stretch to the moon and back.

An early Victorian specimen of three birds in blown and spun coloured glass, perched among flowers enclosed in a glass shade eighteen inches high, realised £13 a few years ago.

STEUBEN GLASS. This famous glass is made at the Steuben Glass Works at Corning, in the state of New York. Its history and rapid development since being re-organised by Arthur Amory Houghton, jun., in 1933, a great grandson of the founder of Corning Glass Works, probably the largest establishment of its kind in the world today, is told in a monograph, *Steuben Glass*, by James S. Plaut, New York, 1948.

For some thirty years the products of the company were marked by reactionary design. No consistent style evolved, glass was blown, cut and engraved into a variety of ponderous and over-complicated forms of indifferent quality in both material and workmanship. In 1933, however, it was decided to concentrate on flawless crystal glass, and the services of Sidney B. Waugh, the sculptor, were engaged to exploit its inherent beauty in imaginative design. The change in policy met with immediate success and two years later the company exhibited pieces in New York and London, and in 1937 were awarded the Gold Medal of the Paris Exposition.

Many of the Steuben products are permitted to retain, wherever possible, the unique blown quality of the glass itself and cutting is held to a minimum. Not all Steuben products are left unadorned, however, and many examples are given incised decoration with the copper wheel. Probably the most notable example is the 'Merry-go-Round' Bowl (Fig. 246), designed in 1947 by Sidney Waugh and presented by President and Mrs Truman to Princess Elizabeth (now Queen Elizabeth II) on the occasion of her marriage. The craftsman who engraved the bowl is seen at work on it in Fig. 248.

Another equally famous specimen by the same artist is the Gazelle Bowl (Fig. 247), now in the Metropolitan Museum of Art, New York. The emblems are engraved by the copper wheel and display craftsmanship of the highest order. A further specimen of excellent workmanship is the Valor Cup (Fig. 245), designed by John Monteith Gates in 1941 for the British War Relief Society to commemorate the Battle of Britain.

The pair of vases shown in Fig. 249, designed by Eric Gill in 1940, also display excellent craftsmanship. These vases are typical of a large group of vessels decorated at Steuben, in which the work is tastefully executed but with the requisite restraint.

In general, the styles created by the Steuben Company show

245. *'Valor Cup' designed in 1941 by John Monteith Gates for the British War Relief Society to commemorate the Battle of Britain.* (*Steuben Works, New York*)

246. *'Merry-go-Round' bowl, designed by Sidney Waugh in 1947, and presented by President and Mrs Truman to Queen Elizabeth II (then Princess Elizabeth) on the occasion of her marriage.* (*Reproduced by Gracious Permission of Her Majesty The Queen*)

247. *'Gazelle Bowl' designed by Sidney Waugh in 1935, now in the Metropolitan Museum of Art, New York.*

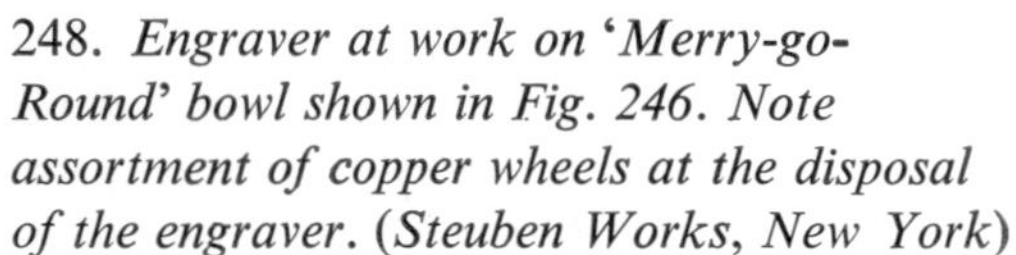

248. *Engraver at work on 'Merry-go-Round' bowl shown in Fig. 246. Note assortment of copper wheels at the disposal of the engraver.* (*Steuben Works, New York*)

249. *Pair of vases by Eric Gill in 1940.* (*Steuben Works, New York*)

250. *Bowl engraved by Simon Gate, one of the famous engravers from Orrefors Glassworks in Sweden.* 251. *Bowl with engraved subject 'The Shark Killer'. The artist is Viktor Lindstrand, of Orrefors Glassworks, Sweden.*

an originality in subject and form. They emerge from the impulse to make the best use of the remarkable crystal medium at the disposal of the American artists, but each specimen is created with three elements in mind—material, workmanship and design—and if any of the three is deficient, perfection cannot be achieved. For this reason, the work may not be as free or as vigorous as some modern Continental creations, where the tendency is to emphasise the element of decoration.

STIPPLING.
See ENGRAVING, Stippling.

STOPPERS. Stoppers for decanters and the like varied considerably throughout the eighteenth and early nineteenth centuries. The earliest style was the so-called 'spire' stopper, which appeared about the middle of the eighteenth century. It was at first uncut, but specimens extant are usually found with cut facets in the form of small hollows whose edges intersect to form a shallow diamond pattern.

Later in the century 'disc' stoppers appeared, which, as the name implies, were flat and circular in shape. The edges of the disc stopper could be plain, but more usually they were scalloped or notched. Decanters with long sloping shoulders were provided with a more elongated form of the disc stopper, referred to as the 'lozenge' style.

The Irish Period was responsible for the appearance of two new styles—the 'mushroom' stopper, so-called because of its resemblance to the mushroom, and the 'target' stopper. The mushroom stopper could be cut, but it was more usually moulded in radial ribs. The target stopper, an elaboration of the earlier disc type, had a plain centre with moulded or cut ridges radiating from the centre to the edges. Both these styles were popular well into the nineteenth century.

The remaining style still popular today is the type of stopper supplied with the square decanters in the so-called 'tantalus'. This is a circular knob of glass completely faceted over its whole surface. It is usually referred to as the 'lapidary' stopper.

Occasionally, a collection of mixed stoppers comes up for sale. A few years ago, a collection of fifty-four of mushroom, lozenge, target, and other shapes, some with cut decoration, sold for £19.

SULPHIDES.
See CRYSTALLO-CERAMIE.

SWEDISH GLASS. Venetian workers penetrated as far north as Sweden and during the sixteenth century a glasshouse was established at Helsingborg, where a Venetian glass-maker was known to have operated.

The style during the seventeenth and eighteenth centuries,

252. *Bowl engraved by Simon Gate at Orrefors Glassworks, Sweden. It is typical of the vigorous muscular figures that have established the Orrefors tradition.*

however, showed little if any Venetian influence and for the most part followed Continental fashions of such articles as the beakers, roemers, and the conical wineglasses of Germany and Bohemia. These articles were copied without variation and without displaying any distinctive national characteristics.

In recent years, however, there has been a great revival of Swedish handicraft; the reformation of industrial art, soon after the commencement of the present century, inspired the Swedish glass-makers with new ideas of form and decoration. From 1917 onwards, art glass from Sweden has become known all over the world.

Prominent among the Swedish glasshouses is that at Orrefors, which was originally an ironworks. It became established in 1898, the early products being the plainest kind of domestic ware and common bottles. Following the first world war, artists were employed to exploit the properties of glass and to express them with artistic effect. In a very short time artists Simon Gate and Edward Hald created their original 'Graal' glass. This was a flushed glass employed to produce delicately tinted motifs very much after the style of Emile Gallé (*see* FRENCH GLASS).

In spite of the resemblance, however, the style was essentially different. Gallé's motifs were produced by applied methods such as that of removing the upper layer of glass to expose a coloured background, whereas the Swedish workers achieved much the same result by work at the furnace mouth. Their methods called into play the inherent properties of the medium; they emphasised its fundamental characteristics after the earliest traditions, and their work was therefore more aesthetically effective than the creations of the French worker.

Nevertheless, applied methods of decoration were sometimes employed by Gate and Hald, many of their better known productions being decorated by wheel engraving. Abstract and figure subjects were a favourite style, and the artistry and originality of such work gained for it an instant appeal. The examples shown in Figs. 250-252 are illustrative of the vigorous, muscular figures which have established the Orrefors tradition.

SWEETMEAT GLASSES. Sweetmeats made their appearance at the closing stages of a meal served at a generous and well-ordered table; to invite attention they required to be delicacies of originality and taste, and attractively served. Most eighteenth-century cookery books devote considerable space to recipes for sweetmeats, which included candied and preserved fruit, trifles, sundaes, chocolate and numerous other items, and glasses for sweetmeats appeared in a great number of eighteenth-century notices.

The serving of sweetmeats at the last courses of a meal is a custom dating back to Roman times, and although there are one or two references in this country to glass vessels for holding sweetmeats, it is doubtful whether glass was used to any extent for this purpose until the advent of Ravenscroft's attractive medium, glass-of-lead, at the end of the seventeenth century.

Before the days of fashionable glass, it is quite clear that silver and oriental china were used for the serving of sweetmeats, but such articles were rare and expensive and the former at least was not improved with the contact of a sticky substance. Glass vessels would, therefore, have provided a welcome change.

Hartshorne (*Old English Glasses*, 1897, p. 466) gives an early reference to what might have been sweetmeat glasses in an

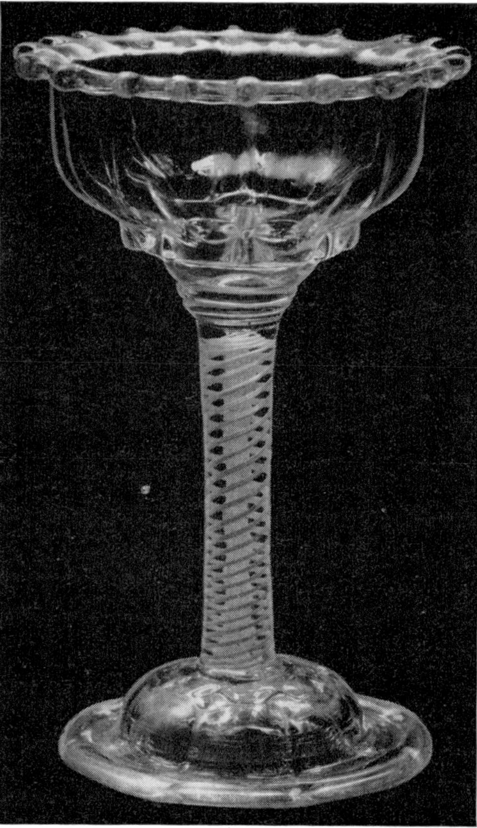

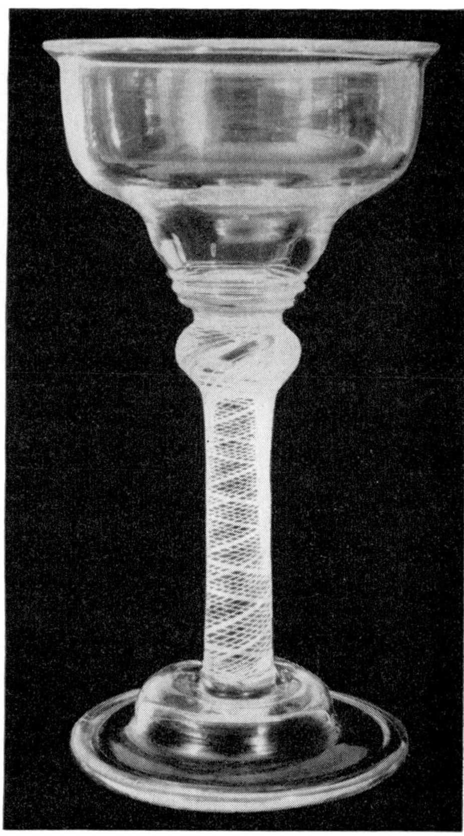

253. *Early sweetmeat glass showing cutting in shallow style on the bowl, stem and foot and scalloping to the rim.* 254. *Sweetmeat glass with double series opaque-twist stem, bowl with denticulated rim, and foot domed and folded.* 255. *Rare sweetmeat glass with multiple spiral opaque twist knopped stem, and domed and folded foot.*

extract from the Private Account of William More of Loseley, Surrey, 20th August, 1556: 'lyttle barrels for sukket'; but apart from the fact that the item appears in a long list of glasses, there is no evidence to prove that the vessels were made of glass.

A reference occurs in the early part of the seventeenth century to what also might have been sweetmeat glasses; an extract from the Inventories for Sir William and Sir Thomas Fairfax, taken 3rd April, 1624, includes: 'Cheney dishes, gally potes, glasses and boxes furnished with sweet-meates' (*Archaelogia*, Vol. xlviii, p. 121).

John Greene, of the Glass Sellers' Company (*See* ENGLISH GLASS, HISTORY OF), who imported glass from Venice between the years 1667 and 1672, ordered some ornamental bowls with waved edges and with handles, supported on a high foot, which were in all probability intended for sweetmeats or fruit.

There can be little doubt that soon after the introduction of lead glass at the end of the seventeenth century, sweetmeat glasses were made either in dish or saucer form with a stem or high foot. From the beginning of the eighteenth century, it was the general custom in fashionable houses to use glass freely in the dessert services. Such vessels included large glass cream bowls or glass baskets for the fruit, glass saucers or glass standing dishes for preserved fruits, candy and dried orange chips.

There is a satisfying view of such dessert services in the early part of the eighteenth century from the Household Books of Lady Grisell Baillie (*see* BAILLIE, LADY GRISELL), the Scottish diarist who kept a careful record of her visits to London, and who described in considerable detail the arrangement, content and character of the various glasses used at the fashionable functions she attended.

The dessert glasses referred to by Lady Grisell as 'scaloped' and 'cornered brim' were obviously decorated by cutting. The former style was the same wavy, undulating finish given to the rim of the bowl as is understood today by the term 'scalloping'; a 'cornered brim', on the other hand, was the cutting of the edge of the rim into a series of sharp angular cuts, more like notching, but on a larger scale.

Sweetmeat glasses appear in great variety and are invariably fashioned and decorated in the best of taste and workmanship. There are also several characteristics which at once give them distinction. The graceful, double-ogee bowl, the domed foot, a symbol of quality and dignity, and the triple collars at the base or top of the stem, or both, are features which adorn many of the most attractive sweetmeat glasses. Other features persisted with sweetmeat glasses long after they had gone out of fashion with other types of glasses; moulding and the elegant Silesian stem may be quoted as examples.

Fairly early in the century, when china became cheaper and more abundant in England, the term 'sweetmeat glass' began to disappear from the trade lists, and to be replaced by 'dessert glass'. The dessert glasses may have included both the sweetmeat glass and the large fruit dish, which later gave place to the epergne, first advertised as being made in silver about 1750 and in glass about 1768.

On the other hand, F. Buckley (*Glass*, 1931, Vol. VIII, (p. 15

256. *A glass salver with a tall sweetmeat glass in the centre ringed by eight jelly glasses.* circa *1745.* (*Laing Art Gallery, Newcastle-on-Tyne*)

257. *Central view of the sweetmeat glass shown in Fig. 256 looking into the bowl showing style of engraving.* (*Laing Art Gallery, Newcastle-on-Tyne*)

258. *Epergne with sweetmeat glasses in basket form, suspended from arms springing from a tall faceted central column.*

points out that it eventually became the custom in the eighteenth century to have stands or pyramids of sweetmeat glasses in which a tall glass in the centre of a silver or glass salver was ringed round with shorter glasses of the same type on which, possibly, other and smaller glasses rested. This was probably the nature of the 'grandest and one of the best Pyramids ever made in England', advertised by a Norwich glass-seller in 1768

Two excellent examples of these *Verres de Parade* are shown in Figs. 256 and 258. The former is of a glass salver with a tall sweetmeat glass in the centre ringed by eight jelly glasses, a style popular about 1745. As will be seen, the salver and glasses were elaborately engraved with the wheel. This specimen is in the Laing Art Gallery, Newcastle-on-Tyne. An example of the engraving itself is admirably shown in Fig. 257, the view of the central sweetmeat glass looking into the bowl; it is engraved with formal trellis border, roses, carnations and poppies.

The second example (Fig. 258) is an epergne with sweetmeat glasses suspended from arms springing from a tall central column, faceted with the wheel in hollow diamond pattern. The glasses themselves are fashioned in basket form and cut in light shallow style.

Articles of the type shown in Figs. 256 and 258 would, no doubt, have been used in conjunction with glass girandoles or table chandeliers fashioned and decorated in similar style.

An idea of the use of luxury articles of this nature in the fashionable houses can be gained from a description in *The Compleat Confectioner*, written in 1753 by Mrs Hannah Glasse: 'A high pyramid of one salver above another, the bottom one large, the next smaller, and the top one less; these salvers are to be filled with all kinds of wet and dry sweetmeats in glass, or little plates, colour'd jellies, creams, etc, biscuits, crisp'd almonds and little knicknacks, and bottles of flowers prettily intermix'd, and the little top salver must have a large preserved fruit in the centre.'

The tall sweetmeat glass lent itself admirably to cutting. The bowl had to be strong and capacious, and the stem and foot, in keeping with the form of the bowl, offered convenient scope for the cutter. The earliest style of cutting was hollow diamonds and edge flutes on the bowl, but the rims were scalloped, an almost constant feature of cut sweetmeat- and dessert-glasses throughout the eighteenth century. An example of the style described is shown in Fig. 253.

The stems were usually cut in hollow diamonds and the feet fluted in fan-shaped panels. It is probable that this was not so much the work of the legitimate glass-cutter as that of the glass grinder, who specialised in looking-glasses and lustres for chandeliers, and who probably made such luxury articles as sweetmeat glasses. For example, Jerom Johnson, whose main trade was the supply of lustres, advertised 'scalloped Desart Glasses' in 1739, and John Challinge, a London looking-glass grinder, advertised in 1767, 'Girandoles, Desart Glasses, Coach Glasses, etc.'

Later in the century, cut sweetmeat glasses were more usually decorated by deeply incised motifs, such as relief diamonds in simple and complex form after the style adopted by Irish cutters.

Sweetmeat glasses with opaque-twist stems are comparatively rare. The stem can be plain or knopped, and of the single or double series twist type. A specimen with the double series twist stem is shown in Fig. 254. It has a denticulated rim and—what is very rare in glasses with an opaque-twist stem—a domed and folded foot.

The specimen shown in Fig. 255 is also of the opaque-twist type. It has an opaque-twist stem, of the single series type, with a knop at the top of the stem surmounted by collars. It will be noted that the foot is also folded and domed as in the case of the specimen in Fig. 254.

Glasses of the type shown in Fig. 255 are sometimes described as champagne glasses because of the tazza-shaped bowl. Champagne glasses and sweetmeat glasses of this type do, indeed, run parallel in general outline; no sure distinction has yet been formulated, or, for that matter, is likely to be. On this matter Haynes (*Glass Through the Ages*, 1948, p. 163) has the following to say: 'Broadly speaking, it is possible to drink conveniently from champagnes, but not from sweetmeats. The terms are used with small discrimination.'

A small sweetmeat glass was sometimes given the alternative name of 'comfit' glass. (*See* COMFIT GLASSES.)

Sweetmeat glasses cover a range of prices from £6 to £125. A sweetmeat glass with wide double ogee bowl with trellis design, with three graduated knops on a domed and folded foot, sold for £31. Another sweetmeat glass with a similar bowl vertically ribbed with an opaque-twist stem, with domed and folded foot, sold for £21. A third sweetmeat glass with cover, both nipt diamond waies, supported on a cushion tier knop and star studded Silesian stem on a domed foot realised £22 a few years ago.

An unusual sweetmeat glass was one enamelled by Beilby in white with foliage design with a double ogee bowl on a Silesian stem and with domed and folded foot. This glass is probably unique and changed hands in 1955 for £125.

An epergne, such as is shown in Fig. 258, sold quite recently for £50. It had a vase-shaped stem on a square base from which sprang eight scroll branches, each carrying a sweetmeat dish cut in hollow diamond fashion and also a central sweetmeat from which were suspended pendent drops.

SYLLABUB GLASSES. Syllabub was an insipid, rather nauseous drink, judged by modern standards, but popular and well appreciated in the seventeenth and eighteenth centuries. It was prepared from cream fresh from the cow, whipped to a froth, to which was added sack, seasoned with ratafia, and spices such as cinnamon. In some recipes, the final feature of the preparation was that of 'stroking' it at the cow's side.

In another recipe, given in the *Compleat Housewife* (1732), whipped syllabub is prepared from cream and sack, with some lemon juice, the mixture being whipped to a froth. As the froth rises, it is taken off with a spoon and then gently laid on the surface of glasses of white wine, claret or sack.

Special glasses were used for syllabub, but there is no doubt that they changed considerably in form during the period in which they were advertised—roughly one hundred years. The earlier practice was to drink syllabub like posset through the spout of a glass or earthenware vessel with two handles, but punch bowls with ladles were also employed.

There was an early reference to syllabub glasses in 1677 (Francis Buckley, *History of Old English Glass*, 1925, p. 114), in connection with George Ravenscroft, when he agreed to supply covers to 'syllabub glasses' at varying rates. The glasses were apparently then made ribbed, plain, diamonded, purled or with 'extraordinary work', the latter referring, no doubt, to some unusual form of decoration. (*See* NIPT DIAMOND WAIES.)

Buckley goes on to say that the syllabub glass was nothing more or less than a posset glass, with two handles and a spout, such as that shown in Fig. 221. (*See* POSSET AND CAUDLE GLASSES.)

The use of posset glasses for serving syllabub is enjoined by Raffold (*Experienced English Housekeeper*, 1769).

There would appear to be no doubt, therefore, that the syllabub glasses of the latter part of the seventeenth century can be identified with the posset glasses of that period. As time went on, however, it became a fashionable drink for ladies at evening functions and, consequently, different glasses were employed. From notices appearing in the newspapers about the mid-eighteenth century, it would appear that there was a difference between the glasses used for the two beverages. 'Whipped syllabub' glasses are mentioned in 1725; syllabub glasses are mentioned frequently alone after 1731. The alternative name, 'whips'—short for 'whipt-syllabub'—also appears.

It is most probable that there was a gradual transition from the posset glass to the jelly glass, first the spout and then the handles being dispensed with. There are some late seventeenth-century glasses extant shaped very much like the early posset glasses, but with no spout and only one handle. (*See* JELLY GLASSES.)

Syllabub and jelly glasses after 1770 were identified together in the same advertisements: 'Jelly and Syllabub Glasses.'

Buckley (*History of Old English Glass*, 1925, p. 115) points out that the idea that the two glasses were practically identical is shown by specimens of bell-shaped glasses engraved with the letter S, as though to distinguish them from jelly glasses of similar shape.

The capacity of syllabub glasses is much the same as that of the dwarf ale—that is, from three to four ounces—and, indeed, without handles, the syllabub and jelly glasses are parallel in appearance, the bowl being bell shaped or bulbous, widely flared at the mouth. In many specimens the stem is absent, but it may be rudimentary or very short.

TAPERSTICKS.
See TEA CANDLESTICKS; BRISTOL GLASS.

TASSIE, JAMES (1735-1799) **AND WILLIAM** (1777-1860). James Tassie and his nephew William became experts in reproducing ancient engraved gems in white and coloured glass pastes. James Tassie also earned world-wide fame in the making of original portrait reliefs in the same medium, and for his reproductions of reliefs by contemporary modellers.

James was born at Pollokshaws, near Glasgow, in 1735, and began his career as a stonemason. He studied drawing and modelling at the Foulis Academy in Glasgow, and at the age of twenty-eight went to Dublin, where he met Dr Henry Quin, who taught him how to make casts of engraved gems from glass paste. After three years in Dublin, Tassie went to London, where he very soon obtained a bounty from the Society for the Encouragement of Arts for his 'profiles in paste'. Tassie's first premises were in Great Newport Street (1767-1771), later in Compton Street, Soho (1772-1777), and eventually in Leicester Fields, now Leicester Square.

His early work was the reproduction and sale of ancient engraved gems in white and coloured glass pastes, some of which were excellent copies of the originals.

The carving of precious and semi-precious stones is an art with a great tradition behind it. The lapidary craftsmen of Ancient Egypt cut and polished natural stones into ornaments and articles of utility; such articles were much in vogue in Imperial Rome, and fetched high prices. Murrhine glass, cut and polished on the lapidary wheel, was fashionable in Italy from about 60 B.C.

Islamic craftsmen of the ninth and tenth centuries practised the art, but it was not until the fifteenth century, after the taking of Constantinople by the Turks in 1453, that it was again introduced into Italy. The practice extended to glass as a medium in Prague, when Caspar Lehmann (1570-1622), lapidary craftsman in the Court of Emperor Rudolf II, was appointed glass-cutter to the Court.

It was the reproduction of the gems and carvings of the ancient craftsmen to which James Tassie first devoted his talents, and in 1755 he issued a catalogue of more than three thousand items. By 1791 the number had grown to fifteen thousand (catalogue prepared by Rudolph Eric Raspe), drawn from many famous collections and including also gems by contemporary engravers.

Between 1767 and 1791, Tassie exhibited many original portrait reliefs in glass paste at the Royal Academy and the Society of British Artists.

Tassie's medium was a finely powdered potash-lead glass, or pâte-de-verre, which was softened by heating, and when plastic, pressed into a plaster of Paris impression of the subject being reproduced. For original portrait-reliefs, a wax impression was first modelled from which a plaster mould was then made. His productions were extremely popular with London jewellers and he supplied cameos and carved glass panels to the Adam Brothers and to Joseph Wedgwood.

His cameo-portraits are among his best work and many are preserved in the Schrieber Collection at the Victoria and Albert Museum, London, and are described in the *Catalogue of English Porcelain, Earthenware, Enamels and Glass*, published in 1930 (Vol. II, pp. 113-120).

The Collection includes (1) casts from gems and medals, (2) medallions moulded with portrait-reliefs wholly in opaque white glass paste, and (3) reliefs in opaque white glass paste mounted on glass or other materials.

The casts from gems and medals include the Head of Bacchus, cast from a gem; Head of Minerva, cast from a gem, with a clear glass ground and mounted as a brooch in a silver frame set with white glass-paste brilliants; and bust of Oliver Cromwell, cast from a medal having a black glass backing. The usual size is about one and three-quarter inches to two and a quarter inches in diameter.

The medallions mounted with portrait reliefs in opaque white glass paste are more numerous; in general they take the form of profile busts. Examples are Queen Anne (1664-1714), Queen Charlotte (1744-1818), Frederick the Great, King of Prussia (1712-1786), George III (1738-1820), Raphael, the Italian painter (1483-1520), and William V, Prince of Orange, son of William IV by Anna, daughter of George II of England (1748-1806).

The medallions vary considerably in size from seven-eighths

to four and a half inches in height and three-quarters to three and a half inches in width. There is sometimes a signature, such as 'T' impressed or 'Tassie F'.

According to Gray (*James and William Tassie*, John Miller Gray, 1894), the larger reliefs were modelled apart from their backgrounds in the early specimens, but later James Tassie mastered the process of casting a large relief and its background as a whole.

The reliefs in opaque white glass paste mounted on glass or other materials are well represented in the collection and include profile busts of Robert Adam (1728-1792), George III (1738-1820), Mary, Queen of Scots (1542-1587), William Pitt (1759-1806), and one of the artist himself. This latter takes the form of a profile bust to left, inscribed: 'James Tassie died 1 June 1799 in his 64 year. W. Tassie F 1799.' It has a matt glass ground, is four inches in height and two and three-quarter inches in width, and has a moulded black wood frame. This portrait relief was executed by William Tassie, the nephew of James.

William Tassie succeeded his uncle and added to the series of casts of gems, but he only occasionally produced portrait reliefs. He eventually retired in 1840 and was succeeded by John Wilson, who had entered William Tassie's employment in 1827, and later became a partner in the business.

TEA CANDLESTICKS or **TAPERSTICKS.** The glass tea candlestick or, as it is more often referred to, the taperstick, was a small-scale reproduction of the glass candlestick. They varied in size from five to seven inches in height and followed their larger counterparts in style; knopped, air-beaded and air-twist styles were followed by the opaque-twist and the cut variety.

The precise purpose of the eighteenth-century taperstick appears to be in some doubt today among collectors. Christopher Haedy advertised in the *Bath Chronicle*, 20th November, 1766: '. . . a great variety of Cut, Engraved and Gilt Glasses, Tea and other Candlesticks.' The same glass seller later advertised in the *Bath and Bristol Chronicle*, 20th November, 1768: 'A great variety of cut, engraved and gilt glasses, cut candlesticks, Tapers.'

There are two explanations of the terms used above. One was that tea candlesticks were designed for the tea or side table. Tea drinking had, of course, by this time become firmly established in this country, and a small candle capable of burning for a short period may have been used in conjunction with the tea set. On the other hand, the taperstick is accepted by some as a small counterpart of the candlestick used for holding the tapers for lighting the candles. Hence the use of the word 'Tapers' in Haedy's advertisement in 1768. (*See* BRISTOL GLASS.)

A typical taperstick is shown in Fig. 259. It is six and a half inches in height and the socket is just wide enough to take an ordinary lead pencil.

The type of taperstick shown in Fig. 259 has changed hands about the £20 mark. Occasionally a taperstick with air-twist stem appears in the sale rooms. In 1956 a taperstick with nozzle resting on a triple collar, with air-twist stem and domed and stepped foot, realised £32.

TEAR GLASSES.
See AIR-TWIST STEMMED GLASSES.

259. *Taperstick or tea candlestick, cut in shallow diamond fashion on the stem. The wide domed foot is also faceted. The specimen is 6½ inches in height, and the socket is just wide enough to take an ordinary lead pencil.*

TIES, GLASS.
See SPUN GLASS.

TOAST-MASTERS' GLASSES.
See FIRING GLASSES.

TODDY LIFTERS. Punch came into fashion during the last half of the seventeenth century. It was a drink introduced into this country in consequence of Dutch trade with the East Indies. There is a reference, for example, in John Evelyn's *Diary* on January 16th, 1662, of his visit to an East India vessel lying at Blackwall Dock, 'where we had entertainment of several curiosities, amongst other spirituous drinks, as punch, etc.'

The 'punch bowl' quickly became an important ritual in the well-ordered household and, indeed, a critical knowledge of the preparation of punch became part of the education of the fashionable gentleman.

In the early days a large silver bowl was called into service, provided with a removable rim scalloped in order to take the glasses; these were placed in the punch bowl with the stems resting in the escallops, feet uppermost.

Ladles, used for serving the punch, were prepared from hard wood, such as beech, willow, or metal, or silver coins

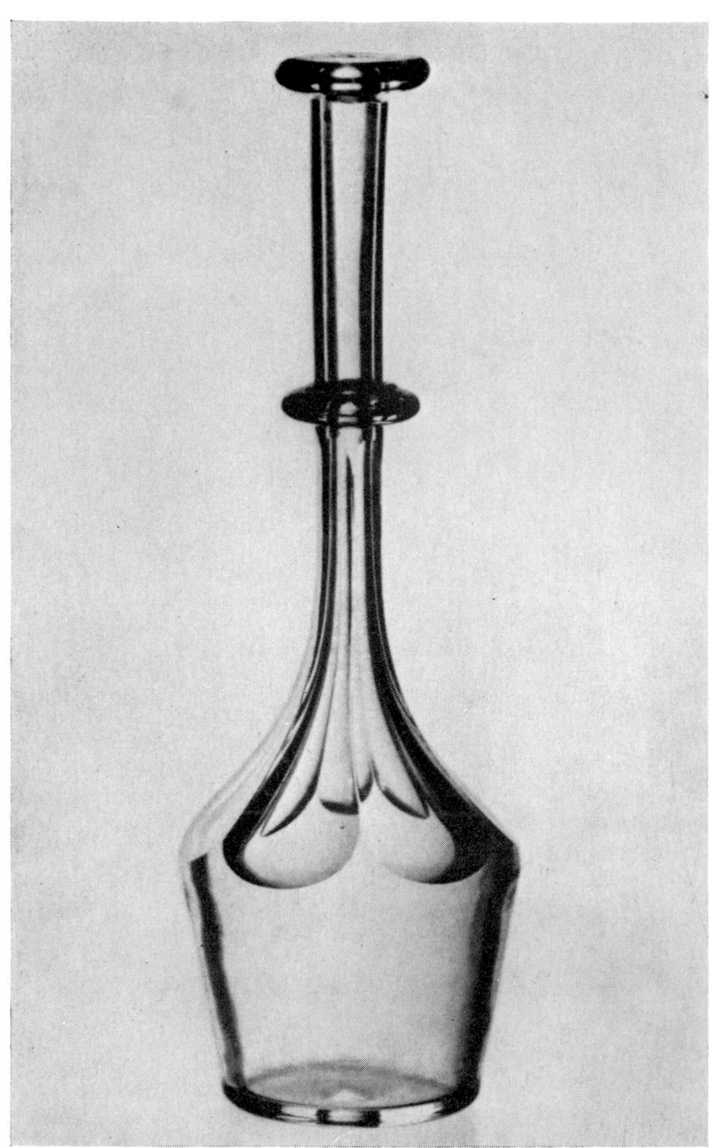

260. *Toddy lifter used for serving punch, popular in England, Ireland and Scotland during the eighteenth century.*

thinned by hammering and shaped, or alternatively whalebone or horn. The glass-maker at first attempted not too successfully, to challenge the popularity of these serving articles in glass, but it was not until the turn of the seventeenth century that he achieved success by striking an entirely new line. This was the so-called toddy lifter, claimed to have been invented in Scotland (Arnold Fleming, *Scottish and Jacobite Glass*, 1938), but later made in English and Irish glasshouses. There are Irish specimens in the National Museum, Dublin.

The toddy lifter, a typical specimen of which is shown in Fig. 260, was something like a miniature decanter in shape, with a body large enough to hold a glassful of liquid. There was a small hole in the base, which enabled the vessel to be used like a pipette. The lifter was dipped into the punch bowl, so that it filled itself rapidly through the hole in the base. The thumb was then pressed firmly on the top of the lifter, much as is done in the use of a pipette after the suction of the liquid into the vessel. The sealing of the contents by pressure of the thumb, of course, prevents the liquid from escaping. The punch, thus contained in the lifter, could then be conveyed safely from the punch bowl to the serving glass, and released at will by removing the thumb from the top of the rim of the lifter. The action is simple and efficient, and they were extremely popular at the time.

They were decorated by cutting, which greatly added to their neatness and pleasing form. Some lifters had a collar round the somewhat long neck, such as the specimen in Fig. 260, which served a practical purpose in use, in allowing a rest or grip for the fingers while the thumb pressure was being applied. The usual size is about six inches.

TRENCHER SALT or **SMALL SALT.**
See SALT-CELLARS.

VASE CANDLESTICK. The term vase candlestick referred to a glass candlestick which was provided with a heavy metal stand of box-like appearance. It was intended, no doubt, to improve stability and so avoid the risk of fire. These articles were first advertised by Christopher Haedy in 1777 (*see* HAEDY, FAMILY OF). The glass candlestick itself followed the current styles of the candelabra. Candle-sockets were scalloped, the grease-pans were provided with pendent lustres, and the stems were heavily cut.

Vase candlesticks remained a popular item well into the nineteenth century; indeed, some were shown at the Great Exhibition of 1851. (*See* CANDLESTICKS.)

VASE LUSTRES. The coloured vase lustres of Victorian and Edwardian days are becoming of great interest to the collector today. These vases, usually in pairs, were accorded a place of honour on the mantelshelf, one at each end. They were more decorative than functional; they could have contained flowers, but one never saw them used for this or any other purpose.

The usual style is a vase up to a foot in height, shaped something like a chalice, with scalloped rims, a typical specimen being shown in Fig. 261. Long prismatic cut-glass lustres, similar to the icicle pendents of the candelabra of the same period, hung from the rim of the bowl in close fringe formation, and gave out a silvery musical note when a gust of wind from an open door or window caused them to collide gently with one another.

Coloured lustres came into fashion shortly after the Great Exhibition, at which the Bohemian glass-makers had displayed vases which excited much comment in the Press. The Bohemian style favoured display and colour, and was a reaction against the vogue of crystal glass set up by the Stourbridge glass-men. The English glass-makers profited from the advice of the Press. They adopted the Bohemian style of decoration, but reproduced it for home consumption with a strong native flavour. The pendent icicle lustre is typical of Victorian over-emphasis, but it paid handsome dividends. A pair of coloured vase lustres graced many suburban mantelshelves.

A popular style was cased or flashed glass, in which a thin casing of coloured glass was superimposed over the transparent glass during the making of the article. The coloured layer was afterwards cut through in a pattern to expose the transparent glass beneath.

Opaque coloured glass was also employed to good effect in treatments of this nature.

A pair of glass lustres, thirteen inches high, similar to the specimen shown in Fig. 261, recently changed hands for £30.

261. *Victorian coloured vase lustre, with cut icicle pendants. Height 12 inches.* 262. *Venetian wineglass with twisted baluster stem, bowl bulbed and winged with flared lip, sixteenth or seventeenth century. Height 7¾ inches, width 4⅝ inches. (By courtesy of the Victoria and Albert Museum)*

VENETIAN GLASS. On the mention of Venetian glass, there at once springs into the mind's eye those tall slender glasses adorned with delicately fashioned side-wings on their stems; light, fairy-like glasses, often tending to the fantastic. They display work of the highest order, for the unique properties of glass were exploited to the utmost limits. Typical specimens are shown in Figs. 262-266.

For their glass-making, the Venetians used white pebbles, *cogoli*, obtained from the bed of the rivers Po or Ticino, as a source of silica. The alkali constituent was obtained by recovering soda-ash from certain marine plants, such as those grown in the salt marshes in the Spanish province of Mucia, and exported from the nearby port of Alicante as *barilla*, or a similar ash obtained from Egypt known as *roquetta*. Most of these forms of soda contained quantities of lime, but this material was introduced into the glass in other forms, such as powdered marble or crushed sea-shells, in order to give the glass its necessary stability and working properties.

It would appear that little glass-making was practised in Venice during the eleventh and twelfth centuries, and it was not until the thirteenth century that it began on anything like a large scale. At the close of the century, work was carried out in a business-like manner, the glass manufacturers being divided into distinct groups. These were the *fioleri*, makers of vessels, *verieri*, makers of glass in mass, *cristallai*, makers of glass for spectacles, *specchiai*, makers of mirrors, *margaritai*, makers of small beads, and *perlai*, makers of large and hollow beads, and the *venditori*, dealers in glass-ware. When the groups became well organised, trade regulations were arranged between the masters and the workmen of each group, and these regulations were later to become very strict and the control rigid.

In order to avoid risk of fire, it was ordered by the Grand Council of Venice in 1291 that all glass furnaces should be demolished in Rialto—that is, the City that is now called Venice. Most of the glasshouses were then erected on the island of Murano and, according to some historians, the glass-makers were encouraged to do so, because, once established on the island, they were virtually prisoners, so strict were the regulations controlling the glass-making industry against the secrets becoming known abroad.

The earliest examples of the skill of the Venetian craftsmen, still extant, would appear to belong to the fifteenth century. A specimen of an enamelled blue glass cup with portraits in medallion is preserved in the Correr Museum at Venice.

263. *Venetian tazza, clear glass with blue edges.* circa *1506.* (*By courtesy of the Victoria and Albert Museum*)

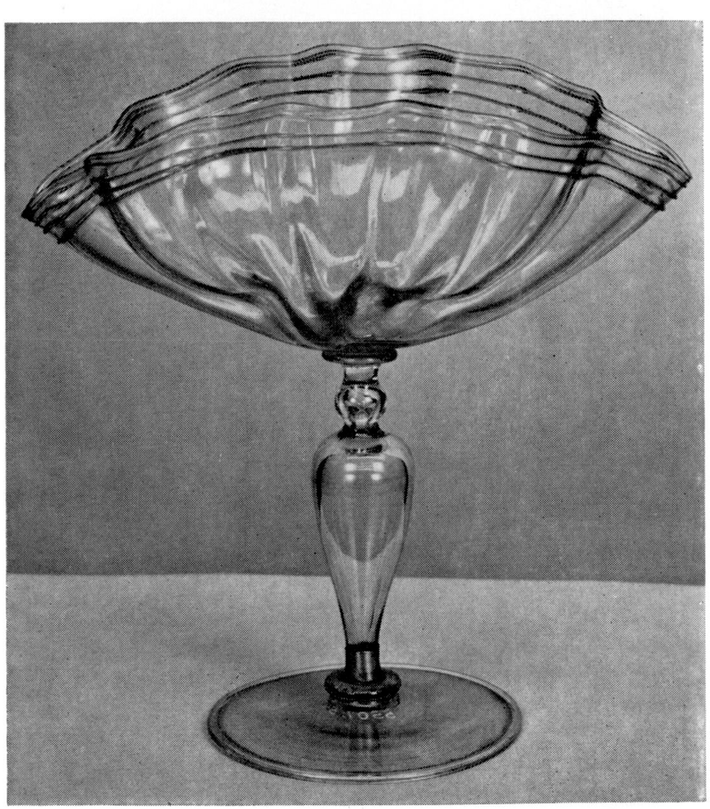

264. *Sweetmeat glass in Venetian cristallo.* circa *1600.* (*By courtesy of the Victoria and Albert Museum*)

It was one of the privileges of the glass-makers to be allowed to coin a number of medals at certain of their functions, and these often formed the inspiration for the decoration on their glass vessels.

A number of specimens of the fifteenth century also exist at the Victoria and Albert Museum. Blue glass appeared to be very popular at this period. One specimen is a cup ornamented with a procession of figures of Venus and other subjects. Another specimen is decorated in blue glass and enamel. It is of plain glass, some sixteen inches in height with an ogee bowl mounted on a foot, the cover and the foot being ornamented with raised gadroons and ribs.

An important specimen from this period changed hands at Sotheby's, London, early in 1959 for the record sum of £4,600. It is referred to as the Fairfax Cup and is a Venetian enamelled glass beaker of pale opaque turquoise colour, and of almost barrel shape with high kick in the base, three and five-eighth inches in height, *circa* 1480. It is enamelled in a continuous band with the story of Pyramus and Thisbe. This specimen is now to be seen at the Victoria and Albert Museum, London.

It was not until the latter part of the fifteenth century, however, when the influence of the classical revival made itself felt in every department of art, that the glass-makers of Murano began to make a close study of Roman models; the heavy covered cups of Gothic form, and the rich and gaudy bowls and tazza, gave way to the more classical shapes.

The demand for artistic work in glass, however, quickly

brought about the production of useless ornaments, any complicated form that took the whimsical fancy of the workman being evolved on the instant; novelties with no practical value, such as ships, birds, belfries, animals of all descriptions, fish, tubs, castles, all were produced in glass and in every conceivable colour, with rich ornamentation in gold and enamel.

The varied productions of the glassworks have been classified by Nesbitt (*Descriptive Catalogue of the Glass Vessels in The South Kensington Museum*, 1878, XCIV-XCV) into six divisions as follows:

(1) Vessels of colourless and transparent glass, or glass of single colours—that is, glass coloured with metallic oxides before being worked into vessels.

Clear white glass is generally used for drinking glasses, but they are not unfrequently decorated with coloured glass laid on in threads externally, or forming parts of the ornaments attached to the stems. These last are very commonly twisted to assume the most fantastic forms. The coloured glasses are usually blue or purple, but green, amber, ruby and an opal white are met with; the last two appear not to be of early introduction. A few examples occur where the two colours are employed, one internally, the other externally.

(2) Gilt and enamelled glass. These methods of decoration were employed on both coloured and colourless glasses. The cups and vases of the fifteenth century are generally rather massive, but in the sixteenth century, when extreme lightness and elegance of form were sought after, the drinking glasses were too thin to bear the heat of the enamelling furnace without losing their shape. The enamelling was, therefore, in a great measure, confined during this century to tazze, bowls or salt-cellars. The decorations are chiefly coats-of-arms, the lion of St Mark, or merely flowers and dots, in place of the portraits, processions and other elaborate subjects employed in the previous century. In later times dishes and tazze were sometimes decorated not by enamelling but by painting on their under surface in oil colour.

(3) Crackled glass. This type of glass has a rough surface divided irregularly by ridges, like ice frozen in the wind. It is supposed to have been made by suddenly cooling the vessel when half blown, and then re-heating and expanding it so as to increase the distance between the sections into which the surface was cracked by the sudden change of temperature. It is believed to date from the eighteenth century.

(4) Variegated or marbled opaque glass, commonly known by the German word *schmeltz*. The most common variety is a mixture of green and purple, which by transmitted light, appears a deep red. Sometimes it resembles jasper and sometimes chalcedony. Other varieties are imitations of lapis lazuli and tortoise shell, and an opaque white, speckled with blue and red, is met with. Aventurine or speckled glass may also be included in this class, and patches of it are sometimes found mixed with *schmeltz*. These appear to belong in great part to the seventeenth century, but the jasper colour referred to was made in the fifteenth century.

(5) Millefiori or mosaic glass. This is made from threads of glass of variegated colours arranged vertically in a pattern forming a geometric figure, an arabesque or more commonly a mosaic pattern usually with a view to forming a small cup. The threads are then united by heat after which the fused mass is subjected to lateral pressure resulting in a homogeneous slab, which, when cut into veneers at any angle, will yield a number of uniform designs. Another method of treatment is to prepare a large number of threads of different colours into a rod on a large scale, and then draw it while hot so that the thickness of the rod is gradually diminished. When cut transversely, the pattern formed by the number of different coloured threads would in some cases be so small as to be beyond the power of the human eye to detect.

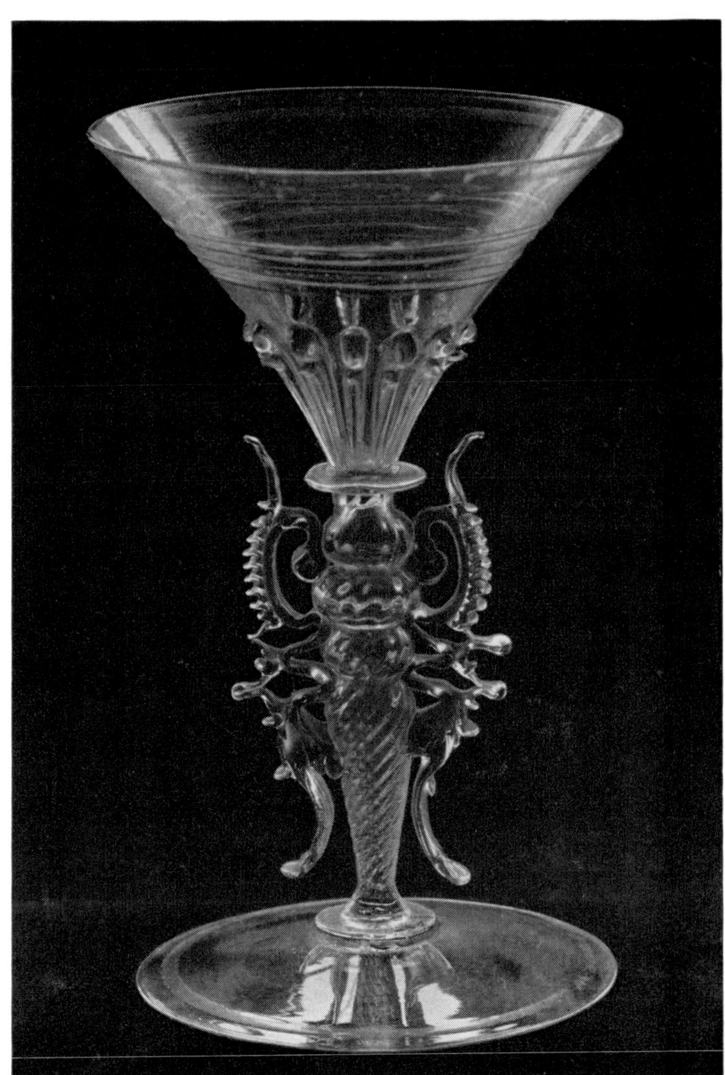

265. *Venetian wineglass in clear blue and white metal. (By courtesy of the Victoria and Albert Museum)*

These wares are clearly imitations of the ancient Roman process, but are not executed with as much taste and success. The process would appear from records to have been introduced in the fifteenth century.

(6) Reticulated, filigree, or lace glass; called by the Venetians *vitro di trina* or a *reticelli*; these varieties contain fine threads of glass, greatly coloured, but sometimes milk-white—latticinio—included in their substance, and are certainly among the most beautiful of the products of the skill of Murano. The idea was, no doubt, borrowed from fragments of Roman glass, but the Venetians far surpassed the ancients, judged from Roman specimens extant.

During the sixteenth century, the drinking glasses were made

266. *Two Venetian wineglasses with scrolled stems, seventeenth century. Height $6\frac{7}{8}$ inches, and $5\frac{1}{2}$ inches, respectively.* (*By courtesy of the Victoria and Albert Museum*)

extremely thin, and decorating with enamel was restricted to the heavier and thicker bowls and tazze. The extreme thinness and fragility of the drinking glasses also made it very difficult for cutting and engraving with the wheel; engraving with the diamond was carried out only to a very limited extent.

It is perhaps possible to attribute the decline of Venetian glass to its extreme fragility and to the fact that much of the production served no other purpose than that of novelty or decoration. The demand certainly grew for artistically decorated glass-ware, but of a more serviceable and robust type, and this demand was eventually satisfied by competitive countries.

Glass-making is still carried on in Murano and visitors to Venice often cross the narrow strip of water to the island, where they may visit the glass-works and watch the descendents of the craftsmen of earlier centuries fashion popular souvenirs.

Rare Venetian glasses, as already pointed out in the case of the Fairfax Cup, command good prices. The Fairfax Cup itself realised £4,600, but it must be recalled that it had an early date—1480. Those of later date and therefore of not such high rarity realise lower figures. For example, a shallow bowl with folded rim and concave base, its lower part with gadrooning and with white and turquoise enamel dot decoration, changed hands for £65 and a similar bowl, somewhat larger, realised £48. Both were early sixteenth century.

VERZELINI, GIACOMO or **JACOB** (1522-1606).

See English Glass, History of; Verzelini Glasses.

VERZELINI GLASSES. The known facts of the life of Jacob Verzelini have been given in English Glass, History of. The following are the descriptions of those glasses which have with some certainty been accredited to him:

1. *The RB-IB Goblet, 1577.* This goblet, illustrated in Fig. 267, was discovered some years ago by Messrs Cecil Davis; it is the earliest dated specimen of any English glass. It has a deep-sided bowl engraved with a hound pursuing a unicorn and another hound pursuing a stag. The animals are equally spaced and divided by four trees. Below are three panels separated by arabesque foliage, two of the panels showing the

I
initials R—B, and the third bearing the date 1577. Above and
B

below the lower decoration on the bowl are lines enclosing a waved line, and below the lower of these borders, at the base of the bowl, is a string-of-pearls border. The bowl is surmounted on a small collar knop.

The original stem and foot are missing and have been replaced with a seventeenth-century pearwood foot with a narrow silver rim, chased with egg-and-tongue motifs. The specimen, seven and seven-eighths inches in height, is now in the Steuben Collection, New York.

2. *The AT-RT Goblet, 1578.* This specimen was brought to light as recently as 1948 by Messrs Delomosne & Son, Ltd., in circumstances sufficiently romantic to give encouragement

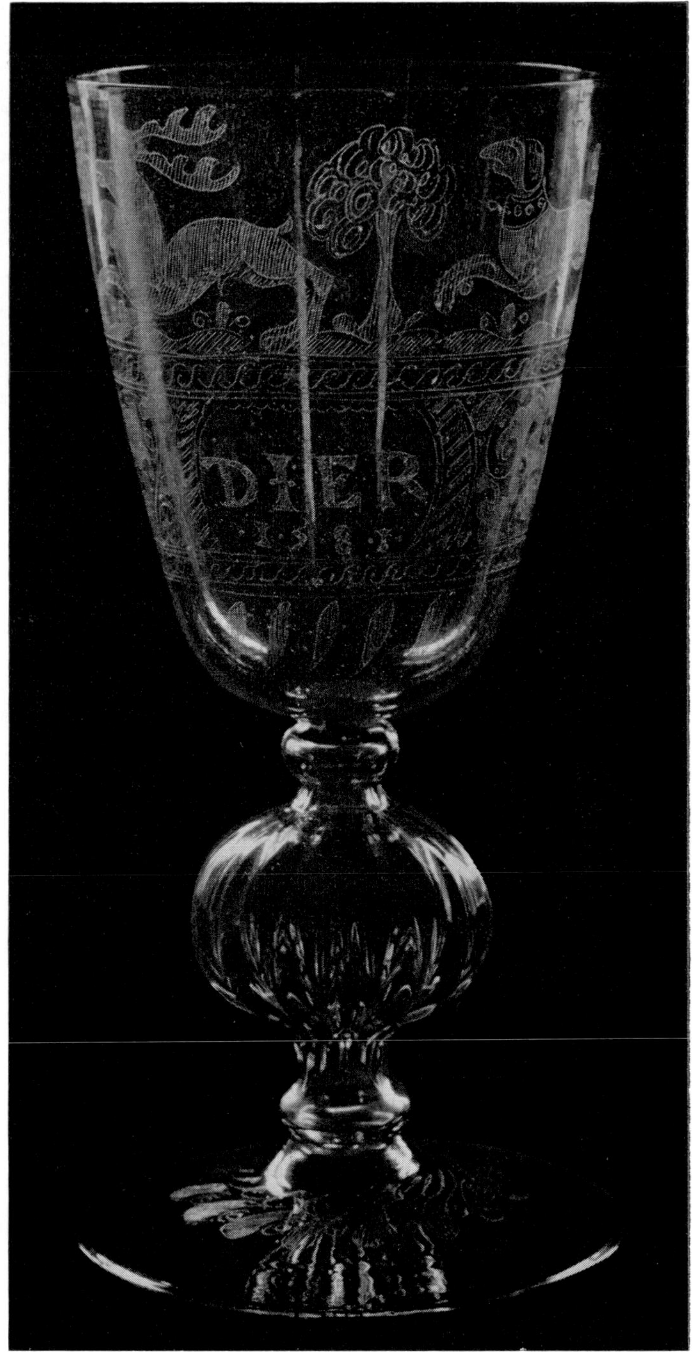

267. *Verzelini Goblet, dated 1577, the earliest dated specimen of any English glass. The bowl is engraved in diamond point work with the initials RB—IB and the date 1577. The subject engraved on the upper part of the bowl is a hound pursuing a unicorn and another pursuing a stag. The original stem and foot are missing, and have been replaced by a seventeenth-century pearwood foot. Discovered some years ago by Messrs Cecil Davis, Ltd., it is now in the Steuben Collection, New York.* 268. *Verzelini Goblet dated 1581. This specimen is better known as the Dier Glass. The bowl is engraved by the diamond with a stag, a unicorn and four hounds. There are three engraved panels with the words JOHN-JONE, DIER 1581 and the Royal Elizabethan Arms in the third.* (*By courtesy of the Victoria and Albert Museum*)

to those sceptics who maintain that all important specimens of old glass were used as cullet after 1745, or repose either in collectors' cabinets or in museums.

It is a goblet eight and three-eighths inches in height, with a straight-sided bowl over a large hollow fluted knop. The foot is folded and engraved with foliage. The engraving round the top of the bowl depicts a stag and hound separated by four trees, and on the lower portion are panels, outlined by arabesque foliage, bearing the date 1578 and the initials AT RT. The interlacing of the initials by a ribbon and the corresponding second letters suggest a marriage glass.

This glass, unlike most of the other specimens attributed to Verzelini, is in good condition.

3. *The AF Tazza, 1580.* This glass is five and one-eighth inches in height, with a wide shallow bowl above a hollow knop. The high conical foot is narrowly folded from above.

269. *Verzelini Goblet dated 1586. The semi-ovoid bowl is encircled by two bands of colourless glass with two bands of white enamel threads, between which is engraved with the diamond IN:GOD:IS:AL:MI:TRVST. In a panel are engraved the initials GS tied with a lover's knot, and the date 1586.* (*By courtesy of the Victoria and Albert Museum*)

There are three panels diamond engraved with arabesque foliage, two bearing the initials AF, tied with a lover's knot, and the third showing the date 1580.

This specimen, shown in Fig. 270, has been broken but repaired. It was formerly in the Collection of Horace Walpole, but is now in the Buckley Collection at the Victoria and Albert Museum, London.

4. *The Dier Glass, 1581.* This is a goblet eight and a half inches in height, with a straight-sided bowl above a large hollow fluted bulb between two small knops. The foot is plain and engraved with foliage. The glass is shown in Fig. 268.

The engraving on the bowl shows a stag, a unicorn and two hounds with four trees. In this specimen there are three panels separated by arabesque foliage, the words John-Jone in one, Dier 1581 in the second, and the Royal (Elizabethan) Arms in the third. This glass is in the collection at the Victoria and Albert Museum, London.

5. *The KY Goblet, 1583.* This glass is eight and three-quarter inches in height, with a deep semi-ovoid bowl above a hollow bulb, ribbed and moulded with four lions' masks. The foot is narrowly folded from above. Below a scrolled border are the words IN : GOD : IS : AL : MI : TRVST, which is the motto of the Pewterers' Company of London. Below are three panels separated by arabesque foliage, the initials KY tied with a lover's knot in one, a merchant's mark in the second, and the date 1583 in the third. The foot has been broken but repaired.

6. *The GS Goblet, 1586.* A goblet just over five inches in height, with a hollow fluted bulb in the stem, and a plain foot engraved with petals. The semi-ovoid bowl is encircled by two bands of colourless glass and two white enamel threads, between which is engraved the inscription IN : GOD : IS : AL : MI : TRVST. Above are three panels separated by arabesque foliage, one with the initials GS tied with a lover's knot, while the other panels bear the date 1586. This specimen is shown in Fig. 269.

7. *The RP-HP Goblet, 1586.* This glass is six and a half inches high, with a rounded bowl nearly five inches in diameter over a ribbed bulbous knop. The engraved foot is folded. The goblet is decorated with a series of eighteen ribbed mouldings and a closed continuous horizontal trailing to the top of the moulding. The border is engraved GOD SAVE QVYNE ELISABETH, and in panels below, spaced in arabesque foliage, appear the initials RP. 1586. HP.

The bowl has been broken and somewhat clumsily repaired. The glass was discovered within recent years by Messrs Cecil Davis, Ltd.

Among other diamond-engraved glasses that have from time to time been associated with Verzelini's name or still remain in some doubt may be mentioned the following:

The Poitiers Goblet, 1578. This glass is five and a half inches high, with a shallow bowl above a large hollow fluted bulb; the foot is folded from above. The bowl is engraved with a stag, unicorn and hounds with six trees. Separated by arabesque foliage are three panels, one with a heart pierced by two arrows, and the date 1578; the second bears the initials AMM DLP, and in the third is the *fleur de lys* of France. The goblet, undamaged, is preserved in the Musée de Cluny, Paris; its English origin has not yet been proved.

The Barbara Potters Glass, 1602. This specimen is in a style quite different from the other glasses described. It has a bell-shaped bowl on a tall stem, consisting of a hollow urn-shaped knop with radial ribs and four lions' masks, above which is a solid baluster. It has a foot narrowly folded from above and is engraved with foliage.

The bowl, decorated with floral borders, is inscribed BARBARA POTTERS, 1602. It is now in the possession of the Victoria and Albert Museum, London. It has been suggested that it was made by Verzelini's successor, Sir Jerome Bowes, who would, no doubt, have continued to employ the same craftsmen after Verzelini's retirement in 1592.

270. *Verzelini Tazza, dated 1580. The shallow bowl is engraved by the diamond with the initials AF tied with a lover's knot and the date 1580. The specimen has been broken and repaired. It was formerly in the Collection of Horace Walpole and is now in the Buckley Collection at the Victoria and Albert Museum.*

The Winifred Geares Glass. This glass has a semi-ovoid bowl engraved with the date 1590, with the arms of the Vintners' Company of London and the name *Wenijfrid Geares* above a fleur-de-lys and other symbols.

The Vickers Glass. This has a cup-shaped bowl bearing an inscription that the glass belonged to Queen Elizabeth.

The Ridley Glass. So named because of its association with John Ridley (1617-1644), Vicar of Preston, near Faversham, Kent.

The diamond engraving of the Verzelini group of glasses has been attributed to Anthony de Lysle, an engraver of pewter and glass. The claim that he was the artist working for Verzelini is not a very strong one and is based on the fact that he was the only engraver known between the years 1508 and 1602. It is thought that he came from France, but it is known that he took out papers of denization in 1582.

The last Verzelini goblet to be sold realised £2,000.

VISSCHER, ANNA ROEMERS (1583-1651).
See DUTCH GLASS.

VITREARIUS, LAURENCE (*c.* 1226).
See ENGLISH GLASS, HISTORY OF.

WALKING STICKS.
See NAILSEA GLASS

WATCH BOTTLES.
See WITCH BALLS.

WATERFORD GLASS.
See IRISH GLASS.

WHEEL ENGRAVING.
See ENGRAVING, *Wheel Engraving*

WINEGLASS COOLERS. Towards the end of the seventeenth century, the idea was introduced of placing a wineglass in a bowl of cold water in order to cool it for the wine. Anthony à Wood (A. à Wood, *The Life of Mr Anthony à Wood*, Oxford, 1730), the Oxford antiquary (1632-1695), records the event in 1683 as follows: 'This year, in the summertime, came up a vessel or bason notched at the brims to let drinking glasses hang by the foot, so that the body or drinking place might hang in the water to cool them. Such a bason was called a "monteigh".'

Dr Johnson in 1773 described the montith (his own spelling) as a 'vessel in which glasses are washed'.

Glass wine-coolers became the fashion in the later eighteenth century, when it was then customary to provide a wine-cooler at the table and two glasses for each diner. After the first glass had been emptied, it was placed upside down in the wine-cooler, while the second wineglass was in use, preparatory to the serving of a different wine.

A typical wineglass cooler of this period is shown in Fig. 36, BRISTOL GLASS. It is in blue glass with a key-fret border in gilt and is signed 'I. Jacobs, Bristol'. Wineglass coolers, as will be noted from this example, were provided with either double or single lips on which the stem of the wineglass rested.

Wineglass coolers, of course, were made in flint glass and many are still preserved.

For prices of wineglass coolers, *see* FINGER BOWLS and IRISH GLASS.

WINEGLASS, THE MAKING OF. For the making of such articles as a wineglass, the methods employed by the early glass-maker have changed little with time. The tools the glass-maker employs today, which are illustrated in Figs. 272 and 273, are very much the same as those of 250 years ago. They are few in number even for the most intricate pieces of work, and are so simple as to appear almost primitive. Indeed, their simplicity only serves to emphasise the glass-maker's dexterity and skill. He judges proportions, like the true artist, by his senses, and creates contour and shape with an ease and perfection that raises his craft to one of dignity.

Nevertheless, an article fashioned in the glasshouse is not so much the effort of an individual as that of a team, known in the trade as a 'shop' or a 'chair'. The article, while it is being fashioned in its plastic state, is passed from one worker to another; each presides over one particular operation in the sequence required to complete the article. It is in this sequence of operations that the unique properties of the metal as a medium are exposed. Lead crystal glass can be made to do almost anything in the hands of a skilled craftsman, but by no amount of coaxing or persuasion can the metal be hurried. The speed of each individual in the team or chair must be regulated to suit the medium, and if an error is made in the judgment of time in one operation, the whole sequence is spoiled.

The making of a stemmed drinking glass is a typical process to use as an example. Such glasses can be made either in three pieces, the bowl, the stem and the foot—a method described in glasshouse parlance as the 'stuck shank'—or, alternatively, the drinking glass can be made in two pieces, the bowl and stem being made in one piece to which a foot is afterwards attached, known more popularly as the 'drawn shank'.

In the three-piece method, the first operation of roughly forming the bowl is carried out by a 'footmaker', the formation of the stem is the task of a 'servitor', and the finishing of the glass is carried out by the 'gaffer', the craftsman presiding over the chair. There are usually one or two boys or apprentice hands who carry away the finished article and generally assist the chair.

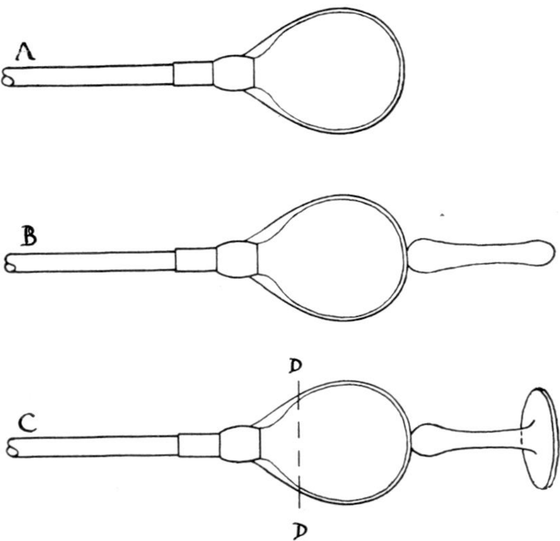

271. *Sketch showing steps in the process of making a wineglass.* A. *The footmaker forms his gathering of glass by marvering and blowing it roughly into the shape of the bowl of the wineglass he is making.* B. *The servitor fixes a knob of glass to the end of the bowl, which eventually forms the stem.* C. *The servitor fixes the foot of the glass. The gaffer detaches the blow iron and shears off surplus along the line.* D/D. *He finishes the rim of the wineglass in his 'chair' as shown in Fig. 273.*

The first operation in forming the glass is carried out by the footmaker, whose task it is to gather or collect the molten glass from the melting pot on a blow-iron. This is an iron pipe about five feet long and an inch in thickness, one end of which is conveniently shaped for blowing by mouth and the other extremity thickened into globular form to facilitate the collection of the molten glass. The footmaker places the end of the blow-iron on the surface of the molten glass and rotates it rapidly with his hands. This action causes the glass to adhere to the blow-iron, collecting upon it like treacle round a spoon. Still rotating his blow-iron, the footmaker carries it to a marver, a heavy slab of iron about two or three feet square with a highly polished surface, as shown in Fig. 272. Such is the consistency of the molten glass in this condition that its shape can be altered at will by a simple rolling motion across the smooth surface of the marver. It is to be noted that, whereas at a somewhat higher temperature the hot glass adhered to the blow-iron, when at the lower temperature at which it is being marvered, there is no tendency for it to adhere to the marver itself.

The marvering operation is interrupted occasionally by the footmaker to blow down his blow-iron in order to distend the mass of glass into a bulb, and he may elongate its shape by holding the blow-iron in a vertical position to allow the bulb of glass to extend slowly under its own weight.

If the operation of forming the bulb proceeds too slowly, however, the footmaker may swing the blow-iron with a pendulum motion or, in some cases, complete a circular movement by swinging it over his head. Alternatively, he may take it to a small auxiliary furnace or 'glory-hole' to reheat the glass before following one or other of the processes just described. The footmaker has, therefore, complete control over the plastic mass of glass and can shape or reshape it with ease. It is in this respect that his judgment is made manifest, for he must time the completion of his process to coincide with those being carried out by the other members of the chair.

The footmaker, having completed his task of forming the bulb roughly into the shape of the bowl of the glass (Fig. 271 A), now hands it to the servitor, who drops a small knob of molten glass upon the extremity of the bowl. After being heated at the glory-hole so that the junction is made complete, this knob of glass is drawn out to form the stem (Fig. 271 B), a small button of glass being left at the unattached end. The servitor now gathers on this extremity an amount of molten glass from the pot to form the foot, which he quickly fashions (Fig. 271 C) by flattening with a pair of wooden 'clappers'.

Having completed his part in the formation of the glass, the servitor passes it to the gaffer, who grips the foot by a spring clip attached to an iron rod popularly known in the glasshouse as the 'gadget', a term used continuously in glasshouse parlance since it was invented about a century ago.

The gaffer now detaches the blow-iron from the bowl of the glass by touching it along the line (Fig. 271 D/D) with a moistened piece of iron, such as a file, and then sharply tapping the blow-iron with it. This causes the bowl to crack completely round its circumference. Still holding the glass by the gadget,

272. *Glass-maker known as the 'foot-maker' who has gathered a mass of molten glass on his blow-iron, and is here seen shaping it on the 'marver', a flat slab of iron.* (*Central Press*)

273. *The gaffer at work in his glass-maker's chair. He is seen trimming the rim of a bowl with a pair of shears. When hot and plastic, glass can be cut with a pair of shears much the same as cloth.* (*Central Press*)

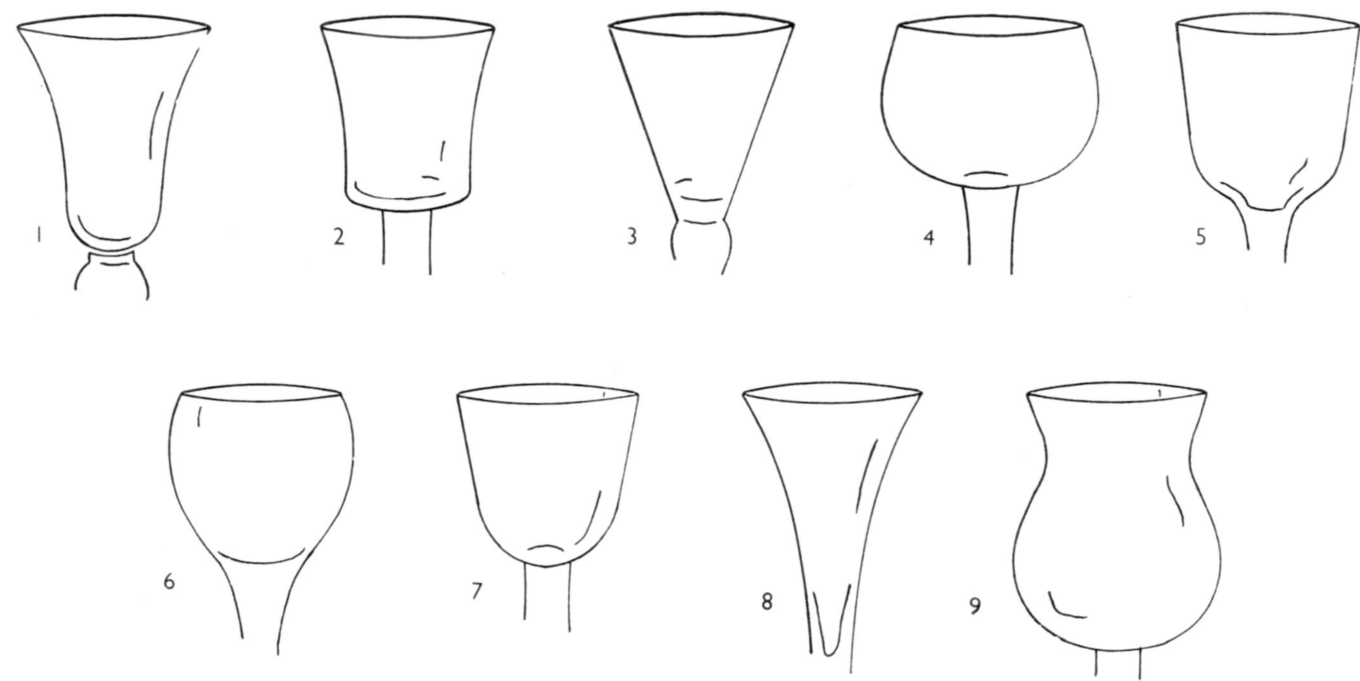

274. *Bowl Forms.* 1. *Bell.* 2. *Bucket.* 3. *Conical.* 4. *Cup.* 5. *Ogee.* 6. *Ovoid.* 7. *Round Funnel.* 8. *Trumpet.* 9. *Waisted.*

the gaffer now reheats it and proceeds to remove the surplus glass from the rim of the bowl with a pair of shears very similar to a large pair of scissors. The shearing operation is shown in Fig. 273 being applied to the rim of a bowl.

After shearing, the gaffer completes the shape, and finishes the edge of the bowl with his 'pucellas', a pair of spring tongs, somewhat similar to a large pair of sugar-tongs, which he also employs to adjust the diameter of the bowl. During this operation, the gaffer is seated in his glass-maker's chair (Fig. 273), which is an ordinary wooden form or long stool, having attached to it two extended flat arms, slightly inclined, along which he rolls either his blow-iron or gadget backwards and forwards with his left hand while shaping the hot article with his right. The spinning motion thus given to the soft glass prevents it from collapsing under its own weight, which it would very quickly do if allowed to remain still. Having completed the article, the gaffer hands it to a boy who carries it to the annealing furnace.

This routine for the making of an article such as a wineglass is not by any means strictly followed in every glasshouse; the methods vary in different localities. In the eighteenth century, before the invention of the gadget, the foot of a three-piece glass was attached to a 'pontil', for the finishing operation in the chair. The pontil is a solid rod of iron about the same length but not quite so thick as the blow-iron. In this operation a small knob of hot glass is gathered on the extremity of the pontil, and at once attached to the underside of the foot. The unfinished wineglass can now be detached from the blow-iron by touching with a moistened piece of iron and tapping sharply, the completion of the glass then being carried out in the chair.

This finished glass is then detached from the pontil by a sharp tap, but the broken edges are apparent where it had been separated from the pontil. This rough mark, referred to as the pontil mark, is characteristic of nearly all eighteenth-century drinking glasses. At a later period, after the advent of cutting, the sharp edges were often removed by grinding and polishing, which left a smooth, hollow depression in the centre of the underside of the foot.

After being completed, the glass article is then annealed, in order to remove any residual stresses. (*See* ANNEALING OF GLASS.)

The various bowl forms employed throughout the eighteenth century are shown in diagrammatic form in Fig. 274.

WITCH BALLS. Glass balls in various colours and lustred inside to resemble silver spheres may still be found in the many curio shops scattered about the country. They are in many different sizes, but are rarely large. The commonest, no doubt, are the green glass balls somewhat larger than a cricket ball, used as floats for holding up fishing nets. Arnold Fleming (*Scottish and Jacobite Glass*, 1938, p. 108) states: 'Glass balls . . . have been employed by generations of fisher-folk who decorate them with scriptural texts and the name and number of their smack. A duplicate is hung in the window of the fisherman's home. If disaster should unfortunately overwhelm the crew, their ball, with its sides well worn and polished by the pounding of the waves upon the seashore, is the only, silent and sad, messenger of their fate. Sometimes the inscription has vanished and only the calligraphy of the green-speckled foam of a sea-wreck, dusted dry with the sand, remains.

'Witch balls are another type. Glass-blowers have ever had a superstition regarding any peculiar tint in the metal, hence the idea of crystal gazing. For some they possess a charm still, as they believe they can ward off things that go bump in the night, and other strange forms of misfortune. The fate of the crystal ball is occasionally connected with a family; while it remains whole, the owner will be lucky, but with the appearance of any flaw, the family fortunes are bound to decline, and before a death the ball becomes misty and dim. Should the crystal be lent, the person fetching it must neither speak, sit, nor enter the home, or be found outside his own home after sunset. In many districts, they still serve to ward off the "evil eye", or cure sickness in man and beast. The glass ball is, after an incantation, placed in water before this is given to the sufferer to drink.'

Fleming's reference to the evil eye finds confirmation in connection with Nailsea glass. H. St George Gray (*Connoisseur*, Vol. XXX, 1911, pp. 85-98) states that glass balls were hung in the cottage of the Nailsea workmen to ward off the evil eye.

Francis Buckley (*Glass*, Vol. VIII, 1931, p. 364) has the following remarks to make on these coloured glass spheres. 'Almost invariably they are described as "Witch Balls". This curious name has been explained as being connected with the old-fashioned superstitions about witches and the "evil eye". These brightly coloured glass balls were intended, it would seem, to attract the witches, or at least, to distract their attention from the other contents of the cottage. They were supposed, in fact, to act as a sort of charm, like the bright brass ornaments on old horse harness.'

It is suggested by Buckley that the original name for ornaments of this kind was most probably 'Watch Bottles'. Their origin may be sought in the following notices, referred to by Buckley. The *Daily Courant*, 14th February, 1704: 'Stolen, two red watch-bottles, rib'd with gold, several gilt watch-bottles and other toys.' *Public Advertiser*, 10th February, 1768: 'John Collet, glass-seller, deceased, in the Minories, London . . . fountain and acorn glasses, watch balls, phials, tumblers.'

It would appear, therefore, that the 'watch bottle' of 1704 was identical in idea with the later 'watch ball'. The ordinary watch ball has a hole in the top for the insertion of a peg and string, by which means it is hung up. The earlier kinds may have had a small neck at the top, for the same purpose, which would have suggested the description 'bottle'. The term later changed from 'watch ball' to 'witch ball', no doubt by the enterprising wandering pedlars, who sold them at country fairs, and who sought to satisfy the curious folk-lore of the countryman. It was good sales talk, as is evident from the fact that these ornaments have survived in large numbers, and also because the term 'witch ball' has remained unchanged to this day.

The majority of these balls are of coloured glass, blue perhaps being the commonest colour. As there is a tendency to describe all coloured glass as 'Bristol', most witch balls are said to be of Bristol or Nailsea origin. This is not the case, however; coloured glass of all kinds was made in most parts of the country. There are many notices in the old newspapers to support this view.

From the appearance of some of the later witch balls, it is clear that they were made in the earlier half of the nineteenth century. This applies particularly to the silvered variety, for a satisfactory and economical method of silvering the inside was not established until the middle of the nineteenth century. The *Magazine of Art* reported in 1852: 'So great is their power of reflection that the entire details of a large apartment are caught upon them in surprising minuteness and clearness of definition and in amusing perspective.'

Some witch balls are found with loops of coloured glass round the surface of the glass after the manner of festooning. *The Pottery Gazette* (1942) gave a description of the method used in the making of these ornaments: 'The worker would first blow a smallish sphere of glass, and his assistant would then wrap around it a thread of softened glass of a different colour, encircling the ball a number of times, spacing the spiral as he went along. With his tool, the maker would then drag the threads at four equidistant points, thus forming four sets of loops. He would then reheat the whole at the pot-mouth, and blow the article to its finished size when the glass was sufficiently softened and the applied threads had merged somewhat into the body of the glass.'

There are many other kinds of witch balls, in all manner of striped and spotted glass, and plain red glass is not uncommon in the north country. Just occasionally a specimen is found made to hang in strings, all except the lowest ball having a hole provided in the base as well as the top.

Witch balls can be found in most antique and curio shops and can be purchased for a pound or so. For example, four similar to those referred to in NAILSEA GLASS, with latticinio loops in opaque white and pink on a translucent blue ground, from five to seven inches in diameter, sold a few years ago for £5.

WOLFF, DAVID (1732-1798).
See DUTCH GLASS; NEWCASTLE GLASSES.

WOODALL, JOHN (1850-1925)
See CAMEO GLASS.

YARDS-OF-ALE. Of all the glasses employed in the consumption of ale or beer, the half-yards or ale-yards are the most curious. These slender yard-long glasses can be traced back to the early part of the seventeenth century when they were known by various names such as the 'Long Glass', the 'Ell Glass', and the 'Cambridge Yard Glass'.

Young quotes in his *England's Bane* in 1617: 'He is a man of

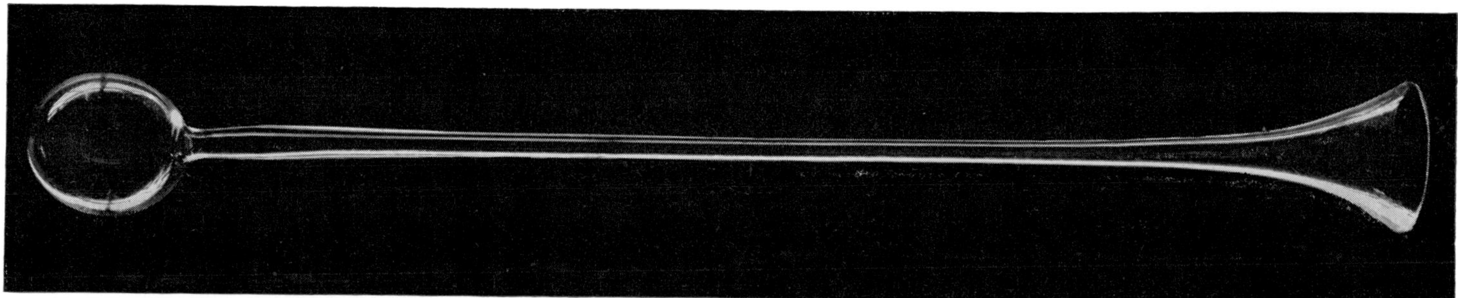

275. *Yard-of-ale glass. These glasses vary from thirty inches in length to over a yard. Some were provided with a foot, but the specimen shown is probably a trick glass. Ale yards are known from the early seventeenth century.*

no fashion that cannot drink by the dozen—by the yard—and so by measure we drink out of measure.'

Mention of yards-of-ale occurs in John Evelyn's diary on 10th February, 1685: 'Being sent to by the Sherriff of the County to appear and assist in proclaiming the King, I went next day to Bromley, where I met the Sherriff and Commander of the Kentish Troop with an appearance, I suppose, of five hundred force—the High Sherriff read the proclaiming titles to his bailiffe—and then after many shouts of the people, his Majesty's health being drunk in a flint glasse a yard long, by the Sherriff, Commander, Officers and chief gentlemen.'

The ale-yards vary in length from thirty inches to over a yard; the capacity is something like one pint. It would appear that in the seventeenth century, when the yard-of-ale came in for a certain amount of popularity, it was provided with a foot similar to other styles of glasses. Owing to their extremely fragile nature, yards-of-ale were obviously only used on special occasions, such as that referred to by John Evelyn, and no doubt much care was necessary in using the glass because of its great length.

The yard-of-ale shown in Fig. 275 was a modification without a foot, and such glasses were employed as trick glasses. They were provided with a bulb at the end such as that shown in the illustration, which increased the difficulty of using them still further. One who had had no experience of an ale-yard would be presented with a full measure. The unfortunate victim could, by exercising great care, overcome the initial stages of emptying the glass until it was finally tilted for the remaining portion. The inrush of air into the now elevated bulb would cause the remainder of the ale to squirt into the face of the drinker as if from the jet of a hose.

Bate (*English Tableglass*, 1905, page 64) issued a warning regarding fraudulent versions: 'Should the collector find a yard-glass engraved "A yard-of-ale is a dish for a King" let him not purchase it as an antique; it will be one of half a dozen made a few years ago to the order of an old friend of mine who being not unconnected with the brewing of good beer, wished to make a few presents to friends and selected this distinctly unconventional form.'

Modern versions were made as recently as 1955 by an English manufacturer.

Very few of the genuine article appear in the sale rooms. A genuine yard-of-ale, three feet in length, of robust construction, trumpet mouth and bulbous end such as shown in Fig. 275, changed hands a few years ago for £10.

YSART, PAUL.

See PAPERWEIGHTS, Modern Manufacturers.

ZWISCHENGLASER.

See GERMAN AND BOHEMIAN GLASS.